Belonging

EARLY AMERICAN STUDIES

Series editors:
Kathleen M. Brown, Roquinaldo Ferreira, Emma
Hart, and Daniel K. Richter

Exploring neglected aspects of our colonial,
revolutionary, and early national history and culture,
Early American Studies reinterprets familiar themes
and events in fresh ways. Interdisciplinary in
character, and with a special emphasis on the period
from about 1600 to 1850, the series is published in
partnership with the McNeil Center for Early
American Studies.

A complete list of books in the series is available from
the publisher.

BELONGING

An Intimate History of Slavery and
Family in Early New England

Gloria McCahon Whiting

PENN

UNIVERSITY OF PENNSYLVANIA PRESS

PHILADELPHIA

Publication of this volume was aided by the
C. Dallett Hemphill Publication Fund
Copyright © 2024 University of Pennsylvania Press

Published by
University of Pennsylvania Press
Philadelphia, Pennsylvania 19104–4112
www.pennpress.org

Printed in the United States of America on acid-free paper
10 9 8 7 6 5 4 3 2 1

Hardcover ISBN: 978-1-5128-2449-0
eBook ISBN: 978-1-5128-2450-6
A catalogue record for this book is available from the
Library of Congress.

Endsheets: William Price, "A new plan of ye great town of
Boston in New England in America, with the many
additional buildings, and new streets, to the year 1769"
(Boston, 1769). Courtesy of the Norman B. Leventhal Map
and Education Center at the Boston Public Library.

To the memory of
Dorcas, Sebastian, Sue, Thomas, Mark, Darby, and
all the others.
I hope I have done your stories justice.

And to my husband, Paul,
and to our children,
Elisa, David, Audra,
and the baby we lost.

CONTENTS

ILLUSTRATIONS

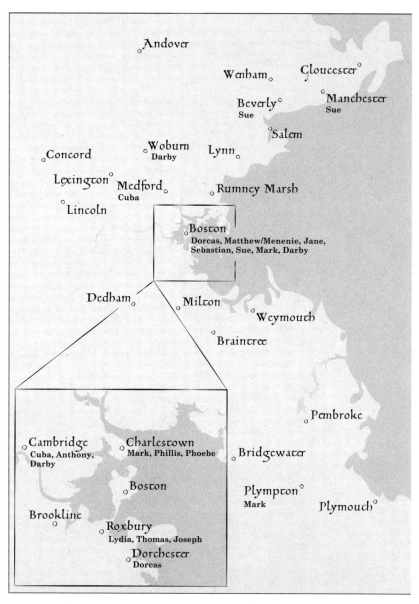

Map 1. Map of eastern Massachusetts. This map shows many of the places mentioned in *Belonging*, with key historical actors listed under the towns in which they lived. Map drawn by Vanessa Knoppke-Wetzel.

ON NAMES AND MORE

The names I have chosen to use in this book will not align with the expectations of many readers. Historians tend to introduce historical actors using both their given names and their surnames (as in "George Washington"), and then they usually refer to these people subsequently by their surnames ("Washington"). When writing about Americans of European ancestry, this works quite well. But when writing about people in slavery, many of whom were denied the distinction of a surname, this method does not hold. By trying to follow the convention, historians find themselves boxed into referring to Anglo-Americans by their last names and identifying most enslaved people by their first names, which creates an inequity ("Washington" versus "Ned" or "Jenny") in their very prose. This echoes what enslavers wanted: to give stature and significance to white people while demeaning bound people of African descent.

In an attempt to address the injustices implicit in the names of those I write about, I have decided to flip the convention. Rather than referring to historical actors by their surnames after I initially introduce them, I refer to them by their given names. This felt awkward at times when I was writing, and it might feel awkward at times to those who are reading. But calling the commander in chief "George" seemed the best course of action in light of the other names set down in the historical record. Perhaps these moments of discomfort in the text will serve as reminders of how slavery assaulted the dignity of its victims by distorting one of the most fundamental parts of people's identities: their names.[1]

I have attempted in other ways to use language that honors my historical actors. For instance, I do not refer to the people about whom I write as "slaves," as such a term serves to reduce human beings to the degrading status imposed on them by their oppressors. Instead, I most frequently use the adjective "enslaved." *Belonging* discusses, for instance, enslaved people, enslaved mothers, enslaved activists, enslaved husbands, enslaved Bostonians, enslaved congregants, and enslaved children. When referring to those who bound others, I favor the term "enslaver" because it indicates that these people actively endeavored to exert dominance over those they bound; theirs was no passive position of authority. I generally avoid "planter," "owner," and "slaveholder." And I use "master" only selectively, mainly with regard to people in term servitude, as in that context in New England the word appears not to have been strongly associated with racial oppression: Both Black and white workers in various short-term labor arrangements—apprentices, servants, maids—answered to people whom they, and others, understood to be their "masters."[2]

*   *   *

I have brought the years found in my historical sources into alignment with the modern calendar, with the new year beginning on January 1 rather than on March 25 (as was the case for much of the period under study). However, all quotations in this book appear just as I found them in the archive (with the sole exception that I have lowered the colonists' superscript letters). This has the advantage of preserving the voices of my historical actors and the record keepers who documented their world, but it also means that capitalization, spelling, and syntax often do not conform to modern usage.

INTRODUCTION

Sometime around the first of January in 1701, a little procession wended its way through the streets of Boston. A group of women was out on errand, one following another following another. The woman leading the way was probably pleased with her day's work; she had made a purchase—"a Bargain," an acquaintance called it—and she expected to put this purchase to good use. The woman trailing the convoy would have considered the transaction differently. She held in her arms a six-week-old baby: her child, but not hers. The enslaver of this woman in the rear had sold the infant to Mary West, the young lady marching in front, and Mary, who lived out of town, would remove the child from Boston as soon as she could make the proper arrangements. Years later, a bystander would remember the now nameless woman perform her final act of mothering that baby: "the Negro Woman the Mother of said child took the child and Carryed it away following . . . Mrs West."[1]

That same year, another mother carried another infant through the streets of Boston. This mother, named Jane Lake, followed another procession. She walked with her enslaver's family to Boston's First Church, turning east onto the road known as "the way to the neck," which they followed deeper into the peninsular town rather than out to the slim spit of land leading to the neighboring village of Roxbury. In less than half a mile, the company reached the aging wooden meetinghouse, at which point it probably split, with Jane filing into a pew in the gallery alongside her husband, Sebastian, and the congregation's other dark-skinned worshippers. But the family would not stay in the gallery today. At the proper time, Jane would hand the infant to Sebastian and watch the two make their way past the pews. Baby Jane was to be baptized, and Sebastian, like all fathers presenting their children to the Lord, would hold her aloft before the congregation while the minister poured symbolic water over her head. Little Jane "is baptised by Mr. Allen," an onlooker would report: "Bastian holds her up."[2]

These two infants had a good deal in common. They were both daughters born at the turn of the eighteenth century to women of African descent enslaved in Boston. And yet, much about their stories differs as well, revealing the complexity of life on the ground in early New England, where gender, race, and enslaved status were not sufficient to predict a child's future. The first baby, who came to be called Sue, was sold away from her mother as a nursing infant and would come of age alone in an Anglo-American household. The second, little Jane, was born to parents who had cultivated white allies in their neighborhood, contracted a formal marriage, and negotiated with those who bound them regarding the care of their children. While each step of Sue's procession through Boston took her farther from her family, Jane's convoy initiated her into her mother's Christian community and provided her father an opportunity to ritually affirm his paternity within one of the town's most significant social institutions: the church. Before either child had the capacity to make sense of her circumstances, Sue had been forcibly separated from her kin, and Jane had been claimed publicly by hers.

Sue and Jane were born in a place celebrated for its legacy of liberty. During seminal moments of American history, New England is commonly associated with freedom. In the seventeenth century, English puritans who sought autonomy to worship as they wished crossed the Atlantic, bound for the Massachusetts Bay. In the eighteenth century, New Englanders who refused to submit to new British demands fomented a revolution that led to American independence. And in the nineteenth century, New England's abolitionists helped push slavery to the center of national politics, instigating the Civil War and the end of race-based slavery in the United States. But New England was not just a cradle of liberty in American history. It was also a cradle of slavery. From the earliest years of colonization, New Englanders bought, traded, and sold people—most of whom were African. *Belonging* tells New England's early history from the perspective of these people: the people who belonged to others and who struggled to maintain a sense of belonging among their kin.

Belonging places special emphasis on the intimate lives of those who belonged.[3] What did it mean for people in bondage to attempt to build families when their ability to do so was hindered by an enslaver's power? The particular circumstances of bondage in New England created a host of problems for the families of the enslaved. Spouses, like baby Jane's parents, ordinarily did not live in the same household. Fathers and their offspring routinely were separated by inheritance practices as well as by sale. Children could be removed from their mothers at an enslaver's whim, as Sue would grow up to understand all too well. And people in bondage had only partial control of their movements through the region, which made more trying the task of maintaining far-flung relationships. The difficulties transcended distance. Parents could not ordinarily support their children, as their labor contributed to the households of their enslavers rather than to the welfare of their offspring. Likewise, children were forced to answer to the authority of those who held them in slavery rather than that of their fathers. How was a bound husband or father to provide for, guide, discipline, or command respect under such circumstances? How was a mother to care for and teach? A wife to submit? A child to learn and grow, to carry memories of the past and craft a vision for the future? *Belonging* explores the ways in which the conditions of slavery in New England influenced the intimate relationships of people like Sue and Jane. How did belonging to enslavers prevent the enslaved from belonging to one another?

But *Belonging* does more than lay bare the obstacles to family stability for those in bondage; it also explores how people of African descent created family and kinship ties despite these limitations. The book charts Afro-New Englanders' persistent struggles for intimacy throughout the century and a half stretching from New England's founding to the American Revolution. Black people approached their white enslavers, neighbors, legislators, and brethren in the church, requesting civil marriage, access to spouses, and proximity to children. They strove to influence the treatment of their family members, they pursued opportunities for economic advancement, and they called for release from bondage. Sometimes these pleas were not well received. Claims were rebuffed, intimate ties severed. Baby Sue, whatever her mother thought of the matter, was sold casually out of town. But sometimes Black New Englanders secured meaningful concessions: the right to marry, protection for a child, a promise of freedom. And the cumulative effect of these concessions was significant. The work of making and maintaining kin ties— work carried out by thousands of Afro-New Englanders negotiating with the white folks around them—influenced the region's law, religion, society, and politics. This work led to the legal protection of enslaved people's right to marry, for example, as well as helped foster uneasiness in the church about spousal separations. Ultimately, the actions taken by people of African descent to fortify their splintered families—and the arguments made by Black activists insistent upon their right to family integrity—played a pivotal role in bringing about the sudden and poorly understood collapse of slavery in

Massachusetts. This book tells that larger narrative through a series of personal stories, pulling together these microhistories to demonstrate their cumulative effect in encouraging broader change in New England society. Bondspeople of Massachusetts played a crucial role in loosing slavery's grip on their region.

*　*　*

Belonging builds on a sustained, creative, and truly monumental outpouring of work on families in slavery. The kin ties that people of African descent forged in bondage have fascinated scholars since the early twentieth century, and generations of historians have plumbed the archive to illuminate how Black family life was at once ravaged by and resilient to the predations of slavery. Especially important to advancing this scholarship was the development of women's history, which made the case for attending to women in the historical record and addressing the difficult pasts to which their archival presence gestures. Gender historians have further advanced work on slavery by questioning long-standing interpretive practices, whether the patriarchal assumptions that shape much historical writing or the tendency in the scholarship to privilege the economic over the intimate. And, recently, scholars have meditated on the silences of the archive, which can make it nigh impossible to tell the stories of those in slavery, especially women and children. Notwithstanding the limitations of the historical record, however, scholars have managed to delineate the family lives of people in bondage with striking clarity. Studies of sexual practices and physical intimacy, marriage and coupling, childbirth and maternal health, education and childrearing, parenting customs and familial authority, sexual exploitation and corporal violence, and matriarchy and matrifocality, among many other topics, have painted an impressively nuanced portrait of family life under slavery.[4] Much of the discussion of bound families in North American history, however, has centered on the experiences of people in the American South, and most studies focus on large plantations in the nineteenth century. Historians know less about how bondspeople built intimate relationships in the context of household slavery—the environment that predominated in New England. By focusing on a region in which the average enslaver owned very few people, *Belonging* sheds light on the intimate experiences of those in slavery who lived more with white people than with Black people.[5] Here there was no demographic foundation for emotional density: People of African descent had to be exceedingly adaptive to avoid utter isolation, formulating an array of strategies in order to counter the fragmentation that marked their family life. Scattered in ones and twos throughout white households, they nonetheless persevered in attempting to create and sustain intimate bonds.

One of the primary strategies that bondspeople deployed in their bids to safeguard the relationships of their choosing was marriage. Central to *Belonging*'s arguments about the intersection of family and slavery in the English-speaking Americas is the evidence it provides of the importance of formal civil marriage to bondspeople in Massachusetts. *Belonging* documents the legal protection of enslaved people's right to marry, it reveals how frequently the enslaved engaged in government-sanctioned marriages, and it furnishes clues from the archive indicating that bondspeople used such marriages strategically to garner community support for and protection of their often-precarious bonds. Of course, it is crucial to note that bondspeople who wed one another were not guaranteed the conjugal rights that Anglo-Americans expected for themselves in matrimony. Their children could be taken from them, even at birth; their spouses could be sold to distant places. However, that the enslaved were allowed to marry by the government—allowed to do so, in fact, over the objections of enslavers—is important. And that those in bondage chose to seek formal marriages in large numbers is significant. All of this runs counter to generations of scholarship that has understood enslaved people in the British Atlantic world to have had access only to informal marriages or, at best, religious marriages.[6] The importance of marriage to bondspeople, and the ways in which the enslaved manipulated the institution, is a central thread weaving the chapters of *Belonging* together.

Belonging does not ground itself only on the scholarship pertaining to enslaved families. The book also makes use of, and seeks to contribute to, the growing field of New England slavery studies. Far more literature reckoning with New England's long history of slavery has been published over the past couple of decades than in the preceding centuries combined. We thus know a great deal about the labor of the enslaved in the region, about the material worlds that enslaved people inhabited, about the resistance of bondspeople to slavery, about the participation of enslaved people in colonial churches, and about the connections linking the enslaved to other people in various states of unfreedom. The ties between racial thinking on the one hand and the political and religious beliefs of Anglo-Americans on the other have become much clearer. The sinews binding New England to slaveholding regions elsewhere, whether the West Indies or the mainland Southern colonies, have been examined with care. And the tortured process of emancipation in the region has received meticulous attention.[7] Yet little of this rich scholarship on slavery and its abolition in New England has given serious consideration to the intimate lives of Black families. Scholars ordinarily relegate the kin ties of bondspeople to a single chapter of larger works, if they treat them at all, and, in those chapters, they often rely on evidence from published primary source material rather than engaging deeply with New England's robust (though fragmented) archives of slavery. This book demonstrates that there is far more evidence about enslaved families in New England than historians have appreciated. By foregrounding the family strategies of New England's bondspeople, I hope to advance our grasp of the intimate and familial. I hope also to show that centering families can provide new insight into slavery and into those caught up in it. Looking at New England slavery through the lens of intimacy can shift our understandings of Black activism, of the losses suffered by those in bondage, of Afro-New Englanders' engagement with churches, of the ways in which both white and Black people thought about race, and more.

Case in point: I set out, in researching this book, to better understand the families of Black people in early New England, only to find, to my surprise, that uncovering the intimate worlds of Afro-New Englanders revealed fresh insight into the end of slavery in the region. *Belonging* thus puts forth a new vision of abolition in Massachusetts, joining scholars who argue for more attention to the roles that people of African descent played in eradicating the systems of bondage that ensnared them.[8] From start to finish, antislavery agitation in the region was linked to the actions and appeals of Black people. At the dawn of the eighteenth century, Samuel Sewall's treatise, *The Selling of Joseph*, which was the first antislavery tract printed in New England, emerged out of the judge's negotiations with Afro-New Englanders who sought to shift the day-to-day realities of slavery to accommodate their family lives. Toward the century's end, the attempts of Black people to highlight the contradictions between slavery and family would push their white neighbors to spurn slavery en masse. Generations of historians have endeavored to explain abolition in Massachusetts by repeating versions of the same story: Slavery ended in the state because the constitution declared all men "free and equal," which allowed bound people to sue successfully for their freedom.[9] However, I have uncovered striking evidence that the practice of slaveholding in the Boston area petered out before the passage of the revolutionary constitution, which means that the constitution *responded to* changes in slaveholding more than it *instigated* such changes. The cessation of slavery followed on the heels of a massive public campaign by Black activists and their allies—a campaign that featured centrally the ways in which slavery compromised families of African descent. Black people drew on ideas about family, therefore, to convince their neighbors in the revolutionary moment that slavery was illegitimate.

But what did family *mean* in revolutionary New England? And what had family meant when Sue and Jane were marched across Boston at the turn of the eighteenth century, or in the decades prior? Among Anglo-Americans in seventeenth-century New England, family was defined by two elements: co-residence and subjugation to a household head. Members of a family inhabited the same dwelling house, and—whether wives, children, servants, or the enslaved—they all answered to the household head (who was usually a man but could be a widowed woman). Evidence suggests that many puritans developed loving relationships with their spouses and children. Nonetheless, families in seventeenth-century New England were economic units more than affective ones. They were also units in which kinship ties were not central; servants, enslaved people, apprentices, and other non-kin workers were all incorporated.[10]

Though aspects of this economic, household-based understanding of the family were enduring, ideas about family life changed meaningfully over the period under study in this book. By the middle of the eighteenth century, the ideal of companionate marriage had emerged. Anglo-Americans began increasingly to place emotional intimacy at the heart of matrimony. The power that fathers exercised over the marriages of their grown children receded. Parents became gentler, and more engaged, when it came to childrearing. Influenced by the culture of sensibility and the language of sentiment that pervaded at the time, white New Englanders came increasingly to regard and experience families as affective spaces of intimate election. It was to their families that the region's colonists turned for strength, for succor, and for mutual sympathy.[11]

By the era of the American Revolution, Black New Englanders were talking about the family using similar terms as white New Englanders. Family was—or should be, they claimed—a haven of domestic affection. And the institution of slavery, they argued, deserved to be castigated for the damage it did to family intimacy. Slavery violently interrupted the "endearing ties" that bondspeople had built with one another. It "stole" children from "the bosoms of tender parents." As one Black father declared, he was driven by "parental Affection" to liberate his daughter. And slavery separated wives from their "affectionate" husbands. One Black couple was said to have stated that separation would be the "greatest evil that could befall them" because it would take from them "all the comfort & enjoyment of the married state." If family was a source of comfort generated by the commitment of a husband and wife to one another and to their children, then family was not out of the reach of New Englanders in slavery. People living under the authority of others could achieve this (though the threat of long-distance separation always loomed). Black New Englanders, including the enslaved, could build the sorts of families that their white neighbors were building by the middle of the eighteenth century. They had at their disposal a deep desire for intimacy, they were willing to do the work of cultivating affection across households, and they had mastered the syntax of sentiment.[12]

It was harder for people in bondage to form families based on the earlier Anglo-American vision, centered as it was on co-residence, subjection to the authority of the household head, and shared economy. Few enslaved husbands and wives lived together in early New England, and rarer still were nuclear families under one roof. A man in bondage could not command authority the way an enslaver could. And, though it was possible for the enslaved to acquire property, the families they built were by no means economic units; bondspeople belonged to Anglo-American households and were forced to contribute to those family economies rather than meeting the needs of their own spouses and children. Nonetheless, evidence suggests that some Afro-New Englanders pursued this form of family—or, at least, variations on the theme. Important here is the embrace of formal marriage. Bondspeople in Massachusetts understood that, for their English neighbors, marriage was crucial to initiating families, to cleaving members from two different families in service of making a third one. Because marriage was seen as creating a new family, only certain people in certain situations were allowed to marry; the access to marriage of household subordinates, such as children, apprentices, and servants, was regulated by law. Enslaved people of African descent were the only dependents of Anglo-American households allowed, against an enslaver's will, to engage in the civil ritual that fractured established Anglo-American families and built new ones. And, indeed, large numbers of them did pursue marriage. They also pursued release from bondage. The desire to form their own families practicing shared economy under the authority of a household head appears to have loomed large in the minds of some. Consider the man who, after obtaining his freedom in the early eighteenth century, saved money to buy the woman he wished to marry. He reportedly explained that he "purpose[d] Marriage" to the woman in question but would not follow through until he had purchased her from her enslaver: He would not have a wife who remained in submission to another.[13]

The ability of the enslaved to incorporate so effectively divergent family forms—all despite the vicissitudes of life in bondage—is impressive. It provides yet more evidence of something to which scholars of New England slavery have already drawn attention: the adaptability of those bound in the region.[14] But these varieties of family—the capacious economic one and the denser affective one—were by no means the only sorts of intimacies to sustain those in slavery. On the contrary, evidence suggests that Black residents of Massachusetts deeply valued other kin, whether aunts and uncles, children-in-law, or grandparents.[15] The enslaved cherished as well the companionship and aid of communities to which they were linked by neither blood nor contract: bondspeople in the household, brethren in the pews, neighbors down the street, friends the next town over. This should hardly surprise, for networks of kin in West African societies were expansive and flexible, incorporating a diverse array of people for the purpose of strengthening the group.[16] The records of early New England make clear that people in bondage were forced to belong to their enslavers—but a careful reading of the sources shows that not all belonging was coercive. The enslaved, time and again, *chose* to belong to companions, to those bound alongside them, to brothers and sisters, to husbands and wives, to parents and children, and to other kin. This book considers these collective decisions to belong within the context of the forcible belonging that was thrust upon Black New Englanders in bondage.[17]

*   *   *

To explore slavery and family in New England, *Belonging* assembles archival fragments primarily from the eastern part of Massachusetts, with particular emphasis on Boston and the surrounding towns. Narrowing the evidentiary focus in this case is strategic. Recent scholarship has suggested that local conditions might have varied widely enough in different parts of New England to allow the development of divergent labor practices and systems of bondage.[18] By refusing to collapse the entire region into a single frame, and instead paying attention to local circumstances, *Belonging* tells a textured story of the development of a place and its people.

Boston and the surrounding towns cannot claim to represent all of New England, of course. However, the area is a particularly useful one in which to explore slavery and family. As the commercial lynchpin of the region and the wealthiest and most populous part of New England, the Boston area had a considerable number of African-descended inhabitants. Boston's Black population very much dominated that of Massachusetts; in the first half of the eighteenth century, approximately one-third to one-half of all Black people in the entire province resided in the town.[19] The numbers are comparatively small, at least early on. Only around 400 people of African descent are estimated to have lived in Boston in the first decade of the eighteenth century. By midcentury, however, the number of Black inhabitants counted by census climbed to 1,541—about 10 percent of the port's population— and scholars have suggested that the actual Black population was higher, composing closer to 15 percent of Boston's total inhabitants. Boston's Black population trailed downward in the third quarter of the eighteenth century, but no town in New England overtook it: The port was, in some sense, the slaveholding capital of New England throughout the colonial period.[20] It was the cultural capital as well, educating the region's leaders, producing printed materials that circulated widely, and generating legislation that influenced neighboring colonies. The area's economic and cultural prominence make it a productive place in which to trace the tactics used by its sizable population of people of African descent to build intimacy within the context of bondage.

Belonging proceeds roughly chronologically from the settlement of the Massachusetts Bay Colony to the era of the Revolution, trawling through some 150 years of history. Its six chapters tell the stories of six different families of African descent. These family narratives display tremendous variety. Just as Sue and Jane started out on quite different paths despite their shared gender, race, and enslaved status, the life trajectories of others diverged enormously as well. And yet, certain threads tie these narratives together. Readers will encounter, time and again, the impediment of dark skin and bound status, but they will see as well people seeking continually to create meaningful relationships and negotiating with Anglo-American people and institutions in order to do so. Sometimes those in bondage conceived of unusual, even counterintuitive strategies, calibrated carefully to a particular historical context. Often, however, the tactics used in different historical eras bear an uncanny resemblance to one another. The echoes through the years suggest powerful continuities in both the obstacles faced by Black families and the activist traditions used to counter those obstacles. The radical claims that bondspeople were broadcasting throughout the region by the book's end—claims that played a role in dismantling slavery during the revolutionary era—had deep roots.

Though each chapter of this book tells a family story, *Belonging* does more than chronicle the experiences of six clusters of people tied by blood, marriage, or affection. Indeed, as you will see, I often leave behind my main characters for many pages at a time. I do this both by necessity and by choice. Occasionally, I am compelled to look elsewhere because the trail my actors left in the historical record has grown cold. I like to think of the work I do as biographical, but the fact remains that I do not have access to the kind of evidence that grounds most biographical writing. I seek to make up for the shortcomings of the historical record by developing the contexts of the stories I tell. Fragments of other people's lives captured in the archive can help me answer questions about my main characters that the historical record does not directly answer. The shards and snippets gleaned from my principal actors' communities are therefore *part of* my central narratives rather than diversions from them, even though they often direct the storyline away from my main cast of characters. This work of building context, of accounting for the experiences of hundreds of others who shared my main characters' time and place, gives my book meaning beyond the six stories it tells. By developing the settings in which its historical actors operated, *Belonging* excavates a larger history of the ways in which people across time and space built and maintained intimate relationships.[21] The many examples the book provides enable each chapter to serve as a deep exploration of a particular aspect of the intimate lives of the enslaved, such as marriage or childhood, even as it tells a family story.

And there *are* many examples. I would like to dwell a bit longer on the topic of evidence: where the evidence in this book comes from, how I use it, and why it matters. When I conceived of this project, I anticipated that it would present evidentiary challenges. Not surprisingly, others, including people I greatly respected, warned me of the same. Uneasy but undeterred, I embarked on research in earnest. Might the archive somehow reveal itself differently to me than it had to others? But this was not to be. What I found, to my dismay, was that the indexes, catalogs, guides, and aids upon which historians usually depend proved my doubters correct. The historical record would allow me to cobble together bits and pieces about how enslaved people and their work fit into the matrix of local labor practices. Likewise, some evidence existed of the participation of bondspeople in churches and of their engagement with courts. And there were certainly clues to the movement of people in slavery within and beyond the region. But the intimate lives of those in bondage? They were obscured almost entirely from my vision.

At this point, it would have been prudent to pivot to a project that was more feasible from a research standpoint. Instead, though, I chose to dig in my heels. What if, rather than change my topic, I changed my methodology? What if I assumed that there were no shortcuts—none at all—to this sort of work? What if I tossed the indexes, which nearly all the time pointed to enslavers rather than to those they enslaved, anyway? And what if, instead, I simply opened the record books and read from the first page to the last? What might I find? I started with local probate court records. Ultimately, I gleaned clues from a page-by-page perusal of 131 weighty volumes—and was stunned. Over 99 percent of the evidence pertaining to people of African descent in these records was not recoverable using the alphabetized indexes or probate dockets prepared by archivists seeking to make the records accessible. Buoyed by my findings, I turned to other courts. Working methodically, I gleaned data from dozens of volumes of the Suffolk County civil court's records. I also read each page of fifty-two volumes produced in the eighteenth century by the high court of Massachusetts. The payoff was clear; by my approximation, more than nine of ten references to Black people in these court records could be found only by means of a page-by-page perusal. My body of evidence grew. I turned to the records of other courts. Likewise, I read volumes of church records from start to finish. I read diaries. I read volumes of papers collected by the town of Boston. And I read records produced by the town selectmen. I worked, page by page, through marvelous tomes compiled by the Massachusetts State Archives, into which are pasted papers documenting every aspect of the state's early history. This list could go on.

Over the years, I uncovered mountains of evidence, much of it fragmentary. In fact, as I went about writing *Belonging*, I realized that my problem had become less one of lack and more one of excess: There was simply too much. Again and again, I made the difficult decision to scrap clues to forgotten people's lives, clues that I had, at great effort, fished out of the oceans of New England's early records. But I have refused to tame and tidy this work too much. This is intentional: The abundance of evidence in *Belonging* serves a purpose. Ours is an era of skepticism about what the archive has to offer to historians of slavery—and for good reason. Nearly all of the written records produced in the early modern Atlantic world were penned by enslavers rather than by those they enslaved. They were generated to document (and often to justify) the actions of those who stole the lives and livelihoods of others.

Frequently, they were created for the very purpose of protecting the institution of slavery. The archive, therefore, is poorly equipped to probe the intimate worlds of the disinherited.[22] But this book argues that it can do so in spite of itself. The profusion of evidence in *Belonging* suggests the capacity of the archive—or, at least, of *some* archives—to offer extraordinary insight when plumbed with a particular set of research methodologies. *Belonging* also argues that the ability to slog systematically through extensive collections is crucial to enabling scholars of the enslaved to do their work. The luxury of inefficiency in one's research is what makes this sort of historical detective work possible.[23]

Reading systematically through hundreds of volumes of records allowed me to cobble together a great deal of evidence—and it did something else as well. My methodical approach turned up *individual people* in the archive. As I worked through different bodies of sources—moving from the courts, to the churches, to the records of municipal government, and beyond—I filed away my findings in a series of databases. Over time, it became clear from the accumulation of this evidence that historical actors who appeared in one archival collection would sometimes reappear in another—and then another, and another. My findings therefore amounted to more than a jumble of isolated anecdotes: From them, I could begin to make out the contours of actual lives. And the sources allowed me not only to glimpse these individual lives but also to uncover clues linking people to one another. In some cases, it was possible to reconstruct networks of kin. From this realization emerged the structure of *Belonging*. When it became clear that I could tell intimate stories of families of African descent in seventeenth- and eighteenth-century New England and that I had the supplemental evidence necessary to help make sense of such stories, I decided that these stories must shape the narrative trajectory of the broader work.

I am glad that I made this decision, and I am glad that I stuck with it over the years of writing and revising, for the simple reason that human narratives are powerful. There are, nonetheless, costs to telling such stories. By committing to narrate the events that my main characters experienced, roughly in the order in which these people experienced them, I have sacrificed certain aspects of my authorial control. Analytically structured chapters can develop and substantiate arguments more or less as the historian wishes. Narratively structured chapters, by contrast, have more constraints. For example, in any given chapter I cannot raise topics in order of importance. Nor can I move from that which is familiar to readers to that which is unfamiliar, or from that which is simple to that which is complex. I cannot dictate my own scheme for introducing material; instead, I must broach my subject according to what the story driving the chapter allows.

A similar issue governs the organization of the book as a whole. *Belonging* moves forward through time, starting with the earliest story and ending with the latest one. Each story discusses the themes that lie at its heart, and each story leaves other matters unaddressed. Certain subjects are therefore discussed early in the book, while other topics are taken up later. Consider the example of sexual violence. This weighty matter does not receive attention until the fifth of six chapters, when the story at hand leads naturally to its discussion. It would be a mistake, however, to conclude because of this arrangement that the intimate violence women suffered in New England slavery is an issue of little significance. My intention in arranging the material this way is certainly not to downplay the importance of sexual violence by foregrounding other items at its expense; instead, I am trying to remain faithful to the stories that I have chosen as narrative vectors for my chapters, each of which deals with a particular historical period and explores a cluster of related themes. So please bear with me as I move chronologically through time, both within each chapter and within the book as a whole.

Now for a glimpse of the people, and their worlds, that each chapter of this book seeks to understand. In the first chapter, "Dorcas and Her Kin," I tell the story of Dorcas, one of the first enslaved Africans brought to New England. Through Dorcas's story, I examine how racial slavery was incorporated into the cultural, legal, and religious fabric of New England, and how this incorporation frustrated the efforts of those who wished to build families within the context of bondage. Dorcas's persistence in mastering Christian beliefs and practices—and her claim that membership in a Christian community should be liberatory in a temporal sense as well as a spiritual one—ultimately persuaded her brethren to free her for the purpose of righting her family life. But Dorcas did not start a trend; people of African descent in New England would continue to be caught between the opposing demands of belonging to one another and belonging to enslavers. The next chapter, "Sebastian, Jane Lake, and Their Children," centers on the problem of marriage for those in bondage, exploring the union that led to the birth of baby Jane, whose 1701 baptism opened this Introduction. The chapter charts the development of an unusual marriage culture in Massachusetts, where civil, legally recognized marriages between enslaved people proliferated, and it argues that the demands of people like Jane and Sebastian, along with puritan misgivings about extramarital sex and spousal separation, led white New Englanders to alter customs of slavery emerging in the British Atlantic world—customs that devalued marital integrity for the enslaved—in ways that sometimes benefited those in bondage. Chapter 3, "Sue Black and Her Sons," turns to baby Sue, sold at six weeks of age, whose final moments with her mother are chronicled in the beginning of this Introduction. Sue suffered a fate common to bound children in early New England: separation from all natal kin. By telling Sue's story and that of her children, the chapter seeks to shed light on what it was like to grow up enslaved in early New England, where the isolation could be numbing.

Record keepers vigorously sorted New Englanders by race in the seventeenth and eighteenth centuries, but Chapter 4, "The Bedunahs," makes clear that people in the past did not always draw such divisions and that sometimes they *could not* draw them. Thomas Bedunah, a man of African ancestry, his English wife, Lydia, and their mixed-race children lived an economically comfortable life among Lydia's extended network of kin, coming over time to be treated quite like white folks—indeed, coming to be *perceived as* white folks. Within two generations, they were altogether indistinguishable from their Anglo-American neighbors. However, even as Thomas accumulated property and achieved standing in his community, other Black New Englanders found the barriers placed by African ancestry and enslaved status intractable. These barriers are on full display in Chapter 5, "Mark, Phillis, and Phoebe." The three central characters in this story found themselves thwarted at every hand by the power their enslaver wielded over their circles of belonging. Tackling head-on the reality that many people in bondage built forms of family that did not adhere to Anglo-American models, Chapter 5 shows the importance to enslaved people of nuclear families sanctioned by neither church nor state; of communities that blossomed in taverns, on the streets, and under cover of darkness; and of kin-like connections that people in slavery nurtured with those bound in the same households. The chapter shows as well the power of enslavers to disrupt the life-giving threads of connection tying one bondsperson to another. And it demonstrates how this power might drive the enslaved to desperation.

Belonging's sixth, and final, chapter, "The Vassalls," follows Cuba and Anthony Vassall and their children from slavery to freedom during the American Revolution. It uses their story to reexamine the narratives that historians have told about the end of slavery in Massachusetts—narratives that privilege the passage of the state's liberatory constitution—and to center instead the actions and arguments of people of African descent leading up to that moment. During the revolutionary era, Black activists and their allies worked to discredit slavery by emphasizing its incompatibility with family. Evidence suggests that this line of reasoning had power: Slaveholding in the Boston area screeched to a halt with the onset of war in 1775 rather than, as scholars have long believed, after the adoption of the 1780 constitution that declared all men "free and equal." These developments built on a foundation that bondspeople had been laying since Dorcas had justified her claims to family integrity in the seventeenth century. Generations of commitment on the part of the enslaved to forging bonds in public meant that every white Bostonian who made a stand against the British in the 1770s had witnessed bound children held up for baptism, had watched Black people make their way across town to visit family members, and had heard ministers announce the marriage plans of enslaved people in their congregations. Clusters of state- and religion-sanctioned Black kin were more visible in Boston than they were in most of the rest of the Anglo-Atlantic world—and this visibility made more compelling the argument that these people deserved the right to family integrity. Generations of faithful family building had put cracks in the foundation of slavery, and, during the Revolution, the edifice, built brick by brick over the preceding century and a half, began to crumble. Finding ways to belong to one another—and to justify that belonging in the public square— helped the enslaved bring into being a world in which they would not have to belong to enslavers.

Belonging is first and foremost a history of individuals and their families in seventeenth- and eighteenth-century eastern Massachusetts. Through telling the stories of these intimate ties—these life-sustaining bonds of blood, contract, and affection—this book sheds light on the unremitting struggle of the enslaved to retain control over their personal lives. In the process, *Belonging* reshapes our understanding of racial slavery in the region. While never underestimating the power of enslavers over those they bound, *Belonging* nonetheless shows that generations of Black Americans both belonged to and belonged in Massachusetts, where they steadily built, and over time made unassailable, their claims to family and to freedom.

CHAPTER 1

Dorcas and Her Kin

Slavery, Family, and the Law in the Seventeenth Century

> There shall never be any bond slaverie, villinage or
> Captivitie amongst us unles it be lawfull Captives taken in
> just warres, and such strangers as willingly selle
> themselves or are sold to us. And these shall have all the
> liberties and Christian usages which the law of god
> established in Israell concerning such persons doeth
> morally require. This exempts none from servitude who
> shall be Judged thereto by Authoritie.
>
> —The Body of Liberties, 1641

Dorcas looked out upon the sea of faces under the thatched roof of the crude logwood meetinghouse. She was there on that day in April 1641 to give voice to the transformation that God had brought about in her life. She might have felt the pressure: This was a crucial step to joining the puritan community. The silence rolled over her; the congregants were waiting. Inhaling sharply, perhaps, the young woman began to speak. We do not know what she said, but many relations of faith given by Massachusetts colonists survive, and we can be confident that Dorcas would have adhered to the basic structure that governed the genre.[1] She likely began with an acknowledgment of the sin that plagued her, even in her mother's womb. Then, she might have gone on to address the misfortunes that had broken down her pride. Perhaps the woman told her listeners, as did another confessant, that "the Lord took away all I had." For Dorcas, such a proclamation could hardly have been an overstatement. The young woman had almost certainly been born in West Central Africa, captured as a girl just reaching adulthood, and sold to the men who packed people into slave ships on the coast.[2]

Or, perhaps Dorcas expressed, in the words of another confessant, that the "Lord brought me through many sad troubles by sea." This would have been truer for Dorcas than any of those circled round could have known; the stench of vomit and sweat and feces had filled the ship's hold. Some spiritual relations delivered in Massachusetts lingered on experiences of illness and death. We "were all sick," one Native American confessant remembered; "my kindred died," recalled another.[3] Dorcas, too, had experienced such troubles. Mortality on a slave ship was inescapable. Any vessel on which Dorcas could have crossed the ocean would have left a trail of Black bodies in its wake; evidence generated by the trade suggests that over one-sixth of captives taken into the Atlantic at this time lost their lives at sea. All of this had to have taken a toll. Perhaps Dorcas acknowledged, as did another confessant, that her heart had become "dead and senseless" from her "hard voyage." A heart that had moved beyond feeling would have revealed to Dorcas's emotive audience the depth of her descent.[4]

The woman's words washed over her listeners. These "straits," this "affliction," such "sad trials," they trusted, could render supple the most unregenerate sinner in the hand of her Maker. Thankfully, the congregants might have observed, God's hand had drawn Dorcas to New England, and here there was instruction on how properly to be humbled. At this point in her relation, Dorcas likely recalled before her audience what she had begun to learn in this strange new land. Did she highlight the words of her minister? The truth captured in a catechism? A powerful passage of scripture? Perhaps, as Dorcas had grown in understanding and as her insight had become keener, she had come to recognize that her motives for pursuing God were mixed. Hypocrisy, after all, knocked at every soul's door.[5] As a woman in bondage, scorned at every turn a stranger, did Dorcas engage in pious practices for impious purposes? Maybe she admitted, as did an Indigenous confessant, that "I therefore prayed, because many *English* knew me, and that I might please them." Seeking to affix tendrils of connection to puritan believers would have made good sense, for nothing in this unfamiliar place could match the intimacy of the community of saints.[6] But God, in His mercy, corrects those whose ambitions are misplaced. Dorcas would have learned over time that the English could not save. No, she must look to Jesus.

Every congregant whose eyes were fixed on Dorcas had begun, at some point, to develop an awareness of good and evil, and they could hardly have forgotten when they first countenanced, in horror, the depth of their depravity. Dorcas would have related a similar experience. And she likely acknowledged, as had those before, her inability to overcome the sin that held her back. But in weakness Christ works. Perhaps it was in Dorcas's very debility, in her very lack, that she "discovered the freeness of grace," as one godly woman put it. Receiving Christ, or "closing with the Lord," in the puritans' turn of phrase, might have brought Dorcas delight. His "sweetness" caused me "to break out to weeping," one of Dorcas's brethren told his listeners; "He let me feel his love," proclaimed one of Dorcas's sisters in Christ.[7] We cannot know how Dorcas chose to conclude her story, but the historical record makes clear that the woman's tale of transformation was compelling. When Dorcas fell silent, the congregation broke forth; one after another commended the woman's "blamelesse and godly" spirit, and her brothers and sisters admitted her to their fellowship with "great joy to all their hearts."[8] The woman had made herself a saint. Of course, Dorcas would have been quick to demur, for no puritan could claim to have worked her own salvation; it was God in her that accomplished this.[9] But perhaps that made Dorcas all the more remarkable. The Almighty had chosen her, dredged her from a sea of souls, leaving so many others—people of education, wealth, and position—eddying among the wreckage of a wicked world. Full assurance was ever elusive, yet Dorcas finally was tethered to something that offered her sea-weary heart some steadiness. The words of a fellow saint might have resonated with the young believer: "I saw although my soul did doubt, yet my soul was a ship at anchor."[10]

The relation that Dorcas delivered on that April day of 1641 represented a major spiritual accomplishment: Dorcas was the first person of African descent received into a congregation in New England. This chapter considers Dorcas's remarkable act of spiritual integration alongside the early development of slavery in Massachusetts. I begin by sketching out potential African pasts for Dorcas; no historical records shed light directly on the woman's origins, but it is possible to piece together plausible beginnings and a likely path to New England. Once Dorcas set foot in Massachusetts, I can pencil in the contours of her life with a firmer hand. I explore the dynamics of the household in which Dorcas was enslaved, a household riven by hierarchy yet intensely intimate: Its many members spent much of their lives together in a single room, synchronized to the rhythm of puritan devotional practices. I likewise explore the process by which Dorcas mastered puritan theology and persuaded her brethren to embrace her as a member of their church. Here I pivot to the political context of Dorcas's faith journey. The colony at the time was debating its first body of legislation, called the "Body of Liberties," which inscribed slavery in law just as news of Dorcas's godliness was spreading in Massachusetts. Dorcas's brethren, that is, chose to label her a forever outsider almost immediately after she had navigated the public process of demonstrating that she belonged. But Dorcas did not let them have the last word. She went about making herself socially legible in a variety of ways, perhaps most importantly by creating a family with an African man in Boston and bearing children. Hers was a family broken by distance, which Dorcas—and the brethren—knew was not what God had intended. Dorcas drew attention to this reality, managing in an impressive act of persuasion to induce the very people who had once endorsed her permanent bondage to devote their time and financial resources to liberating her for the purpose of righting her family life. The woman's story suggests that belonging to a puritan congregation in seventeenth-century New England could bring powerful life change. But Dorcas's tale stands out, as much as anything else, for its singularity. Dorcas's experiences did not echo in the lives of others bound in seventeenth-century Massachusetts; the system of slavery would only become more rigid and robust over the course of the woman's lifetime. Dorcas managed to maneuver herself out, but other bondspeople in the region would struggle for generations with little relief against the very same problems that had plagued her family.[11]

*   *   *

Dorcas probably was not named "Dorcas" at birth, but we cannot know what she was called by the people who brought her into the world and sustained her as she grew. Nor can we discern exactly when Dorcas was born, though clues exist.[12] The girl whom the Dorchester brethren would refer to as "Dorcas ye blackmore" might have spent her early years in the Kingdom of Kongo on the western coast of Central Africa, a strong and centralized state that had long since developed a form of African Christianity.[13] Catholic catechisms and visions of saints would have filled her mind, even as she laid out food for deceased kin and received revelations from the deities who intervened for her in the spirit realm.[14] As a Kongolese child, Dorcas would have known a world of slavery. While her people had once been hesitant to bind their own, captives were the currency of trade with the outside world, and Kongo's elite had contrived many mechanisms for reducing people to bondage by the time

Dorcas was born. The girl could have been fettered as the result of a crime committed by a kinsman, or she could have been sold into slavery by a deceitful family member. She could have been bound for failing to show deference to the authorities, or she could have been seized when a rival political faction outmaneuvered her own.[15] Once reduced to human property, Dorcas would likely have been traded south to the port of Luanda in the Portuguese colony of Angola, where she fell into the clutches of one of the Europeans who sold Africans across the seas.[16]

Or, Dorcas might have had a different West Central African origin. It may be that she was born in the Kingdom of Ndongo, south of Kongo and to the interior of Angola. Coming of age in a village of a hundred people or so, she would have learned to farm from Ndongo's female agriculturalists, perhaps planting corn, an American crop that the Ndongo had recently embraced. If the fields grew dry or seasonal rains caused landslides in the highlands, Dorcas would have petitioned the spirits who controlled natural forces, for Christianity had penetrated the kingdom but little. Dorcas might also have summoned the souls of her ancestors; the Ndongo often turned to those who had predeceased them when they needed help or guidance as they moved through their world. Indeed, one can imagine the girl directing anxious requests to her unseen protectors, for life in Ndongo when Dorcas was a child was particularly perilous.[17] Hungry for captives to export into the Atlantic, the Portuguese in nearby Angola reduced tens of thousands of Ndongo people to slavery with the aid of the Imbangala, a destructive group of marauders who pillaged villages for survival.[18] Kidnapped in the turmoil, perhaps, the girl would likely have been transported down the Kwanza River to Luanda. There, she and the other prisoners would have been locked in pens, chained one to the next, and left to wait.[19] When ships appeared on the horizon, the captives would have been counted, taxed, and hastily baptized. Then, descending into the dark bellies of slavers with names like "St. John the Baptist," "Holy Spirit," and "Good Jesus," they would have sailed west.[20]

We do not know, of course, that Dorcas was from Ndongo; nor can we claim with confidence that she was Kongolese. Dorcas could well have been born into another people group in the region. However, what we *do* know about the movement of people around the Atlantic rim in the early seventeenth century makes fairly certain that Dorcas hailed from West Central Africa and was taken by Portuguese traders to the Americas. At the time of the girl's capture, the Portuguese dominated the Atlantic slave trade, supplying through vessels of death and despair the African labor that had come to power so much of Spanish America.[21] And most Portuguese slavers did business in Angola; packed in their fetid hulls were hundreds of human beings who had been forced on board in the Bay of Luanda.[22] Vessels sailing under the Portuguese flag did not make a practice of transporting human cargo to North America, so peripheral were the fledgling English colonies to the Atlantic economic system. Instead, they plied the Caribbean Sea toward the bustling Spanish ports of Veracruz and Cartagena. There, in the sky-blue waters of the Caribbean, English and Dutch sea captains managed, when their luck was right, to intercept Portuguese ships, stealing the Iberians' treasure—gold, silver, and *people*. Dorcas then, like the other Africans brought early on to the English colonies in North America, doubtless came by piracy.[23]

Dorcas might have been stolen by puritan pirates, in fact. In 1630, the same year one group of puritans settled the Massachusetts Bay Colony, another group formed a colony on Providence Island, a tiny landmass off the Caribbean coast of what is today Nicaragua. The puritans in the Caribbean had high hopes of producing tropical crops in abundance, but, before the decade was out, they had given up on tilling their way to wealth. Instead, they decided to earn their daily bread by plundering Iberian shipping and coastal settlements.[24] These raiders might have been the ones to capture Dorcas, for the earliest recorded shipment of bound Africans to arrive in Massachusetts Bay hailed from Providence Island.[25] In the harbor of that tiny puritan stronghold awash in a sea of Iberian power, a Massachusetts trading vessel called the *Desire* had reportedly met two English warships, both of which held licenses for privateering. These ships had "taken divers prizes" from the Iberians, the story went—prizes that included "many negroes."[26]

If Dorcas was one of these "prizes" seized by the English, she would have sailed toward Boston on the *Desire* in early 1638.[27] Perhaps, braving the bitter sea winds of February, she stood on deck as the vessel, at its journey's end, maneuvered around the pallid frozen islands that punctured the blue of Massachusetts Bay. Had Dorcas from that point gazed landward, she could have spied her destination. We might imagine the girl squinting to make out a harbor shrouded by snow as the *Desire* approached the waters of what Bostonians called the Great Cove, which lapped the docks of the town's North End and soaked the icy marshes along the port's eastern flank. The rough-hewn wharves and piers of the fledgling town would steadily have grown closer to the ship and the girl who stood sentinel on board. Then, as the tide came in, the *Desire* would have docked, dropping anchor, and Dorcas would have disembarked.[28]

We cannot be certain that Dorcas was one of the Africans stolen by puritan pirates near Providence Island and shipped aboard the *Desire* to Massachusetts, but we do know that Dorcas was in the Boston area soon after the *Desire* returned to port. The girl found herself in the town of Dorchester, some five or six miles up the Neponset River from Dorchester Bay, which was itself a mile south of Boston Harbor. She was forced to join the household of Israel Stoughton, a household composed, like middling English families on both sides of the Atlantic, of people related to its head by blood, marriage, and obligation. Israel and his wife, Elizabeth, had four children: Israel, Susanna, William, and Hannah.[29] And others joined them in the wood-frame house on the bank of the Neponset River. Israel's mother-in-law, Elizabeth Knight, lived there, which brought her English servant, John Stringer, under Israel's governance as well.[30] Alexander Miller and John Wipple, English servants who had helped Israel establish his Dorchester farm, were likewise recognizable features of the household. Other dependents, like Robert Way, temporarily resided in Israel's home while the Bay Colony's court sorted out whom they should serve and for how long. And records suggest that Israel added an Indigenous woman to his domestic labor force just before Dorcas entered the household.[31]

Upon Dorcas's arrival, there would have been at least eleven people living in the household. If Israel indeed obtained the Native woman he sought, this polyglot of people bound by ties of dependence to Israel would have numbered twelve. And when Israel was given temporary charge of English people in bondage, the household's count could push to thirteen or fourteen. All were considered part of Israel's family, for a family at the time was defined by two elements: co-residence and subjugation to a household head. Of course, belonging to a family in seventeenth-century Massachusetts did not ensure parity or equivalence of status. Hierarchies defined every relationship in Israel's household, and shared economy mattered more than affection. Nonetheless, this hierarchically ordered economic unit binding diverse dependents to a central authority existed within the context of extraordinary physical intimacy.[32]

The members of Israel's family lived in close quarters. At all times there would have been four people in various forms of bondage—Dorcas, Israel's two English servants, and Elizabeth Knight's bondsman—and often there would have been more unfree people. However, no separate outbuilding existed to house them.[33] Nor was there likely any kind of spatial division within the home between the members of the household bound to Israel by blood and marriage on the one hand and those bound by their obligation to serve on the other. In terms of daily nearness, the experiences of enslaved New Englanders contrasted markedly with the experiences of those bound in plantation regions, where bondspeople most often lived at some distance from their enslavers. Consider the case of Israel's family. Given Israel's social status, his house likely had two rooms, but it is possible that it had only one: The inventory of Israel's belongings, taken after his death in 1650, specified merely the "great Chamber" of his home.[34] Based on the objects recorded in this room, the entire family appears to have slept, eaten, and dressed here. The fire, in its enormous hearth, was tended here. Israel did his writing here, seated in a chair, pulling quill and parchment from a nearby trunk. The children played and were schooled here. The women spun and sewed here. And when the fields were snowed over, the men worked here at carpentry or repairing farm equipment. Each member of the household moved through the small, dark, low-ceilinged room in a complex choreography of daily life, rarely more than an arm's length from another.[35] Nobody in the family would have thought much about privacy; curtains on the bedsteads, intended to insulate sleepers through long winter nights, afforded the only real seclusion from the others, but, of course, one could not expect one's own bed. If Dorcas spent her nights on one of the family's bedsteads, she would have shared it with at least one mate, perhaps more. The girl slept in the arms of strangers.

Together they slumbered, together they awoke, and together they gathered. Israel led them each morning in expressing to God their great gratitude: "thou hast preserved us this night past from all the dangers and feares thereof, hast given us quiet rest to our bodies, and brought us now safely to the beginning of this day."[36] Somebody then read a passage of scripture—family members took turns with this—and Israel explained its meaning. Chapter by chapter they worked through the Bible, starting anew in Genesis upon finishing the book of Revelation. After listening to Israel's teaching, Dorcas and her fellow householders sang psalms by candlelight in the dimness of dawn. Nobody kept time—Dorcas chanted at her own pace, her breath chasing the smoke—but their discordant worship was strangely affecting.[37] The psalms they chose allowed them to give voice to their thanksgiving. Waking in the morning was akin to awakening to rebirth in God, and they started their days by expressing gratitude both for physical life and for spiritual intimacy with their maker.

Mealtimes provided further opportunities for spiritual reflection. Before eating, puritans centered their minds on their weakness: They needed food,

Figure 1. Fairbanks House hearth. Dorcas might have tended fires in a hearth similar in expanse to the one in the Fairbanks home: six feet wide by four feet tall. Built in Dedham, Massachusetts, around the time of Dorcas's arrival in the Bay Colony, the Fairbanks house has little glazing and low ceilings. Courtesy of Sharmin McKenney and the Fairbanks House.

day after day, else they would perish. They meditated on God's power: It was He who provided, through every season, what was necessary for their sustenance. And they asked God to use their physical hunger to kindle their spiritual appetite: "grant . . . that as we do hunger and thirst for this food of our bodyes, so our soules may earnestly long after the food of eternall life." After they ate, they honored God for sating their spirits and their stomachs: "To thee, O Lord, O God, which has created, redeemed, continually preserved, and at this present time fed us, be ascribed all honour, glory, power, might and dominion, now and evermore."[38] Meals always were prefaced and concluded with prayer. Never did the household partake without acknowledging the One who provided. And the evening meal, at the day's end, served as a prelude to nightly devotions. Scripture was read again, Israel exposited once more, and then the family entered a prayer of repentance. Everyone in the shadowy room thought back on wrongdoings—even that very day's—

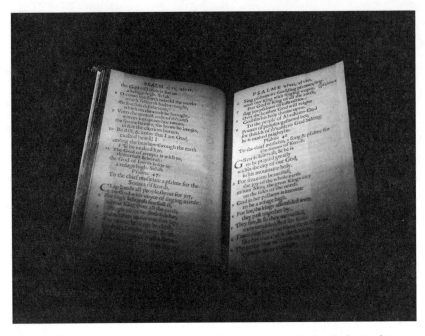

Figure 2. Bay Psalm Book. Dorcas would have sung from the Bay Psalm Book in both Israel's home and the Dorchester meetinghouse. Published in 1640, this metrical translation of the Psalms was the first book printed in English North America. Courtesy of Timothy Clary/AFP via Getty Images.

and confessed hearts that were full of "*too much* love of our selves, and the world" and "*too little* love of thee, and thy Kingdome." They sang psalms that dwelled on death, and they prepared to sleep, to rest in the care of God. He would, they trusted, wake them anew in the morning.[39]

Cycles, all tied to and interpreted through Christian faith, gave form to the life Dorcas lived with the puritans in Dorchester. The setting of the sun and its rising; the lying down each evening and morning's rousing; the nightly dying—"My Bedde is like my Grave so cold"—and the rebirth that came at the dawn of each day.[40] And there were others. After each week's toil, Dorcas observed the Sabbath at the Dorchester meetinghouse, immersed for most of the day—some six hours—in a retelling of the epic story of humanity's fall and redemption. Midweek she joined the congregants for more teaching and to worship: "lecture day," they called this. And, as the weeks turned to months, as the ground thawed or the air grew crisp, the puritans marked the passage

of the seasons with reminders both of their own frailty and of God's provision. Fast days, clustered in the spring, encouraged self-examination, for this
was a time of death, when seeds were sown—buried—in anticipation of new
life, of resurrection. And thanksgivings, often held in the autumn, provided
the saints with opportunities to celebrate the harvest of God's bounty.[41]

There must have been an early period, soon after her arrival, in which Dorcas struggled to understand the rituals of her new life, for much was strange.
The hours of formal teaching. The rows of pews in the meetinghouse. The om-
nipresence of books—Bibles, of course, but also devotional manuals, psalters,
theologies, commentaries, and published sermons. These would have struck the
girl as curious. Soon, however, Dorcas appears to have learned her part in the
household's spiritual practices, and she seems to have come to grasp the worldview that gave them meaning. She had a teacher who was both able and exact-
ing. Pious and learned, Israel had joined the Dorchester Church in 1633, right
after migrating to Massachusetts, and he would go on to serve as an elder.[42] The
man would long be remembered for his faithfulness. Decades later, one of his
brethren in the Dorchester Church would include him on a list of religious lu-
minaries mostly made up of ministers. (They were "good and holy men," the
aged colonist recalled, sent by God to Massachusetts to "chear our hearts.")[43]
In the end, Israel would give his life for his faith, taking up arms alongside
other puritans in the English Civil War and dying an ocean away from his
family.[44] He was just the sort of household head to take seriously his responsibility to educate those under his authority in the ways of the Lord.

But Israel would have known the real bounds of his tutelage. The enslaver
could, in good conscience, require Dorcas's attendance at meetings and insist upon her participation in household worship; indeed, he had to. However, he could not compel the girl to be saved, for it was the Lord who called
the godly—the elect—to himself. Dorcas, for her part, was clearly a student
of extraordinary capacity; that she mastered the intricacies of puritan theology on short order in a non-native language testifies to her intellectual dex-
terity. But she was more than a linguistically talented woman capable of
intricate thought. She was also someone who believed, or professed to believe, herself chosen. At some point—perhaps two years after she arrived in
Massachusetts—the devotional practices of home and church bore fruit:
Dorcas testified to her conversion.[45] The girl had become learned in the ways
of the Lord. As a Massachusetts minister reported, Dorcas was "indued with
a competent measure of knowledge in the mysteries of God." This knowledge had led to conviction; Dorcas had become burdened by "her miserable

estate by sinne," the minister related. And conviction had led to transformation; Dorcas had reached out to Him who offers healing for souls and "experience[d]," as the minister put it, the "saving work of grace in her heart." This grace imbued Dorcas with a quality that other saints could recognize. As one puritan teacher explained, those "who have the *Spirit* of God in them" were capable of sensing "the workings and *manifestations* of the same *Spirit* in others."[46] It was a quality that the saints savored. The "Blackmore maid" bound to the Stoughton household had "a sweet favour of Christ breathing in her."[47]

Naturally, Dorcas wished upon conversion for communion with her spiritual equals. In the words of a minister who wrote about her transformation, Dorcas "longed" to join the church. But puritan congregations did not admit just anyone to their covenanted assemblies. In order to be united with the Dorchester fellowship, Dorcas needed to convince the brethren that she had, in fact, been redeemed by the blood of Christ. This would be no simple course of action. Puritans believed, in the words of Richard Mather, Dorcas's minister in Dorchester, that "all members of churches ought to be saints." That is, nobody should be admitted to fellowship who had not received assurance from God of salvation. Therefore, as Richard put it, congregations needed to "use all . . . means whereby God may help us to discern, whether those that offer themselves . . . be persons so qualified or no."[48] For Dorcas, a girl plucked from Africa just as she was edging into adulthood, demonstrating herself to be "qualified" to join a puritan congregation in the stony New England soil in which she had been planted would mean embarking on a lengthy journey of persuasion.

Dorcas started by seeking out the elders of the Dorchester congregation and explaining to them her desire to join the church. They examined her, which was standard practice: A "trial of her [was] taken in private," a minister noted. After the elders were satisfied with Dorcas's account of her religious experiences, it fell upon the ruling elder to inform the congregation of Dorcas's desire to join and to request that members investigate whether her behavior was consonant with her claim to know Christ. If this inquiry turned up any transgressions, Dorcas would have been required to repent of the wrongdoing. Even if it did not, however, there was more work to be done, for merely avoiding grievous misconduct was insufficient; various brethren had to attest publicly to the goodness of Dorcas's behavior. Finally, the young woman, already thrice vindicated, was brought before the church to deliver her relation of faith. Fragments of this part of the process made their way into the historical record. As a minister recalled, Dorcas "was called before the whole Church, and there did make confession of her knowledge in the Mysteries of Christ and of the work of Conversion upon her Soule." The woman's story more than satisfied. She was "admitted a member by the joynt content of the Church," the minister wrote, emphasizing that the brethren experienced "great joy" in welcoming her to fellowship.[49] Opening the heavy leather-bound volume of his church's records, Richard dipped his quill in ink and scratched "Dorcas ye blackmore" on the congregation's list of members. In the quiet reverence of puritan worship on that April day in 1641, much had changed, both for Dorcas and her wider world. Never before had Richard entered into his weighty tome the name of a person who was not of English descent, and his inscription on this day represented an important reality: The Dorchester congregation had become the first puritan body on "these remote Coasts of the earth," as Richard put it, to covenant with a "blackmore."[50]

* * *

The coasts of New England were indeed remote coasts—at least from certain vantages. Geographically, the region was distant from the core wealth-producing areas of the so-called New World: the Spanish and Portuguese settlements in South and Central America, and the Caribbean, where the English were on their way to building their first lucrative colony in Barbados. But New England was not just an outlier in terms of geography. Unlike most colonial regions in the Atlantic, New England was formed by people who had chosen to exile themselves from their country over matters of conscience. Colonists like Israel Stoughton decided to build new lives in what they called a "hidious & desolate wildernes" in order to worship as they wished.[51] The religious motivations underpinning this migration influenced the sorts of migrants that came—and they influenced as well the sorts of societies those migrants built. Whole families crossed the Atlantic, rather than individuals; newcomers to the region were more educated than migrants to other English colonies; and those who disembarked on New England's shores skewed wealthier than those who landed elsewhere, with skilled craftsmen and sturdy farmers predominating among them.[52] Together they built a society that was unusually egalitarian. Terms like "Equall," "Equallitie," and "equity" peppered their writing, and a sense of proper parity shaped their decision making, whether they were divvying up land, levying taxes, or administering justice in the courts.[53]

Some participants in this communal experiment felt that New Englanders were "already in heaven," as one put it, but the commitment to ethical values had its limits.[54] Not all were welcomed into the godly commonwealth, and though the incorporated towns that proliferated across the landscape were a blessing to some, they were a curse to others. Native people suffered acutely. The New England experiment could not subsist without the land of the region's Indigenous inhabitants, and the flow of immigrants across the Atlantic quickly put pressure on Native holdings. Between the initial settlement of the Massachusetts Bay Colony in 1630 and the year 1633, more than 3,000 English migrants poured into the colony, and by 1634 many of these people had moved far inland, building settlements up and down the Connecticut River and competing with Native people for land, resources, and access to trade. The English instigated a bloody war with the Pequot tribe less than a decade after the founding of the colony, ostensibly to avenge the murder of two Englishmen, and they slaughtered their Pequot opponents, including women, children, and the elderly. They also took captives. Bay Colony leaders lacked legal justification for binding the Pequots, but, soon after the war, they sanctioned slavery in the colony's inaugural legislative code, titled—ironically, with respect to the Pequots—the Body of Liberties.[55]

The passage of the Body of Liberties, which this section of the chapter explores, might have justified the enslavement of the Pequots, but it did not restrict slavery in Massachusetts to Native people. There is no indication that the colonists considered Indigenous people especially suited for slavery; it is much more likely, in fact, that they associated people of African descent with lifelong bondage.[56] Indeed, the enslavement of Indians led rapidly to the enslavement of Africans in the region. New England was remote from centers of Atlantic wealth, but the little settlement on the northeastern coast of North America was inextricably linked to the commerce and trade in African bodies that had come to power the Atlantic system, and the region's colonists had any number of trading partners who could swap Indians for Africans. Consider, for example, the *Desire*. The vessel had left New England stocked with Pequot captives, whom her captain had exchanged for cotton, tobacco, and "negroes" on Providence Island—one of whom might well have been Dorcas.[57] From the perspective of Massachusetts colonists, this was a strategic exchange. Scholars have long recognized both the difficulty of enslaving local populations and the utility of distance as a tool for marginalizing those in bondage—twin realities that New Englanders understood from experience.[58] Native captives deserted their English enslavers in large numbers, for they were familiar with the region's terrain, had access to potential allies in their nations of origin, and benefited from their ability to blend into communities of free Indians—all of which advantaged them vis-à-vis enslaved Africans.[59] As Massachusetts enslavers saw it, then, what better than to send Pequot women to the Caribbean in exchange for women, like Dorcas, who were utter strangers to the region?

Dorcas therefore crossed the Atlantic (in bondage) for the opposite reason Massachusetts colonists did (of their own free will). Estranged from their mother country, puritans had set sail for New England because they wished to create a place of belonging; Dorcas, conversely, was brought to Massachusetts for the very purpose of alienation. The contrast must have been made all the starker to Dorcas because of her vantage point in the Stoughton household, which provided as intimate a window as any into the process by which rights expanded for ordinary English colonists while autonomy was stripped away from the foreigners meant to serve them. Israel had an outsized influence on Massachusetts governance. He had cemented his position among the colony's political elite around the time of the Pequot War and would be elected one of the ruling magistrates for years to come. And the man was not a passive member of the court. He used his standing to advocate for a number of issues "on the countrys behalfe," as he put it: issues of great importance to the "freemen"—ordinary voting colonists—rather than their leaders. In 1634, for instance, he had worked to incorporate local representatives into the governing body of Massachusetts, reducing the power of the small cadre of magistrates elected at large who had wielded unchecked authority in the colony.[60] But incorporating town-based deputies did not solve what Israel seems to have considered the fundamental problem: The freemen were still subjected to judicial rulings that depended on the discretion of their elected representatives, which—though often just and fitting—were therefore unpredictable. The solution was simple. Israel's neighbors needed protections grounded in law.

Israel was deeply invested in the process of encoding in law what the freemen came to call their "liberties"—their safeguards against unwarranted government intrusion. He was the only magistrate to join the colony's governor, deputy governor, and treasurer in the task of vetting the draft body of legislation.[61] But revision of the colony's proposed legal code did not stop with Israel's elite cohort; once the men had compiled suitable laws, they distributed them to the colony's towns to be vetted by the freemen. As Massachusetts governor John Winthrop described the process, the laws were "published by the constables to all of the people" so that "if any man should think fit, that any thing therein ought to be altered, he might acquaint some of the deputies therewith." It was a plan wrought "at length" in order to "satisfy the

people," a "democratical procedure" that ultimately exceeded what some of
the colony's leaders found reasonable—but it likely pleased the patriarch who
ruled Dorcas's household on the Neponset River.[62]

Israel must have had many conversations about this body of laws—the
Bay colonists' Body of Liberties—with his neighbors. Surely Dorchester's freemen stopped by the house to talk to the magistrate, one of the code's chief
proponents and principal architects, before trekking to Boston to make an
appearance at court. What did Israel think of the laws? Were they comprehensive enough to protect the people from the magistrates, should they
become overzealous? Were they faithful to biblical precepts? Were they
fair? How would *he* change them if he could? Dorcas would have overheard
Israel's exchanges with the freemen as she fetched them water from the nearby
well or swept the mud they tracked into the home's great room. The young
woman had mastered English by then, and conversations about the laws that
God gave the Israelites—and the laws that God's people in the Bay Colony
deserved—must have struck her as familiar. As a result of Richard's teaching in Dorchester's First Church and Israel's instruction in his home, Dorcas
knew a great deal about the saga of God's chosen people in the ancient world.
And because of her location in the household of a prominent and active leader
of the colony, Dorcas was familiar with the tension between the freemen, who
were eager for their legal protections, and their magistrates, who were reluc-
tant to codify wholesale a body of law.

If Dorcas knew about the development of the Body of Liberties in the colony, so too did the people debating the legislation know about her. News of the
African woman's godliness had spread with speed throughout the region.
When Dorcas stood in the Dorchester church and gave her testimony before
the brethren, John Winthrop was trying to govern a colony in the midst of cod-
ifying a wide-ranging body of legislation against his counsel, but he took time
to mention Dorcas's acceptance into Dorchester's First Church in his journal.
His admiration of the woman is clear: "A negro maid, servant to Mr. Stoughton
of Dorchester, being well approved by divers years' experience, for sound
knowledge and true godliness, was received into the church and baptized."[63]

The brief notation indicates the importance of the event in two ways. First,
it shows that reports of Dorcas's baptism had traveled throughout the colony
by word of mouth. John, who lived in Boston, almost surely did not witness
the event, as he rarely left his own congregation, Boston's First Church, in
order to visit others.[64] John heard of Dorcas's baptism from somebody else,
then, which indicates that the event was significant enough to become grist

for discussion among the colony's leaders. But John's mention of Dorcas's baptism does more than reveal that people outside the Dorchester community discussed the African woman's faith confession; it shows as well that Bay colonists considered Dorcas's participation in the church enormously significant. John did not ordinarily record baptisms in his journal, either infant baptisms, which were standard, or adult baptisms, which happened more occasionally. Very early on, when John's journal functioned as a day-to-day record of his life, he noted two baptisms in his Boston church, and he alluded to the admission of a prominent new settler.[65] But, besides these early references, all to people in his own congregation, John failed to remark on baptisms in the 724-page tome that historians have come to call his "journal"—with one exception, of course: that of Dorcas.[66]

The reason John neglected to write about baptisms, particularly after the early years of settlement, is simple: He began increasingly to conceive of his so-called journal as an account of puritan settlement in America rather than a chronicle of daily affairs. He never actually titled his opus a "journal," though historians have called it that ever since because it begins very much like one, with short daily entries. Instead, John conceived of what he wrote as a *history*, especially as time went on. When he began his second (of three) notebooks in October of 1636, he inscribed "A Continuation of the History of N: England" at the top of the first page, and when he began his third notebook, he titled it the same. By the time of Dorcas's baptism in 1641, John composed only about one entry a month, and these entries were longer and more retrospective than the regular brief entries he had penned a decade before.[67]

John's entries had also become more intentional. The volume had become a public book that needed to be edited for proper voice and content. John occasionally made such edits explicit in his text. Soon after Dorcas's baptism, for example, he prefaced an entry with a "Query," asking "whether the following be fit to be published." Not long after that, he deemed an event "not unworthy to be recorded," as it was "the first of its kind." And in the summer of 1643, he cancelled an entire passage, noting in the margin that "this were better left out."[68] John's largely retrospective composition of his *History*, and the active process of revision to which he subjected it, are significant to understanding Dorcas and her place in the fledgling colony. Neither the African woman's determination to join the congregation nor the Dorchester church's acceptance of her relation of faith were trivial fragments from John's daily life, casually jotted in a private account. Instead, when reports of Dorcas's baptism reached the magistrate, he deemed it news worth

remembering, and he intentionally inscribed it alongside the other notewor-
thy events of the colony in the story of New England's founding that he was
carefully crafting. The "negro maid, servant to Mr. Stoughton" had, in a
small and anonymous way, made history.

When Dorcas stood before Dorchester's First Church and shared her story
of faith, she looked out on a group of freemen engrossed in thought about
their "liberties." Not long before, they had received copies of the colony's proposed code of laws, and they had evaluated the legislation in the General
Court. Now, even as Dorcas spoke, the laws were continuing to be revised.
Both the elite cadre of legislators to which Israel belonged and the freemen
who sat in the meetinghouse pews had opportunities to alter the laws before
they were passed by the court in December of 1641. John's *History* provides
the best summary of the revision process: The court "revised" the laws (this
was the work of Israel's committee) and distributed them to "every town" to
be "further considered." Acting on the advice of "all the people," the court
then "revised" the body of legislation further before finally ratifying it.[69] On
the tenth of December, the court's records read: "the bodye of laws formerly
sent forth among the ffreemen . . . was voted to stand in force."[70] Records of
the court were kept, with few exceptions, by the colony's secretary, but John
himself scratched these lines into the court's register. He also noted the occasion in his *History*. The court "established 100 laws," he wrote, "which were
called the Body of Liberties."[71]

In certain respects, the Body of Liberties was aptly named. The Bay Colony's first legal code was more a bill of rights than a guide for government. It
laid out in detail the people's "liberties"—liberties that included freedom of
speech and movement, right to trial by jury, and protection against cruel and
unusual punishment. And the people's new liberties did not extend merely
to the freemen; the Body of Liberties included liberties for women, children,
servants—and even animals. The code also included liberties for "strangers"
like Dorcas, the "blackmore" who stood before the Dorchester First Church,
the "negro maid" who trod the page of John's *History*. The legislation guaranteed relief to "foreigners" and "strangers" should they shipwreck on the
colony's coast and promised shelter should they flee persecution, famine, or
plague—provided they profess the "true Christian religion."[72] And it granted
them a third "liberty": "There shall never be any bond slaverie, villinage or
Captivitie amongst us," the ninety-first "liberty" began, "unles it be lawfull
Captives taken in just warres, and such strangers as willingly selle themselves
or are sold to us."[73]

Emphasizing its first clause—"there shall never be any bond slaverie . . . amongst us"—some have pointed to this "liberty" as an early statement of anti-slavery sentiment in the Americas.[74] But the "liberty" that ostensibly eliminated slavery in the Bay Colony instead set forth not one but three scenarios in which slavery was legal. This had the effect of making the law sanctioning slavery in Massachusetts more capacious than legal measures passed in various places that would become major centers of slavery. For instance, when Barbados had legalized slavery several years prior, the applicable decree only allowed enslavement for the third of the three scenarios set out by the Bay Colony's legislation.[75] Would-be enslavers in Massachusetts therefore had options. Bay colonists could lawfully claim the lifelong labor of other human beings as long as they were "Captives taken in just warres," like the Pequots shipped to Caribbean slavery aboard the *Desire*; "strangers" who chose to "selle themselves"; or "strangers" who were "sold to [them]," like Dorcas. Dorcas's various transfers—from African soldier, perhaps, to Portuguese merchant to English privateer to puritan captain to Massachusetts colonist—these apparently legitimated in her captors' minds her fitness for "bond slaverie."

Two distinctions were emerging in the infant colony's legislation, distinctions that would prove enormously influential for the decades to come. The first distinction differentiated colonists from England and other countries that practiced Christianity from "people of other Nations." The second distinction separated debt peonage, which was finite, from slavery, which lasted for life. These two distinctions—between European and foreign, limited servitude and lifelong slavery—worked in tandem. That is, the bondage to which European colonists could be reduced was temporary, while the servitude to which "strangers" could be subjected was permanent, or at least could be. The Body of Liberties made sure to avoid confusion between the two types of residents and the two types of bondage by grouping the "liberties" by status: The rights of strangers were delineated beneath the label "Liberties of Strangers," while those of servants (who were, by implication, European—indeed, nearly all English) were demarcated "Liberties of Servants." Importantly, the three instances in which slavery was legal pertained only to strangers. The clause about "bond slaverie" was inscribed under the "strangers" category rather than the "servants" category, and its text reinforced that it was relevant only to foreigners. Those subjected to slavery could only be "Captives taken in just warres," something an Anglo-American in Massachusetts would never be, or "strangers," something an English colonist by definition was not. Servants had altogether different rights than strangers. Under the category "Liberties of Servants," the Body of Liberties made sure to clarify that servants who served their masters "deligentlie and faithfully" for seven years should be rewarded upon their release.[76]

The Bay colonists were not the first to exempt their own from lifelong bondage while allowing others to become chattel slaves. These practices were common in the ancient Near East, and the Old Testament contains nearly identical legislation. Israelites could not bind other Israelites for longer than seven years. After seven years of faithful service, any "Hebrew servant" had to be allowed to "go out free for nothing."[77] And the freed Israelite should not "go away empty"; masters were instructed to bless former servants "liberally out of flock, and out of floor, and out of winepress." Failure to do so could provoke God's wrath.[78] But the standards applied to "strangers" or those from "the heathen . . . round about" were very different. These people were the "possession" of their masters, and the Israelites who owned them could "take them as an inheritance for [their] children."[79] According to the laws God gave Moses, recorded in Leviticus, strangers "shall be your bondmen for ever: but over your brethren the children of Israel, ye shall not rule one over another with rigour."[80]

Distinguishing between English servants and enslaved foreigners, then, would have been natural both for Israel and his committee as they vetted the legal code, and for Dorchester's First Church brethren as they pored over it and proposed changes to their deputies. But the distinction in their minds would not have been one of theory, based on ancient biblical decrees of questionable applicability to their society in the American wilderness. Dorcas was present in all these peoples' lives, whether as ephemerally as a report carried north by a visiting magistrate or as corporeally as a dark body stooped in labor or uplifted in worship. Tales of the young woman's "true godliness" circulated the little colony while it worked on refining its inaugural code of laws, and Dorcas had undergone the rigorous public process of joining the community of saints in the Massachusetts Bay at the same time that this community was in the midst of determining who belonged in the colony and who did not, who could one day enjoy liberty and who could not. But the fact that the young woman had been mastering puritan religion and colonial lifeways in Massachusetts for years did not persuade those around her that the colony's legislation could afford to elide the distinction between English and foreigner. Dorcas had been brought to Massachusetts for alienation, and her alienation had been inscribed in law precisely when she showed that, on some deep level, she actually belonged. The freemen's great legislative accomplish-ment, the triumph of their legal protections over the discretionary judicial rulings of their leaders, had ensured, for their sister at Dorchester's First Church, perpetual bondage.[81]

*   *   *

Nowhere are Dorcas's thoughts preserved for posterity, but we might imag-ine what passed through the woman's mind as she reflected on the perma-nence of her position. Perhaps she felt despondent that her status was now fixed in law. "And so my heart was saddened," she could have confessed to a confidant, in the words of a fellow believer; "this increased my sorrow."[82] She might have considered herself betrayed by the brethren who saw fit to pass such a measure. Likely, she was angry as well: It would have been no small matter to find oneself suddenly condemned by the law to a lifetime of bond-age. Or perhaps she simply shrugged. Dorcas had come to know the English and their ways, experiencing firsthand their treatment of bound people of Af-rican ancestry, and she might therefore have understood her enslaved status to be permanent even before the Body of Liberties was enacted. It may be that the colony's inaugural legal code changed things for the English—justifying as it did the actions that colonists had already taken with regard to captive taking and slave trading—but did little to alter the realities of the so-called strangers in their midst. Unfree people who were not of European descent might have known that they would be forced to live their lives out in bond-age well before anything about "bond slaverie" was actually on the books.

Still, the Body of Liberties now removed any ambiguity. With the rigid-ity of Dorcas's status crystal clear, the challenge facing the woman if she were ever to extricate herself from bondage, or even merely to ameliorate her con-dition, was to make herself socially legible to the English people with whom she lived. Joining the church was a vital first step to participating in puritan community life. It was also an extraordinary one. By meeting the puritans' high standards for congregational admission, Dorcas set herself apart, for even among the English only a minority were admitted to the Bay Colony's churches. Attaining membership in puritan congregations had involved a rigorous process from the colony's earliest days, and many came to find admission altogether beyond reach when, several years after the colony was founded, ministers began to require that candidates narrate the story of their salvation. Dorcas told her tale to great acclaim, but public confession stood in the way of many of her English neighbors. In some Massachusetts towns, fewer than one in five English people earned membership status in their local churches.[83]

And Dorcas, for her part, did more than simply join the privileged circle of believers. She went on to become a celebrated evangelist. According to the report of a local minister, Dorcas marveled at God's decision to give "free grace" to "such a poore wretch as she," and she labored to help Native people experience that grace as well. A promotional tract titled *New Englands First Fruits*, which publicized the puritans' initial spiritual harvest among Indigenous New Englanders, made much of Dorcas's conversion and subsequent spiritual toil, casting her as a saint engaged in effective work for the Kingdom of God. The woman—"with teares," according to the report— "exhorted some other of the Indians that live with us to embrace Iesus Christ, declaring how willing he would be to receive them, even as he had received her."[84] News of Dorcas's efforts circulated through England, where it provided evidence of the fledgling colony's spiritual success, defending Massachusetts from those who questioned the slow progress of its mission to evangelize Native peoples. Dorcas, apparently, was one of very few: The tract's authors could point to only seven or eight non-English adults whose lives had been changed by the colonists' good news—and three of them had died before *First Fruits* went to press.[85] Including Dorcas in the count doubtless helped give confidence to those reporting on this rather meager return that God would bring "a greater *Harvest* in his owne time."[86] Dorcas's godliness served to vindicate the puritans and the colony they were building on Massachusetts Bay.

Becoming a church member in good standing, furthering the mission of Massachusetts to local Native people, and helping, through both, to justify the colony's raison d'être, Dorcas quickly made herself meaningful to the puritan project in New England. But the woman worked in still other ways to give lie to the claim that she was a "stranger" in her new home. Though she lived five or six miles up the Neponset River from the Dorchester Bay, which was itself at least a mile south of Boston, Dorcas did not confine her geographic movement to Israel's holdings, her immediate neighbors, and Dorchester's First Church; nor did she limit her social circle to Israel's Anglo-American neighbors and their bound laborers. Somehow, the woman managed to maintain contact with other Africans in Boston. The population of Black people in the area was very small at the time. The *Desire* had brought the only recorded shipment of Africans to labor in the region back in 1638, though people of African descent likely had trickled in on other ships in the interim.[87] Eventually, Dorcas began to build a family with one of the people in her little group of African acquaintances, a man named Matthew. They probably married—something that the biblically knowledgeable and reputedly pious Dorcas would undoubtedly have wished to do—but marriages in the town of Boston were not recorded prior to 1651, so it is impossible to know with certainty. It is clear, though, that the two had entered into a long-standing relationship by the early 1650s. This was a relationship that would bring about new life: offspring of African ancestry born on American soil.

As the days began to cool at the end of summer in 1652, Dorcas, now likely nearing thirty years of age, gave birth to a son named for his father, Matthew. Not surprisingly, the child's spiritual welfare was a priority for her; she made sure that Matthew was baptized by her Dorchester congregation at that time. Curiously, though, the records of another congregation, Boston's First Church, discuss Matthew's Dorchester baptism: "Mathew a Negro sonne to Dorcas a Negro a sister of the Church of Dorchester was baptized into the fellowship of that Church on the 12th day of . . . [September] 1652."[88] The decision of the Boston church's record keeper to reference the infant's baptism was unusual. While the church had been logging the baptisms it performed since its 1630 founding, not once had it recorded a baptism that took place in a *different* meetinghouse. But the circumstances of little Matthew's birth differed from those of the other infants baptized in the Bay Colony. The issue was simple: Matthew's parents dwelled apart. They broke the cardinal rule of puritan family life that "husbands and wives . . . [must] cohabitat[e]."[89] They did not do so by their own choosing, of course, but they did so nonetheless.

Because the elder Matthew lived in Boston and Dorcas lived in Dorchester, they attended different churches: Matthew the Boston congregation, and Dorcas the Dorchester one. So the leadership of both churches would have known about—and cared about—the child's baptism. Matthew, it seems, did not experience a coming to the Lord in quite the way Dorcas did. Unlike Dorcas, he was not baptized in Massachusetts, and he never formally joined his congregation, though he did attend meetings, for church attendance was required by law. This does not mean, of course, that Matthew was never baptized, nor does it mean that he did not consider himself a Christian; he might well have been baptized in his African nation of origin, as were various other enslaved New Englanders.[90] But the elder Matthew's position on the periphery of the Boston congregation *does* explain baby Matthew's baptism in Dorchester. The infant was baptized in Dorcas's meetinghouse because the colony's churches only baptized children into their congregations if their parents were members. Dorcas's membership, then, was her child's ticket to initiation into the community of saints. Nevertheless, the Boston church probably chose to record Matthew's remote baptism because the infant's father, though not a member, was a regular participant in the congregation. Which records ought to be logged where? The churches' ministers did not know, as they had never navigated such a situation before.

Confusion about baptism and congregational belonging was only one of many difficulties to crop up as Dorcas and Matthew tried to hold together an African family that not only bridged separate households but spanned town borders as well. The documentary record is not as rich for Matthew as it is for Dorcas, but the man almost certainly was enslaved, for Afro-New Englanders ("strangers" who were "sold to us") were condemned by the Body of Liberties to lifelong servitude. The ramifications of this legislation and of its broader Atlantic context—in which Africans were understood by enslavers throughout the Americas as especially fit for bondage—manifested themselves in palpable ways. The divergent status of "negro servants," as they were often called, and English servants is evident in the Bay Colony's early records. Probate records for Suffolk County, the Massachusetts county that contained both Boston and Dorchester, reference hundreds of servants in the seventeenth century, most of whom were European or African. Strong patterns distinguish white servants from Black ones. Almost without exception, bound people of African descent were considered significantly more valuable than white servants; Black laborers were assessed at up to four times the value of white laborers of comparable age and gender, which suggests that the service they were expected to render was far more protracted. And the language used to discuss Black and white laborers differs substantially as well; decedents' wills bequeathed the "time" of white servants to their heirs, but they bequeathed the persons of Black ones. The following example illustrates the broader trend: Around the time of Dorcas's baptism, a colonist named Henry Russell gave his wife the "remainder of the time of my servant, John Comstock," while a man named William Brimsmead bequeathed to his son "my Negro Symon."[91]

Matthew's bondage would have made the circumstances confronting the fledgling family trying. His presence in Dorcas's life was probably limited to brief visits, for he certainly would not have had more than one day a week free from labor, and that day was not reserved for him to do as he pleased: It was the Sabbath, and he belonged in the meetinghouse. Moreover, even if

Matthew could find the time, his enslaver might have prohibited him from undertaking the journey to Dorchester once snow heaped up in piles along the paths connecting Boston to its hinterland. Dorcas, then, likely assumed by herself the responsibilities associated with caring for a newborn while she attempted to perform whatever duties were expected of her in the Stoughton household. The woman faced sleepless nights and long workdays; the demands of soothing, breastfeeding, and diapering her child; and the loneliness of doing it all on her own. Perhaps worst was her lack of hope. Time would not ameliorate the family's situation, after all. Dorcas and Matthew's condition was permanent.

Dorcas knew this was not how a puritan family was to work. Wives were not supposed to be removed from the governance, care, and protection of their husbands. Infants were not intended to be separated from their fathers. Children were not meant to be raised alone by devout but struggling mothers, burdened by the weight of slavery. What Dorcas was experiencing did not align with what she had been taught by her minister about the structure of godly families or what she had gleaned from the scriptures read morning and night in the Stoughton household. But Dorcas knew where to turn to make things right. A dozen years before, the young woman had approached the elders of the church with a request: She wished to tell them her tale of salvation for the purpose of gaining admission to their intimate fellowship. They had complied; she had spoken to the brethren; and her godly comportment ever since had brought the congregation acclaim. Now, the historical record suggests, Dorcas went to the elders again, bringing with her a humble but firm entreaty. She wished to be released from slavery so that she could right her upturned family life.[92]

If anyone in the colony would have considered undertaking such a rescue mission for Dorcas, it would have been the Dorchester brethren. Week after week over the course of years, these people had worshipped, prayed, and pored over scripture with the bondswoman. And they had solemnly bound themselves to her, as had she to them. Any person who joined the congregation pledged to "further . . . the best spirituall good" of the other "members of this Congregacon." Engaging in "mutuall Instruction[,] reprehension, exhorta[ti]on, [and] consola[ti]on," those who covenanted with the church would "watch . . . over one another for good."[93] But promises of mutuality notwithstanding, there were plenty of reasons to doubt that the brethren would come to Dorcas's assistance. Obtaining release from slavery with the aid of a local body of believers was wholly uncharted territory at the time.

No one else of African descent had joined a Massachusetts church; no other congregation had enacted the emancipation of a bondsperson; not a single enslaved person, for that matter, had yet been liberated in the colony. And the Dorchester brethren had long tolerated Dorcas's enslaved status. None had protested when Israel originally brought the bound "stranger" to the congregation—at least, the minister's records do not mention any objection to either the woman or her enslavement. None had complained about the woman's perpetual bondage when she joined the congregation and was baptized twelve years prior. And none of the Dorchester freemen had effectively opposed the "liberty" that bound their sister in Christ to perpetual slavery when they were given the opportunity to assess the body of legislation that would govern the colony around the time of Dorcas's baptism. Condemning a baptized believer to a state of perpetual bondage had not struck them as problematic.

Eventually, however, the same people who had once assented to Dorcas's slavery began to see things differently. Dorcas had changed, and her situation had changed, in ways that made her continued bondage more difficult to justify. A decade earlier, when she had first approached the elders, Dorcas had been a stranger less rooted in New England's rocky soil. But she had gone on to turn herself into a congregant, acquiring full membership in the church. She had made a practice of sharing the good news with local Indigenous people, helping to fulfill what many Bay colonists understood as their colony's true purpose. She had built a family, orienting it according to puritan norms as best she could by living faithfully in a monogamous relationship, bearing a son, and bringing that boy under the authority of the church. The woman had borne fruit, and that fruit spoke of whom she was. "Ye shall know them by their fruits," the Lord had said. "Do men gather grapes of thorns, or figs of thistles?" The words echoed in the minds of the godly: "Even so every good tree bringeth forth good fruit; but a corrupt tree bringeth forth evil fruit."[94] There was no mistaking what sort of tree Dorcas was. There was no questioning her piety. The Sower had sown her where He willed, and, seemingly against all human odds, the woman had burst into blossom. Dorcas the stranger had done an extraordinary work of integrating herself into a system that defined her as an outsider. She had sunk her roots deep into inhospitable ground. And she now asked, in light of this, one thing of her brethren: that they would enable her to follow the teachings they all professed by intervening to remedy her troubled family life.

The leadership of the Dorchester church found Dorcas's request compelling. Soon after little Matthew reached his first birthday, when the child could be seen toddling across the wooden floor of the meetinghouse, the very same people who had long tolerated Dorcas's bondage, even endorsing legislation that grounded her enslaved status in law, became concerned about the "bond slaverie" that would keep their African sister tethered to the Stoughton household for life. They became so concerned, in fact, that they called a meeting. A dozen years had passed since the African woman had stood in the low-ceilinged log meetinghouse and professed her faith in Christ before the men and women of the congregation, and for a dozen years Dorcas's fellow believers had condoned her bondage, but in December of 1653, seventeen men gathered to address a situation that had become pressing. Dorcas's minister, Richard Mather, was present, of course, along with Henry Withington, the church's ruling elder; John Wiswall, a deacon; Richard Baker, a town selectman; and Hopestill Foster, captain of the Dorchester militia. A dozen other sturdy freemen absorbed in the affairs of the congregation joined them. The men met to take a vote on a matter of great importance: the "redemption" of the African woman with whom they had so long worshipped. The decision was unanimous. "[T]hey were all willinge that Dorcas was to be Redeemed."

But redeeming Dorcas was no small task, and Dorcas's First Church brethren had no guarantee of success. They could not simply pronounce the bondswoman free by purchasing her from her enslaver (who by this point was probably one of Israel's heirs, as the man had passed away a few years previously). Unfortunately for the church and the woman it sought to liberate, the process of freeing enslaved laborers in the colony was not so simple. Dorcas's brethren depended for success on the will of the Bay Colony's magistrates. These men had played a role in the process by which servants were freed from their masters since the colony's founding.[95] In 1631, for instance, the magistrates' court, called the Court of Assistants, ruled that a man named Phillip Swaddon should be "sett free" from his master in exchange for ten shillings, and it "sett at liberty" John Webb from his master two years later. The following year, it adjudicated the process by which Robert Fibbin was freed from bondage to his deceased master's heirs in recognition of "some service [he] p[er]formed att sea."[96]

The role of the court in the early years seems to have been limited to arbitrating disputes between masters and their freedom-seeking servants, but, beginning in 1636, the magistrates claimed for themselves far more authority in overseeing the process by which bound laborers became free-men. In December of that year, the General Court forbade masters from liberating their servants before their terms of indentures expired. "[N]o servant shalbee set free," the court ruled, "until hee have served out the time covenanted." The court would inflict a fine on any master who liberated his servant prematurely and, presumably, nullify the liberation.[97] The magistrates left for themselves room for discretion, though, as they were wont to do: They could "remit" the fine if they "s[aw] cause." And sometimes they did. A few months later, they declared James Hayden free because his master had promised to liberate him "before the act of the Court made against it."[98] They subsequently fined Israel himself for "releasing his man before the expiration of his time," but they later canceled the fine.[99] Not long after, they freed Hester Ketcham from her master and allowed William Tyng to buy his liberty from the man who claimed his labor.[100] In the fall of 1640, they approved the emancipation petitions of Ralph Wilmott and John White, but they subsequently fined several masters for "selling [their] servant[s] [their] time."[101] The court selectively freed a number of bound laborers in the following years: It "granted . . . power" to Joane Oliver to free her servant; it approved the petition of Captain Bridges to "sett free" George Millard; and it "granted leave" to Mr. John Gore to free Thomas Reeves.[102] Records of the court do not explain why the magistrates approved some emancipations and denied others, but they make abundantly clear the power that the magistrates exerted over the ability of masters to release their servants.

The first step in the First Church brethren's elaborate plan to emancipate Dorcas, then, involved convincing the magistrates that Dorcas could, in fact, legally be freed. Dorcas's advocates probably expected this to be difficult because the woman's situation differed from those of the other bound laborers liberated by the court since its 1636 prohibition of early emancipations. Unlike the servants freed before her, Dorcas was a stranger, so the legislation stipulating that servants must be released after seven years of service did not apply to her; she would have already received her freedom if it had. As a stranger, she was one of the few Bay colonists subjected to a lifetime of "bond slaverie" according to the body of legislation brought into being by her First Church brethren and their fellow freemen a decade before. Therefore, Dorcas's Dorchester brethren were not asking the court merely to move an already scheduled emancipation to an earlier date; they were asking the court to bring about an emancipation that would never have happened without their intervention. They were requesting that the magistrates intervene to alter the status of someone whose status was fixed.

But the leading men of the Dorchester congregation were hopeful, and they were not about to let Dorcas's redemption fail for lack of planning. They selected three men to initiate the process: Hopestill Foster and "the 2 deacons"—probably John Wiswall, who was present at the meeting, and Robert Clap, a long-standing deacon not in attendance that day. Hopestill and the deacons would go to Boston and ask the magistrates what they "could doe by power." Would the magistrates be willing to sanction the emancipation of their First Church sister? Would they make an exception to the 1636 legislation and allow a servant for life to assume an identity as a free woman? Would they use their judicial prerogative to enforce law—or to override it? If the magistrates looked upon their venture with favor, Hopestill, John, and Robert would then come to agreement with somebody of authority—it could be "Liuetennant Cooke or any other," the brethren noted—as to what, precisely, the price of Dorcas's "Redemptio[n]" ought to be. The three First Church representatives would then furnish Mr. Robert Howard, one of the brethren present at the meeting that December day, with an ox and a cow. He was to hold the livestock as payment for Dorcas, presumably until the transaction was completed. But Hopestill, John, and Robert would not alone be responsible for the financial outlay to secure Dorcas's freedom. The records Richard inscribed in the First Church's annals were clear: The "Rest of the bretheren above named," the minister wrote, "doe p[ro]mise to Laye down for the present amonge them the sume" that Hopestill, John, and Robert put forth. And the men at the meeting planned to share the cost still further. In due time, the "whole church" would put forth a "Contribution" to reimburse them for their expenses. This was not the deed of a solitary benevolent individual; it was the action of an entire faith community. A whole body of people would take on together the burden of liberating one of their own.[103]

Dorcas's fractured family life, which kept her from living the way a pious wife and mother ought to live, appears eventually to have caused her brethren to reevaluate their embrace of her bondage. The men who in 1641 had been comfortable with the idea of slavery, limited, of course, to "strangers," now pledged their finances, and those of their fellow congregants, to free the African woman in order to allow her to engage in family-building as God intended it. They risked sacrificing status as well as financial resources, for the colony's ruling elite could look upon their errand with favor or spurn their request with disdain. When the brethren intent on redeeming Dorcas gathered in the meetinghouse on that December day, they were by no means certain of the magistrates' minds; plenty of petitions for early liberation had been denied over the course of the prior decade. But the magistrates seem to have tilted toward magnanimity when they considered the appeal on Dorcas's behalf. Though their records from this period do not survive, notes taken by Boston's town clerk indicate that the African woman moved from Dorchester to Boston in the months to follow, probably during the early part of 1654, and she resumed her family duties there, presumably alongside Matthew.

Dorcas soon bore another child, a daughter named Martha. By choosing a biblical name, the couple (perhaps with Matthew in the lead, as naming was a male prerogative in puritan New England) paid homage to the importance of puritan Christianity to the young family, or, at least, to Dorcas. In Martha's most memorable biblical appearance, described in the Gospel of Luke, Jesus made a visit to her home. Saddled with household preparations, Martha asked her guest to tell her sister Mary, seated at his feet, to help her. But Jesus corrected Martha rather than Mary. "Martha, Martha, thou art careful and troubled about many things," he responded, yet "but one thing is needful."[104] No matter how pressing the demands of the world, he affirmed, the most important task was to rest at the feet of the Lord. Perhaps the decision of Dorcas and Matthew to name their daughter after a worried and overworked woman who had been freed from her daily toil by the Lord himself gestured to the liberation, both spiritual and temporal, that Dorcas had found in Christianity through Dorchester's First Church.

Unfortunately, baby Martha did not live long. According to the records of Boston's clerk, she died in October 1654, less than a year after her mother's emancipation.[105] No surviving evidence sheds light on how Dorcas and her family dealt with the loss of little Martha, a girl who seems to have represented the shards of hope to which her parents clung at that juncture of their lives—hope for rest and redemption, family and freedom on the shore of Massachusetts Bay. And, for a time, the archive yields little on Dorcas and her family: No more baptisms were registered in the region's churches, no more deaths were recorded by the town clerk, no more observations were inscribed in the accounts of puritan grandees, and no more pious deeds were touted in promotional tracts. The little African family lived a quiet life, abiding by the law, worshipping with the nearby Boston congregation, and, presumably, finding enough employment to make it through each year with food on the table, a roof over their heads, and clothing sufficient to keep them from freezing in New England's winters, which must have felt harsh indeed to people born and bred in West Central Africa.

*   *   *

In the fall of 1675, Dorcas, now beyond middle age, resurfaced in the historical record. Her husband had died in July, and Dorcas appeared before the colony's governor and deputy governor with an inventory of the man's estate in late September. The man was free, he left an estate, and this estate was formally entered into the records of the probate court. Each of these things set him apart from most men of African descent in the region. The estate, however, was humble; the man's entire inventory totaled less than ten pounds sterling, coming in at nine pounds, fourteen shillings, and twenty-six pence. He owned no land, so the family must have lived in a rented chamber or in the corner of a sympathetic neighbor's home. Besides his clothing, Dorcas's husband possessed a bed and bedstead as well as a modest collection of furniture: a chest, two stools, three chairs, a small table, and a looking glass. He had the necessary equipment for tending and cooking on an open fire—tongs, a pair of andirons, and a spit—and he possessed an assortment of cookware and utensils: pots, skillets, dishes, bottles, and a collection of pottery described simply as "earthern things." On the last line of the account, the appraisers noted "old tubs" and "lumber," items that may provide clues to the family's survival. Dorcas probably used the tubs for cleaning. Did she take in neighbors' laundry to make ends meet? Or do wash for a landlord in exchange for housing? Did her husband work as a handyman around town, using his small stock of lumber to repair the homes and outbuildings of his neighbors?[106]

Curiously, Dorcas's husband was not referred to as "Matthew" in the inventory of his estate. Instead, the record rendered him "Menenie." And Dorcas had acquired his name as her surname: "Dorcas Menenie." We should not allow these naming modifications to throw us from Dorcas's trail, for abundant evidence indicates that Dorcas Menenie was the Dorcas who served in Israel's household, covenanted with the Dorchester congregation, and received her freedom as a result of the church's concerns about her fractured family life. Records from both the Boston and Dorchester congregations indicate that the Dorcas whom Richard baptized in 1641 was still alive, still living in Boston, and still attending Boston's First Church as late as 1677, two years after Menenie's possessions were inventoried. And she was one of an exceedingly small group of Africans in the port at the time; no more than fifty Black women resided in Boston when Dorcas Menenie probated her husband's estate, and the number could have been much lower.[107]

Menenie's inventory yields other clues linking Dorcas Menenie to the Dorcas who once labored in slavery on the Neponset. For instance, Jacob Elliot and Theophilus Frary, the two men who appraised Menenie's estate for the court, would have known Dorcas well, as they were longtime members and lay leaders of Boston's First Church, the congregation that Dorcas attended after moving to Boston. It would have been natural, then, for the woman to lean on them as she worked to settle her husband's affairs after his passing; perhaps she suggested their names to the judge of the probate court, who was in charge of recruiting the right people for such a task.

Menenie and Matthew, like Dorcas Menenie and Dorcas, were likely one and the same. The strong phonetic resemblance of the two names suggests that the designation "Matthew" may have been given to—or taken on by—Menenie upon his arrival in the Bay Colony. Perhaps Menenie willingly changed his name, or at least used Matthew in certain social circles, in a bid to adopt the outward trappings of his new culture. Such a decision could have been strategic. As Dorcas's case shows, making radical accommodations to puritan life had the potential to pay off for even the most exploited of early New Englanders. Regardless of the way in which the man acquired his new moniker, the naming of baby Matthew suggests that the anglicization of Menenie was probably not coerced. Children born to bondspeople at the time of little Matthew's birth were not bound themselves, so Matthew's naming almost certainly would have been his parents' prerogative—and it seems unlikely that the couple would have bestowed upon their child a name that was imposed on Menenie by his enslaver. Why did the inventory record the possessions of "Menenie" rather than "Matthew"? Likely, the man went by both names, presenting himself by turns as either Matthew or Menenie, depending on his audience.

Menenie, like Dorcas, almost surely hailed from West Central Africa. His name strongly resembles *munene*, a common word in dozens of languages across central and southern Africa. This word is rendered by linguists as meaning either "big" or "tall." And the word was integral to the system of government prevalent in the Kasai region to the north and east of the Kingdom of Kongo; the *ngongo munene* was an association of men that exercised authority over each neighborhood jurisdiction.[108] Menenie was given, then, or perhaps took for himself, a name that could be related either to his social standing in the Kasai, if he indeed originated there, or to his physical stature if he originated elsewhere. Regardless of how Menenie acquired his name, it is one that evokes strength and authority, traits that the man would have needed to move from being a captive sold into the Atlantic slave trade to being a free man heading a free household in a place unimaginably distant from his native land, both geographically and culturally.

Menenie's death brought to an end a relationship that spanned close to three decades, but it did not leave Dorcas altogether adrift in the Massachusetts port, unmoored from meaningful relational ties. Dorcas decided to formalize her church affiliation after her husband's passing, which suggests that she found her congregational community a significant source of support. For decades after her move to Boston, Dorcas had remained a member of the Dorchester congregation that redeemed her, but, after Menenie's death, she made her change in affiliation official. In August of 1676, a full thirty-five years after Richard had noted that "Dorcas ye blackmore" had been baptized and joined his First Church, the African woman appeared in the Dorchester congregation's book of records for the last time. Dorcas had formally requested dismissal from the congregation in order to join her longtime home church in Boston, and the Dorchester brethren approved: "Dorcas ye neger being formerly a member of this Church was dismissed to joyn to ye first Church at boston," the entry read. The record keeper's unusual formulation—that Dorcas was "formerly" a member—makes sense in light of Dorcas's long-ago move to Boston and its First Church. Dorcas had been absent from the Dorchester meetinghouse for an extended period of time, and her affiliation, she decided at last, ought to match that reality.[109]

Dorcas was received into Boston's First Church in July of 1677. She was the first non-European admitted to membership, but the records of the congregation do not show any special interest in or disdain for her. The African woman had attended the church for nearly a quarter of a century, after all, and the strangeness of this godly "stranger" had surely diminished over time. Extant church records suggest that the men and women who had long worshipped with Dorcas had no qualms about the woman's fitness for fellowship. She was admitted alongside an Englishman named John Dyer, who had recently relocated to Boston from neighboring Weymouth. Both presented letters of dismission from their prior churches: that is, assurances they had left in good standing and were free to join another congregation. Dorcas's letter from Dorchester's First Church was undoubtedly satisfactory, as the Boston brethren voted to receive her without debate. The notes taken that

Figure 3. Communion cup.
This humble beaker was
owned by Boston's First
Church during the years
Dorcas worshiped with the
congregation. It was likely
used for communion, which
means that Dorcas, as a
baptized believer and full
member of the church, would
have drunk from it alongside
her fellow believers. Photo-
graph © 2024 Museum of Fine
Arts, Boston.

day dwell instead on an undisclosed "something" that was "more than usuall in the Letters for John Dyer" and might have kept him from being "safely accepted." While the members ultimately received John "according to their old and usuall manner," it was John who prompted discussion, not Dorcas.[110]

Dorcas had bound herself yet again to a body of puritan believers in Massachusetts, and she had been found, once more, to be exemplary in belief and practice. A woman of great piety and deep knowledge, Dorcas altered irrevocably the temporal course of her life by embracing the spiritual commitments of the colonists. Her story demonstrates the impressive liberatory potential of the puritan church in early Massachusetts. Congregations could take radical actions to enable believers in slavery to right their disordered family lives. They could neutralize the strangeness of godly strangers. They could transform the life prospects of their most oppressed members. But Dorcas's story also shows the capriciousness of the emerging system of slavery in New England. Congregations could accomplish these ends only if they so chose—and ordinarily they did not. Finally and fundamentally, Dorcas's tale lays bare the deepening chasm between slavery and freedom in early Massachusetts. When Dorcas was brought to the Bay Colony, no law set her aside as a bondswoman for life. But precisely when she showed that on the most important of registers she truly belonged, Dorcas found herself decreed a permanent outsider. The freedmen had triumphed: They had established a robust body of "liberties" to protect themselves from leaders who might overstep—and in so doing they had condemned their celebrated sister in Christ to perpetual bondage. That Dorcas ultimately managed to extricate herself from slavery is testament to her extraordinary powers of persuasion, which were aided by a set of circumstances that made the contradictions between slavery and godly living particularly glaring. But it is crucial for us to note that Dorcas did not start a trend: The woman was not one of many. Indeed, the story of this godly stranger stands out more for being *strange* than it does for representing experiences broadly shared by the enslaved. No surviving records indicate that other Massachusetts congregations redeemed people in bondage during the middle of the seventeenth century, and the institution of slavery became only more entrenched in New England over the course of Dorcas's lifetime. Dorcas got through, but the system hardened.

In the early eighteenth century, a free Black man named Charles Meneno made his home in Boston. Might Charles have been a descendant of Dorcas and Menenie? This is a strong possibility, as Charles's surname closely resembles "Menenie," and Black children in New England fathered by men without surnames were often given their father's first name for a last name. Perhaps Charles was the son of Dorcas and Menenie's child, Matthew, whose entrance into the world had laid bare to the Dorchester brethren the contradiction between the demands of puritan family life and the binds of slavery. Unfortunately, the historical record yields no certain answers as to Charles's parentage—but the man's presence in Boston is abundantly clear. There, Charles labored to maintain the thoroughfares that the town selectmen called "Highwayes"; he hustled to local shops to buy needed provisions; he took his seat in the meetinghouse—the very one, it might be, that Dorcas had once joined.[111] As he did these things, the man moved through a human and cultural landscape that had changed much since Dorcas's time. Far more enslaved people walked the town's streets than Dorcas would ever have seen. People of African descent, once substantially outnumbered by indentured Europeans, had come to dominate the region's pool of bound laborers.[112] The enslaved were now ensnared by a more robust body of legislation than the simple ninety-first "liberty" passed by Dorcas's brethren. And churches remained in the business of redeeming people from spiritual bondage, but none appeared to be in the business of redeeming people from temporal bondage; slavery, despite its depredations on the family, did not spur liberatory congregational action. These changes shaped indelibly the intimate relationships of African-descended people in bondage. Over the course of the eighteenth century, most enslaved wives would live apart from their husbands, and most bound children would be separated from their fathers. Black Bostonians who made the kinds of claims about family and slavery that Dorcas had made would not meet with consistent success until the revolutionary era. Then, finally, enslaved people would convince their white neighbors that their right to properly order their family lives eclipsed the right of their enslavers to claim them as property. But that stood some five generations away. For the long slog to come, people caught in the mire of slavery would struggle for access to loved ones, for the time to build intimate relationships, for the material resources needed by their chosen communities, for the right to develop their kin networks as they wished, and for recognition as members of the families they had made. Few would share Dorcas's extraordinary success in these endeavors, but many would take part in the common project, giving the lie to the fallacy that people of African descent were "strangers" in New England. Belonging to enslavers would not prevent the enslaved from belonging to one another.

CHAPTER 2

Sebastian, Jane Lake, and Their Children

Marriage, Gender, and Power in Slavery

> It is most certain that all Men, as they are the Sons of
> *Adam*, are Coheirs; and have equal Right unto Liberty,
> and all other outward Comforts of Life. . . . These
> *Ethiopians*, as black as they are; seeing they are the Sons
> and Daughters of the First *Adam*, the Brethren and Sisters
> of the Last ADAM, and the Offspring of GOD; They ought
> to be treated with a Respect agreeable.
> —Samuel Sewall, *The Selling of Joseph: A Memorial*, 1700

As Jane Lake crossed Marlborough Street, the central artery connecting the south end of Boston to the north, she might have heard the call of a huckster marketing his wares: poultry, eggs, butter, cheese. The growl of the dog that trailed him was perhaps audible as well. And one can imagine the air ringing with the laughter of children scampering over the icy cobbles, lost in play. Picking her way between the piles of dung that clung to the frozen thoroughfare, Jane might have greeted an enslaved woman carrying an armload of firewood or an African coachman guiding the carriage of a local merchant. Perhaps she paused when she reached the far side of the street, hugging the snowbank to give wide berth to several cows lowing unsuspectingly toward the slaughterhouse. Had she lifted her gaze at the right moment, Jane might have spied the silhouette of a neighbor boy, dark against the wintry world, disappearing down a side street in the direction of the grist mill. The wind was bitter that morning and the sun's rays too weak to offer warmth, but the streets were busy. Bostonians, as always, had much to do. Suppressing a shiver, Jane likely pulled her cape tight to guard against the biting cold and hastened past a few houses, glad that her destination was near. And then she was there: her neighbor's water pump.[1]

Jane likely repeated this walk, which took just a few minutes, day in and day out, in months warm and cold, over the course of years. Her purpose? To fetch water, of course. This is what she doubtless would have told anyone who asked. Her household could not do without water for even a morning: The teapot had to be filled; garments needed laundering; a basket of root vegetables, remnants from the fall harvest, wanted broth in which to boil. But Jane might have had other aims as well. Perhaps she hoped that, when the pump came into view, so too would a man. Her neighbor, Sebastian, who was also in bondage and regularly out on errand, managed to get to the pump often enough that Jane had come to find fetching water an occasion for friendly banter and neighborly gossip. For a woman in slavery, a trip to the pump was never just a trip to the pump.[2]

The water pump was not their only place of rendezvous. Jane and Sebastian also found themselves together at Boston's First Church, the meetinghouse that Dorcas Menenie and her husband had attended in the mid- to late seventeenth century. In 1677, Dorcas had been the first African to affiliate with the congregation, and Jane followed in her footsteps, joining the church and becoming baptized in 1691. Though Sebastian never became a member of the First Church, he accompanied the family that enslaved him on Sabbath days, so he must have crossed paths with Jane inside the aging wooden edifice. Segregated along with children in the upper galleries opposite the pulpit, people of African descent suffered the indignity of inferior seating based on their race, but they might have enjoyed less oversight than usual as a result of their distance from those who enslaved them.[3] And perhaps the First Church held special meetings for its Black parishioners as other congregations in the region did. For instance, the African-descended congregants in Boston's Second Church formed a "religious society" in the late seventeenth century that convened every Sabbath evening, often, it seems, without oversight.[4]

Besides trips to the water pump and treks to the meetinghouse, there would have been glimpses, glances, and snatches of conversation at other times as well. Sebastian almost surely guided the livestock of the man who bound him past the house in which Jane lived, as that was the most direct route to the Boston common. Jane might have shuttled to and from her enslaver's home the girls who came at tender ages for lessons in reading

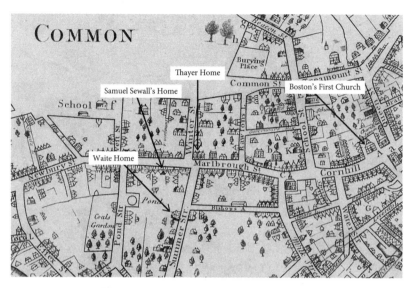

Figure 4. Map of Jane and Sebastian's neighborhood. This facsimile of a 1722 map shows the Boston neighborhood in which Jane lived with the Thayers and Sebastian lived with the Waites. The water pump, which was located by the home of their neighbor, Samuel Sewall, stood roughly between them. And Boston's First Church, which they both attended, was about a third of a mile down the street. Collection of the Massachusetts Historical Society.

and knitting. Both Sebastian and Jane ran errands for the same neighbor, Samuel Sewall, a local judge who lived just a stone's throw away. And, no doubt, the two seized other opportunities to see one another as well. Bondspeople in Boston—both male and female—were extraordinarily mobile, delivering messages and goods for their enslavers throughout the town and the villages surrounding it.[5] It is therefore easy to imagine Jane and Sebastian encountering one another in the byways of what was, at the time, the largest town in North America. Unfortunately, we cannot make out across the centuries the words the two exchanged. But one thing is clear. The pair came to an understanding as the frozen landscape began to thaw in the final year of the seventeenth century. By the spring of 1699, Jane and Sebastian were quite sure of it: The two had decided that they wished to marry.

In this chapter, I tell the story of Jane and Sebastian's marriage, the struggles that came before, and the developments that followed—developments that altered the intimate landscape not only for Jane and Sebastian but also for other bondspeople in the region. I begin by examining the context in which enslaved partners pursued wedded intimacy in Massachusetts. Bound people seem to have initiated their own marital relationships, and they ordinarily did so, by necessity, across households. I then explore the negotiations between hopeful couples and those who bound them. When Jane's enslaver sought to prevent their union, Jane and Sebastian recruited as an advocate Samuel Sewall, whose antislavery pamphlet, *The Selling of Joseph*, emerged from this mess of bickering neighbors and thwarted intimacies. But Samuel's support was beside the point: The marriage was made possible only by the sudden and unexpected death of Jane's enslaver. Here I explore the meaning of the formal unions of Jane, Sebastian, and other Afro-Bostonians—unions announced in their churches and vetted by their communities—and I examine as well the authority that many bound men enjoyed in the families they formed. Finally, I consider a Massachusetts law, passed soon after Jane and Sebastian wed, that guaranteed enslaved people the right to marry. This legal measure was at once immaterial and truly important. On the one hand, some enslavers flouted it, and the unions of those bondspeople who *did* marry were utterly bereft of conjugal rights: The right of enslavers to do what they wished with those they claimed as property always eclipsed the right of the enslaved to marital integrity. On the other hand, though, the law enabled some bondspeople to obtain the marriages they desired, and it helped to foster an unusual marriage culture among Boston's enslaved population. Many people in bondage appear to have seen government-sanctioned unions as a tool by which they might safeguard their intimacies.

*   *   *

Jane and Sebastian appear to have followed a path toward intimacy common to people of African descent in turn-of-the-eighteenth-century New England. Though few sources shed light on the process by which bondspeople obtained marriage partners, fragmentary evidence suggests that others at this time—at least other men—initiated their own unions. In 1691, for instance, Thomas Sungo, a man of African descent who had managed to obtain his freedom, sold himself as a servant in an attempt to secure access to the woman he wished to be his wife. Thomas promised to serve a Charlestown mariner named Nathaniel Cary for four years, and Nathaniel, in turn, pledged to fulfill the standard duties of a master, providing food, clothing, and lodging as well as "all other Necessaries Meet & Convenient" during Thomas's term of service. That, however, was not all: Nathaniel also pledged that he would "permit" Thomas to marry Nathaniel's "Negro Woman Servant named Penella." Ultimately, Penella would go free with Thomas at the expiration of his service.[6]

Penella and Thomas's marriage was not forced on them by Penella's enslaver; on the contrary, Thomas had to give up a great deal in order to persuade Nathaniel to allow the union. Nor was the marriage of Onesimus, who was enslaved by minister Cotton Mather, arranged. Cotton noted that he "allowed" Onesimus "the conveniences of the Married State"—language that suggests the minister was responding to Onesimus's request rather than dictating orders.[7] Cophee, a man enslaved by Ebenezer Pemberton, minister of Boston's Old South Church in the early eighteenth century, also took his marriage into his own hands. He paid Ebenezer 40 pounds to secure his freedom so that "he might be with his wife." Thomas, Onesimus, and Cophee all took the initiative in establishing and sustaining their marital relationships. Unfortunately, the roles played by their wives in courtship are essentially invisible. But these unions suggest that local residents who enslaved people of African descent at the turn of the eighteenth century did not, as a matter of course, dictate whom they should marry.[8]

Jane and Sebastian appear to have been typical not just in the initiative they took when it came to seeking out a spouse; they were typical, too, in the cross-household nature of their union. The two were forced to live with and serve different Anglo-American enslavers. Sebastian was bound by the Waite family: John, Eunice, and their four children. John was a Boston merchant of modest means, and the papers filed upon his death in Suffolk County's probate court refer to Sebastian, whom appraisers valued at twenty pounds in 1702, as his "One Negroman." Jane, enslaved by Deborah Thayer, a Boston widow and mother of five children, was almost certainly the only bondsperson in that household as well; accounts relating to the administration of Deborah's estate in the early years of the eighteenth century refer to Jane by name but do not mention any other laborers.[9] The living situations of Jane and Sebastian, both of whom resided alone in their enslavers' homes, mirrored those of many bondspeople in the Province of Massachusetts Bay.

Most enslavers in Boston at the turn of the eighteenth century bound just one laborer. Records produced by the probate court, which systematically documented the property of those who died, make this clear. Between 1670 and 1740, 1,070 bound people appeared in Suffolk County's probate records, divided into 622 different households. Among these households, 379 claimed only one enslaved resident; 142 households claimed two people in bondage;

53 claimed three; 24 claimed four; 13 households claimed five bondspeople; three claimed six; four claimed seven; two claimed eight; one claimed 11, and one unusual household—that of an extraordinarily successful Boston merchant who married a wealthy widow—claimed 14 enslaved people. With 61 percent of slaveholding households asserting ownership over merely one person, the opportunities for Jane, Sebastian, and their Black neighbors to build families under the same roof were quite limited.[10]

This picture is not complete, though, without taking gender into account. Fortunately, most of the 1,070 bondspeople found in turn-of-the-century Suffolk County probate records can be identified by sex, and it is possible to ascertain the approximate age of most; only 143 are listed akin to the "four Negroes" bound by innkeeper Thomas Selby, in a manner that obscures their gender, their age, or both. Among adults in bondage, men outnumbered their female counterparts by a meaningful margin; the records list 327 adult men and 260 adult women, which means that men made up 56 percent of the total bound population. The problem for Black people looking to find a co-resident partner in Boston at this time, however, was less the gender distribution of bondspeople in the region than the gendered division of the enslaved by household. Of the 408 households probated during this period that left gender-specific references to bound adults, fewer than a quarter (99 households, or 24 percent) contained both men *and* women—and therefore potential co-resident couples. It is hardly surprising, then, that more than four-fifths of enslaved Afro-Bostonians who chose to marry fellow bondspeople found themselves in situations similar to that of Sebastian and Jane: They were claimed by different enslavers than were their spouses and they were forced to labor in different homes.[11]

Jane and Sebastian are representative of their neighbors on a variety of counts. That they pursued intimate relationships on their own terms with those of their choosing appears customary, though the evidence on this is slim. That they both lived on their own in Anglo-American households, separated from other people of African descent, was all too ordinary. And that each of them sought to marry someone bound in a different household from their own was commonplace. In these ways, Jane and Sebastian's relationship, and the circumstances that gave it birth, were unexceptional. Only one thing about the couple's story, in fact, is truly unusual: the extent to which it can today be told. The copious notes of their neighbor, Samuel, preserved for posterity the extended negotiations that preceded the couple's union, and these, together with court records, documents produced by local ministers, logs kept by town officials, and evidence from newspapers, enable us to piece together Jane and Sebastian's story and consider its meaning. The pair's marital saga can therefore instruct us on the challenges faced by bound couples who wished for wedded intimacy in early Massachusetts.

*   *   *

When Jane and Sebastian decided they wanted to marry, a hindrance held them back: Deborah opposed the match. Deborah probably felt amply justified in preventing Jane from marrying. From Deborah's perspective, the marriage could only mean trouble. Should Jane wed Sebastian, children would almost surely follow, which would mean more mouths for Deborah to feed and more bodies for her to clothe. These dependents would not benefit Deborah economically, at least not for a long while. To make things worse, Jane's usefulness would be diminished by the demands of bearing and tending to her offspring, and a pregnancy gone wrong could bring about her death. Deborah had five children of her own to raise—her youngest was still just seven when Jane and Sebastian were discussing marriage in 1699—and she had no husband to help her do so; Nathaniel Thayer had died six years earlier. A widow with slim resources already overburdened by the task of rearing children, Deborah had little to gain, and plenty to lose, from allowing the marriage.

But Jane and Sebastian would not take no for an answer. Part of their determination might have been a matter of morality. Jane appears to have been deeply religious, with a meaningful faith and a robust knowledge of scripture. We know, at least, that her testimony of God's work in her life persuaded the brethren of Boston's First Church to receive her as a member and baptize her, which means that she succeeded in obtaining a status in the church that surpassed that of most Anglo-Americans in New England.[12] For such a devout woman, entering a marriage-like relationship without actually marrying would have been out of the question. Surely, she knew St. Paul's commendation of marriage as "honorable" and his caution: "to avoid fornication, let every man have his own wife, and let every woman have her own husband." Even if Jane had been tempted to stray from these teachings, her relationship with the First Church might well have tethered her. She had covenanted with the brethren, after all: "I do promise," the pledge went, "by the grace and help of the Lord Jesus, that I will forsake all my former lusts and corruptions." The brethren, for their part, aimed not to let her slip, vowing "holy watchfulness" over each member.[13] If Jane wished to remain in good standing with the local body of believers, she needed to discipline her own body accordingly. Intimacy with Sebastian had to be sealed by marriage.

But the impulse to marry was probably rooted in more than a desire to follow Christian mandates. As a full member in good standing with the church, Jane likely expected a formal union with Sebastian to yield tangible benefits: a minister angered by an enslaver's decisions and willing to say so directly, or brethren who registered with stony stares their disapproval of an enslaver's actions.[14] Knowing that Deborah opposed the match no doubt made Jane and Sebastian anxious. Would she try to prevent the two from spending intimate time together? Or, worse, decide to sell Jane and procure in her place a worker who would not be slowed by pregnancy, childbirth, and the rearing of infants? Would she send away children whom she found useless? Perhaps. But she was less likely to do these things if her community deemed them unacceptable. If Deborah's brethren believed that Sebastian and Jane ought to be allowed to see one another, the woman might cave to their pressure. If others in the pews decided that the two should be permitted to order their marital lives aright, maybe she would let it be so. A formal marriage, that is, would serve two purposes: It would allow Jane to enter into a sexual relationship without violating her Christian covenant, and, by legitimizing Sebastian and Jane's union in the eyes of Jane's community of believers, it might compel Deborah to support them—or at least to refrain from sabotaging their relationship.

Whatever their motivations, Jane and Sebastian were determined to wed. But how, when an enslaver had prohibited the marriage? To proceed, the pair needed to find someone capable of persuading Deborah to change her mind. That the two settled on their neighbor, Samuel Sewall, an inveterate scribbler and noter of events great and small in his neighborhood, was a stroke of luck for historians. It was also a decision that made good sense for the couple. Not only was Samuel a justice of the peace who often married his fellow Bostonians, but he was uncomfortable with slavery, which Jane and Sebastian likely knew and doubtless appreciated. And, conveniently, Samuel lived right between the two: His home was just a few houses south of the Thayers' and directly to the north of the Waites'. Samuel lived so close to Sebastian, in fact, that drops from his russet apple trees littered the threshold of the Waites' orchard each fall.[15]

Geographic proximity bred relational intimacy. Samuel entrusted Deborah with the education of at least one of his daughters, and he might have discussed business matters with John while they walked down Summer Street to the wharves in the South End of Boston. On Sabbath days, the Sewalls, Waites, and Thayers all worshipped in the neighborhood. The Sewalls' Old South Church was less than two-tenths of a mile from the First Church that the Waites and Thayers attended, and both were situated on the neighborhood's main thoroughfare, so the families doubtless crossed paths on their way to meeting. Sebastian and Jane, of course, were knit into this web of relationships. They, too, would have seen Samuel when passing the Old South en route to the First Church on Sabbath days, and we know that they interacted with the judge at other times as well. It was at Samuel's pump that Jane filled her pail with water, and Sebastian regularly helped the judge with odd jobs, whether at his house, in his orchard, or around town.[16]

Jane and Sebastian's intimacy with Samuel, born of proximity, seems to have convinced them that he would be a useful ally. The Waites agreed. Likely at Sebastian's urging, both John and Eunice began to visit the judge in the spring of 1699 to advocate for the couple, seeking to enlist his help in endorsing their marriage. Samuel's diary chronicles some of the instances in which they came to his home. On the first of April, Samuel noted that John visited him and "express'd his earnest desire that Bastian might have Jane, Mr. Thair's Negro." A week later, Eunice visited Samuel's house to repeat the plea. She "expresse[d] her desire that Sebastian might have Mrs. Thair's Jane," Samuel noted. The woman had clear instructions for Samuel. "She would have me promote it," he wrote of the match, even though she had nothing to gain from it: "she said 'twould be to their prejudice in some respect." Samuel began immediately to investigate. It was clear that Sebastian and the Waites supported the marriage, but what did Jane think? "I spake to Jane," Samuel reported in his diary just two days after John first asked him to facilitate the marriage. He did not record what Jane said, but his continued efforts to bring about the match suggest that the woman indeed wished to marry Sebastian.[17]

So Sebastian, Jane, and the Waites apparently supported the marriage, but Deborah did not—and it was Samuel's job to persuade the widow to change her mind.[18] This was a job in which the powerful neighbor—merchant, magistrate, justice of the peace—apparently failed. Samuel's diary provides little insight into the initial stages of this bargaining process, but it makes clear that Jane and Sebastian's effort to formalize their union hit an impasse. The months ticked by. April turned to May, and Samuel made note in his diary of the votes cast at a town meeting. Still no progress. May turned to June, and Samuel registered his approval of his minister's preaching. Still no progress. June to July, and Samuel mentioned his wife's travels along the Massachusetts coast. Still no progress. The following April, a year after John and Eunice had first spoken to Samuel, Jane and Sebastian were still stealing moments in the orchard, at the water pump, and on the common, apparently no closer to marriage than they had been the year before. Deborah's obstinacy seems to have frustrated the efforts of all those involved. April turned to May, and Samuel commented on the rain. Still no progress. May to June, and Samuel remarked on local baptisms. Still no progress. Something simmered inside Samuel.[19]

That month, June, when the neighborhood's gardens began to bear what Samuel called the "First Fruits" of the season, the judge ruminated on slavery. This was not new. According to his diary, Samuel had "been long and much dissatisfied with the Trade of fetching Negros from Guinea." Now, however, he was convinced that he needed to go public with the conviction: He confided on June 19 that he believed he had been "call'd of God" to write on behalf of the Africans enslaved in the Americas.[20] Just five days later, his treatise was published by Boston printers. Titled *The Selling of Joseph*, Samuel's tract set forth a proposition that was radical in the British colonies at the turn of the eighteenth century: the proposition that slavery was wrong. "It is most certain," he wrote, "that all Men, as they are the Sons of *Adam*, are Coheirs; and have equal Right unto Liberty, and all other outward Comforts of Life." Samuel asked in his diary for God's "Blessing" to "accompany" his words.[21] *The Selling of Joseph* needed whatever blessing it could get. As it crossed the Atlantic on ships bound for England and made its way, by land or sea, to colonies on the American mainland, it found many skeptical readers. Samuel's tract was one of the few antislavery pamphlets circulating in the Atlantic world at a time when British colonies throughout the Americas were hardening the line between Black and white, between enslaved and free; in fact, only one English-language antislavery tract had been printed in the Americas before Samuel's words went to press.[22] Historians ever since have marveled at the merchant's ability to articulate an argument for liberty in a world becoming dependent on unfree laborers of African descent—and they have pondered what prompted such foresight.

According to some scholars, explanations of Samuel's antislavery activism can be found in the man's person himself—that is, in his psychology. According to others, Samuel's activism can be explained by his vast transAtlantic networks of communication.[23] However, I would like to suggest that we can best understand the actions that Samuel took in midsummer

1700 by focusing on a different scale: a local one. Samuel's diary indicates that a confluence of town events preceded his decision to write against slavery. Samuel's friend and neighbor, Cotton Mather, had told him that he intended to publish a tract encouraging enslavers to take seriously the task of converting those they bound. Samuel had also learned that plans were afoot among Boston's town leaders to impose a duty on African arrivals, with the aim of discouraging their importation into the increasingly multiracial port.[24] Buoyed both by efforts to Christianize the town's bondspeople and by attempts to reduce Boston's traffic in bound Africans, Samuel was finally spurred to compose his antislavery treatise by another local circumstance: the unjust enslavement of two Africans in town. The judge apparently "began to be uneasy that [he] had so long neglected doing any thing" about slavery when he was reading a commentary by an English puritan clergyman on the Epistle to the Ephesians, which mentioned "blackmores" in a discussion of servants and masters. Then, precisely when he was "thus thinking," Samuel wrote, "in came Bro[the]r Belknap to shew me a Petition he intended to present to the Gen[era]l Court for the freeing [of] a Negro and his wife, who were unjustly held in Bondage."[25] Hearing from his friend and fellow parishioner at the Old South Church that local people were wrongly deprived of liberty solidified Samuel's "unease" with slavery spawned by the commentary on Ephesians.

But conflicts had arisen over the wrongful enslavement of other Black people in Boston without spurring such action on Samuel's part.[26] What, then, gave this particular appeal such power? We do not know the names of the petitioners; not a trace of this petition, or any action taken on it, survives in the court records. It is therefore difficult to flesh out the story. But we do know what seems to have mattered most to Samuel: that the people in question were married. These were not just any Africans. To have earned recognition by a churchman like Joseph Belknap as a "Negro and his wife," they had likely married formally, which means that they made commitments to one another that were difficult to live out while enslaved. Puritan husbands and wives were supposed to cohabit, and puritan husbands were expected to provide for their wives. As Jane's minister at the First Church, Benjamin Wadsworth, would posit in a series of sermons published in the opening years of the eighteenth century, it was the "*duty*" of husbands and wives to "*cohabit or dwell together with one another.*" Regarding provision, Benjamin contended that "The Husband should indeavour, that his Wife may have Food and Raiment suitable for her. He should contrive prudently, and work diligently, that

his Family, and his Wife particularly, may be well provided for."[27] Slavery
made it nearly impossible for husbands and wives to fulfill these cardinal duties of marriage. Most bound couples in the region were split between two
Anglo-American households and so could not cohabit, and enslaved men
were unable to ensure that their wives were well cared for. Therefore, whoever wrongfully bound the man and woman in the petition did not just de-
prive them of personal liberty; he deprived them of the ability to order their
familial lives in a godly fashion.

It was not news to Samuel that slavery posed special problems to pious
couples. The man had been mulling this over for some time when his friend
appeared at his front door, petition in hand. In fact, Samuel had been thinking about the conflicting demands of slavery and marriage in puritan New
England—and talking about them with his neighbors—ever since he had first
learned of Sebastian's desire to wed Jane some fourteen months prior. The
plight of the wrongly enslaved couple discussed in the petition could not have
failed to have reminded Samuel of this matter, a matter that was, quite literally, close to home—and a matter about which he probably felt some disquiet.
Samuel had been charged with negotiating the marriage between Jane and
Sebastian more than a year before. Yet, month after month, the hoped-for
marriage dragged nearer to nothing.

That Samuel penned *The Selling of Joseph* in the middle of a prolonged
attempt to work out the family life of two of his bound neighbors makes good
sense when one reads the treatise with care, for families are all over it. The
tract's central metaphor is a familial one: that of the family of God. "[A]ll
Men . . . are the Sons of *Adam*," Samuel argued; "Originally, and Naturally,
there is no such thing as Slavery" since all "*are the Offspring of GOD.*" Moving
to the biblical family of Joseph, Samuel expounded that "*Joseph* was rightfully
no more a Slave to his Brethren, than they were to him."[28] It was a clever move,
for the statement was self-evident, but its ramifications radical. By placing
bound Africans in the position of the wronged Joseph and putting Anglo-
American enslavers in the position of Joseph's vengeful brothers, Samuel
suggested that his slaveholding neighbors were engaging in a wicked traffic
that pitted brother against brother.

Samuel next launched into a detailed discussion of the problematic nature of slavery in the New England context. Again, families were central. Slavery
brought sin into New England households, Samuel insisted; he complained
that enslavers concealed the extramarital sex of those they bound, "lest they
should be obliged to find them Wives, or pay their Fines" for fornication. (A

touch of disdain here for Deborah Thayer and people like her, who obstructed the efforts of those seeking lawful Christian marriages.) And not only did slavery thwart the endeavors of most Afro-New Englanders to build families, but the slave trade tore apart the families of Africans in Africa: "It is . . . most lamentable to think," Samuel wrote, "how in taking Negros out of *Africa*, and Selling . . . them here, That which GOD ha's joyned together men do boldly rend asunder . . . Husbands from their Wives, Parents from their Children." Though extant evidence sheds no light on the lives of Sebastian and Jane prior to their arrival in Boston, the judge surely knew bondspeople who had been torn from their kin by the Atlantic trade. Time and again Samuel contended throughout the treatise that slavery was incompatible with family life rightly conceived—whether the families in question were the family of God, the family of the biblical Joseph, the families of Anglo-American enslavers, the families of bondspeople in New England, or the families of those in Africa who were caught up in the slave trade.[29]

If we neglect to piece together Jane and Sebastian's story, *The Selling of Joseph* appears to be the product of an inexplicably forward-thinking colonist or an international network of radical Anglo-Protestants, and the marginalized people who shaped this remarkable writing remain marginalized in the tales we tell of it. However, when we recognize that the judge was negotiating Jane and Sebastian's marriage at precisely the same time he wrote the text, it is possible to see the fingerprints of Jane and Sebastian throughout. By grounding Samuel's antislavery writings on the actions and aspirations of his Black neighbors, I hope to build on the work of historians who have shown how people of African descent shaped abolitionism. In the Anglo-American context, much of this scholarship deals with the late eighteenth and the nineteenth centuries, but the case of Jane, Sebastian, and *The Selling of Joseph* shows that Black people's demands gave form to antislavery thought from the very beginning. Of course, though, I cannot claim to be original in centering Jane and Sebastian in this story, for I am by no means the first to envision the two at the heart of *The Selling of Joseph*. Far more clearly than we, enslaved people understood their importance to the happenings in their neighborhoods, and, more than three hundred years ago, Sebastian saw himself in Samuel's radical writing. He would name his first son John, presumably out of deference to John Waite, who appears to have freed him upon his deathbed. But his second—and last—he would name Joseph.[30]

* * *

Marriage could provide enslaved men with power in the familial context, as Sebastian's naming of baby Joseph suggests. However, at this juncture for Sebastian, patriarchal authority still lay in the future. When *The Selling of Joseph* went to press, Jane and Sebastian were yet unmarried. On September 26, 1700, more than three months after Samuel wrote his treatise, the enslavers were in his home haggling over who would support the couple's children (should they have any) and by what means. Deborah demanded that the Waites allow Sebastian "one day in six . . . for the support of Jane, his intended wife and her children, if it should please God to give her any." John, Samuel wrote, "wholly declin'd that," but he "freely offer'd to allow Bastian Five pounds, in Money p[er] annum towards the support of his children p[er] said Jane (besides Sebastians cloathing and Diet)." Ultimately, Samuel "persuaded" Deborah and Jane to agree to the arrangement. The matter seemed settled: The Waites would contribute five pounds annually to help defray the expenses of raising the couple's children. With a touch of satisfaction, Samuel put a period to the saga: "and so it was concluded." But the matter was not, in fact, concluded just yet. When Deborah died months later, Jane and Sebastian were still not married, and John visited Samuel yet again, "earnestly desir[ing] me to hasten consummating the Marriage between his Bastian and Jane."[31] Finally, on February 13, 1701, nearly two years after the bargaining process had begun, the couple was married by Samuel himself.

For Jane and Sebastian, entering into marriage was not a casual affair; nor was it a private one, carried out in the presence of friends in bondage, accompanied, perhaps, by an enslaver's family. The union the two entered was far more formal than this and far more visible to their broader community, features that set it apart from marriages between enslaved people in much of the English-speaking Americas.[32] According to Samuel's diary, John delivered a "Note of Publication" both to Boston's town clerk and to a man named Williams, who likely was connected with the First Church. The objective, Samuel wrote, was for the couple to be "published according to Law." Jane and Sebastian were taking part in the ordinary process required to marry legally in early New England, where a couple's intention to wed was to be filed with the town clerk and made public through the process of asking, or publishing, banns. On three consecutive Sundays prior to the wedding, a minister would proclaim before the congregation a couple's plan to marry and inquire whether anyone had a fitting reason to prevent the union. Should somebody object to a pairing—say, one spouse was already married or the union was incestuous—that person could "forbid" the couple in question from proceeding.[33] With their "Note of Publication," Jane and Sebastian invited the community to vet their relationship in the same way it vetted the relationships of their white neighbors. The two also made sure that their marriage—and its legitimacy—was well advertised around town.

Perhaps there was power in that proclamation of conjugal commitment from the pulpit. Hearing Benjamin Wadsworth, the First Church minister, announce thrice over Jane and Sebastian's decision to become husband and wife likely lent a kind of gravitas to their union. This might explain why those with whom Jane and Sebastian shared life in turn-of-the-century Boston appear quickly to have come to view their marriage as valid.[34] The community's widespread recognition of the couple's marital bond was made manifest in Jane's very name: After her marriage to Sebastian, the woman, once known as "Jane Lake," was called "Jane Basteen." That is, Jane lost the surname she had once possessed and gained a corruption of her husband's given name as a replacement. Jane's name change seems to have been immediate and firmly fixed: Jane Lake was referred to as Jane Basteen not just in 1701, the year of her marriage, but also in 1703, 1706, and 1708. And in 1711, Samuel, who by then had known the woman for more than two decades, referred to her as "Jane Boston" in his diary—modifying her surname to parallel the continued transformation of Sebastian's name, which had earlier been "Bastian" but by then in records most frequently was "Boston."[35] Jane's initial name change and its subsequent modifications show that the woman was securely linked in the minds of her neighbors to the man she married.

The name change shows something else, too. It suggests that Jane and Sebastian's community, unlike many slaveholding communities, recognized and sought to bolster Sebastian's patriarchal authority in the marriage.[36] What about "Lake"? Jane had a bona fide last name, recorded in her marriage record, in which "Jane Lake" married "Bastian"—though it is likely, of course, that this name was originally inherited from an enslaver. Still, why not use *that* to mark the couple? Unlike his wife, Sebastian had no last name—at least, no extant records indicate that he did. In such a situation, unknown to white New Englanders, all of whom possessed surnames as well as given names, it might have been logical for Sebastian to take Jane's name, seeing as it was the only last name either of them could claim. But no evidence indicates that Sebastian was ever called "Sebastian Lake." Instead, Jane for the rest of her life would be marked by versions of Bastian, Basteen, and Boston.

The patriarchal patterns of naming that rendered Jane a "Basteen" do not seem to have been unusual in Massachusetts. Other women of African ancestry lost their surnames when they married Black men without last names, and, like Jane, they gained their spouses' given names as replacements. For instance, an enslaved Bostonian referred to variously as Katherine or Kate came to be called Katherine Cornwall after marrying a bound man of African descent named Cornwall. Similarly, a free Black woman of Bridgewater named Margaret received as a surname her husband's given name—Sash—when they married. And Dorcas, from Chapter 1, who lived in Boston and attended Jane and Sebastian's First Church in the middle to late seventeenth century, would come to be surnamed Menenie, which was her husband's given name.[37]

Jane Basteen, Katherine Cornwall, Margaret Sash, and Dorcas Menenie were no outliers; this patriarchal pattern of naming operated on a population scale throughout the region. The burgeoning port of Boston, again, serves as a useful example. More than 200 surnamed enslaved and free people of African descent were registered in Boston's church and vital records from the late seventeenth century through the year 1730, and many of their last names, like Jane Basteen's, were derived from given names common to Afro-New England men. Some of these names, such as Anthony, were of Luso-Spanish origin akin to Sebastian. Others, like George, Lewis, Edwards, and Richards, were conventional English names. Still others were classical; for example, Caesar, Primus, and Titus. Some names, such as Sampson and Simons, were biblical in origin. And a significant number were African. Coffy derived from Kofi, the Akan day name for Friday; Cojoe from Cudjoe, the day name for Monday; and both Quakee and Quaquo were probably versions of Quaco, the Akan name for Wednesday. Mingo and Sanco (a distortion of Sango) were also given names of African origin that doubled as surnames in early eighteenth-century Boston, as was Cumin, which likely derived from Kumina, a Kikongo word originating in the Kongo region. And not only did wives, at least on occasion, receive as surnames their husbands' given names, but children did so as well; the African practice of adopting the given name of one's father as a surname appears to have flourished in early New England, where the patriarchal naming customs of Africans melded easily with those of their Anglo-American neighbors.[38]

Jane and Sebastian negotiated their relationship within the context of a patriarchal culture, one that not only assumed Sebastian would pass his first name on to his children as a surname (trumping his wife's bona fide last name in the process) but also expected that Sebastian would choose his children's given names. Eight and a half months after the couple finally managed to wed,

Jane gave birth to their first child. Samuel recorded the infant's arrival in his diary, noting of Sebastian that "He calls her Jane." It might well be that Samuel was simply projecting his own cultural assumptions onto the enslaved couple; Anglo-American fathers in early New England typically named their children, sometimes without seeking advice from their wives. But Samuel's statement is eminently believable: Sebastian lived in a society that recognized naming as the father's prerogative, and he likely hailed from a society that gave men the right to name their children. Of course, we cannot glimpse Jane and Sebastian's interior lives, and it is possible that Sebastian consulted Jane while making his decision; the chosen name certainly demonstrated a deep respect for her. However, the people with whom Jane and Sebastian lived out their lives—leaders in the church, local civil authorities, and neighbors up and down the street—would have understood the act of naming to be rightfully Sebastian's, and Sebastian's alone.[39]

From the perspective of white New Englanders, Sebastian not only retained rights to naming—both of his children and, in a way, of his wife—but he also could partake in public rituals that cemented his authority in his family. This can be seen in the sacrament of baptism. On the first Sunday of November in 1701, Sebastian found himself standing before the First Church congregation. His infant daughter was to be baptized and Sebastian, like all fathers presenting their children to the Lord, would hold her aloft before the congregation while the minister poured symbolic water over her head. Little Jane "is baptised by Mr. Allen," Samuel would write in his diary later that day: "Bastian holds her up." When Samuel noted that Sebastian held little Jane up before the First Church, he was recording Sebastian's participation in an important symbolic practice. The holding up of children was hugely consequential to Samuel; he wrote on numerous occasions about holding up his own children as they were baptized. And when eleven of his fourteen children had been born, Samuel took time to list them by name in his diary, noting that "All the above-named Eleven Children have been by their father, Samuel Sewall, (holding them in his arms,) Offered up to God in Baptisme, at the South-Meeting-House in Boston . . . upon the Sabbath Day in the Solemn Assembly of God's Saints."[40] Holding up the child, as Samuel saw it, represented the offering of that child to God. And familial ties eclipsed legal ownership in this situation: Fathers, rather than enslavers, momentarily claimed the position of family head. As was the case for Sebastian's family, the child may have been considered the legal property of somebody else, but that did not negate the right of Sebastian—and Sebastian only—to stand before the church and be recognized, if merely for a moment, as the true authority over that child.

Besides providing enslaved men with a fleeting opportunity to wrest authority over their children from the Anglo-Americans who claimed ownership of them, baptisms may well have reinforced the clout of these men within their own families. The practice of offering children to the Lord in baptism seems to have been carried out exclusively by men, or nearly so; in Samuel's many references to baptisms, not once did an infant's mother hold her child up before the congregation. This was an offering that only the father, as the head of the household, could make. Puritan conceptions of family life gave wives a good deal of power within the home, but the husband ultimately was "the Head of the Wife." As Samuel's minister put it: Both husbands and wives "have each of them a share in the government of them [children and servants]; tho' there is an inequality in the degree of this Authority, and the Husband is to be acknowledged to hold a *Superiority*."[41] Maintaining what puritans considered proper gender relations was important within the church. Even though Jane had been baptized in the meetinghouse and was a long-standing member of the congregation, it was Sebastian—a man with no official relationship to the First Church at all—who held aloft their infant child for baptism.

There were other ways in which Black men might have found their positions vis-à-vis their wives bolstered by the realities of life in New England. Unlike enslaved men in the antebellum South, bondsmen in Massachusetts were considered responsible for supporting their kin by their broader society—at least in certain instances. This can be seen, again, in Jane and Sebastian's story. Remember that Deborah suggested, when bargaining with the Waites over the prospective marriage of Jane to Sebastian, that "Sebastian might have one day in six allow'd him for the support of Jane, his intended wife and her children."[42] Sebastian's labor, in Deborah's mind, ought to help feed and clothe his dependents. And the Waites apparently agreed; though they refused Deborah's request that Sebastian use the proceeds of one weekly workday to provide for his wife and children, they offered to furnish Sebastian with five pounds annually, a sum equal to one quarter of Sebastian's assessed value in John's 1702 inventory. With this yearly payment, Sebastian would be able to sustain his family, at least in part. Significantly, John agreed to give *Sebastian* the annual allowance. He could have simply provided the cash to Deborah himself, but he did not. And Deborah did not ask to manage the payment. Apparently, both enslavers thought it appropriate for Sebastian to feed and clothe his wife and children using money he earned through his labor, and they gave him leeway to use the five pounds as he saw fit. Even though Sebastian was in bondage, the Anglo-Americans around him considered him responsible for maintaining his family.

New Englanders expected other men in bondage to provide for their offspring as well. Unfortunately, descriptions of the arrangements enslavers made concerning the marriages of those they bound almost uniformly have not survived—indeed, Jane and Sebastian's story would have been lost if not for Samuel's unusually prodigious note-taking and fortuitous role in mediating the relationship. Therefore, the expectation that enslaved fathers provide for their offspring can be seen most readily in cases of bastardy, which were documented by Massachusetts courts. It was not unusual for bound men convicted of fathering children out of wedlock to be required to pay for the support of their offspring. In the early eighteenth century, for example, an enslaved man named Cesar admitted to fornication with Mary Goslin, a white woman who bore a child as a result of their relationship. The two were convicted by the court and summarily punished: each was whipped ten stripes and ordered to pay court costs. But Cesar alone was required to post a twenty-pound security to the towns of Boston and Dorchester in order to provide for his child.[43]

The case of Cesar and Mary not only provides evidence of the expectation of Anglo-Americans that at least some men in bondage help maintain their offspring, but it also sheds light on the degree to which the enslaved internalized the patriarchal assumptions of their society regarding male provision within the family. Cesar took it upon himself to support materially his partner and their infant. Cesar and Mary were not the only ones convicted as a result of their crime; the court ferreted out a cadre of people whom Cesar had recruited to care for Mary and their newborn child. Sometime before the baby's birth, Cesar had approached an Anglo-American woman from Dorchester named Abigail Trott and persuaded her to "receive" Mary "into her house." Abigail apparently tended to both Mary and the child, who was born in her Dorchester home. In return for her services, Cesar compensated Abigail with "money and other things." Two free Indians, Andrew and Anne Johnson, were fined by the court along with Abigail; at some point they had "receiv[ed] and entertain[ed]" Cesar and Mary's child in their Boston home. As these records show, not only did Cesar take the initiative in assembling an interracial network of people to care for his sexual partner and their child, but he also supplied financial incentives to compensate Mary's caretaker for her time and trouble. Enslaved status notwithstanding, Cesar insisted on providing for his kin.[44]

Men in bondage worked in a variety of ways to provide materially for their wives and children. The most visible of their efforts revolved around the process of obtaining freedom, which generated a paper trail and therefore at least sometimes can still be traced. Men appear to have acquired their freedom more frequently than women in New England. This is unusual; manumissions in societies throughout the Atlantic world tended to favor women, in large part because male enslavers emancipated women with whom they had sexual relationships (and sired children) at higher rates than they did other people in bondage.[45] Coercive intimate encounters between women and those who enslaved them appear to have been less common in New England than in many other parts of the Anglo-Atlantic world, though they certainly happened and will be discussed in Chapter 5. Perhaps as a result, enslavers who lived in the region did not preferentially manumit women in bondage. During the first half of the eighteenth century, for example, about two-thirds of people emancipated by their enslavers' wills in Suffolk County were male.

Fragmentary but consistent evidence indicates that, once free, Black husbands and fathers went to work liberating their family members. They labored, usually in the most menial of occupations; they saved their money, occasionally investing it with sympathetic Anglo-Americans; and, in some instances, they even sold themselves into term servitude in an attempt to acquire the funds to free their families. The reality that opportunities for freedom came more readily to men than to women and could subsequently spread from husbands and fathers to wives and children influenced the gendered division of power in enslaved families. The bound fathers and husbands who lived alongside Jane and Sebastian were not so consistently deprived of the opportunity to protect and provide for their families as historians have understood enslaved men in much of the Anglo-Atlantic world to be. Abetted by a labor system that valued men's work over women's, they lived with the knowledge that they might manage one day to secure their family's welfare as a free family, even if the chances were slim. Quite the opposite was true for enslaved women. Wives and mothers in the region were less likely than men to manage to liberate themselves, and they appear to have succeeded in unshackling their kin only very rarely.[46]

Despite the relative power accorded to bondsmen vis-à-vis their kin, men like Sebastian under ordinary circumstances were forced to watch their families grow from a distance. Enslaved status was heritable through the

maternal line in New England, which means that whoever claimed ownership of a bound woman was recognized as the rightful owner of that woman's
children as well. New England's practice of inheriting bondspeople through
the maternal line, combined with the dispersal of the enslaved in extraordinarily small holdings throughout the region, led to the creation of what might
have been the most matrifocal of living arrangements for bondspeople in the
Atlantic world. In places where enslaved fathers were able to cohabit with
their wives and children, nuclear families could proliferate, but not so in
New England; in Boston, at least, the vast majority of bondspeople who chose
to marry others in slavery were, like Sebastian and Jane, claimed by a different
enslaver than their spouse. This means that in most families any children
born to the couple would live with their mother in one Anglo-American
household while their father lived in a different household altogether.[47]

Matrifocality and patriarchy make unexpected bedfellows. Historians
have observed that enslaved households with absent fathers tended to produce families in which women wielded power, and they have argued that
two-parent, nuclear households in bondage generally yielded families with
patriarchal, or male-dominated, gender relations. That is, scholars have understood the structure of bound families to define the power relations within
those families. The evidence that enslaved children in New England lived with
their mothers rather than with their fathers in families that were considered
by their broader society to be subject to the authority of bound men like Sebastian therefore undermines a central assumption in much scholarship on
families in slavery.[48] But the archive of slavery in New England seems clear:
Husbands and fathers appear to have retained important elements of authority even in families that were centered geographically on mothers.

Given the reality that husbands and fathers did not ordinarily live with
their families, it is hardly surprising that Sebastian was gone when Jane gave
birth to baby Jane in 1701. His enslaver had sent him to work for the provincial government in Boston Harbor, where he helped construct the fort that
would come to be known as "Castle William."[49] Sebastian appears still to have
been on this assignment when Jane gave birth to their second child, a boy, in
August of 1703.[50] This infant, John, might have been named by Sebastian in
honor of John Waite, who seems to have worked out a manumission agreement with his bondsman, but the child remained firmly secured with
his mother in bondage.[51] Then, in 1706, Sebastian stood before the First
Church congregation once again, offering his daughter, Mary, to the Lord.
He repeated the ritual with Jane in 1708, likely named in memory of her older

sister, who had died in 1703. The couple's next child was born in 1712, and he was christened Joseph in what may have been intended as a reminder to those around him that he was as wrongly enslaved as was the biblical Joseph. Finally, Sebastian held Elizabeth up for baptism in 1714. In thirteen years of marriage, the man had fathered six children. He must have had regular intimate contact with his wife during these years in order to produce children so rapidly, which means that he would have been present in his children's lives, even if he did not live with them.[52] And when those six children were born, Sebastian had named them, at least as his neighbors saw it. He had stood before the First Church to dedicate each of them to the Lord. All the while, during this time of family growth he had somehow managed to extricate himself from slavery. Sebastian's children might have lived with their mother, but gender relations within the family did not necessarily skew toward providing Jane with power. The fragmentary extant evidence suggests that Sebastian had authority—at least at certain times and in certain situations—over those in his family.

*   *   *

Jane and Sebastian's story shows the ability of enslavers to prevent those they bound from marrying in turn-of-the-eighteenth-century Boston. Deborah apparently refused to heed the pleas of the couple, the requests of John and Eunice, and even the entreaties of the neighborhood's leading citizen. And there was no recourse for the aggrieved: It took nothing less than the hand of God to clear the way for Jane and Sebastian's marriage. Other evidence indicates that enslavers could claim for themselves the right to delimit bondspeople's intimate affairs. The case of an enslaved man named James Mills is a good example of this. Accused by Bostonian Thomas Berry of "frequenting the company of his Negro woman contrary to his mind," James was sentenced by the Suffolk County Court to be whipped for the deed.[53] And not only could enslavers put a stop to visits between partners in bondage, but the law made abundantly clear that they could prohibit bondspeople from formalizing relationships. Justices of the peace and ministers were allowed to solemnize the marriages only of people who had the "consent" of "those whose immediate care and government they [we]re under." For dependent people—whether in slavery, in servitude, or simply the children of household heads—marriage was off-limits without permission, and the enslaved, unlike other people under family government, never aged or staged into autonomy. Dependents from cradle to grave, those bound by slavery were the only people in turn-of-the-eighteenth-century Massachusetts who could legally be prohibited for life from joining in matrimony.[54]

The entire debacle of Jane and Sebastian's attempted marriage—and his ineffectiveness at bringing it to a satisfactory conclusion before Deborah's demise—appears to have haunted Samuel. Some things ought not be disallowed by slavery, Samuel believed, and marriage was one of them. Late in the year 1705, as Jane and Sebastian approached five years of matrimony, Samuel had an opportunity to make his views known to the Massachusetts General Assembly. The Assembly at that time was debating new legislation governing marriage in the province, and Samuel prevailed upon his fellow representatives to do something quite extraordinary for Black people in Massachusetts: He persuaded them to establish in law that the enslaved had a right to marriage. "No master," they ultimately decreed, "shall unreasonably deny marriage to his negro with one of the same nation[,] any law usage or custom to the contrary notwithstanding." In one stroke, the Assembly overwrote the legislation requiring consent for those under the "government" of enslavers, and it nullified "customs" that allowed people like Deborah to dig in their heels and withhold lawful marriage from those in slavery. This "clause about their Masters not denying their Marriage," as Samuel described it in his diary, was really quite extraordinary. Bound and dependent white people in the province still required permission in order to marry lawfully, but enslaved people of African descent could now wed one another, even if those who bound them preferred that they did not.[55] Black people ensnared in slavery no longer could be condemned to singleness for life—at least not legally. And enslavers like Deborah no longer could waylay with such impunity the marriage plans of those they bound.

To Samuel, this legislation made perfect sense. How could people who considered themselves Christians justly deny marriage to those they held in bondage, thereby condemning them to sexual sin? After all, as he had explained in *The Selling of Joseph*, bound Africans were "Men and Women," and the "Offspring of GOD" as much as English people were.[56] What is more, sexual sin did not merely harm those who indulged the flesh; it also polluted the households in which they lived. Puritans and many of their eighteenth-century descendants believed that they were responsible for rooting out the evil in their homes, and, if they failed to do so, God's punishment might come upon their entire family. As Thomas Shepard, minister in nearby Cambridge, had argued, God would "impute" the sins of "children, servants, [and] strangers who are within our gates" to the household head "who had the power . . . to restrain them and did not." The result: "our families and consciences [will] be stained with their guilt and blood." This way of thinking is ubiquitous in the writings of the province's early religious authorities.[57] If the wrongdoings of bondspeople imperiled Massachusetts households, then letting them marry could safeguard those households. By endowing the enslaved with conjugal rights, Samuel and the rest of the Massachusetts General Court could stop the dangerous progression of sin.

But changing the law was one thing; changing "customs" and "usages," as the legislation put it, was another altogether. There is no indication that this 1705 legislation was publicized, so knowledge of it, to the extent that there was any, must have spread by word of mouth from one hopeful bondsperson to the next, or, perhaps, from one anxious enslaver to another. Not surprisingly, evidence suggests that some enslavers defied the law, refusing to let bondspeople contract formal marriages. They did not do this publicly. Enslavers did not as a matter of course prohibit those they bound from marrying once they got to the point of publishing banns; only one Boston couple was formally forbidden from marriage during the eighteenth century because an enslaver posted a complaint.[58] To the extent that Anglo-Americans kept the people they enslaved from entering formal unions, they did so quietly, through persuasion or punishment, in the confines of their homes. Evidence of this kind of treatment can be found in the annals of Boston's New North Church, where, in 1764, long after Jane and Sebastian's time, a woman named Dinah informed the church's minister that she and her husband had not been married "according to the forms prescribed in the law of the Province for White people." The reason? As Dinah explained, "the Master of the Negro man [would] not consent to such marriage." Although the two had "contracted" to one another "by the consent of both their masters & mistresses," they had not been allowed to solemnize their marriage as they ought to have been according to the 1705 law.[59]

Dinah doubtless stands in for many others denied marriage contrary to the law, but the archive yields little on this matter. What the sources that survive show far more amply is the utter lack of conjugal rights that accompanied the formal unions of those in bondage. Enslaved people might have had the right to civil marriage in Massachusetts, but their enslavers did not forfeit the right to do as they wished with those over whom they claimed ownership. And when the property rights of enslavers conflicted with the rights of people in bondage to marital intimacy, the enslaved were at a deep disadvantage despite the efforts they put forth to obtain legitimate marriages. To make things worse for bondspeople who sought lawful unions, the assumption that marriage nearly inevitably would bring with it geographic division seems only to have grown stronger over time, perhaps as the region became more intensively integrated into the Anglo-Atlantic commercial world and as its homogeneous religious culture began to splinter.[60]

The extent to which white New Englanders accepted the notion that slavery brought with it spousal separation is evident by the middle of the eighteenth century in the way that ministers altered traditional marriage vows when marrying people in bondage. In the "Negro marriage vows" used by Samuel Phillips, who ministered north of Boston in Andover, the husband promised to "be True & *Faithfull* to [his wife] and . . . Cleave to her *only, so long* as God, in his Provid[en]ce, shall continue your and her Abode in Such Place (or Places) as that you can conveniently come together." The wife promised likewise. Samuel then declared them "*Husband* and *Wife*," but only "so long as God shall continue your Places of Abode as afore-said." Other ministers in the region, such as Robert Hubbard in Shelburne, Massachusetts, and Roger Newton in Greenfield, Massachusetts, amended marriage oaths as well, seeking to account for the fact that bound people of African descent lived apart.[61]

The evidence all points in the same direction: Those who joined bondspeople in marriage throughout the region appear regularly to have shifted expectations of marriage to match the compromised ability of the enslaved to access their spouses. People of African descent were painfully aware of this reality. When Flora and Exeter were married, the minister informed them that "they were not discharged from Servitude or in any Manner freed from their obligations to their respective masters." That is, their marriage in no way impinged on the right of their enslavers to do what they wished with them, including selling them away—which is what happened. Flora and the couple's children were shipped to Virginia, and Exeter, who never learned of his family's whereabouts, spent his waning years wandering New England in vain pursuit of his missing kin.[62] Black Bostonians writing in the revolutionary era would bemoan this ability of enslavers to override conjugal rights: "we are no longer man and wife than our masters or Mestreses thinkes proper."[63] The marriages of the enslaved offered no guarantees. Husbands and wives in bondage might be separated at a moment's notice, and for any reason, from those who mattered most.

Yet, the 1705 legislation providing enslaved people the right to marry nonetheless had significance. The historical record reveals that Samuel's marriage clause provided recourse to some enslaved people who sought formal unions. For instance, in 1709, the province's lower criminal court considered the petition of Jack, a man bound by a Boston butcher named Samuel Bill. Jack wished to marry Esther, a woman claimed by Robert Gutteridge, a Boston "Coffeeman." According to Jack, his "Master and Mistress [we]re Consenting," but "the said Mr. Gutteridge refuse[d] to give his Consent."[64] Citing the 1705 law by name, Jack declared that it "provided That no Master shall unreasonably deny Marriage to his Negro with one of the same Nation." The petition asked the court to interrogate Esther's enslaver. If the man had no "reasonable objection" to the match, Jack requested that he "& s[ai]d Esther may be Marryed together." The justices ruled in Jack's favor, ordering, with an unmistakable reference to the 1705 legislation, "that the said Jack Negro be not denied marriage provided he attend the Directions of the Law; for the Regulation of marriages." Esther's enslaver had no choice but to capitulate, and Jack and Esther were married in 1710 by the minister of Jane and Sebastian's First Church.[65]

Other bondspeople seem to have appealed to the 1705 legislation when it was in their favor to do so. The diary of Henry Flynt, a longtime tutor at Harvard, contains several passages about a man named Toney. Henry very nearly had an agreement in November of 1737 to sell Toney to a man named Thomas Crosbey for ninety pounds, but Thomas backed out at the last minute, insisting that he "would not be Obliged to Marry [Toney] to his Brothers Negro woeman." Thomas would only buy Toney if he could "dispose of" his brother's bondswoman at "some distance" beforehand. But who would have "obliged" Thomas to marry Toney to the enslaved woman claimed by his brother? Certainly not Henry, who just wanted to complete the sale, or Thomas's brother, whose own bondsperson seemed to be at Thomas's disposal, or Thomas himself, who opposed the match. Thomas clearly was worried about contact between the two people of African descent; they needed to be separated by "some distance" before he would buy Toney. Henry's frustrated jottings suggest that Toney himself—or the "Negro woeman"—had the power to compel Thomas to consent to their union, which raises the possibility that the province's 1705 protection of marriages of the enslaved still had legal clout more than three decades after Samuel advocated for it before the General Assembly.[66]

Other white residents of Massachusetts appear to have felt obliged by the 1705 legislation—or the religious culture that helped birth it—to allow their bondspeople to marry. Consider the quandary of Longmeadow minister Stephen Williams. Stephen's bondswoman, Phillis, who had been baptized in his church, wished to marry a local man in bondage, but Stephen's wife opposed it. Stephen's diary betrays his suspicion that his wife's position did not honor God. "[Th]e affair of marrying o[u]r negro Girl—is somew[ha]t p[er]plexing—I beg God w[oul]d be pleas[e]d mercifully to direct therein—SO as that his holy name—may not be dishonor[e]d," he wrote on one occasion. "I pray God to direct me to my Duty, in this affair—of Difficulty," he pleaded on another. The angst continued: "I am afraid—we do wrong," he admitted; "I pray God to direct [us] to—[our] Duty—in this affair." Still more: "I am in a Strait respecting Phillis," he wrote, asking God to keep the family from "dishonouring his Great name." Stephen was not alone in recognizing the injustice of the situation. His congregation apparently took Phillis's side: "I am yet in great p[er]plexity—upon acc[oun]t of o[u]r negro—Girl," Stephen wrote, adding that "people are uneasy." Finally, nearly eight years after he first discussed Phillis's desire to wed, Stephen married Phillis to the man of her choosing.[67] Stephen's diary leading to the time of Phillis's marriage has been lost, so we cannot know what finally persuaded the man to allow the match, but his tortured scribblings over the years make undeniable his anxiety about the spiritual ramifications of denying marriage to godly people in bondage.

Further evidence suggests that people with strong religious convictions took seriously the marital unions of the enslaved. When Benjamin Colman, pastor of Boston's Brattle Street Church, asked Samuel Sewall about the baptism of a man named Scipio, Samuel wrote Benjamin a letter expressing hope that Scipio would indeed be baptized. Yet he "has had a Child," Samuel wrote, and "I never heard that he was married." To Samuel, the situation demanded a remedy: "If he should desire a Wife, I should forward him therein so it might be conveniently [accomplished]."[68] Likewise, Cotton Mather and fellow minister Thomas Prince recognized the union split between their two households. Ezer, enslaved by Cotton, and Dinah, enslaved by Thomas, had two children in 1722, when Ezer was baptized by Cotton and joined his Second Church. Because Ezer "was Received into the Covenant of GOD, and Baptised Lately with us," Cotton requested that Ezer's offspring, lawful as they were, be baptized in Thomas's church. Thomas seemed happy to comply; the two children were baptized in the Old South Church the following day.[69] In another example, John Gyles, a parishioner at Samuel's Old South Church, worked diligently to rescue the marriage of Jethro Boston and Hagar, both bound in his household. After Hagar committed adultery, John recalled using "all possible Endeavours to reconcile the said Jethro & Hagar." A neighbor remembered the man doing what he could to mediate "but all in vain."[70] Though John was ultimately unsuccessful at preserving the marriage, his decision to seek reconciliation suggests that he cared about the union, that his reputation as an upstanding household head might be sullied by his inability to enforce monogamy among his dependents, or perhaps both. Conjugal bonds between enslaved people mattered to at least some enslavers.

Because marriage could matter, many bondspeople embraced the institution. Marriages among the enslaved show up in historical records of all types. For example, the newspapers that flooded Boston's streets referenced wedded bondspeople in a variety of ways. Some were victims of unfortunate accidents, as the "Negro Man and his Wife" struck dead in bed by a bolt of lightning in the garret of an enslaver's home.[71] A number of married couples were advertised for sale. A "Negro Man aged about 40 and his Wife 30" were to be "disposed of." A "Negro Man and his Wife" were to be sold "at a reasonable rate." A "Negro Man" was to be auctioned alongside the "likely Negro Woman" described as "his Wife." And a "likely Negro Man" was to be sold "with his Wife."[72] Still other wedded bondspeople were sought by enslavers. For instance, the poster of one notice wished to purchase "a Negro Fellow . . . with his Wife." And some married couples, like Caesar and his "Wife," took to the road in flight from slavery.[73]

The documents produced in the process of settling enslavers' estates also mentioned bound husbands and wives. Examples of married couples referenced in probate records include Richard and "his wife Grace"; "Negro Caesar" and "his wife Sarah"; an unnamed "Negro-man & his Wife"; Andrew and "Hannah his Wife"; "Pompey and his Wife Fidelia"; "Joseph and Tabitha being Husband and Wife"; and "Robin & his Wife."[74] Probate records also show that the marriages of bondspeople could influence the actions of enslavers. One man ordered his "Negro Woman Esther" to be sold after his death but stipulated that she should be "not far distant from her husband." Likewise, "Negro Man John" was left to an heir because he was married to the bondswoman of that heir.[75] Furthermore, probate records show that enslavers, at least on occasion, thought about the marital prospects of those they bound. That is, contracting a formal union was anticipated of at least some people in slavery. One will writer left land and a variety of personal effects to a man he bound, named Pompey, and to "his Wife if any he should have." The hope was that "Pompey & Wife" would one day "be able to support themselves."[76]

Married people of African descent also appeared before the bar, suing, being sued, and giving testimonies in the region's courts. Anthony, a bound African man, and "Mariah his Wife" charged an Anglo-American man with unlawfully enslaving their daughter. James Lancashire, a free man of African descent, and "Katherine his wife" sued to recover a debt. A man named Joseph was found guilty of murdering "Nanny Negro his s[ai]d Wife." Titus, a free Black man, sued for the liberty of "Dinah his wife." Quaco was accused of poisoning a fellow bondsman at the home where "his wife," Jenny, was enslaved. Seymour and "Kate his wife" went to court to recover money owed to Kate. Geoffs and his "Wife," Parthenia, both enslaved and of African descent, were accused of theft. Roger and Peg, the "wife of the said Roger," were prosecuted by the man who bound them when they left his service. Lewis and Martha "his wife" were accused of having sex before marriage. Exeter Turner, a free Black man, and "his wife," Luce, were convicted of receiving stolen goods. John Jackson and Jone "his Wife" filed suit for Jone's liberty. Betty, "wife to Richard Price," was convicted of "being in Bedd with another Negro man." Primus Freeman "& Marget his wife" turned to the court to recover an unpaid debt.[77] And there are more: Many other married couples of African descent interfaced with the Massachusetts court system.

Evidence of the marriages of enslaved people can be found in many places, but perhaps the most powerful testimony to the region's unusual marriage culture is the sheer number of bondspeople who married. In just the town of Boston, well over a thousand enslaved and free Black people were married by ministers and justices of the peace over the course of the eighteenth century.[78] And when high mortality rates cut their unions short, some of these people asked local officials to perform their second, or even third, marriages. For instance, a woman named Patience married first a man named Bristow, and then a man named Boston. Joshua Gee, pastor of Boston's Second Church, officiated her first marriage, and Andrew Eliot, minister at the town's New North Church, officiated her second. Patience seems to have passed away not long after her marriage to Boston, as Boston married—again in the New North Church—a woman named Susanna. His final marriage, to Phillis, would be solemnized by New North's pastor as well. After each of these marriages, the presiding minister dutifully relayed a record of the marriage to Boston's town clerk, and the unions were inscribed in the clerk's records alongside the unions of Patience and Boston's white neighbors.[79] Examples of bondspeople who married in a formal capacity only to do so again upon the death of their spouse abound in the records of eighteenth-century Boston.

The unusual marriage culture among enslaved people in eastern Massachusetts appears to have been made possible by the hesitation of at least some white people to deny bondspeople marriage. Having a law on the books guaranteeing the enslaved the right to marry surely helped; so, too, did the belief that those in bondage, however low on the social hierarchy, deserved the right to order their intimate lives in a God-honoring fashion. However, these things do not explain why people of African descent embraced formal marriage—and the process leading up to it—with such vigor. Of course, deeply religious people in bondage, like Jane, might have wished for a formal marriage in order to align their intimate lives with their spiritual convictions. But the embrace of marriage on the part of the enslaved was not about legitimizing sexual behavior—at least not primarily. For bondspeople less pious than Jane, there were other options for sexual intimacy, whether casual encounters or long-term informal partnerships without civil standing that paralleled English common law unions.[80] Demanding government-sanctioned marriages was, for the enslaved, strategic.

In a region where most bound families were stretched between multiple Anglo-American households and had to respond to the wishes of two (or more) different enslavers, couples seized civil marriage to claim legitimacy for their bonds—and to seek protection for their intimate relationships. This was not jumping the broom; it was jumping through a lot of administrative hoops.[81] For Jane and Sebastian, achieving government-sanctioned bonds entailed cultivating allies in their neighborhood to advocate for their union, delivering a notice of marriage intent to the town clerk, asking a local minister to thrice announce their desire to wed, and finding a justice of the peace to marry them. Doing these things took time, money (some officials charged couples for marrying them), and literacy—or at least access to people with literacy. But the effort could pay off. Some evidence suggests that these legal unions mattered to the Anglo-Americans living alongside bondspeople, who took formal marriages more seriously than informal ones and, at least in certain circumstances, felt obliged to protect conjugal ties sanctioned by the provincial government.

The case of Hannah and Bostan, who were bound in different Massachusetts households, is a good example of the protection that could result from a marriage. When the two decided to wed, their enslavers drafted a legal agreement that would "Bind and Oblige" themselves as well as their heirs forever to keep Hannah and Bostan in close proximity to one another. Nobody, according to the contract, would have the right to "oblige" Hannah or Bostan "to serve further Distant appart from Each Other then the Bounds of the Parish."[82] Hannah and Bostan might never live in the same household, but this legal instrument ensured they would always reside in the same town. Similarly, Francis Foxcroft, a judge from Cambridge, sought to preserve the marital union of a man named Exeter whom he had freed some years earlier. Francis petitioned Boston's selectmen in the early eighteenth century when he learned that they wished to expel Exeter from the town. The judge declared that Exeter had "been married many years to his present Wife named Leucey." It was true. Exeter and Leucey had been married thirteen years earlier by a local minister. Francis continued: The two had "cohabited in Boston ab[ou]t two years," he wrote, and the selectmen ought to allow Exeter to remain. "I think no man, wou'd draw upon himself the Curse of parting man and Wife," Francis concluded.[83] Perhaps unwilling to risk divine retribution, the selectmen yielded. Marriage for the enslaved conferred no conjugal rights, but there was nevertheless power in the vows that Jane and Sebastian, Hannah and Bostan, and Exeter and Leucey proclaimed.

*   *   *

Jane and Sebastian's union might have played a role in bringing about the unusual marriage culture among people of African descent in eighteenth-century Boston. Their determination to wed—and the near impossibility of their quest to do so—appears to have influenced the thinking of their neighbor, Samuel, who would go on to disseminate arguments against slavery in The Selling of Joseph and work to establish in law the right of the province's bondspeople to marry. Regardless of the extent to which Jane and Sebastian's marriage influenced the ability of others to wed, however, this union, and the vistas it opens into the practical problems bondspeople faced when it came to formalizing their relationships, are worth careful consideration. The reality that civil marriage was available to enslaved people in Massachusetts—and that these people embraced such marriages with gusto—runs counter to scholars' claims that the unions of enslaved people throughout the Anglo-Atlantic were informal or of a purely religious nature.[84] In the region where Jane and Sebastian lived, people in bondage sought out local officials to administer their vows in impressive numbers. They embraced marriage in part because it was often available to them, thanks to the 1705 legislation and the religious culture that undergirded it. But pursuing civil unions was more than a knee-jerk reaction to their availability; Black people who sought to be "Lawfully married," as one man in slavery put it, appear to have acted strategically to bolster support for their often-precarious marital relationships.[85]

As for Jane and Sebastian's marriage, we know much about its tortured inception, but we know little about its later development. Church and town records reveal only the barest contours of the family as it entered its second decade. Sebastian labored during this time for the town of Boston, which required free Black men to maintain local streets and highways in lieu of militia duty: The selectmen included some form of "Boston Waite" on every inventory of laborers taken between 1708 and 1725.[86] He labored as well for Samuel, whose diary reveals that Sebastian helped him continually with odd jobs. As for Jane, she gave birth to her sixth and last child in 1714 and then disappeared from the historical record. None of the couple's children can be traced into the third decade of the eighteenth century. Their firstborn, Jane, died in 1703; Samuel noted on March 20 of that year that "Little Jane, Bastian's daughter, died last night 2 hours after midnight." Mary passed away four years later; Samuel mentioned going to her funeral. The couple lost a third child in 1709; town records state that a "Negro ch[ild] of Bastian" was buried that March.[87] Neither of the couple's final two children can be traced in the historical record at all. Perhaps they, too, died as young children. Rates of infant mortality were high across the board in turn-of-the-century Boston, but Jane and Sebastian's family seems to have been hit particularly hard.[88] Despite Jane's continual childbearing, the family grew only modestly. At least three of the six children died in their early years, and the couple may well have lost more children, as the town's death records from the time are spotty.

All vestiges of Sebastian's family life seem to have disappeared in the second decade of the eighteenth century, but extant sources show that the man was alive and active until 1729. He performed faithfully the labor required of free Black men by the town of Boston, and he maintained a close relationship with the Sewall family. His errands for the judge became increasingly intimate in nature. In 1721, Samuel noted that his granddaughter was "brought home" ill from the smallpox. Sebastian—now called "Boston" rather than "Bastion," "Bastian," or "Basteen"—went to get the girl, but he did not drive her home in Samuel's carriage; instead, he "carried her in his Arms." A few years later, Samuel's daughter died in his home. She had sustained significant injuries to one of her legs, and a "noxious Humour" flowed from her lifeless body. Samuel tried to use lime to "suppress and absorb" the foul fluid, but apparently he was not successful. The girl died in mid-August, so the stench must have been awful. Somebody apparently suggested that the corpse be placed in the cellar—the coolest and least-occupied room of the house. But Sebastian would not let it be so; "Boston will not have her put into the Cellar: so she is . . . remov'd into the best Room," Samuel wrote. Because they would need to open the coffin's casements "for Coolness" in the stifling room, custom required that the exposed body be watched. Sebastian, according to Samuel, "would watch all night."[89]

As Samuel aged, he seemed to depend more and more on Sebastian. Near the end of his life, he referred to the man as "a considerable prop to my declining Cottage." In the late 1720s, Samuel's metaphorical "cottage"—his "earthly house," his "outward man"—was fading, and he knew it. But Sebastian would die before the old judge. The former bondsman passed away on the fourteenth of February in 1729 at six-thirty in the evening. Sebastian likely had his wife on his mind in his waning hours; he breathed his last on the day following the twenty-ninth anniversary of his hard-fought-for marriage to Jane.[90]

Sebastian's wife and children had faded silently from the historical record over a decade before, but Sebastian's death was broadcast to the city of Boston. Samuel noted that a minister at Sebastian's First Church prayed publicly for the ailing man just before he died. And Samuel himself hosted a remembrance of Sebastian after his passing. The aged judge opened his home to the community—perhaps facilitating a viewing of Sebastian's body, according to custom—and he treated those who came liberally with alcohol; as Samuel put it, he "made a good Fire, set Chairs, and gave Sack" before Sebastian's funeral. What is more, the *New-England Weekly Journal*, one of the town's newspapers, published a rare obituary for the man, mourning his "much lamented" passing and describing his "very decent" burial. Over the course of his long life, Sebastian had apparently endeared himself to many; the paper reported that he had "acquir'd . . . the general Love and Esteem of his Neighbours by a Readiness to do any good Offices in his power for every

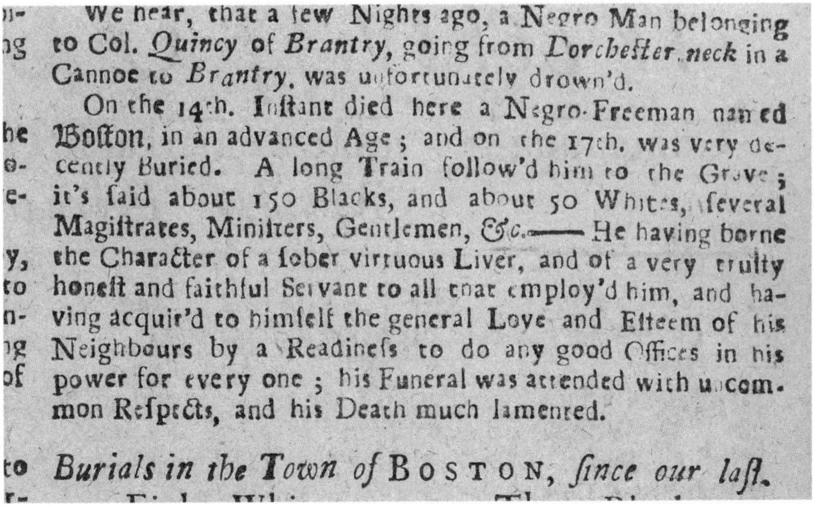

We hear, that a few Nights ago, a Negro Man belonging to Col. *Quincy* of *Brantry*, going from *Dorchester neck* in a Cannoe to *Brantry*, was unfortunately drown'd.

On the 14th. Instant died here a Negro-Freeman named Boston, in an advanced Age ; and on the 17th. was very decently Buried.   A long Train follow'd him to the Grave ; it's said about 150 Blacks, and about 50 Whites, several Magistrates, Ministers, Gentlemen, &c.—— He having borne the Character of a sober virtuous Liver, and of a very truly honest and faithful Servant to all that employ'd him, and having acquir'd to himself the general Love and Esteem of his Neighbours by a Readiness to do any good Offices in his power for every one ; his Funeral was attended with uncommon Respects, and his Death much lamented.

Burials in the Town of B o s t o n, *since our last.*

Figure 5. Sebastian's obituary. Sebastian's obituary brought news of his death and impressive funeral procession to readers throughout the region. Collection of the Massachusetts Historical Society.

one." Sebastian had earned the respect of the "Magistrates, Ministers, [and] Gentlemen" who accompanied his coffin to the grave—men, like Samuel, of great wealth and influence—but he also had strong connections to the city's oppressed: Approximately 150 people of African descent, most of whom were enslaved, attended his burial.[91] About fifty Anglo-Americans attended his funeral as well; he was, after all, a "sober" and "virtuous" man and a "very trusty honest and faithful Servant to all that employ'd him." But the newspaper yields no clues regarding his family. Did any kin join the throng, 200 strong, at Sebastian's graveside? Was Jane still alive at the time? Were any of their children? Elizabeth would have been fifteen; Joseph, seventeen; Jane, twenty-one; and John, twenty-six—easily old enough to have started his own family. Did any grandchildren march in the "long Train" that snaked behind Sebastian's coffin as it was carried to the burial ground? Or did the elderly African, one-time patriarch of an expanding family on New England soil, depart Boston as kinless as he had likely arrived many decades before?

CHAPTER 3

Sue Black and Her Sons

Childbirth, Child-Rearing, and Childhood in Bondage

A Negro Infant Girl about Six Weeks Old, to be Given for
the Bringing up: Inquire of John Campbell Postmaster,
and know further.

—*Boston News-Letter*, 1706

Her cries cut the air: plaintive announcements to the household of the arrival of new life. Held by sturdy arms, perhaps those of the local midwife,
she was wiped clean. Neighbor women lifted her mother from the squatted
position of delivery to the comfort of a bed—or maybe the mistress of the
household did this with the help of her oldest daughter. Somebody removed
blood-soaked linens. Someone else might have plastered the mother with a
poultice of new-laid eggs and rose oil to aid healing. A third person, perhaps,
brought the mother chicken broth and thin wine, both to be drunk warm. A
fourth may have stoked the fire, lest the late November chill enter the woman's
womb and cause the "torments and inflammations" that worried physicians.
A lactating woman in attendance likely gave the infant her first nurse, as
mothers' early milk was thought to be "curdled" by the "great Commotion" of
labor. The work of the female helpers in the room was no doubt lightened by
a collective sense of relief, for they had toiled with success toward a happy
outcome: The mother had survived her painful ordeal—her "travail," they
aptly called it—and brought forth a living child. Yet the mother, whom records never name, might have felt a sense of unease as fall crept toward winter in the year 1700. She had brought into the world a daughter whom she
was powerless to protect. This child—her child—belonged to another.[1]

The baby was named Sue, or so she would come to be called by those who enslaved her: Sue Black. The man with power to shape her life prospects was named Elizur: Elizur Holyoke. Sue was an infant of African descent, as the surname she was given later in life proclaimed to the world—a girl born to a woman in bondage whose name New England's record keepers never set down for posterity. Elizur was a man of English ancestry, as the surname he inherited proclaimed to the world—a man fathered by a well-known official whose name recurs in the province's annals. As a prosperous merchant, town selectman, and representative to the Massachusetts legislature, Elizur trod heavily across the historical record.[2] The people over whom he exercised mastery, however, are today far less visible.

Sue entered a full household, for Elizur had many dependents. Elizur's wife, Mary, had given birth to eleven children, eight of whom were still alive when Sue's cries rang out. The oldest was twenty-one; the youngest had turned three just weeks before. And neighbors frequented the Holyoke home. The family's unusually large collection of chairs—dozens arranged in six different rooms—suggests that the Holyoke residence was a local gathering place. As mistress, Mary was responsible for ensuring that the innumerable daily tasks required to sustain those in her care were executed with efficiency. In the home there were fires to tend, meals to cook, clothes to sew, garments to wash, and, always, children to mind. Just outside was a garden to cultivate, a cow to milk, and an orchard to harvest. And in the outbuildings, barley awaited malting, beer brewing, and cider pressing.[3] Mary likely depended on her older children for help, and she might have had the aid of hired girls or apprenticed servants, though existing records say nothing of this. We do know, however, that Mary benefited from the coerced labor of Sue's mother.

No bill of sale documents the day on which Elizur came to claim ownership of the woman who bore Sue, nor does a surviving will show the passage of this woman from one generation of an Anglo-American family to the next. But a sliver of evidence raises the possibility that Sue's mother had served the Holyokes for some time before she gave birth to Sue on that November day. Nearly eight years earlier, a local diarist had mourned the loss of one of the Holyoke children. "This day in the Afternoon One of Mr. Holyoke's Twins falls into the Well and is drownd," he wrote, adding by way of explanation: "no body but a Negro being at home."[4] Might the so-called "Negro" on whom rumors blamed the death of Elizur's son have been Sue's mother? The connection certainly is conceivable.[5]

Eight years before Sue's birth, the Holyokes lost their son in a devastating accident; their bondswoman, by contrast, would lose her daughter in a matter-of-fact transaction. Not long after Sue's birth, Mary Holyoke began to scour the town for buyers. She alerted a group of Boston women, who passed the information on to female contacts of their own. "[M]rs Hollyoak ha[s] a Young Negro Child to sell," the town buzzed, and she was offering a "bargain." A deposition filed in court years later allows us to glimpse the news traveling along one tentacle of this female network. Mary informed a woman identified as "Mrs Leathers"—almost surely Boston resident Susannah Leathers—of her wish to sell Sue. Susannah later made her way to the home of a woman named Mrs. Peacock, who kept an inn in town. There she found Mary Norton, an unmarried woman who had recently traveled twenty-five miles by sea from her Manchester home on the north shore of Massachusetts. Susannah might have known Mary, and she might have expected her arrival in Boston; not long before, Susannah had lived in the same sleepy fishing village from which Mary hailed.[6] It is also possible, however, that the two Manchester women simply happened upon one another in Mrs. Peacock's Boston inn. From Mary Holyoke to Susannah Leathers to Mary Norton the news spread. As middlewoman, Susannah did not mince words in pursuit of a buyer. Another woman staying at the inn later would recall that Susannah "Advise[d]" Mary Norton to purchase the child, for "Mrs Holloak would sell it a Pennyworth"—that is, for a nominal price.[7] Sue would be sold on the cheap.

Six shillings. In Boston around the turn of the eighteenth century, one could purchase a pair of shoes for such a sum, or a petticoat; two old teapots or a large skillet; half a dozen "course towells" or a wheelbarrow.[8] One could also buy a child. After Susannah led Mary Norton and two other women to the Holyoke home, Mary "made a bargain" for baby Sue. Six shillings passed from one Mary to the other, providing the former with a laborer for life and relieving the latter of an unwanted infant.[9] Did Sue's mother stand by and watch the two women haggle over her daughter, barely six weeks old? Did she hand Sue over so that Mary Norton could inspect the baby who presumably would provide her with ease and financial security in the years to come? Did she appeal to anyone in the Holyoke family in an attempt to stop the transaction? Or did she accept Sue's departure as just one more feature of the cruelty of life in bondage? Many questions about the moment of Sue's exchange remain unanswerable, but we do know that Sue's mother was close at hand and that she stayed with her daughter to the last. Mary Norton did not take the child from the Holyoke home when she returned to Mrs. Peacock's inn. Neither did her female companions. Rather, Sue's mother held the infant as they marched across Boston. A quarter of a century later, an onlooker would still remember the woman's final moments with her daughter: "the negro woman the mother of said Child took the Child and Carryed it away," following Mary Norton "to . . . [her] Lodging."[10]

In this chapter, I explore Sue's childhood—the childhood that her own mother never had the opportunity to glimpse. I begin by considering what might be the most striking feature of Sue's early years: the utter isolation she experienced as the sole person of African descent in an Anglo-American household. Such isolation was common. Most enslaved children in the region found themselves in households with no natal kin. A number of factors can account for this, but two are principal: the lack of conjugal or parental rights that accompanied the marriages of those in bondage and the unusually low economic value assigned to youngsters in slavery. Taking babies from their families, of course, removed them from their natural source of sustenance, which means that infants in bondage regularly depended on women other than their mothers for survival. Here I probe the unusual intersections between slavery, race, and wet nursing in New England, where free white women nursed bound Black infants, like Sue. I then go on to explore the dynamics of the home in which Sue was raised. Like most enslaved children, Sue lived in extraordinary physical intimacy with those who bound her, and, in certain respects, the archive suggests that Sue was relatively well cared for. However, Sue's childhood nonetheless must have been deeply damaging: She was verbally assaulted, physically abused, and constantly reminded that she did not belong. Despite it all, though, Sue survived; she formed intimacies in the little town; and she eventually gave birth to children of her own. At this point, I discuss labor and delivery for bound women in New England, which paralleled in most ways the process of childbirth for white women in the region. The results of enslaved women's travails, though, were wholly dissimilar. Women in bondage brought children into the world whom they were powerless to protect and from whom they were apt to be separated. So it was with Sue, who would be parted, one after another, from each of her three sons. Alone she had embarked on her journey of childhood, and alone they would embark on theirs.

*   *   *

Why separate a baby from her mother? It is tempting to connect Sue's sale at such a tender age with the Holyoke family's unfortunate loss of their four-year-old son, a boy named Samuel. If Sue's mother was indeed the "Negro" at home when Samuel tumbled into the well—the one whose supposed carelessness could explain the untimely loss of a "very lovely Boy"— then Mary Holyoke's decision to pawn baby Sue for the price of a petticoat could have been vindictive. Perhaps Mary decided that the bondswoman whose presumed negligence deprived her of a treasured son ought not to enjoy the privilege of raising her own offspring. Child for child, flesh for flesh. But the story almost surely is not so simple. Taking into account the broader landscape of slavery and family in Massachusetts around the turn of the eighteenth century suggests that much more was at work in this transaction. Sue, after all, was not alone in her aloneness.

When Sue sailed from Boston to Mary Norton's Manchester home, she suffered a fate common to enslaved children in early New England: separation from all natal kin. Children bound everywhere in the British Atlantic world endured the breakup of families, but intimate ties were particularly precarious for young people in New England.[11] Reading the wills written by enslavers and the inventories taken of their possessions after death allows us to grasp just how ordinary Sue's experiences were. In the late seventeenth and early eighteenth centuries, the majority of children mentioned in these documents appear to have lived in homes without enslaved adults: 120 youngsters were bound in households that did not claim grown people, while 103 lived in households that did.[12] This suggests that the greater number of children enslaved in the Boston area at the turn of the eighteenth century found themselves in circumstances akin to Sue's after her mother turned from Mrs. Peacock's inn and headed, empty-handed, back to the Holyoke home: These children lived without mother, father, or parent-like bondsperson.[13]

Mapping with more precision the distribution of bound children throughout the region's households reveals the constancy of young people's fractured familial circumstances over time. According to probate records, in the last quarter of the seventeenth century, 53 percent of bound children found themselves in households with no adults in slavery. The first quarter of the eighteenth century was the same; 53 percent of bound children lived on their own in Anglo-American homes, cut off from bondspeople who could have played a parental role. This percentage decreased to 47 percent between 1725 and 1749 as the bound population in the region rose and enslavers expanded their holdings a bit, but it did not continue to fall.[14] In the third quarter of the eighteenth century, 48 percent of enslaved children lived apart from their fathers, mothers, and all bound parental figures. In all, over the course of the century stretching from 1675 to 1774, nearly half of bound children in the region—323 of 654—found themselves very much alone in the homes of their enslavers.[15]

To what can we attribute this persistent pattern? The vagaries of the Atlantic slave trade explain why many young people in the region were separated from elders. New England imported proportionately more children than the rest of the British colonies. This was partly of necessity: Enslavers in the southern colonies and especially the Caribbean preferentially selected workers who could immediately be put to hard labor. And it was partly of inclination: New England colonists tended to favor bondspeople who had passed the age of needing care but had not yet reached adulthood, as they found them teachable.[16] Traders therefore deposited small groups of young people on Boston's town dock, who were then purchased, often alone, by Anglo-American enslavers. Kin ties were severed from the start. The "Young Negro Girl born in Barbadoes" offered for sale by a Boston merchant in 1712 almost surely was separated from family long before she set foot in Massachusetts. Similarly, the "Very likely Negro Boy" advertised in 1716 as having been "3 years in the Country" must have lost meaningful relationships long before Bostonians could take them from him. And the "several Negro Boys and Girls" who in 1719 had just arrived from Jamaica likely were torn from parental figures before their forced journey north.[17] The unforgiving currents of the trade stole countless young people from their kin.

Other children bound in New England, however, found themselves alone because a local enslaver willed it. People like Mary Holyoke could—and did— break up families at whim. Depositions filed in court occasionally furnish evidence of this practice. An infant called Toto still "sucked" when she was given by her enslaver to his daughter in the late seventeenth century, and the baby boy of a woman named Moll was "given a waye" in the first part of the eighteenth century just a "few Dayes after It[s] Bearth."[18] Newspapers, which provide still more insight into the separation of children from their parents, suggest that Mary Holyoke did well with her six shillings; scores of advertisements offering enslaved children "to be given away" were posted over the course of the eighteenth century.[19] The first notice offering a child for the taking was placed in the *Boston News-Letter* in 1706, soon after the *News-Letter* inaugurated the practice of selling enslaved New Englanders through print.

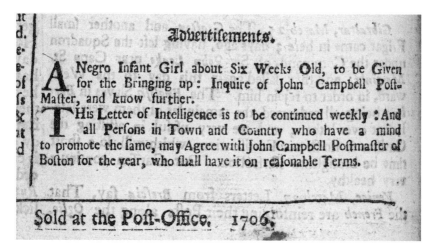

Figure 6. Advertisement of enslaved girl. In 1706, the *Boston News-Letter* circulated information about a girl, like Sue, who was to be sent away from the place of her birth—and, doubtless, from her mother—at six weeks of age. Described by its printer as a "Letter of Intelligence," the *News-Letter* would print similar advertisements until the eve of the Revolutionary War. Photography © New-York Historical Society.

It could have described Sue when she was handed over to Mary Norton half a dozen years before: "A Negro Infant Girl about Six Weeks Old, to be Given for the Bringing up."[20] Such offers would be posted in Boston newspapers until the revolutionary era.

Children of African descent must have been linked in the minds of the reading public with the act of gifting, for across Boston's vast corpus of eighteenth-century newspapers the two went hand in hand. When a newspaper offered to give something away, that "something" was nearly always a bound child. For instance, of 101 advertisements with the phrase "to be given away" placed in Boston's newspapers during the first half of the eighteenth century, 95 offered bound children for the taking. And the trend continued. In the third quarter of the eighteenth century, 202 of 238 notices advertising people or possessions "to be given away" involved children in bondage. Over the course of the first three-quarters of the eighteenth century, then, 88 percent of those who used Boston newspapers to find takers for property freely offered sought to divest themselves of enslaved children.[21]

The formulation can be reversed. If advertisements of people or property "to be given away" almost always offered bound children, advertisements mentioning bound children usually were placed by people attempting to dispense with those children. That is, when children of African descent showed up in Boston's weeklies, they ordinarily appeared not because someone was trying to buy them or sell them; they appeared because someone was trying to give them away. In the first half of the eighteenth century, over 95 percent of advertisements referencing a "negro child" sought to send that child to whomever would take him or her.[22] And in the third quarter of the eighteenth century, of the 228 advertisements that mentioned a "negro child," 207 endeavored to give the child away. During these years, then, more than nine of ten people to advertise a child of African descent in Boston newspapers did so in hopes of passing that child along, gratis, to another household.[23]

But newspaper advertisements indicate that not all children were considered worthless by those who sought ready labor: The value placed on youngsters in bondage varied according to age. Exceedingly few enslavers bothered to advertise for sale bondspeople age six or under. The notice announcing the availability of a "likely Negro Girl about 5 Years of Age, to be Sold" is highly unusual; rare, too, is the advertisement placed by a person looking to purchase "a Negro Boy of about two or three Years of Age."[24] If enslavers included young children in the advertisements they drafted, they most often listed them as appendages to women who were likely mothers, the implication being that these children, who lacked independent value, would follow their kin. But the age of seven appears to have marked a turning point—the point at which enslavers began to believe that marketing bound children would turn a profit. Whether the "likely NEGRO GIRL, about Seven Years of Age" listed in Portsmouth, New Hampshire; the "NEGRO BOY this country born about 7 years of age" publicized in Hartford, Connecticut; or the "Very likely healthy Negro boy, about 7 Years of Age" peddled on the north shore of Massachusetts, children who reached the age of seven seem to have become profitable across New England.[25] Eight-year-olds in bondage were advertised similarly. And notices for youngsters of nine and ten were placed with still more frequency. Numbered among the ten-year-olds in Boston whom enslavers expected to sell were a "*likely Negro Boy*"; a child "sold for no Fault, but for want of Employ"; a "strong, healthy Negro Girl"; a boy who spoke "good English"; a youngster who had recently arrived from West Africa; a child who had been born in Boston; and a girl offered for sale only because there were "too many Servants in the Family."[26] The list could go on.

It makes sense that children around the age of seven began to be valued by New England's household heads. Infants and toddlers were difficult to care for, and they could not contribute to the household economy in even minor ways. Likewise, children of three, four, or five were more apt to slow one down in the home, garden, or shop than they were to really help. But eighteenth-century New Englanders believed that a well-trained child of seven or so—whether bound or free, Black or white—could accomplish tasks with reasonable efficiency.[27] Of course, there were instances in which enslavers sought out children younger than this. Mary Norton, after all, was willing to pay for the trouble of raising six-week-old Sue. But the six shillings she proffered make sense in light of her geography. Details in the historical record suggest that enslavers from rural parts of New England were more apt to value young children in bondage than were those in places like Boston. Newspapers again provide evidence of this. For instance, a woman deemed "too good a Breeder" was recommended to "any Person in the Country[side]," while a woman considered a "very poor Breeder" was "therefore not fit for the Country"; she was advertised instead *"To Be Sold only in Town."*[28] Likewise, enslavers offering infants for the taking sometimes marketed them to rural people, as when a nine-month-old girl was offered gratis to *"any Person who lives up in the Country."*[29] Colonists in the countryside had more land and needed more people to work that land than did most Bostonians—and many did not have the financial wherewithal to purchase bondspeople who were considered valuable on the open market. Instead, they looked for bargains among the very young, who might cost just six shillings or, perhaps, nothing.

The children whom Boston's enslavers tried to give away—those they "dispos'd of," as one advertisement put it—tended to be exceedingly young. Most notices offering children for free did not specify their ages, but those that did provide a sense of how very new—and how vulnerable—these bondspeople were. The *Boston Gazette* offered "A Negro Child a few Days old, to be given *away*," and the *Boston Evening-Post* printed a notice for *"A Likely, healthy Negro Child, a Week old, to be given away."*[30] A man named Stephen Hall, who styled himself an esquire, asked readers who were interested in "a likely Negro Child about a Week old" to "Enquire" at his Medford home: The infant was "to be given away." The *Boston News-Letter* advertised "A Likely Female Negro child about 10 Days old, to be given away," and the *Boston Evening-Post* circulated an offer for a *"Fine Female Negro Child, about 3 Weeks old"* to be *"given away."*[31] The advertisement for this three-week-old infant, posted in March, emphasized that she was *"well cloathed."* What, one wonders, were most of these newborns wearing?

Over the course of the eighteenth century, multiple newspapers posted notices offering month-old children, and Boston readers learned in 1740 that a "Fine Negro Male Child, about Five Weeks old" was free for the taking. More than one advertisement tried to find takers for children who, like Sue at the time of her sale, were six weeks old.[32] And a *"Very healthy Female Negro Child"* of seven weeks was *"to be given away"* at mid-century, as were a number of children old enough for their enslavers to reckon their age in months: The *Boston Post-Boy* marketed "Negro" children of both three and nine months of age.[33] The child of nine months—*"A Strong Healthy female Negro Child"*—was advertised alongside *"a Negro Woman who is a very good Cook."* The baby was *"to be given away"* and the woman *"to be hired out by the Year."* Wherever the two ended up, they quite likely ended apart; their enslaver, at least, appears to have made no effort to ensure that the two went to the same household. And enslavers occasionally were explicit about their willingness to separate mothers and children, as when one advertised a bondswoman with a "fine Child" to be sold "either with or without the Child."[34]

Parting mother from child might have been necessary in order to make the woman's sale viable, for it could be difficult to find people willing to receive bound infants into their households. The advertisements themselves provide abundant evidence of this. One notice offering a "very likely Female Negro Child" beseeched "Whoever" would be "willing to take it" to get in touch with the newspaper's printer.[35] Advertisements such as these often ran for multiple weeks, indicating that takers were in short supply. Enslavers turned to a host of descriptors in an attempt to make the children they wished to dispose of more attractive. Some children were "Likely," others were "Very likely," and more than one was "Extraordinary likely." Various infants were "lusty." A number were "of a very good Breed," several were "of an excellent breed," and one was "of as fine a Breed as any in America." Some were "well," several were "in good Health," many were *"healthy,"* scores were *"Fine,"* and a number were "hearty."[36] Multiple enslavers made sure to state that the infants being offered were at no risk for smallpox. One child had been "kept remote from the Small-Pox," an advertisement declared, and another notice took care to specify that the child "to be given away" was *"lately Born in a Family where the Small-Pox hath not been, nor is at present in the Neighbourhood."*[37]

Glowing descriptions of children were not always enough to persuade anyone to take them, though, so some enslavers resorted to offering incentives. One posted a "young Negro Child to be given away," furnishing forty shillings to whomever would accept the youngster. Another offered a "lusty Negro child," promising to bestow upon a willing recipient the "Necessaries for it." One advertised "Money and Cloaths to be given away," adding the caveat, in fine print below, that they came with "a Likely, Healthy Female Negro Child, of an excellent Breed." And one enslaver advertised "a Male Negro Child of an excellent Breed," assuring those who might have interest in him that he was not just to be given away, but "To be given away upon good Terms to the Receiver."[38] It was a sly move; readers hesitant to commit to raising a bound infant may well have wondered what those terms were and how those terms might be shaped to their advantage.

The lengths to which enslavers in New England went to rid themselves of the babies born in their households set them apart from those in much of the British Atlantic world. Historians have suggested that the very young offspring of women in bondage were valued—at least nominally—elsewhere. Consider, for instance, the Virginia man who celebrated in 1721 his purchase of "young breeding negroes" or the North Carolina observer who noted that enslavers "esteemed" the "numberous Issue" of fertile bondswomen.[39] In New England, however, particularly in the semi-urban areas of New England, enslavers were hesitant to take babies in—even babies freely given.[40] Young children were a special burden in the region because of the difficulties posed by rearing them in households that, on average, claimed merely one adult in bondage. This adult in most cases represented a considerable share of the household's labor force; in fact, this one adult might have been the only other full-grown worker in the home besides the household head and his wife.[41] Therefore, if an enslaved woman became pregnant, gave birth, and nursed her child, or if she cared for another bondswoman's newborn, or if a mistress decided to bring up an infant in bondage, the entire family economy could suffer. Compare this to plantation contexts, where babies could be raised largely without sacrificing productivity. After mothers were sent back to the fields following an all-too-short postpartum period, bondspeople incapable of hard labor—usually elderly women—could care for their infants. Very young children in places like Virginia, South Carolina, Barbados, and Jamaica could often be minded until they were old enough to work without straining the plantation economy.[42] Not so in New England.

The comparative values of children on New England smallholdings therefore differed from those on plantations elsewhere. This difference is evident
in a careful reading of wills. Wills authored by enslavers who lived in eastern Massachusetts during the seventeenth and eighteenth centuries contrast
starkly with those written around the same time in South Carolina and Barbados, where attention to the reproductive capacity of bondswomen has led
one historian to argue that "speculation about women's childbearing capacity was a natural outgrowth of slaveownership." As early as the 1650s, enslavers in Barbados began to bequeath the "increase" or "produce" of those they
bound, as when the man who enslaved a woman named Diannah endowed
his heir with both the woman and "her future increase." All told, nearly one
in five wills bequeathing women in Barbados during the seventeenth century
used the term "increase."[43] Settlers in South Carolina likewise recognized how
important the procreation of Black women could be to their estates. By the
second quarter of the eighteenth century, almost a third of decedents who
left wills mentioning bondswomen mulled in ink over the "increase" of those
women.[44] But wills written in Massachusetts at the same time provide no evidence of this line of thinking. Of the 329 wills discussing bondspeople composed in Suffolk County during the second half of the seventeenth century
and the first half of the eighteenth, not one considered the "increase" of enslaved women.[45] And this divergence cannot be chalked up simply to language; no decedents used alternative phrasings—such as the "issue" of women
or their "produce"—to get at the same idea. When these Massachusetts enslavers sat down, quill in hand, to ponder their present and future assets, not
one speculated in writing about the offspring the women in their households
might bear.[46] Children yet to be born apparently were not valuable enough
to merit mention.

The ambivalence with which enslavers regarded bound infants sets Massachusetts apart from geographically closer places as well. People in Boston
and the surrounding villages devalued young children to the point that they
sometimes were willing to pay to publicize youngsters free for the taking; they
were even willing, in some cases, to pay takers for their trouble. By contrast,
enslavers in other northern urban centers, such as Philadelphia and New York
City, did not beg in print for the babies born in their households to be taken
off their hands. Searching newspapers in the mid-Atlantic region for the
phrase "to be given away" yielded not a single example of a Philadelphian or
New Yorker offering to pass along a child free of charge. And the regional
distinction can be drawn still more clearly. Searching for the phrase "negro

child" in Philadelphia and New York newspapers unearthed no evidence of enslavers offering to give such children away, though the same phrase pointed to more than three hundred occasions on which Bostonians sought to gift youngsters.[47] Colonists in Philadelphia and New York sought at times to *sell* infants and toddlers of African descent, but they apparently did not routinely attempt to give these children away.[48] In urban places where enslavers commanded somewhat more labor than they did in the Boston area, raising bound children was not as disruptive to household economies.[49] Babies in bondage seem to have posed less of a problem.

In the Boston area, however, infants caused enough inconvenience that enslavers regularly tried to sell women who bore them too quickly.[50] One woman was advertised for sale because she "*breeds like a Rabbet.*" Another was described as "an Excellent Breeder, for which Reason she is to be disposed of." Still another was "offer'd to Sale for no other Reason but her frequent Pregnancy."[51] The list could go on. One woman was to be sold because she was an "excellent Breeder," another because she was a "notable Breeder." The fault of a third was "being too good a Breeder," and of a fourth was "*Breeding too fast.*" Still another woman was described as "a considerable Breeder, for which Reason *only* she is to be sold."[52] One enslaver revealed that the woman in question "breeds too fast for her present Owner," while another explained that the "only Reason" he was offering his bondswoman for sale was because of her extraordinary fertility.[53] Frustrated by the reduced productivity of women who were pregnant, nursing, or raising their young, some enslavers sought to rid themselves of "breeders" and acquire, in their place, adult workers who could contribute without interruption to the household economy.

Children therefore could be rendered motherless in a number of ways. Infants born to women deemed "breeders" could effectively be orphaned when the women were sold away by enslavers displeased with their regular pregnancies. And youngsters considered superfluous to the households of their enslavers could lose their mothers when, like Sue, they were sold away—or simply given to whomever would take them. These partings, at least occasionally, were disquieting to those who inflicted them; details in the archives suggest that enslavers sometimes sought to soften the blow of separation. Some placed requirements on potential takers. One requested a "careful Person" to raise the "Young Negro Child" advertised. In what could have been a bid to place a child near her mother or other kin, another proposed that a "Person in Town" would be the "most agreeable" recipient of the "likely Negro Female Child" he planned to send from his home.[54] Indeed, enslavers at times stated that the children they wished to discard had to remain with their mothers. One offered for sale a *Very likely healthy Negro Wench,*" adding, "*She has a fine Female Child, which must go with her.*" Another announced a bondswoman's availability, noting that "A healthy Negro Male Child" would be "given to the Person who may buy her."[55] Other enslavers placed advertisements that coupled women with children. A three-week-old was paired with her mother; a child "about 10 Months" with a twenty-year-old woman; a boy of eleven months with a "*healthy Negro woman*"; a one-year-old with a "*likely Negro wench*"; a "very likely Boy" just past his first birthday with a young woman; and two youngsters—ages two and six—with a woman "about 24 Years *of Age.*"[56] One advertisement sang the praises of an African-descended woman who was "fine," "healthy," and could "do all sorts of Houshold Work." Promising that she was "of a good Temper" and "faithful and honest," the notice included, almost as an afterthought, that she "has a Male Negro Child."[57] The child, the advertisement implied, would go wherever his mother went.

It is important to remember, though, that even in situations like these, when enslavers tried to peddle infants and their mothers in pairs, the transfers were not benign: Black families were still dissolved to convenience white ones. What of the women's partners? The children's fathers? The siblings, if there were any? The other bondspeople who, though not related by blood, played meaningful roles in the lives of the mother and child? Some enslavers, recognizing the devastation wrought by the frequent sale and gifting of enslaved children in the region, tried to retain all the infants born in their households, as Deborah Thayer had apparently planned to do with Jane and Sebastian's children (see Chapter 2). But threats to enslaved families were everywhere. Even when enslavers opted not to sell bound children one by one as they were born, the kin units they preserved in their homes could well be divided upon their death. This was the case for the household of Peter Thatcher, a minister who lived in Milton, a town south of Boston. Peter was more benevolent than many; he retained during his lifetime three young children, who appear to have been born to Hagar, the bondswoman he claimed, and he stipulated in his will that Hagar should be freed after a period of service to his wife.[58] However, the man also provided instructions for the dispersal of Hagar's children. Peter's son, Peter, would receive "Little Sambo"; his daughter, Theodora, would inherit Jemmy; and another of his sons, Oxenbridge, would be given "Little Hagar."[59] By distributing Hagar's children among his own children, Peter was at least keeping them in an extended family and thus closer to one another than might otherwise have been the case. This was, perhaps, the most a child in bondage could wish for. But it was not much. Liberty for Hagar brought with it the task of parenting children dispersed into three separate Anglo-American households, subject to the authority of three different enslavers.

Hagar, unfortunately, was just one of many. Other enslavers inclined toward freedom split up groups of Afro-New Englanders who might well have been tied by blood or affection, emancipating some in their wills but not others.[60] What is more, even when Anglo-Americans sought to preserve enslaved families through the process of estate settlement, they sometimes managed to sever bondspeople from their kin nonetheless. For instance, in the process of dividing up the property of John Floyd, a well-to-do yeoman living north of Boston in Rumney Marsh, the man's sons distributed eight bondspeople among five heirs. They apparently took care to safeguard a family unit: John Floyd Jr. received "Ceesar & Sarah and their youngest Child called James."[61] But they did not protect it fully; if James was Ceesar and Sarah's *youngest* child, then the couple must have had older children as well. Perhaps the "negro girl called Lydia" was James's older sister. Maybe some of the boys or men named in the document—Jack, Tom, Dick, and Harry—were James's older brothers. All of these people were distributed to different heirs, so, while part of the family survived the estate settlement intact, part of it was torn apart. These children, like baby Sue, were robbed of their kin. Bound in a region without demand for large slaveholdings, youngsters in New England were less valued by enslavers than bound children just about anywhere else in the English-speaking Atlantic world. And their parents—even those who contracted formal marriages—lacked the marital or parental rights that could have ensured access to their offspring. Some enslavers were troubled by the breakup of families that became commonplace in the region. For many, though, the sight of a bound woman walking across town to deposit her six-week-old in the arms of a stranger was too ordinary to be especially distressing.

*   *   *

Six-week-old Sue was in trouble when her mother left Mrs. Peacock's Boston inn—and not simply because she faced a lifetime without the aid or comfort of her mother. No, Sue was in trouble for a far more immediate and material reason. Her new enslaver was in trouble, too. Sue's chances of survival were dismal without the physical sustenance that could be provided only by a lactating woman, and Mary Norton, for her part, stood to lose her investment—however modest it may have been—if Sue wasted to nothing. So Mary recruited a wet nurse. For the sum of five shillings, a woman named Penelope Hadlock, who was staying at Mrs. Peacock's inn and happened already to have plans to sail to Manchester, agreed to "give the Child suck."[62]

We know these details about Sue's early life because, decades later, Mary would launch a series of lawsuits to recover ownership of Sue and the sons Sue would later bear. As a result, close to a hundred documents preserving the testimony of dozens of witnesses would be collected by various Massachusetts courts. This archive documenting Sue's childhood shows that Penelope's commitment to nursing the baby was short-lived. Once in Manchester, Sue needed a replacement nurse. Mary therefore approached a neighbor named Abigail Allen, who later remembered that "Mary Norton asked me to take a young negro Girl Child about six weeks old and Desired me to nurse it for her." Abigail, though, was not able to do so. "I could not take it," she recalled, using language that made Sue sound like a brass kettle or a barrel of cider. Mary then asked another Abigail, a local woman named Abigail Williams, to do the job. This Abigail agreed—she "took it," the record reads—and baby Sue entered the Williams household. Decades later, Abigail's daughter remembered that her mother had "brought [Sue] up for some time," while her son-in-law recalled that his "mother in Law nursed the said Child about three Months."[63] As with most wet-nursing arrangements, this was a financial transaction: Abigail's children remembered hearing their mother say that she was paid for her work.

Penelope Hadlock, Abigail Allen, Abigail Williams. The three women whom Mary sought out to nurse baby Sue were all Anglo-American, which means that, with the exception of the six weeks Sue spent with her mother, the child passed her infancy at the breasts of white nurses, drawing from them the nourishment she needed for survival. Though little evidence sheds light on the ways in which bound infants were fed in the region, Sue's story suggests that white women might have been more important to the sustenance of Black babies in New England than they were in many other Atlantic slave societies.[64] Indeed, clues to the dependence of non-white infants on wet nurses are scattered throughout the region's archive. For example, an unfortunate "malatta" baby living just outside of Boston was suffocated by a wet nurse who fell asleep while suckling him, according to a report filed by a local coroner. Likewise, infants of African descent in the Boston area were occasionally advertised in local papers as in need of lactating caregivers. In 1749, for example, someone posted a notice in the *Boston Gazette* seeking a woman to "take" a child of African descent "to Nurse."[65]

The demographics of the region support the interpretation that babies in bondage were often dependent on the labor of hired nurses. Six in ten children enslaved in Suffolk County did not live with women in bondage, which means that enslavers who took in newborns from other households in most cases could not rely on bondswomen in their homes to nurse them.[66] These households could not take advantage of the brutal economies of scale that governed life on large plantations, where infants could be passed on to bondswomen tasked with nursing the children of mothers who had been sent out to labor in the fields.[67] No, the heads of New England households realized that the children in their homes could subsist only through the labor of wet nurses—and most of the lactating women in the area were white. Wet nurses of European descent in many cases must have helped enslaved infants survive their early months.

Of course, the labor of breastfeeding could go the other way as well, with women in bondage nursing white children. In the late 1680s, for instance, a Boston woman called Kila nursed one of her enslaver's sons at the same time she nursed her own daughter.[68] Based on what we know of bondswomen whose milk was stolen in other parts of the English Atlantic, it is tempting to assume that Kila's circumstances were replicated in household after household throughout New England. This is certainly possible, and it could help explain the rampant giving of infants in eastern Massachusetts during the eighteenth century. Enslavers in need of bound women's milk might have disposed of unwanted babies in order to secure greater nourishment for their own children. Occasional evidence does imply that enslavers rid their households of bound infants in order to use lactating women for personal profit. The placement of two notices in a 1739 Boston newspaper, for example, is suggestive: Directly below an advertisement offering the services of a "Nurse . . . with a good Breast of Milk," another notice announces "A Likely Negro Child to be given away."[69] Might the aim have been to divest the household of the bound child in order to hire out the mother?

Perhaps. Yet the pairing of such advertisements in newspapers was exceedingly rare, and, since the work of nursing was poorly remunerated in eighteenth-century Boston, enslavers would have been better off directing the labor of lactating women to other ends. After all, wet nurses abounded in the town; the supply of women eager to exchange milk for money far outweighed the demand. Newspapers provide evidence of this lopsided market.

Between 1700 and 1750, women seeking work as nurses were featured in 162 advertisements placed in the city's weekly papers, while, during the same stretch of time, merely 34 advertisements sought the services of lactating women.[70] For every notice requesting the aid of a wet nurse, nearly five were printed in an attempt to secure employment for women with ready milk.

Who were these women with their "good Breasts of Milk"? It is possible that the nurses advertised in the papers were enslaved, but the occasional bits of identifying information supplied by these notices suggest a population of poor white women with families of their own. Some women emphasized that they were "*married*." Others stated that their husbands were "*at Sea*."[71] One woman claimed to be "*Reputable*," another "of good Character." More than one sought a child to take into "*her own House*" or "her Family," using language that suggested the women in question were integral to their households. And, very occasionally, advertisements provide clear evidence of the racial background of the wet nurse in question. For instance, a fisherman of European descent named Daniel Merrow offered to a "*Gentleman's Family*" his daughter's "*very good Breast of Milk*."[72]

In one unusual advertisement, a woman seeking employment requested to be contacted only by a "*white Person that has Occasion to put out a Child to Nurse*."[73] This woman, doubtless of European descent, apparently wished only to provide nutritive care to a white infant. The advertisement is revealing on multiple counts. It suggests that a substantial number of non-white children were in need of wet nurses—enough, at least, that one nurse who wished to avoid caring for such infants felt she needed to specify that explicitly. And it shows that racial background could matter to nurses. At the same time, however, by virtue of its singularity, the advertisement implies that most women were willing to breastfeed children of African descent. Of 162 notices announcing the availability of wet nurses in early Boston newspapers, this is the only one to include a racial restriction. Apparently, most of the women who made money from milk in eastern Massachusetts were, like Penelope Hadlock and Abigail Williams, willing to feed children of African descent. Notwithstanding pervasive ideas about the inferiority of Black people, nurses of European descent were inclined to care for children, like Sue, left motherless by slavery—provided it netted a reward in sterling.

Mary, for her part, was willing to forfeit only so much sterling. Sue would be cared for by her lactating neighbors, but no longer than was necessary: When the baby approached six months of age and was able to transition fully to solid foods, Mary fetched her from her wet nurse and brought her home.

Sue likely would have continued to breastfeed for at least a few more months had she been allowed to remain with her mother in the Holyokes' Boston household. Instead, twenty-five miles north of her birthplace, a caregiver would spoon into her mouth pap or panada—English baby foods that combined flour or breadcrumbs with water, animal milk, or broth.[74] There, in the Manchester household headed by Mary's father, Sue would take her first toddling steps. There she would utter her first intelligible words. Under the wood-shingled roof of George Norton's dwelling house, or perhaps beneath the canopy of apple trees in the nearby orchard, Sue would form her earliest memories. Fleeting images of a world in which she was reckoned different.[75]

What was it like to grow up enslaved in the family of a shipwright on the north shore of Massachusetts? Details recalled decades later by Manchester residents suggest that, in a number of ways, Sue was relatively well cared for in the Norton household. She was bundled against bitter drafts; a neighbor who saw her that first winter remembered her being "wrapt up in Cloths or blanketts." She was held; an onlooker recalled seeing the child "Lye on [Mary's] lap." She was taught to walk; a local man remembered that Mary paid him to build a contraption that would allow Sue to "Learn her to goe alone."[76] This toy of sorts—its maker called it a "swing"—seems to have worked. A laborer employed by the Nortons remembered how the little girl would "run about" the house.[77] Sue may have been given a rudimentary education; occasional details in the historical record suggest that some enslaved children were.[78] In certain respects, Sue's treatment seems to have paralleled that of Anglo-American children subject to the authority of their parents or apprenticed to a master.[79] But, of course, Sue was not an Anglo-American child, and she would never belong in the Norton family the way such a child could. Sue was different, and her difference was made palpable at every turn.

Visitors to the Norton home peppered its residents with questions about the girl. Many revolved around the child's ownership. Indeed, inquiries into who owned Sue appear to have been incessant. A woman who lived in the Norton household "often heard" family members tell people that Sue belonged to Mary.[80] A neighbor who claimed to be familiar with the family heard Mary's parents say with frequency that "a Negro Girl . . . named Sue Black was their Daughter Marys." Another neighbor remembered hearing each of Mary's parents say "several times" that "the Negro child was their Daughter Mary's."[81] And a man who worked for the Nortons remembered "People Coming into the house" and asking Mary's mother whether "it"—by which he meant Sue—was "her Child." This would continue throughout

Sue's lifetime. A woman who visited the home after Sue had grown to adulthood remembered hearing Mary's mother declare "that the negroe Woman Called Black Sue was Mary['s]."[82]

The obsession was not just with Sue's ownership; little Sue would have heard other questions as well from those who stopped by the Norton household for work or for pleasure. If Sue belonged to Mary, then how did Mary acquire her? A visitor recalled asking Mary's mother "whose black Child that was" and "how much . . . [was given] for the black Child" and "whose money bought the negro Child." These were common questions asked by those who set foot in the Norton home. One neighbor discussed with Mary's mother Sue's selling price in Boston; another heard Mary explain that she "bought the said Black Child in Boston."[83] And the chatter about Sue was not confined to the Norton household; Sue was fodder for discussion in other homes and among people from other families. One local woman remembered her mother explaining that Mary "pa[id] six Shillings . . . for said Negro while [Sue was] a Child." Another neighboring mother declared in her daughter's hearing that she "saw the money paid to Mrs Holyoke of Boston . . . for said Negro."[84]

Sue could not have failed to recognize her status as an outsider in the household. As people asked who owned her, where she had come from, and how much she had cost, Sue would have seen the confusion etched across their faces. What, these neighbors seemed to wonder, was the point of putting up with this child? Why did the Nortons bother to keep Sue in their home at all? One recalled raising the issue explicitly: "I asked old mrs Norton what they Did with that Black Child here."[85] Members of the Norton family apparently wondered the same thing. In fact, they did not simply question Sue's presence in their home; they resented it. Mary's mother, matriarch of the Norton household, seems to have had an aversion to the baby from the beginning. After telling a visitor to the house that Mary "brought [Sue] from Boston" and "Gave a Piece of Eight for it"—that is, Mary paid for Sue a sum equivalent to six shillings—the woman added that her daughter "had better gave a Piece of Eight to have Lett it alone."[86] The aging matriarch evidently did not want to be bothered with caring for a motherless infant in bondage. Did Sue sense this antipathy as she grew up in the Nortons' home?

It is hard to imagine that she could have missed it. Sue lived in extraordinary physical intimacy with those who bound her. Her presence in the household was ubiquitous, whether as an infant lying on an enslaver's lap, a toddler steadying herself against the old blanket chest, a child dashing in with fresh milk from the barn, a growing girl raking coals in the fireplace, or a young woman drifting off to sleep in one of the home's three beds after a day of toil.[87] This kind of proximity between bondspeople and those who bound them was typical of New England. It was not, of course, unique to the region, but comparatively few people of African descent in the British-Atlantic world found themselves as fully immersed as Sue in the rhythms of an Anglo-American household.[88] In Sue's case, intimacy did not necessarily breed fondness. Not only did members of the household, like old Mrs. Norton, belittle Sue with sharp words, but physical violence gnaws at the margins of the girl's story. A woman who knew the family well—she described herself as "often Conversant at the house of George Norton"—mentioned offhandedly that Mary's brothers, Shadrach and Joseph, "often kick[ed] the said Negro and bid her be gone to her Mistress."[89] This abuse was regular, and it happened in the open. Did anyone step in to shield Sue from the boys' wrath? The record does not say.

Mary, for her part, did nothing to protect the infant she had plucked from her mother's arms in Boston. The woman, putative owner, was not present to intervene, even if she had wished to do so, for she had left her parents' home in the early days of 1702, soon after Sue's first birthday. In what was likely a hurried marriage—she was five months pregnant—Mary pledged herself to a mariner named Samuel West, leaving the sandy beaches and craggy outcroppings of Manchester for those of Beverly, the next town over.[90] Mary apparently had wanted Sue to come with her, but Mary's mother implored her to let the girl remain. The woman who had bemoaned the presence of the bound child in her household not long before now pledged that she would "bring it up"—here she meant Sue—for she "had taken such a ffancy to it that she did not know how to part with it."[91]

Had old Mrs. Norton truly developed affection for Sue? It is possible. But affective attachments were probably not the primary forces driving the arrangement. Mary had motivation to dispose of the bound child, at least for a time: Raising her own newborn while she looked after a bound one-year-old likely sounded wearying. And Mary's mother, for her part, may have begun to envision a productive future for Sue. The two seem to have worked out an agreement that took into account both the logistics of their present arrangements and their joint expectation of profit in the future. If Mrs. Norton went to the trouble of raising Sue, Mary would allow her to profit from Sue's labor until her death—at which point ownership of the bondswoman would revert to Mary. The two women explained this to curious neighbors, who later

Figure 7. Embroidery showing bound child. We have few images of enslaved girls in colonial New England—really, few images exist of enslaved people in the region at all. This embroidery, however, shows a bound child rocking an infant in eighteenth-century Connecticut. Sue would not have done this sort of work when she was young, as she did not live with children, but she doubtless was put to toil in the Norton household as soon as she was able. Courtesy of the Connecticut Historical Society.

remembered Mary saying that she had allowed her parents to keep Sue "during their lives" in return for the money and effort they expended "bringing [the] said Negro woman up." Recognizing that rearing a bound child in a New England home was labor intensive, Mary gave her word that she "would not take [Sue] away from her mother as Long as her Mother Lived."[92]

This was a promise Mary kept. In the Nortons' Manchester home, Sue grew from a little girl to a bigger one. She mastered all sorts of household tasks for Mary's mother, learning to do the wash and to iron; to cook, brew the household's beer, and milk the cows; to make candles; and to spin and sew.[93] The weeks turned to months; the months to years. Mrs. Norton bent with age and the girl she commanded grew in stature. And still Sue worked. By the time she was a young woman, Sue had made herself indispensable to the household. She was so useful, in fact, that old Mrs. Norton had to fend off neighbors who wished to purchase her.[94]

And then, Mary's mother decided to sell Sue away.

The thin slip of paper deeding Sue to another does not explain why the old woman chose to give up such a valuable bondsperson just as she herself was becoming more feeble. Perhaps Mrs. Norton had financial motivations. The woman had been widowed by her husband's death nearly six years before, and selling Sue could pay for needed staples: stacks of firewood to stave off winter's biting cold, barrels of corn to stock an empty root cellar, lengths of cloth to replace a tattered cloak.[95]

Or, possibly, the decision reflected a tinge of concern for Sue, who had now lived more than two decades with Mrs. Norton. In her waning years, the elderly matriarch might have brooded over the agreement she had made with her daughter so long ago. Sue, Mrs. Norton knew, would soon be sent to Beverly, where she would live out the rest of her days in slavery, subject to the will of Mary. Sue's bill of sale suggests that Mrs. Norton wanted to chart a different course for the woman who had come of age in her household. The document required Sue to labor until the age of forty-one and then promised her liberty: Sue would at that time "be free & clear not to be Commanded by any Body."[96] Of course, the agreement was not altogether magnanimous. It compelled Sue to work an additional two decades before acquiring her freedom, and it might well have placed her in a threatening situation, as her purchaser, Elizabeth Norton, was the wife of Mary's brother, Shadrach, who had made a habit of harassing Sue in the Norton home while growing up.[97] But the bill of sale nonetheless provided for the bondswoman a path out of slavery.

Why, then, part with an indispensable helper? Perhaps Mrs. Norton needed ready cash. Perhaps she regretted consigning Sue to a lifetime of bondage with her daughter. Or, perhaps, she did not want to trouble herself with the young woman and the little body taking shape inside her. For Sue, who had already given birth to one child, was, the records suggest, once again pregnant.[98]

*   *   *

Becoming pregnant required a partner, of course, but all evidence suggests that Sue was very much alone as she came of age. What kind of isolation might Sue have suffered as the sole person of African descent in an Anglo-American home? How would it have felt to be the outsider whom strangers gaped at and asked about when they crossed the Nortons' threshold?[99] It is difficult to imagine the depth of Sue's loneliness in the shipwright's home. And leaving the premises would have provided little solace, for the shadow of seclusion extended far beyond the Nortons' modest holdings. Whether surveying the throng at the market, taking her seat in the meetinghouse, or greeting neighbors on the town common, Sue would have seen few faces like hers. The girl must constantly have been aware that she was different.

Unlike Boston, where there was a sizable and growing African-descended community, the north shore of Massachusetts had exceedingly few Black people. In fact, not a shred of evidence indicates that other people of African ancestry lived in Manchester during the years Sue grew from a toddling child to a young woman; notes jotted by the clerks and ministers who kept the town's annals preserve fragments of other Black people's lives, but only after Sue was grown. A man named Jethro, described as a "Negro Ser[van]t," was baptized in Manchester's meetinghouse in 1728. A woman named Dille or Dilla married Stephen, a fellow bondsperson, and mothered four children in the 1730s. Taff bore two children in the 1740s. And a child named Phillis was baptized in 1741, likely following her birth, though the record keeper made no mention of her mother.[100]

Whether or not other Black folks lived in Manchester while Sue was coming of age, smatterings of African-descended people found themselves in the neighboring communities. For instance, in Beverly, Mary's new hometown, a child named Stephen Black was born in 1707, and Cato and Puelah Black were born to a bound woman the following decade. Robin Mingo wed in 1707 a local Indian woman, and an African-descended man named Anthony, designated in the records as "ye freedman," registered twice his intent to marry: first in 1710 and then again in 1715. A man named Mingo was baptized in the Beverly meetinghouse in 1722 upon his "publick profess[io]n of faith," and four adults described as "negro" joined the church the following decade. The town's death records show evidence of African-descended residents as well: a man named Enos perished in 1718; three people with the surname Woodberry died in the 1720s; Oxford passed in 1731; and Cornelia in 1735.[101] By the time the first census was taken of the region's enslaved population, half a century after Mary carried baby Sue to Manchester, Beverly had twenty-eight adults of African descent in bondage. Wenham, which also bordered Manchester, had sixteen, while Gloucester, the third contiguous town, had sixty-one.[102] The Black population in each of these towns appears to have dwarfed that of Manchester, whose selectmen noted only six bondspeople in the return they submitted to the government of Massachusetts.

It might have been in one of these towns, then, the towns pressing Manchester into the sea, that Sue found a Black man she liked well enough: a man fit to bear children with.[103] Records are silent on his name, but he shaped, unmistakably, the course of Sue's life. As the bondswoman approached the end of her second decade, her body swelled with their child. Then, a torrent of events. Sue became unwell; Mrs. Norton sent word; a midwife arrived; the pangs of childbirth quickened; neighbor women hurried over; and, just as her mother had borne down in labor in the Holyoke household, bringing into the world a little girl who belonged to another, Sue brought forth a baby boy. Her firstborn. Her child who was not hers.

Delivering this child was an experience of intense physical intimacy with people in some measure unlike her. Sue gave birth in the arms of her neighbors. Local women named Anne Bennet and Elizabeth Whittier were there, records tell us, and perhaps Mary Peirce and Elizabeth Warring as well. The twin realities of Sue's status and race—that she was enslaved, and that, as her helpers put it, she was a "negro"—did not set her outside the bounds of the community when it came to childbirth; biological needs eclipsed social hierarchies as the neighbor women rushed to the Norton home. Sue, who was safely delivered, benefited from about the same number of birthing assistants as did white women in rural New England.[104]

Other evidence suggests that labor and delivery for the enslaved in the region more or less mirrored labor and delivery for the free. This sets Sue and New England's other Black mothers apart from enslaved women in much of the rest of the British Atlantic. Bondswomen in New England did not give birth in slave quarters, plantation birthing huts, or under the care of African practitioners; they labored according to Anglo-American customs with the assistance of English midwives and neighbors.[105] For instance, when a Boston woman named Flora approached labor, her enslaver sent for local women "to Look to Examine her." Likewise, a free woman of African descent named Abigail Morsemore was accompanied by a Boston midwife and at least one other Anglo-American woman at her childbirth. An unnamed enslaved woman who lived south of Boston was attended by a midwife named Hannah Briggs. And consider the case of Nanny. When the time seemed right, her enslaver "fetched" a group of local women "to assist his negro Slave Nanny in Her then Expected travel." There appear to have been three, one of whom was a midwife, all of whom were Anglo-American. Nanny's labor subsided, so they returned home, but, on the following day, the son of Nanny's enslaver "fetch't Back" the midwife and another. These two, together with Nanny's mistress and three additional neighbors (likewise "fetch't"), stayed with Nanny until she gave birth.[106]

Childbirth for women like Nanny and Sue may have paralleled, in certain ways, childbirth for their free neighbors, but the outcomes of Black women's travails were wholly dissimilar. Twenty years before, Sue's mother had brought into the world a child whom she was powerless to protect. Now Sue had done the same. As Sue held her tiny son in her arms, did she ponder the precarity of their closeness? Did she wonder in anguish where he might be taken, and when? Did she mull over what the future might hold for a little boy with dark skin—and shudder when she considered whose hands might hold that future? Or did she resent the child who made her nights unquiet and strained her weary body with his demands? Yet another possibility: Did she look with indifference upon a boy whose life might be fleeting, a boy who—should he survive infancy—would live out his days in service to someone else in some other place?[107] We cannot know.

The baby would be called Abijah, a royal name yet not an auspicious one. The biblical Abijah, grandson of Solomon, was King of Judah. However, he reigned for only three years and, according to the biblical account, he "walked in all the sins of his father."[108] It was ironic to associate an enslaved boy with a biblical king, but that was likely the intent. Records do not tell us who named the child, but a woman who tended to Sue in labor later recalled that Sue was "delivered of a Boy" who was "afterwards named Habijah." *Afterwards.* By separating the act of naming from the act of delivery, the witness raises the possibility that Abijah was named by another. At the very least, the word suggests that Sue did not christen the infant in the presence of her female helpers. And the word links the first days of Abijah's life to Sue's own infancy. Sue had not been named at birth, either, and her mother certainly did not have the privilege of choosing what she would be called. As one woman later remembered when describing the five-month-old baby, "the said Negroe Girl" was "afterwards . . . called Sue Black."[109] *Afterwards.* Five months old, Sue had still been nameless.

Sue's past showed up in her son's present in other ways. Twenty years before, Sue's mother had stood by, helpless, watching women haggle over her child. Now Sue stood in her mother's place, unable to maintain proximity to her own offspring (had she wished for it). Like Sue, Abijah did not spend much time in the home of his birth or the arms of his mother. One neighbor recalled seeing a man named William Dodge "carry away" Abijah from the Norton house "some time after" the boy's birth. Another remembered Mrs. Norton saying that "she had sold s[ai]d Negro Child to one Mr William Dodge of Wenham for thirty pounds." A bill of sale confirms the details of the transaction: "Bigah black" was indeed purchased by William Dodge for thirty pounds, and he was taken from his mother in October of 1723, around the age of three.[110]

William did not keep the boy long. Within a year, he had traded Abijah to his son, Richard Dodge. Abijah sold for a "suit of Cloaths," just as Sue had once been peddled for the price of a petticoat. Then, two years later, when Abijah was about six, Richard sold him to his brother, William Dodge Jr.[111] From old Mrs. Norton to William Dodge, from William Dodge to Richard Dodge, from Richard Dodge to William Dodge Jr. Bound by four different enslavers by the time he was six, Abijah must have found the transitions dizzying: new homes, new routines, new expectations. In some respects, though, he could count himself fortunate; these dislocations had brought him only one town away from the place of his birth and the residence of his mother. Still, a boy in bondage could never be confident that the future would allow him to maintain any kind of proximity to his family. When Abijah reached the age of seven and his enslaver's right to him was called into question, the man's wife knew just what to do: "I will send this Negro boy to Virginia," she threatened.[112] There were no guarantees for a child bound in Massachusetts.

*   *   *

The year Mrs. Norton allowed William Dodge to "carry away" Abijah was the year she sold Sue, once again pregnant, to her daughter-in-law, Elizabeth. Along with Sue, of course, went her unborn child. This child, a boy who would be named Jethro, would take his first breaths in the household headed by Elizabeth's husband, Shadrach, the man who, when growing up, would "often kick" Sue and "bid her be gone to her Mistress." But Shadrach did not keep the boy. In December of 1725, when Jethro was nearing three, Shadrach sold him to Aaron Bennet, a neighboring miller. Jethro's price was thirty pounds—exactly the sum Mrs. Norton had pocketed for selling Abijah at the same age.[113]

With all this buying and selling of bondspeople in the little seaside community, one might assume that the practices that made slavery work were firmly established. And, in some ways, they were. There seemed to be no question, for instance, that a woman's enslaver ought to enjoy the right to her offspring. Likewise, the identical selling prices of Abijah and Jethro at around the age of three suggests, first, that the market for humans rested on an agreed-upon economic logic and, second, that young bondspeople in rural places were in somewhat greater demand than they were in urban ones. But the documents that Anglo-Americans drafted to sell Sue and her sons reveal that, in certain respects, the systems that made it possible to own people on the north shore of Massachusetts were still being worked out in the opening decades of the eighteenth century. How was one to convey title to a human being? Shadrach was not sure. He was familiar with the practice of selling land, though, so he modeled Jethro's bill of sale on a real estate agreement. It was an awkward fit. Rather than declaring himself master of a bound child, Shadrach pronounced himself the "Lawfull owner of ye Bargined Premises." And instead of asserting the buyer's right to a person, the document upheld Aaron's "poseson of ye Bargined Premises." Equating a boy to an acreage of salt meadow or a parcel of woodland, the document obscured what was at stake in the transaction, but this was, in a way, appropriate. By considering enslaved people as on par with real estate, these enslavers were reaching in a fumbling and indirect manner toward the systems that already had been enshrined in law in places like Barbados, Virginia, and South Carolina.[114] Most important for Shadrach's purposes, the document accomplished what he had intended. Jethro was taken from the home of his birth, "carryed . . . away," as his toddling brother had been a few years earlier and his mother had been more than two decades before that.[115]

Sue bore her third child, Matthew, in 1725, just before her second was sold to the Manchester miller. Once again, Sue's mistress sent word that the time had come. Once again, neighbor women descended on Shadrach's home to aid Sue in childbirth. This was a familiar routine; some of these women had been helping Sue since Abijah was born six years earlier. This time, though, the baby came fast: At least one of Sue's attendants was "Sent for" to help in Sue's labor but did not make it to Sue's bedside until after Matthew had been born.[116] And another thing was different about this little boy. Shadrach would not have the opportunity to sell him. Sue had been sold at six weeks; Abijah at around three years; Jethro when he, too, was close to three. Perhaps Matthew likewise would eventually have been taken off by the highest bidder, but Shadrach lost control of him before this could happen.

For Mary had set out to reclaim the human beings whom she considered her property.

Mary sought Sue first. Clearly, she knew that demonstrating ownership over the mother would be necessary to claim the children. In March of 1726, some twenty-five years after Mary had traded six shillings jingling in her pocketbook for a baby in bondage, she sued her brother for the right to the grown woman. Shadrach "unjustly detaines" Sue, Mary argued in court, for Mary was "well Intituled" to the woman and had been for a long time. After all, she "had honestly bought & p[ai]d for her."[117] The jury agreed; Mary ought rightfully to recover the woman. Nobody mentioned the fact that Sue would thus never enjoy the freedom promised her in old Mrs. Norton's bill of sale. We might imagine that this blocking of Sue's path out of bondage, likely forever, was a heavy blow. But it is possible that the bondswoman was heartened when Mary next sued, in rapid succession, the three men holding her three boys in bondage. Perhaps this was the solution to the family's dispersal? Echoes of Sue's past thundered in her sons' present; a quarter century after Sue's mother had last laid eyes on her infant child, Sue's own family had been scattered. Abijah was in Wenham, Jethro and Matthew were in two different Manchester homes, and Sue was with Mary in Beverly. Wenham, Manchester, and Beverly were contiguous, forming a triangle of land on the north shore of Massachusetts, yet the distance would have been great enough to keep Sue and her children from engaging in any kind of daily interaction.

Mary was successful before the bar, winning the right to all three boys. But it is not clear that Sue and her sons ever lived under one roof for long. Abijah, for his part, was forced to stay in the household of William Dodge Jr., with a mistress who had threatened to sell him to Virginia and children who ordered him about the house: A forty-pound payment from William to Mary cleared the boy's title.[118] And, while it is possible that Jethro and Matthew came of age in the company of their mother, nothing in Sue's story gives reason to hope that Mary prioritized keeping Sue and her sons together.[119] If Mary had felt that bound children ought to live with their mothers, she would not have sold Abijah back to William after winning the boy in her lawsuit. She would not, for that matter, have bought Sue in the first place. So Mary likely dispensed with her bound property in whatever way maximized her convenience and profit—which almost certainly means that family members were divided, one from another.[120] We could surmise that the continued fracture of Sue's family would have come as a disappointment to her. *Perhaps. It is likely. We could surmise.* My language here is full of hesitation because Sue is silent in the documentary record. We *see* her, time and again: a six-week-old exchanged for six shillings; an infant wrapped in blankets;

a growing girl who could "go or run about"; a young woman bearing down in labor. But not once do we *hear* her.[121]

Still, the archive does yield clues. Others in Sue's time and place found themselves in situations similar to hers, and we know more of their thoughts and actions. There was Kate Humphrey, a woman of African descent who appears to have extracted a promise from her daughter's enslaver: The girl "shall have her Liberty," the enslaver ordered, "and return to her mother Kate Humphrey according to my promise to her."[122] There was Anthony, an enslaved father who initiated a legal battle that lasted four years to free his daughter, Molly, from bondage.[123] There was Lettice, a bound woman who approached a local notary, asking that he record and notarize her enslaver's promise to manumit her son, James.[124] However, for every parent in the region who managed to secure better prospects for, and, perhaps, greater access to their children, there were doubtless far more who could not. New England slavery created proximity between bound people and members of the families that enslaved them, but, at the same time, it consistently placed sustained intimacy with their own kin beyond the reach of those in bondage. And so, bound children beyond number would grow up like Sue Black and her sons: alone.

CHAPTER 4

The Bedunahs

Sex and Family Across the Color Line

Be it enacted by His Excellency the Governour, Council
and Representatives in General Court assembled, and by
the authority of the same . . . That none of her majesty's
English or Scottish subjects, nor of any other Christian
nation within this province, shall contract matrimony
with any negro or molatto; nor shall any person duely
authorized to solemnize marriages presume to joyn any
such in marriage, on pain of forfeiting the sum of fifty
pounds, one moiety thereof to her majesty for and towards
the support of the government within this province, and
the other moiety to him or them that shall inform and sue
for the same in any of her majesty's courts.
                —An Act for the Better Preventing of a Spurious and
                                            Mixt Issue, 1705

In the first days of October in 1703, a man and a woman trudged through
Boston's snow-covered streets. They were heading to the home of the well-
known judge, Samuel Sewall. The two had come some distance; they were
not Samuel's neighbors, nor did they, in fact, even live in the town of Boston.
Instead, they hailed from Roxbury, which was connected to the busy seaport
by a narrow strip of land skirting Boston's harbor on one side and the Charles
River on the other. An unseasonable storm had blown through earlier in the
week, blanketing the region with snow, but the early appearance of the "sad
face of Winter," as Samuel put it, had not deterred the couple from traveling

to Boston on that October day.[1] The two had an important errand, one that they wished to accomplish sooner rather than later. They desired to marry, and they apparently had determined that Samuel, a justice of the peace, would be the right man to perform the nuptials.

Why Samuel? Both ministers and justices of the peace could legally join Massachusetts residents in marriage in the early eighteenth century, so the couple had a range of options. They could have asked someone closer to home to wed them, such as the Reverend Nehemiah Walter, pastor of the Roxbury church, or a justice of the peace who resided in their town, like Paul Dudley or James Bailey.[2] But Samuel, apparently, was worth the walk. The man was not just any justice of the peace; he possessed an unusual intellect, a keen conscience inflected by puritan sensibilities, and a voracious appetite for broad reading and deep reflection. He also held perspectives that were unusual in the world in which he lived—and growing more so with each passing decade. Samuel believed, for instance, that slavery was wrong. In a tract written three years earlier, he had declared, "It is most certain that all Men, as they are the Sons of *Adam*, are Coheirs; and have equal Right unto Liberty, and all other outward Comforts of Life."[3] And he worried about the obstacles faced by his Black neighbors, both enslaved and free. One of the major challenges that people of African descent encountered in New England revolved around establishing and maintaining families, and Samuel had assisted some of them in this respect. Just two years earlier, he had wed Sebastian and Jane after working to devise a marriage arrangement that was satisfactory to their enslavers (see Chapter 2). Soon after, he had joined in marriage a man named Sambo and a woman named Elinor, both described as "negroes" in the records of Boston's town clerk. And shortly after that he had married two other Afro-New Englanders: one named Thomas Finnan and the other Maria.[4]

The man and woman who traversed the narrow corridor from Roxbury to Boston that wintry morning therefore had good reason to hope that the justice of the peace would grant their request. They were not asking him to do anything expressly prohibited by provincial decree or local ordinance, of course; as a judge and justice of the peace, Samuel was committed to enforcing rather than thwarting the law. But they *were* asking him to do something that turned against the tide of custom and popular sentiment. They were asking him to join in law a "Negroman" with an "English woman."[5] And this Samuel did. According to the records kept by Boston's town clerk, Thomas

Bedunah and Lydia Crafts were married by the justice of the peace on October 4, 1703.[6]

When the town clerk recorded in his book of records the marriage that Samuel performed on that wintry day, he created the first piece of evidence documenting Thomas Bedunah's presence in Massachusetts—at least, the earliest evidence of the man that survives. But Thomas's story, of course, did not begin in 1703 at Samuel's house on Marlborough Street in the port of Boston. A long chain of events had brought Thomas to the judge's stoop—a history that today can be reconstructed in only the faintest of ways.

Thomas's story likely began in Africa. Though no record reveals this with certainty, the man's surname provides a crucial clue to his origins. *Bedunah* was not an English name. With the exception of Thomas's offspring, no other seventeenth- or eighteenth-century inhabitant of Massachusetts appears to have possessed the surname. *Bedunah* has various possible African origins, however. It could have derived from Bandundu, a place name near the convergence of the Kwango and Kasai Rivers in Central Africa (present-day Democratic Republic of the Congo), which was sometimes rendered "Baduna." *Bedunah* could suggest other African origins as well. "Duna" meant chief or noble in southern African languages, and Badu was a common name given to tenth-born children on the Gold Coast.[7]

Whether Thomas originated in West Central Africa, as the currents of the transatlantic slave trade make likely, or on the Gold Coast, or elsewhere in Africa, his marriage to Lydia suggests that he was taken to the Americas as a boy. Lydia almost certainly would have chosen a spouse who was deeply acculturated to English ways, somebody who could navigate the world of provincial Massachusetts with relative ease. As for the boy's trans-Atlantic journey, it probably did not take him directly from the African coast to New England. Instead, Thomas likely went first to Barbados. This tiny island in the eastern Caribbean directed the flows of the British Atlantic economy. Its prolific sugar production paid for an ever-expanding workforce of enslaved Africans as well as provided planters with the financial means to import food and building materials from the North American mainland. Trade with Barbados was crucial to New England's economy in the seventeenth century.[8] Merchants from Massachusetts traversed the Atlantic, some supplying Barbados with bondspeople they had purchased on the coast of Africa and others supplying Barbados with provisions they had brought from New England. Vessels returning home hauled Barbadian molasses to feed New England's rum distilleries, and they carried bound Africans to sell to the region's residents. Over the course of the seventeenth century, small shipments of bondspeople brought from Barbados gradually built up New England's enslaved population. They came in groups of "two or three," as one New Englander put it, or "3 or 4," as another claimed.[9] One such ship doubtless carried Thomas on the final leg of his protracted journey, depositing him on the town dock of the area's principal port: Boston. It would have been a bewildering ordeal. Likely born in Africa, reduced to slavery, shipped to Barbados, and from there taken to Boston, Thomas had survived tremendous and terrifying change. But his crossing was hardly unique. The man was but one of countless swallowed into the vicious Atlantic trade during the seventeenth century. In some ways, the most unusual parts of Thomas's life—the particularly remarkable aspects of his experience—began in New England *after* he survived this harrowing turn of events. There the enslaved African man became free, he acquired an English name, he married an English woman, he gained a measure of wealth and standing in his community, and he presided as patriarch over a family that seems to have grown more English with every passing decade.

In this chapter, I explore the family that Thomas and Lydia built in Roxbury, examining through their story sex and marriage across the color line in eighteenth-century Massachusetts. I begin by sketching some of the ways in which Thomas might have acquired his freedom, as liberty was an essential precondition to his 1703 marriage to Lydia. I then consider a body of legislation that Massachusetts lawmakers passed soon after Thomas and Lydia's marriage—legislation that outlawed marriages such as theirs and made harsher the penalties for sex between Black people and white people in the province. This legislation represented an effort to curb interracial procreation at a moment in which the importation of Africans was reaching unprecedented levels. However, it did little to alter sexual behavior in the province; residents continued to form interracial liaisons, and the courts seemed hesitant to enforce the laws to the full extent of their severity. As for Thomas and Lydia, they went about raising their four sons and three daughters in a province that had banned unions such as theirs in an attempt to stop the proliferation of children such as theirs. One might expect that daily life in such a climate would have been acutely difficult for them, but the evidence suggests that Thomas and Lydia's near neighbors were little bothered by Thomas's African heritage. The man, after all, lived quite like them. He raised his children in the church, he provided comfortable support for his wife, he accumulated property, he did business in the community, and he paid his taxes. Over time, the evidence suggests, folks with whom he interacted seem to have come to regard and treat him not as a Black man but as a white one. Thomas's children and grandchildren were described in the records in ways that suggest the community considered them white as well. Crucial to the family's ability to assume the status of white citizens, I argue, was the embrace of Lydia's family of origin; the woman's relatives seem to have chosen to integrate the Bedunahs into their extensive and well-connected network of white kin. The occasional willingness of white people to accord those of African descent the privileges of whiteness in Massachusetts is surprising in light of the discriminatory legislation passed during the early eighteenth century, but, in the case of the Bedunahs, family and status helped to override the limitations imposed by race.

*   *   *

How did Thomas, who was almost surely enslaved when he first set foot in Massachusetts, acquire his freedom? The historical record yields no direct clues; Thomas is not mentioned in surviving sources until 1703, when he trekked to Samuel's home to marry Lydia, and by that time he was already a free man. But it is possible to reconstruct the experiences of other African-descended people in the region who acquired their freedom, and it is possible, therefore, to consider the options that might have presented themselves to Thomas.

People in Thomas's time and place could extricate themselves from slavery in a variety of ways. Some, such as running away, carried great risk; others, such as suicide, offered certain demise; still others, such as purchasing one's freedom or persuading one's enslaver to pursue manumission, were safer options—though certainly not accessible to all. In order to purchase their freedom, or, as they put it, to "buy their time," bondspeople needed to find a way to earn money. They could do this by working in the evenings; by growing provisions for resale on their own little garden plots; or, if their enslavers hired them out to neighbors, by pocketing (should they obtain consent) a fraction of their earnings. Enslaved people who managed to secure substantial sums by these means could then buy their liberty if—and only if—their enslavers were willing to release them. Unfortunately, there is no way to assess how common self-purchase was in Massachusetts. Because it was a private transaction between the enslaved and those who bound them, clues to people "buying their time" have largely been lost.[10]

However, a good deal of surviving evidence documents the experiences of African-descended people who obtained their freedom by manumission rather than by self-purchase. Because enslavers sometimes chose to liberate bondspeople in wills, and because those wills were registered in the probate court, many manumissions have been preserved in county court records. For instance, in the century stretching from 1661 to 1760, 120 Suffolk County bondspeople were liberated in the wills penned by their enslavers. This is a group large enough to allow scholars to trace some of what appear to be the common experiences of those who moved from slavery to freedom as the result—at least in the eyes of the law—of an enslaver's final wishes.[11]

The nature of these manumissions varied a great deal from case to case. Some bondspeople, like Pheeba, were freed immediately upon the passing of their enslavers. The will of Ruth Beate proclaimed: "I give to my Servant Maid Pheeba her Freedom at my Decease." A number of enslavers did not stipulate precisely when bound laborers ought to be freed but seemed to assume that the manumissions would proceed as a matter of course when the estate was processed by probate court. Rachel Gatcombe stated simply, "I Give to my Negro Rose her Freedom" and "I Give to my Negro Caser his Freedom." Hannah How used similar language to emancipate Peter: "I Give My Negro man Peter his Freedom forever." And Margaret Blackadoor wrote, "I manumit & Set free from a State of Slavery & Bondage my two Negro Men, namely Thomas & Surinam."[12]

Other bondspeople received their freedom only after a delay.[13] Occasionally, this interval was quite short. Brill, the "Negro Servant" of Rebecca Dudley, would be freed within a year of Rebecca's death. Sometimes the wait was longer. Richard was required to serve each of the three sons of Hugh Floyd for a year before he would be "made a free Man." Jack had to serve Sarah Beard's daughter for five years before he tasted freedom; an unnamed African man had to serve Joseph Simpson's wife for eight years after Joseph's death; and Sambo was required to serve the wife of Henry Brightman for a full decade after Henry passed away. Other manumissions were predicated on the deaths of heirs. Primus was to "have his freedom" only after Elizabeth Mason's son passed away. And Prince, Jenney, and Boston could not enjoy their promised liberty until the wives of their late enslavers had been laid to rest.[14]

Sometimes manumission was delayed until those in bondage reached a certain age. Some enslavers might have believed that such a requirement existed for the benefit of their bondspeople. John Frizell's will stipulated that Sapphina should "go out free forever" but not before "attain[ing] the age of twenty four years." As Sapphina could have become self-supporting before that point, the provision might have reflected elements of self-interest, but John likely considered himself beneficent for liberating a grown woman who could make her way in the world. Nicholas Paige and his wife, Anna, seem to have had similar intentions. They bequeathed Jethro to their cousin, John Gerresh, instructing John to "teach the Boy his Trade perfectly" until Jethro turned thirty. Jethro was in his early twenties when their will was processed by the court, so he had to work for about eight additional years before becoming "Free for himself" and receiving five pounds from the Paige estate. Though Jethro's marketable skills would have eased his transition from slavery to freedom, it is hard to imagine that he wished to prolong his servitude. Samuel Wales promised Toby his freedom, but Samuel stipulated that Toby, then seventeen, would have to wait until he turned twenty-eight. Samuel made no effort to mask the delay in benevolent garb; he simply wanted his heirs to benefit from eleven more years of Toby's toil. Moses and Miriam faced similar requirements; their enslaver, Mary White, ordered that they be "Discharged and made free," but each had to wait until the age of thirty-two.[15] Moses, Miriam, and the other people of African descent who received delayed emancipation provisions resembled more closely in status the European and Native indentured servants in Massachusetts than they did their enslaved African neighbors.

Suffolk County probate records show that promises of manumission could be explicitly manipulative. Although most wills freeing bondspeople did not place conditions on their manumission, a sizable minority of decedents made offers of freedom contingent on the actions of those they held in bondage. Occasionally, a will promised liberty only if the person in question could make a specified payment: Dege and Hagar were freed if they paid Hope Allen's wife thirty pounds "for the educating & bringing up of my Children," and Jack was to be liberated eight years after Mary Hunt's death, provided he pay her executrix six pounds annually. Such manumissions were essentially pledges to allow bondspeople to purchase their freedom—should they manage to acquire the needed funds. More often, however, freedom was held out as a prize for a bondsperson whose behavior was deemed satisfactory. For instance, Mingo was promised his freedom ten years after Joseph Rock's

Figure 8. Will manumitting
Sapphina. John Frizell manumitted Sapphina after he had penned
the rest of his will, squeezing the
notation in small print between the
body of his will and his signature
and seal. Courtesy of the Massachusetts State Archives.

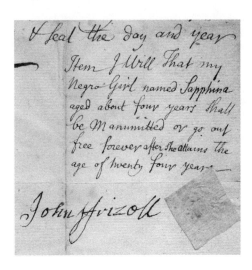

decease, but if he was not a "good faithfull and obedient Servant" he could
be sold. This scenario repeated itself. Sambo was offered liberty if he served
for ten years after Henry Brightman's death but was ordered to be "disposed of" if he did not do so "well and faithfully." Nanny was promised
freedom following the death of Joseph Baxter's wife—provided she "Carry
& behave herself dutifully and well." And Manuel was given to William
Webster's brother to be "br[ought] up . . . to some Trade" and offered his
freedom "if he shall deserve it by his good behaviour."[16]

Freedom did not necessarily sever ties of obligation binding enslaved
people to their enslavers. Wills filed in the Suffolk County Probate Court
show both the staying power of these bonds and the ambiguity of liberty. Brill
was to be freed "within a year" after the decease of Rebecca Dudley, but she
stipulated that "after his ffreedom" he be "ready to wait on my Children so
that they may have the Refusal of his Service." Similarly, Phillis was
"Manumitt[ed] and sett free," but Martha Bridge directed that "she would
Live with my said Cousin Mary Russell." Though Martha insisted that Phillis
have some say in the arrangement—she and Mary were to "agree" upon
"Terms"—Phillis's whereabouts obviously were limited by her erstwhile enslaver's wishes.[17] Obligations could go both ways. John Staniford instructed
a prominent local man to "inspect" the "Conduct and Behaviour" of Vio-
let, Titus, and Minsa once they were "Liberated & sett free," but he also
directed the man to help them transition to freedom: He was to "Assist

and Advise them in what he can, that they may live honestly & Comfortably." Thomas was supposed to be "comfortably Maintain'd & Provided for"
by John Otis's brothers, and Margaret was ordered to be "Assist[ed]" by the
executor of Andrew Lane's estate so that she "may live Comfortably." Likewise, Pompey, Cuffee, and York were to be sustained by the heirs or estates
of John Barns, Ephraim Bosworth, and John Larrabee, respectively, if they
became needy.[18]

The wills filed in probate do more than show that the process of obtaining freedom could be tortuous; they also tell us something about the actions
and behaviors of those who were ultimately manumitted. Some people in
bondage managed to cultivate traits and abilities that convinced enslavers
that their claims to human life were illegitimate. Take, for instance, the case
of Rose. The woman, according to Nathaniel Byfield's will, was purchased for
him as a child in the West Indies and arrived very ill on a ship that docked
in Bristol, then part of Massachusetts. In Nathaniel's household, Rose learned
to read and became educated in religion. Over time, she "persuaded" Nathaniel that she "truly fear[ed] God," which presented him with a moral dilemma: He found himself, as he put it, "oblige[d] . . . to set her free from the
Servitude she stands obliged to Me." To the young woman who had been his
"faithfull Servant," he gave "all her Cloaths" as well as "those that shall be
Given her at my Decease" and "the Bed & Bedding she Useth."[19]

Other people in bondage manipulated circumstances in ways that pro-
pelled enslavers to manumit them. Susan cultivated "good will" on the part
of Mary Anderson, which led to her "full Liberty." Boston performed "faithful Services" and therefore, George Lane concluded, he should "be set at Liberty, and have his full freedom." Ceasar proved himself "very Industrious &
diligent," William Waters decided, and deserved to be "manumitted &
made free." Pompey put forth such "cares & labours," John Barns declared,
that he ought to "be a free Man at his own dispose." And through "faithful
Service" Cuffee persuaded Ephraim Bosworth to "liberate and set [him] free"
and provide him with a bed, bedding, furniture, land, and buildings "to be
holden by him his Heirs, & Assigns for ever." Looking at this partial list of
the instances in which being "faithfull" and "behav[ing] well" paid off for
people in bondage, one could demean their efforts as slavish gestures, evidence that they accepted their subordinate position. But "Fidelity," or apparent fidelity, can also be understood as strategic—and these wills, which
discuss the deeds of the enslaved, or the attachments enslavers formed as a
result of their bondspeople's conduct, not only illuminate the actions of

people in bondage but occasionally even begin to suggest the aims that might have spurred those actions.[20]

Thomas Bedunah might have obtained his freedom from an enslaver grateful enough for years of faithful service to release his bondsman. Or perhaps Thomas's manumission came from a master manipulative enough to bet on the short-term gains of a long-term promise. Or maybe the person who claimed ownership of Thomas felt guilty enough for holding human property to liberate the man—only to insist that he continue to fetch wood and water for his heirs. Any of these scenarios is plausible. If Thomas was extraordinarily fortunate, he might have obtained, in addition to his "time," a bequest to help him make his way as a free man in a world hostile to people of African ancestry. Occasionally liberated New Englanders received legacies from their former enslavers. Some obtained clothing. Joseph West deeded Will "such cloathing and Apparell of mine as my Executor shall think fitt."[21] Others received household items like bedding or cookware. Elizabeth Pierce gave Peg her bed along with "ye old green Curtins about my Bed, and a Kettle & a pott."[22] A number of people were given sums of money, most of which were modest, as in the five pounds Susanna received from Ruth Willys.[23] Sometimes, though, freed people enjoyed legacies of significant value. Ruth Beate granted Pheeba "the use and Improvement of my House and ground where I now Dwell," as well as "the use and improvement of my Household Goods during the term of her Natural Life."[24] Ceesar received two parcels of land and a heifer from Samuel Read.[25] Likewise, Primus received George Raisin's feather bed with curtains and furniture, as well as a sizable bequest: George ordered the executors of his estate to invest 100 pounds and pay Primus the interest each year. Primus thus benefited from financial security that eluded most Black people—indeed, most New Englanders of any race—in the early eighteenth century. And should the man become sick or disabled, George ordered that his executors "call in" the 100 pounds and use it "for the support of the said Primus."[26]

The enslavers of those people who received bequests as well as manumissions recognized an important reality for liberated people of African ancestry making their way in New England at the turn of the eighteenth century: Freedom was no panacea for African-descended people. Nonetheless, freedom was significant. Free people like Thomas had the ability to move about with much more autonomy than their enslaved neighbors. They did not have to creep down from their garrets and slip out the door to rendezvous with their spouses or partners in hidden places. Nor did they need to keep off the road after dark when Boston's constables or night watch ambled by, for free people were not subject to the legal codes that limited the nighttime movements of the enslaved.[27] They had more control over where they lived, where they traveled, and where they worked. And they could finally enjoy the fruits of their labor. Whether they hauled barrels on Boston's wharves, planted corn on Roxbury's farms, or stitched together garments for their neighbors in Charlestown, liberated people of African descent at last received compensation for their work. This was significant because earning even a small income increased a formerly enslaved person's ability to support a family. Everyone in the Boston region at the turn of the eighteenth century, including those in slavery, free townspeople of African descent, and Anglo-American inhabitants like Lydia Crafts, knew the same thing: One's chances of building a family with any stability were much better in freedom than they were in slavery.

Indeed, it is hard to imagine that Thomas's free status did not play a role in Lydia's decision to marry him. Lydia was the youngest child in a large Roxbury family, and her mother, who had been widowed when Lydia was only four, probably struggled to make ends meet. Still, the family was not wholly destitute: Her father had left behind him a home, an orchard, and a variety of possessions, as well as an expansive network of well-established kin.[28] Twenty-two when she made the trek to Samuel's home, Lydia was a young woman of small means, but she was not entirely without options. Marrying an enslaved man would have consigned her to poverty forever. Marrying Thomas, though, might offer something better.

*   *   *

Lydia Crafts's journey to Samuel Sewall's home on that unseasonable October day in 1703 was doubtless difficult, but not merely because of the snow piled along the narrow isthmus connecting Roxbury to Boston. The woman who picked her way through the icy streets was pregnant. She might have wished to hide this from the judge who met her at his door, but she would have been hard-pressed to do so. Nearly eight months along, her state was probably evident to all, despite the fact that this was her first pregnancy and she was bundled in heavy garments to protect against the cold. Lydia's pregnancy posed a problem for the couple. In puritan-inflected New England, sexual activity outside of marriage was not simply frowned upon by neighbors and reprimanded by churches; it was punished aggressively by the province's judicial system.[29] Couples routinely were tried for fornication in the province's lower-level criminal court, where they were disciplined according to their marital status at the time of their child's birth. Unmarried offenders—male as well as female—generally had to pay fines of two to three pounds each or consent to be whipped, usually ten stripes at the public whipping post. And the men in these liaisons typically were required to provide large sums of money to the town in which they lived in order to ensure that their extra-marital children would not burden its poor relief system. The requisite payments could reach as high as fifty or even a hundred pounds, a sizable sum for most men in the region during the early years of the eighteenth century. Couples who conceived prior to marriage but had wed by the time of their child's birth faced reduced sentences. They still were required to pay a small fine or suffer a whipping, but the fathers in these liaisons were not expected to give their towns money in order to provide for their offspring because the children in question, shielded within intact male-headed households, were at much lower risk of landing on the dole.[30]

Lydia and Thomas must have had this in mind as they trudged to Boston. Marrying on that October day would ensure that they faced a lesser punishment for fornication, and it would also enable their child to avoid the stigma of bastardy: The baby had been conceived out of wedlock, and nothing could be done about that now, but she would be born within the bounds of a lawful marriage. Samuel was sympathetic to Lydia and Thomas's desire to form a household prior to their child's birth. He married the couple, and apparently he found Thomas's African ancestry immaterial; he did not bother reporting to the town clerk the man's racial identity.[31] However, as a justice of the province's highest court as well as a local justice of the peace, Samuel might have made a mental note that the Bedunahs ought to be held responsible for their sexual misconduct by the court in the months to come.

Regardless of whether it was Samuel, somebody pointed out the couple's transgression to the authorities, and the Bedunahs were called to court to answer for fornication the following spring. On the fourth day of April, Thomas stood before the justices of the General Sessions of the Peace, the lower-level criminal court, with Lydia by his side. The court's clerk described Thomas as "a Negroman belonging to Roxbury" and he described Lydia as Thomas's "wife," taking care to add that she was "an English woman . . . formerly [known as] Lydia Crafts." Thomas and Lydia were accused of fornication, and they admitted their guilt, or, in the language of the court, they "owned the same."[32] There was no denying the charge: Lydia had given birth to their daughter, Elizabeth, less than six weeks after Samuel had married the couple.[33] The two received the standard sentence: a fine of three pounds each or "ten Stripes" at Boston's whipping post.[34] Though the clerk made note of the couple's unusual racial makeup—Thomas was a "negroman" and Lydia an "English woman"—the interracial nature of the union did not appear to influence the justices' ruling. The couple had committed one crime and one crime only: fornication. They therefore deserved the same punishment as white people who had engaged in the same behavior.

The evenhandedness with which the court treated Thomas and Lydia was typical. Other cases registered in the record book of Suffolk County's General Sessions of the Peace show that interracial fornication was punished just like fornication between people of English descent in the early years of the eighteenth century. For example, in July of 1702, Essex, a "Negro man Servant," and Mary Goslin, a "servant" who can be presumed white based on her English surname and lack of racial identifier, appeared before the justices of Suffolk County's General Sessions of the Peace. Confessing to fornication, they received a standard sentence: "Ten Stripes" or a fine of two and a half pounds sterling.[35] Three years later, Mary appeared before the court again, having committed fornication with another enslaved man. This time, though, the act resulted in the birth of a mixed-race child. She reported that Cesar, a "Negro Man servant or slave," was the father, and he readily confessed. Mary was again sentenced to ten stripes at the whipping post, as was Cesar. In addition, because their extramarital sex resulted in the birth of an infant outside the bounds of marriage, Cesar, as the male responsible for maintaining the child, was assessed a fine of twenty pounds in order to relieve the town of having to care for his offspring—a penalty that was typical if somewhat moderate.[36] Mary's infractions show that the court punished extramarital sex in the opening years of the eighteenth century without considering whether the offenders crossed racial bounds.

But the court's comparative lack of concern about interracial sexual and marital liaisons was about to change. In 1704, when Thomas and Lydia were prosecuted for fornication, the General Sessions of the Peace did not punish them for engaging in sex across the color line; it merely disciplined the two for engaging in sex outside of marriage. Nor had the court shown any interest in penalizing the couple's ultimate marital union: Marriage between Black and white people was entirely permissible according to the province's legal codes at the time. The very next year, though, Massachusetts passed legislation to prevent procreation across racial lines—or, as the law put it, to keep "negro[es] or molatto[es]" and "English . . . or [those from] any other Christian nation" from producing biracial children.[37] This act, titled "An Act for the Better Preventing of a Spurious and Mixt Issue," made the penalty for interracial fornication harsher than that for fornication with a member of one's own race. Black people who engaged in extramarital sex across the color line were now to be "sold out of the province." White offenders, both male and female, as well as Black male offenders were now to be "severely whipped" rather than charged a fine or given ten stripes at the whipping post.[38] And the law strictly prohibited marriage between Black people and white people. Whoever presumed to "joyne any such [persons] in marriage" would face a fine of fifty pounds. Samuel Sewall detested this legislation; he feared it would "promote Murders and other Abominations" as interracial couples sought to conceal the human evidence of their sexual relationships. Nevertheless, as a man of the law, he likely felt some compulsion to follow it. The judge's answer to Lydia and Thomas would probably have been different had the couple appeared on his doorstep in 1705, after the act had passed, rather than in 1703.[39]

The members of the Massachusetts General Court who passed the act to prevent "Spurious and Mixt Issue" were not the only legislators in the Anglo-Atlantic who feared procreation across the color line, and they did not invent legislation to discourage racial mixing out of thin air. Lawmakers in Massachusetts were working from a template: Legislation penalizing interracial sex had been enacted throughout the Anglo-Atlantic world for decades. In 1662, Virginia criminalized interracial fornication, putting in place harsh punishments for English colonists who had sex with people of African descent: They were obliged to pay double the fine required of white people who committed fornication with one another.[40] The next year, Bermuda prohibited both marriage and extramarital sexual relations between "free borne subjects" and "Negroes, Mulattoes, or Mustees." Violators could be banished from the colony.[41] And, in 1664, Maryland sought to prevent marriage and sexual relations between "freeborn English women" and "Negro[es] or other slave[s]" by condemning to bondage both the children of those liaisons and their formerly free mothers.[42] In 1691, Virginia lawmakers expanded the colony's legislation criminalizing interracial sex, which previously pertained only to fornication, to prohibit interracial marriage. Any free "English or other White man or woman" who married a "negroe, mulatto or Indian man or woman bond or free" would be removed from the colony within three months of the marriage. As for women who bore mixed-race children out of wedlock, they were to be heavily fined and sold into servitude for five years if unable to pay. Lawmakers in Massachusetts clearly drew inspiration from this Virginia act when they crafted the province's 1705 legislation, with its allusion to "Spurious and Mixt Issue"—a reference that paralleled, in somewhat milder form, the Virginia law's "abominable mixture and spurious issue."[43] And just two months before the passage of the Massachusetts act, Virginia ratified a legal code that fined ministers who married white and Black people, parts of which appeared nearly verbatim in the Massachusetts legislation that followed it.[44]

Massachusetts legislators were fairly late to prohibit interracial procreation, following some four decades after the first enactment of such laws in the Chesapeake. But the timing made sense for Massachusetts, as the province was in the midst of its first major influx of Africans at precisely the moment its legislature acted to prevent "Mixt Issue" in 1705. Samuel had composed his antislavery tract, *The Selling of Joseph*, in 1700, partly because of "the Numerousness of Slaves at this day in the Province." And this was not just rhetorical flair; other Bostonians noted the rapid influx of Africans at the time and attempted to stem it. In 1701, Boston's selectmen asked the province's elected representatives to "promote the bringing of white serv[an]ts and to put a Period to negros being Slaves."[45] Five years later, a prominent piece in the *Boston News-Letter* argued that "the Importing of Negroes into this or the Neighbouring Provinces is not so beneficial either to the Crown or Country, as white Servants would be."[46] In 1708, Governor Joseph Dudley reported to the English Board of Trade that 200 Africans had arrived in Massachusetts between 1698 and 1707.[47] This was quite a large number considering that the entire population of enslaved people in Boston totaled merely 400 that year. In fact, according to the governor, only around 550 bondspeople lived in the entire province.[48] By his reckoning, then, over a third of the province's total African population had arrived in the last ten years. And if most of the new arrivals had stayed in Boston, which is likely, as it was the Massachusetts town with by far the greatest demand for bound labor, close to half of Boston's Black population might have disembarked over the course of the prior decade.

As people of African descent spread throughout the greater Boston region, opportunities for interracial sex—and interracial procreation—increased. Not only did enslaved people rendezvous with Anglo-American servants under cover of darkness, but Lydia and Thomas, and perhaps others like them, produced racially ambiguous offspring in an entirely legal, even respectable, way: They were married, they were free, and they were economically self-sufficient members of their community. After Lydia wed Thomas in October of 1703 and gave birth to Elizabeth in November of that year, she bore the couple's second child, Benjamin, in January of 1705. The Bedunahs' neighbors would have come to know this boy as they had his older sister. Those who attended the Roxbury meetinghouse would have watched the English woman care for her mixed-race children during Sabbath meetings. And, as the weather thawed and little Benjamin grew sturdier, white and Black people throughout the region would have encountered the growing family on the street, perhaps at markets or among the crowds that thronged the common during open-air sermons or public executions. In all these places and more, the presence of the African patriarch, his English wife, and their "mixt" children had the potential to normalize cross-racial unions in a way that was terribly unsettling to those who believed that Africans like Thomas Bedunah should form a separate and racially distinguishable servant class.

The Massachusetts legislators' approach to preventing "Mixt Issue" in 1705 was two-pronged. Not only did they criminalize interracial sex, but they also enacted measures to reduce the Black population in the province. Enslaved Africans brought into Massachusetts had never been taxed in the past, but now every person importing an African into the province, "male or female, of what age soever," was required to pay a duty of four pounds "per head." The objective was not to stymie commerce. Merchants and shipmasters could freely import enslaved people, avoiding the four-pound fee, provided they exported them again within twelve months. Importers were also spared the tax if their human property died within six weeks of entering Massachusetts. According to the new legislation, then, as long as the enslaved died or passed out of the province, merchants could conduct their business without intervention from the provincial government. The problem was with the people of African descent who stayed. They were the people with the potential to bear interracial children who blurred boundaries in perplexing ways. Not exactly African in appearance, these people were not English either, and they were free nearly as often as they were enslaved. What is more, their numbers seemed to increase with every passing year. By the end of the seventeenth century, there were enough people who did not fit any of the conventional racial categories that they had become a legal problem in Massachusetts. Starting in 1693, the province began to name mixed-race people—"mullatoes"—as a distinct group of people in legislation governing the enslaved. Other New England colonies would follow suit in the early eighteenth century.[49] In 1705, in the midst of significant importation of Africans, there was no sign that this mixing would stop or even slow; instead, the evidence indicated that it would escalate.

Though the Massachusetts General Court enacted the 1705 statute to reverse this trend, the legislation was unable to put a stop to sexual relationships between Black and white people. Before long, a number of African-descended residents had been sent out of the province as punishment for defying the new law—probably to Barbados or other Caribbean colonies, where they perished from the brutality of life on sugar plantations. A woman called "Negro Bess," who was enslaved by a Boston shopkeeper named Jonathan Waldo, was one of those who faced these penalties—penalties that Samuel mourned as "extraordinary" in his journal.[50] In 1710, she stood before the bar, answering to the accusation of fornication. Bess had given birth to a child out of wedlock six months before, and she now claimed that Andrew Walker, a Boston laborer described in court records as a "Whiteman," was the father. Andrew successfully defended himself, producing witnesses who testified that Bess did not accuse him during childbirth—"in the time of her Extremity"—which was necessary in order to establish paternity. Bess had no defense and was summarily ordered out of Massachusetts.[51] Three years later, Coffee, a man belonging to Peter Boylston of Brookline, was also deported, but not before a thirty-stripe whipping. He had committed fornication with Katharine Horton, a "Singlewoman," who could not deny the charge because she had a child to prove it. Katharine received twenty stripes and was given the responsibility of maintaining her child.[52] And a few years after that, an enslaved woman, another Bess, was shipped away in punishment for having given birth to mixed-race children.[53]

As these cases show, the courts were clearly aware of the 1705 act and legislated accordingly. However, they also seem to have moderated the harshness of the law by hesitating to find people of African descent guilty of the crimes for which they stood trial. In 1721, Samuel and the other justices of the province's Superior Court of Judicature decided that John Humphers, a "Free Negro man," was innocent of "wickedly Committ[ing] Fornication with an English Woman against the . . . Law." The case had landed in the high court because the woman in question, Jemima Colefix of Boston, was married. Jemima's "Molatto" baby was proof therefore not just of illicit interracial sex but also of adultery, which was a capital crime. After a "full hearing of the Case," however, the jury summarily discharged John.[54] In another case adjudicating interracial adultery, the Superior Court of Judicature declined to prosecute the individuals involved, declaring the evidence insufficient to support a verdict. A white woman named Mary Cuthbert, wife of a tailor from southeastern Massachusetts, faced the charge of adultery. She had given birth to a mixed-race child fathered by an African man named Jeffery, who was enslaved by her mother. When the jury returned "ignoramus," the parties in the convoluted family crisis were discharged.[55]

The court cited lack of evidence on still other occasions, allowing sexual offenders who crossed racial bounds to go free. In 1713, for example, a white servant named Ann Staples was "found in Bed" with an enslaved Black man named Alexander. But the jury declined to convict the defendants because there was "not sufficient evidence" of fornication.[56] In yet another instance, a "Single Woman Servant" named Ann Hardgrove accused an enslaved man named Chester of fathering her mixed-race child. The year was 1707, and Chester, perhaps afraid of the consequences of the 1705 legislation, had "absconded" when Ann went to court. The jury ordered Ann to be "severely Whipped Twenty Stripes" and to serve her master, a Boston cordwainer named Savil Simpson, for an additional two years beyond her original term.[57] But when Chester was hauled before the bar the following year to answer Ann's accusation, the jury apparently could not find evidence suitable to convict the man of fornication. Chester was declared not guilty.[58]

*   *   *

People of African descent managed from time to time to evade the consequences of their interracial sex, but it is clear that liaisons across racial lines ran against the tide of popular opinion in Massachusetts by the eighteenth century. Such relationships certainly countered the visions held by elite lawmakers of an orderly society. The legislators who passed the 1705 act clearly wished to stop families such as Thomas and Lydia's from proliferating in the region. The act, after all, explicitly outlawed marriages such as theirs. And evidence suggests that the Bedunahs were viewed with suspicion by at least some ordinary people in the early years of the eighteenth century. This is apparent in court records from the fall of 1707, when witnesses reported that a woman named Margaret Lattimore ought to be brought before the bar to answer for fornication. Margaret, they reported, had given birth out of wedlock at the home of a Frenchman named Lacorne, who lived in Cambridge. Now, apparently, Margaret was in Roxbury: "'tis said" the witnesses reported, that she "is at Nurse at the house of Tom a Negro that Married an English Woman."[59]

This brief and indirect reference to the Bedunahs provides several clues to the nature of the family's relationship with its broader community. It shows that Thomas and Lydia were associated with behavior that many Massachusetts residents considered questionable: harboring a sexual offender in their home. And it indicates that accounts of their apparent complicity in Margaret's transgression circulated widely. The witnesses who brought the report to court, after all, were Bostonians rather than the Bedunahs' Roxbury neighbors, and they reported not on what they had observed firsthand but rather on what others had "said" to them. The statement also reveals that people in the region considered the Bedunahs' interracial marriage extraordinarily unusual. In their testimony in court, the witnesses relied on that union to identify the couple: Margaret was nursed at the home of "Tom a Negro that Married an English Woman." Tom, or Thomas, was a common name, so nobody would have known which household was caring for Margaret without the witnesses' references to the racial identities and marital status of Thomas and Lydia. Of course, the witnesses who reported to court could have chosen to identify the couple by using their surname. There were no other Bedunahs in the region, so that would effectively have singled out the family responsible for housing Margaret. But they chose not to, and that choice is significant. By reducing Thomas Bedunah to "Tom" and by failing to name Lydia altogether, the rumors that circulated through Boston reveal a lack of respect for the couple. Even the Frenchman who harbored Margaret at the time of her childbirth was identified in reports by his last name, but Thomas was identified by *what* he was—"a Negro that Married an English Woman"—rather than *who* he was.

Yet Thomas and Lydia's racial differences, which appear to have loomed large to these purveyors of gossip in Boston, seemed to trouble the Roxbury community very little as the years passed. Thomas's status as a "Negro" did not, apparently, define his relationships with his neighbors or circumscribe his children's life chances. Records kept by the town clerk show that the family grew rapidly during the two decades following Thomas and Lydia's marriage. After Elizabeth was born in 1703 and Benjamin in 1705, Joseph arrived in 1708. Then, in 1711, came Abigail. And Lydia in 1715, Ebenezer in 1719, and Moses in 1722.[60] The sources that provide evidence of the family's growth give no inkling that there was anything unusual about the family. They do not indicate that it failed to conform to the racial norms of the Anglo-American families around it. They do not reveal that it was headed by an African man. They record nothing whatsoever about the Bedunah children's race or color.

Perhaps the families in Thomas's neighborhood simply began to accept the Bedunahs as one of themselves. Thomas worked hard, after all, to support his wife and seven children. He accrued through his labor enough money to purchase a home and outbuildings in 1714, and in 1727 he expanded his holdings significantly, buying five acres of adjoining land from one of Lydia's kinsmen. Part of this land, Thomas plowed to plant crops to feed his family—corn, wheat, and an array of vegetables, no doubt—and the rest he reserved for pasture to feed his swine and small herd of cattle. On the two acres adjacent to his home and barn he cultivated an orchard, and when the apples swelled red and ripe each fall, he sold cider to people near and far.[61] The man did well for himself. He owned a cart with which to transport barrels of cider or surplus produce to market. He possessed an assortment of pans, kettles, skillets, and other cookware, which Lydia used to prepare meals for the family. He acquired a collection of furniture, allowing the Bedunah children to sleep each night in real wooden beds rather than on the crude pads that their less fortunate neighbors rolled out on the floor each evening.[62] And Thomas owned more than land, farming instruments, and household goods: He also owned *books*. Was Thomas literate? The fragmented historical record makes it difficult to answer this question. If Thomas wrote a will, it was lost prior to his death. If he penned letters to family members or petitioned the Roxbury church for prayer, these slivers of the past have long since vanished. But a receipt adrift in the papers collected by the Suffolk County Court of Common Pleas indicates that Thomas had, at a minimum, a rudimentary capacity to read and write. It shows as well that Thomas had at least a basic understanding of numeracy and accounting—skills that would have enabled him to navigate the credit-based economy. And, of course, we know from Thomas's inventory that he kept in his home, and likely encouraged his children to read, what the appraisers of his estate recorded with maddeningly little detail: "Books."[63]

Thomas's 1733 inventory reveals impressive economic success. The man had acquired the trappings of a middling New England farmer. According to those who called themselves his "near neighbours" and claimed they were "well acquainted" with his "Real Estate," Thomas was a "husbandman."[64] He owned the land he cultivated, and he produced, through the fruit of his labor, enough to support his family. Husbandmen stood beneath yeomen on the social ladder, but they garnered more respect, and had significantly greater access to material resources, than the common laborers who thronged the streets of Boston and its neighboring towns. Thomas's status as a husbandman was sure; records filed in Suffolk County's probate court refer to him that way not once in passing but ten times in ten different documents. Yet these ten documents, which so clearly spell out Thomas's occupation and rank in the community, say nothing about the man's racial status.[65]

This is surprising. Record keepers in this time regularly referenced Black people—even free Black people—using racialized language. They did this in all types of documents: court, church, town, print, and private records. People of African descent were "negro laborers," "negro servants," "negro slaves." They were "negro men," "negro fellows," "negro boys"; "negro women," "negro wenches," "negro girls." The label haunted them from first breath: "negro infants." And it followed them to the end of life: "old negroes." During Thomas's life, racialized language clung to people of African descent like a shadow in the region's historical record. And racialized language was used to identify other non-white people as well: Terms such as "Indian," "mulatto," and "Black" proliferate in the archive. For those of European ancestry, however, the conventions were very different. Euro-Americans alone had the dignity of avoiding racial categorization in the records; people of African or Indigenous ancestry were so identified as a matter of course, but people of European descent were racialized only in the very rare instance in which a record keeper wished to make a point of their white status.

Therefore, the lack of racial identifiers with respect to Thomas is redolent with meaning. By consistently declining to racialize Thomas explicitly as Black, the men who oversaw the division of Thomas's estate among his children were implicitly racializing Thomas as white: They were according to Thomas the standing of a white man. This fits a broader pattern—a pattern that becomes clear when one steps back and takes into account the entire body of evidence related to Thomas's racial status. The records indicate that those who personally knew the man came to accept him, for all intents and purposes, as being white and entitled to the privileges of whiteness. These people also recognized Thomas as a self-supporting landowner, calling him a "husbandman" or even, in a couple of instances, a "yeoman."[66] Strangers, by contrast, spoke about Thomas in a markedly different way. People outside Thomas's community—those with whom Thomas did not worship or socialize or transact business—racialized the man as Black. And such outsiders produced more cynical assessments of Thomas's occupational standing than those who knew him. They demeaned Thomas as a laborer, overlooking entirely his status as a landowner.

The records filed in probate court display starkly the distinction between the perception of Thomas's community and that of strangers looking in from the outside. The ten documents submitted by Thomas's neighbors to the probate court—the documents that referred to Thomas as a husbandman—did not racialize the man. Nor did an additional document filed in the court, which was also written by members of the Roxbury community; this document referred to Thomas simply as Lydia's "Deceased Husband."[67] Compare this body of evidence with the two documents generated by the court to initiate the probate process following Thomas's death. An administrative bond and a letter, these boilerplate pieces were produced by the register of probate, a Bostonian named John Boydell. In these documents, John called Thomas a carter rather than a husbandman, failing to acknowledge the reality that the man had accumulated enough property to support his family through farming. John racialized Thomas as well, and abbreviated his name, referring to the man time and again as "Black Tom Bedune." But this language did not last. As soon as Lydia and her Roxbury neighbors began to submit documents to the court describing Thomas as "Thomas Bedunah," calling him a "husbandman," and declining to racialize the man explicitly, the probate court's language shifted accordingly, and it dropped the racial descriptors entirely.[68]

Town records, deeds, and the papers produced by other courts reinforce the pattern evident in probate records. These sources indicate that those who lived outside of Roxbury and did not know Thomas personally sometimes racialized the man as Black. Recall that Thomas was labeled a "Negro" when he was hauled to Boston with Lydia to answer to fornication charges. Recall as well that Thomas was referred to as "Tom a Negro that Married an English Woman" when Boston gossips discussed the support he was providing to the mother charged with fornication.[69] But people acquainted with Thomas spoke not as the Boston rumormongers nor as the remote keepers of the court; those who knew Thomas personally racialized him as white and conferred upon him the status of a self-supporting landowner. To Roxbury's farmers, Thomas was a husbandman, a neighbor, a hard-working household head married to an English woman, just as they were. And Roxbury's farmers were not the only people to take little notice of the man's African heritage. Others in Thomas's community did so as well. A slew of documents mentions Thomas during the last twenty-five years of his life: The man surfaces in town records, civil court records (he sued a neighbor for non-payment of debt), the county's registry of deeds, and probate records. But not one record maker in Thomas's community—and not one of the people with whom he did business—described the man as a "Negro." He was, simply, "Thomas Bedona of Roxbury in the County of Suffolk[,] Husbandman."[70] The man's status as a propertied member of Roxbury's community; as the husband of an English woman; and as a self-sufficient, tax-paying citizen who contributed to the public good seems to have trumped his status as an African. Rank and family appear, for Thomas, to have made race.[71]

* * *

Given that Thomas appears to have been accorded the privileges of whiteness by his neighbors, it is hardly surprising that his children were discussed in the historical record as if they were white as well. The Bedunah children were not racialized in any of the documents related to the settlement of Thomas's estate. Benjamin, the oldest, was referred to alternately as a "Labourer" and a "Husbandman," while Ebenezer was described as a "minor . . . son of Thomas Beduna, late of Roxbury in the County of Suffolk[,] Husbandman."[72] Moses, the youngest son, was described identically. The other children were simply named, with no racial descriptors attached: Joseph Beduna, Elizabeth Bilboa, Abigail Robinson, Lydia Beduna. Nobody called the Bedunah children "Molattoes," nor were they "Negroes," nor "Blacks." In surviving documents, Thomas's heirs are altogether indistinguishable from their white neighbors.

Perhaps their father would have been pleased that his community made so little of his children's African ancestry. He had done what he could to make them more Anglo-American, after all, first by marrying a woman of English descent and then by making sure to give them—every one of them—English names. The patriarch might have passed on to his children his African-derived surname, but there were no Bedunahs named Juba, Quaco, or Cuffy. Instead, Thomas chose Elizabeth, Benjamin, Joseph, Abigail, Lydia, Ebenezer, and Moses. What is more, these were not just any English names. They were names that repeated themselves over and over in the Crafts family. Thomas named his children for his wife's kin.

Besides baby Lydia, whom Thomas clearly named for his wife, all of the names that Thomas chose for his children were the names of Lydia's family members. Thomas's naming practices suggest a desire for inclusion in Lydia's extended family—and they imply as well that both Thomas and the marriage were accepted by Lydia's kin. Over the course of two decades of naming children, Thomas used almost exclusively the pool of names that Lydia's uncle, Samuel Crafts, had used for his own children: *Elizabeth, Benjamin, Joseph, Abigail, Ebenezer.*[73] These names were repeated elsewhere in the family, as well. Elizabeth, for example, was the name of Lydia's aunt and two of Lydia's cousins by marriage as well as the name of two of Lydia's nieces.[74] It was also the name that Lydia's cousin, Ebenezer, chose for *his* daughter, whose birth came the year before that of Thomas and Lydia's Elizabeth.[75] Joseph was the name of Lydia's half-brother, the name of her uncle by marriage, and the name of yet another cousin.[76] And Abigail was the name not only of Lydia's aunt and Lydia's sister but also four of Lydia's cousins: Indeed, with the exception of Lydia's childless aunt, all of the children of Lydia's paternal grandfather bore an Abigail.[77] As for Thomas and Lydia Bedunah's final child, Moses, born nineteen years after his parents walked through the snow to Samuel Sewall's home, he appears to have been named for Lydia's uncle and for the man's two sons, both of whom died young.[78] Altogether, in the three generations tracing their lineage to Lydia's paternal grandfather, close to fifty of Lydia's relatives had the names that Thomas chose for his offspring. Thomas's children might have been the only Bedunahs in the province, but their father made sure to signal that they nonetheless were embedded within a rich network of kin.

Thomas's embrace of the Crafts family, so evident in the naming of his children, appears to have been reciprocated. A sense of mutual obligation bound Lydia's extended family to her children; Lydia's relatives cared for their Bedunah family members in times of need much as they would have supported white family members in duress. This can be seen plainly in the aftermath of Thomas's death, when Lydia's kin played important roles in helping to manage her affairs. Three men drew up the inventory of Thomas's estate, all of whom were Lydia's relatives: James Shed (or Shield), Edward Ruggles, and Joseph Ruggles. James Shed was Lydia's relation through marriage; he had wed the widow of Lydia's cousin, Samuel Crafts.[79] And Joseph and Edward Ruggles came from a family that had been intimately connected with the Crafts family for generations.[80]

James Shed, Edward Ruggles, and Joseph Ruggles did not just assess Thomas's estate for the probate court. They also determined that Thomas's property holdings were not large enough to be divided effectively among his seven heirs, and they worked out an arrangement, typical in the era, that would allow Thomas's oldest son, Benjamin, to inherit the land and homestead intact, provided he pay each of his six siblings a sum equal to their share of the real estate. Then Edward Ruggles and another relative, Joseph Williams, put themselves and their financial welfare on the line for the Bedunah family. Alongside Benjamin, the two men signed a bond promising to pay the judge of probate a combined total of 524 pounds should Benjamin fail to fulfill his obligation to pay his siblings the agreed-upon shares. And there was more. Edward Ruggles, working with his brother, John, helped Lydia and Benjamin come to an agreement as to which part of Thomas's estate would remain accessible to Lydia while she was a widow and which part of the estate would pass immediately to her oldest son.[81]

Lydia's male relatives did not abandon the Bedunahs once they had ensured that the value of Thomas's holdings would be divided fairly among his children and that his widow would be cared for adequately until her death or remarriage. More work remained to be done. Two of Thomas's children were underage, and they needed guardians to protect, provide for, and educate them. James Shed and John Ruggles agreed to take on this responsibility. Each had to post bond to ensure that they would be faithful in discharging their duties as guardian, and each needed to obtain two others to post bond on their behalf. For this task, they recruited other members of the Crafts-Ruggles family. In all, six Roxbury men were involved in the settling of Thomas's estate and the adoption of his minor children.[82] All six were Lydia's relatives. The woman might have married outside her Anglo-American kinship networks in Roxbury, but the union resulted in her family integrating Thomas rather than rejecting Lydia. Nor did Lydia's family shun her offspring of mixed English and African ancestry. Indeed, by the time of Thomas's death, Lydia's kin seem to have regarded the man as white—or at least considered him entitled to the privileges of whiteness. And as Lydia's children and their descendants intermarried with their white neighbors in the decades to come, Roxbury's farmers appear to have cared less and less that the family's patriarch had been an African.

*　*　*

Thomas and Lydia's son Joseph left more evidence in the historical record than any of his brothers or sisters, even though, as the second son, he received no land from his father. According to the agreement Lydia's kin helped work out in the aftermath of Thomas's death, the real estate went to Benjamin, the oldest. Hence, Joseph was a laborer rather than a husbandman: He toiled for his neighbors when they had need, rather than laboring for himself on his own soil. It was not an easy life. Fragments of evidence indicate that the man worked hard for uncertain reward. Neighbors, even those who might have been well-meaning, could be unreliable employers. In 1739, Joseph sued Hezekiah Turner, a Roxbury miller and member of the First Church, which Joseph had attended since he was a child. As Joseph explained to the court, Hezekiah had asked Joseph to work for him, promising to pay Joseph "as much as he should reasonably Deserve" for his labor. Joseph consequently helped Hezekiah for more than a year, but he received only paltry compensation in return. He deserved fifty pounds, he claimed, but the salary Hezekiah had paid him barely exceeded twenty-six pounds. The case went to the province's superior court, where Joseph won the balance he claimed. But this accomplished little, as Hezekiah apparently had not the money, the goods, or the real estate with which to pay. The Roxbury miller was jailed, and Joseph lost months of wages.[83]

While Joseph eked out a living laboring for his Roxbury neighbors, he also built a family. In May of 1747, he married a white woman named Mary Ducee in Boston's King's Chapel.[84] Though they wed in an Anglican church in Boston, Joseph neither moved to the port city nor changed his church affiliation. Instead, he brought Mary home to Roxbury, where together they attended the local meetinghouse. For four decades, Joseph had worshipped at the Roxbury church, but he had never completed the requirements to join the congregation; he had always remained outside the circle of saints who affirmed the congregation's beliefs and made professions of faith. Finally, though, just after he passed his fortieth birthday, the man formalized his commitment to both the congregation and the Christian faith. "Joseph Bodoono," the Reverend Nehemiah Walter wrote in the congregation's annals on November 11, 1748, had "owned the covenant," consenting to live according to the faith community's agreed-upon beliefs and practices.[85]

There was good reason for Joseph's decision to affirm the terms of the covenant that governed the church he had attended for the past forty years: His family life demanded it. Mary was at this point very pregnant with the couple's first child, and Joseph would have known that infants in the congregational churches of Massachusetts could be baptized only if one of their parents could endorse the church's covenant and agree to submit to its authority. Joseph took this spiritual step, then, so that his children could be covenanted to the church through baptism, so that they, too, could belong to the community. It was a common strategy for families in New England churches.[86] In fact, Joseph's brother, Ebenezer, had done precisely the same thing three years before, owning the covenant in the Roxbury church less than three weeks before the birth of his first child, a son named Benjamin.[87]

Joseph's wife, Mary, gave birth to their daughter, Lydia, just a week after Joseph owned the covenant.[88] Curiously, there is no indication in the church's records that baby Lydia was baptized. Perhaps the minister forgot to note the event. Or perhaps, for whatever reason, Lydia was not baptized after all. Regardless, less than two years later, Joseph and Mary's second child was baptized. The couple seems to have gone to great lengths to ensure that little Mary's baptism took place. According to the church's book of records: "Mary, [the] daughter of [Joseph] Beduna ... [was] baptised by ye Rev[eren]d Mr. Walter at his own house, during his confinement before his death."[89] Joseph and Mary took the infant to the home of their dying minister. They brought her to the man who had long ago received Joseph's mother into the congregation, to the man who had watched Joseph grow up in the First Church pews, to the man who had preached for decades to the African patriarch, his English wife, and his mixed-race offspring.[90] And, as one of his final acts of ministry, the ailing pastor initiated Mary Bedunah into Roxbury's community of believers.

Little Mary was born to a man who was half African and a woman of European ancestry. She was therefore one-quarter African. However, no records indicate that anyone ever considered her a person of African ancestry. Apparently, her sister was never perceived as African-descended, either. And consider the case of their half-African father. Joseph was not explicitly racialized in his legal squabble with the miller Hezekiah Turner; he was referred to simply as "Joseph Bedunah of Roxbury in the County of Suffolk[,] Labourer."[91] Nor did his marriage record indicate that he was a person of African descent, as marriage records at the time often did. Likewise, when he received a bequest from his neighbor's estate, he was called simply "Joseph Bedunah" in contrast to the woman referred to as "Betty negore" in the same document.[92] And when Joseph formalized his commitment to Roxbury's First Church, Nehemiah apparently did not consider the man of African lineage. The minister was not color-blind; he described the woman listed just three names above Joseph in the church's records as a "negro," so he was certainly capable of documenting racial distinctions among the church's congregants.[93]

Nonetheless, the records logging the births and congregational commitments of Joseph's offspring implicitly racialized the man as white. Just as the Roxbury community apparently regarded Joseph's father, Thomas, as a white man, it seemed to accept Joseph as white as well.

Joseph, after all, lived quite like a white man. He married a white woman. He was received by the church. His children, apparently, were considered white as well; at least, no surviving records indicate that they were regarded as anything else. And, though he stood a step down from where his father had stood on the economic hierarchy of the town, Joseph apparently possessed civil rights that eluded most Black people in New England. Neighbors and coreligionists in the Roxbury church called the man a "Constant Voter."[94] As a free man with personal property, Joseph evidently frequented the polls with his white neighbors, using his ballot to elect the leadership of both Roxbury and the province more broadly.[95] In a small but powerful way, Joseph played a part in molding the legislation that governed his life and shaped his family's prospects.

Being white brought untold advantages in eighteenth-century Roxbury. However, it came with one responsibility that Joseph was not eager to accept: military service. From the early decades of the Bay Colony's history, Black and white people in Massachusetts had played divergent roles in the local militia. Beginning in 1656, legislation prohibited people of African and Indigenous ancestry from training with the military.[96] Curiously, though prohibited from *training*, they were not prohibited from *serving*; people of African descent can be found on regimental lists from the seventeenth century on.[97] But men of African and Indigenous ancestry do not seem to have been obligated by law to fight, as white men were.[98] Joseph's racial status, then, had the power to determine his military responsibilities. If Joseph was a white man, he could have been conscripted to serve in the militia in normal wartime circumstances, while if he was a man of African descent he could not have been obliged to serve; he would instead have had the *option* of serving in the military if he so chose.

Joseph did serve willingly, for a time. He belonged to Roxbury's infantry regiment in 1747, when Francis Brinley, the wealthy Roxbury farmer appointed colonel of the regiment, was ordered to impress four "able Body'd men" from his troop to "goe Easte in Service."[99] The New England colonies were immersed at the time in King George's War, a conflict between the British and the French that played out on American soil, and, as summer turned to fall, they were assembling troops to counter the French threat in Canada.

William Shirley, the governor of Massachusetts, had just directed New England forces to Nova Scotia, where an enormous French fleet was purportedly heading.[100] And Francis, the Roxbury colonel, ordered Joseph to join the effort. Joseph was, after all, on the "List" of the regiment, and Francis had been instructed to impress out of that regiment men for the mission. Perhaps Joseph's low economic status, combined with his liminal racial identity, made him seem vulnerable—a likely candidate for impressment. But Joseph would not go.

Why? At that moment, in September of 1747, Joseph's family life had just begun to blossom. He had wed Mary only four months before. Now was not the time to combat the French in Nova Scotia, and Joseph wished to recuse himself from the expedition. It was well within his rights to do so; as a man of African descent, he was required by law to report for duty to his local military company only "in case of alarm." This was no urgent threat, no local emergency: Francis simply needed to drum up four participants for a distant offensive. Joseph therefore ought to have been excused from involvement altogether. Even if this *had* been a "case of alarm," though—if Joseph had refused to bear arms in the face of invasion—the man of African ancestry could by law have been levied a fine of only twenty shillings or eight days' labor.[101] But Joseph was not treated according to the laws governing "Negroes" and "Molattoes." He was fined ten times that much: ten pounds, which was the sum of money that white men in the province were forced to pay if they evaded impressment.[102] It was a large figure for the Roxbury laborer, and the man must have been livid at having to make the outlay. But Joseph calculated that staying was worth the cost. He handed over the requisite funds, and he remained in Roxbury with his wife while others fought. Then he sued Francis for attempting to impress him.

The surviving evidence related to Joseph's suit indicates that Joseph's racial status was the point on which the case pivoted. If Joseph was an Anglo-American citizen, Francis's actions were legal, but if Joseph was a man of African descent, Francis's actions were criminal. So Thomas's mixed-race son was in the unusual position of trying to convince white judges and a white jury that his white neighbor had wronged him by treating him as he would a white man. Joseph was not white, he insisted; he was of African descent, and to prove his point he presented evidence to the court showing that he had, in the past, been subject to regulations governing Black people in the province— regulations that, according to the law, should have excused him from marching with the Roxbury regiment.

Joseph's evidence of his African heritage came from Roxbury's town selectmen. They certified that "for more than Seven Years Past" they had "from
time to time Ordered Joseph Bedunah and Every other free Negro or Molatto man able of Body Dwelling within the said Town" to work four days
annually at road repair.[103] This was, for these Black men, "an Equivalent for
Trainings." The document was clearly written with Joseph in mind, as it references him by name but does not mention any of Roxbury's other men of
African ancestry. And it confirmed two things that would have been very
helpful for Joseph as he sought to prove that Francis had wrongly impressed
him: first, Joseph belonged to the category of "free Negro or Molatto man,"
and, second, Joseph had served his town by maintaining its roads *in lieu of*
obligatory military training since before King George's War began in 1744.
All free Black and mixed-race men in the province were required to perform
hard labor in place of drilling with the local militia. Black men repaired highways, cleaned streets, or did "other service" for the towns in which they
lived while white men cocked their muskets on the local training fields.[104] By
obtaining this document from Roxbury's selectmen, then, Joseph was gathering evidence that he was, in fact, a man of African ancestry, and that he
had been faithfully performing the duties that the legislature had assigned
men of his station.[105]

Francis, meanwhile, sought to show that Joseph in fact played the role of
a white man in his community, even if his complexion was somewhat darker
than those of his neighbors. He admitted that Joseph was a "Mollatto," but
quickly added that he was a "freeman," he was a "Voter in s[ai]d Town of Roxbury," he was "on [th]e List in s[ai]d Regim[en]t," and he was "a Man Married to a White Woman." In Francis's view, Joseph assumed the position—and
the responsibilities—of a white man by obtaining free status and by doing
things Anglo-Americans did, such as voting, participating in military
activities, and, perhaps especially, marrying white women. It is worth remembering here that the 1705 prohibition of Black-white unions in the
province, which followed on the heels of the marriage of Joseph's parents,
expressly prohibited those of mixed African-European heritage from marrying white people. Therefore, the fact that Joseph was "a Man Married to
a White Woman" indicated that his community—the people who heard the
public announcement of his impending marriage, the minister who performed the nuptials, those who attended the wedding festivities—all saw
Joseph as sufficiently white to wed a white woman. Francis made his case
powerfully: Joseph had free status like white people; he played a civic role in

his town by voting like white folks; he contributed to the local militia by volunteering for military service like other white men; and he acted like a white man when it came to building a family, by marrying a white woman. The way Joseph lived and the people with whom he associated had led Roxbury residents to reassess the man's racial status. Local men had begun to consider him neither a Black man nor even, really, a mixed-race one, but instead a white man like themselves.

With Joseph insisting that he was a man of African descent, subject to the requirements of Black and mixed-race people, and his adversary maintaining that he played the role of a white man in his Roxbury community, the lawsuit went all the way to the province's Superior Court of Judicature. Finally, nearly two years after Francis had ordered Joseph east, the mixed-race laborer won his case in a Boston courtroom. As a person of African descent, he had been wrongfully impressed into military service by the colonel of the Roxbury regiment.[106] Curiously, though, while the outcome of the suit hinged on Joseph's ability to prove his non-white status, the language used by the court's clerk did not racialize the Roxbury laborer as one might expect: He was merely "Joseph Bedunah of Roxbury in our County of Suffolk[,] Labourer." The second son of an African man, Joseph teetered on the brink of whiteness.[107]

* * *

The Bedunahs were not the only residents of the province who approached whiteness through interracial liaisons. Occasional evidence suggests that the offspring of Black-white relationships in eighteenth-century Massachusetts could slip from the category of mixed-race to the category of white. In 1716, for instance, an enslaved woman gave birth to two children out of wedlock, claiming that an Anglo-American man fathered them. The "negro" woman's children were apparently half African and half English. But the court did not describe them as mixed-race. No: The children were "white."[108]

Likewise, in various instances, Massachusetts courts chose not to prosecute people of mixed African-European ancestry who formed sexual liaisons with white people, even though the 1705 legislation prohibited such liaisons between white people and all people of African descent—both "negroes" *and* "molattoes."[109] For instance, when Elinor Waters, a "molatto" woman, confessed to fornication with an "English man" named John Perkins in 1707, she was given the punishment reserved for white people who fornicated with other white people: ten stripes at the whipping post. The court did not even record a punishment for John.[110] According to the law, Elinor should have been sold out of the province, and John should have been "severely whip'd" and fined five pounds. But Elinor's racial background—already mixed—seems to have made her relationship with a white man less troubling to the justices. She was, according to their verdict, white rather than "molatto."

The court made an exception to the law in another instance while adjudicating a case involving a liaison between a mixed-race person and a partner of European descent. In 1724, Samuel Miles, Boston's clerk and the pastor of one of the town's Anglican congregations, was called before the bar to answer for acting "contrary to the Peace and the Law." His crime was "marry[ing] Simon Meers (or Seers)," a man described as "Molatto," with a "Whitewoman" named Jane Osborne, and "knowing them to be so at the time of their Marriage." Though Samuel should have been subjected to a fifty-pound fine according to the stipulations of the 1705 act, the court declared that the "s[ai]d Presentment is Quashed" and permitted the minister to go on his way.[111] Apparently, mixed-race inhabitants of Massachusetts like Elinor Waters, Simon Meers, and the Bedunahs' offspring were at least sometimes considered "White" rather than "Molatto."

This occasional willingness to overlook African ancestry is surprising. Evidence suggests that Massachusetts residents were fairly consistent in their application of racial labels to those who lived in their communities through the mid-eighteenth century; that is, there was not much shifting of people from one category to another.[112] Furthermore, at the time Joseph's father, Thomas, had married his mother, Lydia, free Black people in the province formed a social underclass that was on its way to becoming a legal underclass. After the Massachusetts General Court in 1705 singled out people of African descent as unfit to marry white people, establishing harsh penalties for those who engaged in sex across the color line, it moved to hedge in and separate Black people from their neighbors still further. Free able-bodied "negro or mollato" men were required to maintain the roadways of the towns in which they lived.[113] New legislation also restricted the social interaction of both free and enslaved Black people; any free person of African descent who invited an enslaved person into his or her home without consent of the enslaver would be fined. In addition, Black people in the province faced special penalties for "smit[ing] or strik[ing]" white residents; they were punished more harshly than either Indigenous people or Anglo-Americans who perpetrated the same violence.[114] And Black inhabitants of nearby Boston—which is where a significant proportion of the province's Black population lived—encountered special discrimination. In the aftermath of an alleged "negro plot" to burn the town in 1723, Boston's selectmen passed a series of provisions to "Better Regulat[e]" non-white people, which banned their weapons, restricted their ability to sell food and drink, prohibited them from receiving goods of any kind from enslaved people, regulated their funerary practices, forbade them from carrying canes unless they were truly "Decrepid," and denied them the ability to raise their children.[115]

Some of these legal changes hampered the lives of African-descended people in meaningful ways. For instance, we know that certain Black men sacrificed months of their working lives to maintaining Boston's roadways because, year after year, the records of their labor were submitted to the Boston selectmen. Tom Cowell worked seventy-eight days between 1708 and 1723; Joseph Jollow worked seventy-six days between 1708 and 1725; and a man who went by the name Great John worked sixty-seven days between 1708 and 1721.[116] Some of the legal changes of the early eighteenth century, however, appear not to have been enforced and therefore likely had more limited influence on the lives of the region's Black inhabitants. Take, for instance, the requirement that free non-white Bostonians bind out their children to white households. Parents who failed in this obligation were to have their children bound to masters by either the town selectmen or the overseers of the poor, and children bound this way were to serve until the age of twenty-one. The statute is stated clearly. We would be remiss, though, to assume that, as a result of this town directive, no free Black Bostonians raised their children. I have found no evidence indicating that non-white parents worked out such agreements with potential masters in eighteenth-century Boston. I have uncovered no indication that the selectmen involved themselves in the binding out of Black and Indigenous children as a result of this mandate. And not even Boston's overseers of the poor—who bound out children at a steady clip during the eighteenth century—involved themselves in this business. In a stack of more than 700 indentures put in place by the overseers between 1734 and 1780, more than 99 percent bound out white children. Just four non-white children, a set of siblings of African descent, were indentured during this time, and they appear to have been bound out not because of their race but for the same reason that white children were: Their family of origin was impoverished. These children were "poor," the documents read, and, as one indenture put it, their father was "deceased."[117]

It is important to recognize, therefore, that policies put in place by town selectmen and laws passed by province assemblies might not have been enforced. The fact that they were enacted at all, however, suggests that racial differences were becoming more and more significant to Massachusetts residents during the years Thomas and Lydia raised their children on their Roxbury farm. Black people, even those who were free, faced a barrage of discriminatory legislation in the first quarter of the eighteenth century, legislation that set them apart from their white neighbors. And the province's lawmakers did what they could to separate legally people of African descent from Anglo-Americans, thereby preventing the production of "Spurious" offspring, of "Mixt Issue." Still, the story of the Bedunahs points to ways in which the law failed to describe reality. Factors besides color and descent appear to have shaped notions of whiteness and Blackness in eighteenth-century Massachusetts. Thomas obtained his freedom and became economically self-sufficient, which set him apart from most Black people in the province, who were bound to white households and enjoyed no measure of personal wealth. But Thomas did other things as well, which seem to have encouraged his neighbors to think of him as a white household head. He married a white woman, he evidently gained the acceptance of her family, and he raised light-skinned children. To people in Thomas and Lydia's community, the couple appears to have become nearly indistinguishable from others in the region. Record keepers who knew Thomas personally never noted that Thomas was a "Negro" when they mentioned the man. In an era in which race was becoming increasingly salient to society, Thomas, through his extended family, apparently managed to transcend the line separating people of African descent from Anglo-Americans—the line that lawmakers had drawn so starkly in their legislation. Bonds of kinship could override racial limitations.[118]

If the African patriarch managed to approach whiteness through the years in the eyes of his neighbors, this was even more true of his descendants. His son, Joseph, apparently played the role of a white man in the Roxbury community. He was free, he voted in elections, he joined the local militia, he wed a white woman (which would have been illegal had he been considered of African descent), and he fathered children who were merely one-quarter African. In fact, he so resembled an Anglo-American household head that he was conscripted by local officials for a duty normally required only of white men: military service. In order to gain compensation for being wrongfully impressed into service, Joseph was obliged to go to Boston and establish his Blackness before the bar. The son of the African man had to stand before white judges and white jurymen and convince them that he was not white and therefore not liable to perform the obligations of a white man. He was, instead, a "Molatto man," and that came with its own set of obligations.

In a time in which racial exclusions were drawn increasingly starkly, first Thomas and then his son appear to have functionally moved from Black or mixed-race to white. Thomas's interracial union provides a lens through which it is possible to view the power of kin and community to shape not just social but also racial relations in eighteenth-century Massachusetts. Intermarriage with white people had the power to influence the degree to which those of African descent were considered "Negro." By exchanging vows with white women, joining white kin networks, and bearing mixed-race offspring, Thomas and his children could edge into whiteness in the eyes of their neighbors. And their descendants could meld quite easily into their broader white society if they so chose. Not one of Thomas and Lydia's grandchildren was ever characterized in the historical record as "Negro," "Black," or "Molatto."[119] Perhaps the descendants of Thomas Bedunah were a bit darker than their neighbors; Thomas's grandchild, Moses, for instance, was described variably as "dark" and "light" in complexion, as if onlookers couldn't quite decide which he was.[120] But Moses nonetheless was understood to be a man of European descent.

In 1800, a census taker stood on Moses's stoop and carefully inscribed the name "Moses Budona." Moses had been born forty-seven years before, so the man marked "1" in the column reserved for free white men of forty-five years and older.[121] He drew another "1" in the column reserved for free white women between the ages of twenty-six and forty-five, presumably for Moses's wife. And he scratched out a "2" in the column for free white boys under the age of ten. Then another "2" for free white girls the same age. Moses, a husbandman like his grandfather before him, had, also like Thomas, married a white woman. Then he had fathered four "white" children.

One wonders if the man, described by his contemporaries as brown-haired and blue-eyed, passed on to his sons and daughters the stories he had heard growing up of his African grandfather.[122]

Or whether he simply chose to forget.

CHAPTER 5

─────

Mark, Phillis, and Phoebe

Community, Kin, and Other Intimacies

> My Master let me live in *Boston* with my Wife, and go to
> work. I have most grievously provoked the great GOD to
> Anger, by repeatedly breaking his holy Day, in going out of
> his House and resorting to private Places with my wicked
> Companions in drinking and Carousing on that holy Day,
> a Time I should have improv'd in Meditation and Prayer. I
> have most sinfully abus'd and misimprov'd his manifold
> Favours to my fatal Disadvantage, and have wilfully
> neglected to work out my Salvation; all which Sins GOD
> has call'd into Remembrance, and has justly left me to the
> perpetrating this horrid Crime.
>
> —The Last & Dying Words of MARK, Aged about
> 30 Years . . . Who was Executed at Cambridge,
> the 18th of September, 1755

Holding the vial to the light, Phoebe would have seen that the powder had
sunk to the bottom. Not to worry—smooth but swift turns of the wrist
upset the layer of white, scattering a flurry of flecks throughout the water
filling the vessel. It was now ready. Phoebe reached for the chocolate pot
and lifted the lid, letting loose a heady aroma: cocoa laced with vanilla, cin-
namon, and orange peel. *He will never know.* Likely moving quickly, Phoebe
poured the white-flecked liquid into the pungent concoction. Then she returned the vial to its place in the closet, where it rested, out of sight, in a
corner behind a black jug. Finally, back in the kitchen, she frothed the mix-

ture in the pot using a wooden stirrer. The steamy mug of chocolate looked altogether ordinary when Phillis entered the room, but Phoebe told her, doubtless in a hushed whisper, that it was not so. When their enslaver, John Codman, sat down to breakfast, Phillis could not keep herself from staring. She would later remember with striking clarity the moment the man brought the poisoned beverage to his lips on that Monday morning in late June of 1755.[1]

Two days passed before Phoebe tried it again. On Wednesday, the woman slipped into the closet, reached behind the jug, and pulled out the vial once more. Giving its contents a few swirls, she emptied all that remained into John's morning chocolate. Phillis looked on, perhaps shifting her weight from one foot to the other in unease: That was a lot, all at once. Phoebe's hand was "heavy," Phillis thought. And she told her so as they stood there, alone, in the kitchen. We do not know how Phoebe responded to Phillis's concern, but Phillis would later explain, "I thought she pour'd in too much, more than she should." And: "I wasn't willing she shou'd put in so much and that he should be kill'd so quick." Nonetheless, the chocolate promptly was put at John's place, and soon the man had swallowed it down.

The vial now stood empty. To replenish it, Phoebe picked at the twine knotted around a folded white paper that held more powder, then gingerly measured in the snowy flakes using a narrow piece of iron fashioned for this purpose by Mark, her fellow bondsman. A trickle of water completed the task. Phoebe then administered another dose of the solution into John's breakfast chocolate: his third. The following morning—it was Saturday now—Phillis made gruel for breakfast, a thin porridge of oats or wheat, and into it she dribbled some of the vial's contents. Then she hesitated. As she later claimed, "I felt ugly and threw it away, and made some fresh, and did not put any into that." Phillis tried again that afternoon, doctoring John's gruel and plums with more tainted liquid, but she ended up disposing of those as well.

By this point, the enslaver was clearly unwell. He was given an "infusion," probably some healing herbs steeped in hot water, but that was poisoned, too, purportedly by Phoebe. And on Monday, a week after Phoebe first poured the white-flecked liquid into John's breakfast chocolate, his bondspeople were instructed to prepare him sago, a starch imported from the East Indies often recommended for invalids. But the concoction did John little good; as it simmered in the small iron skillet that Phillis had set upon the fire, Mark surreptitiously stirred in lead. Sitting at a little round table in the kitchen of his Charlestown home, John feasted, meal by meal, to his death.

Figure 9. Chocolate pot. This chocolate pot was made around the time of John's death by a Charlestown-born silversmith who may well have known the people enslaved on the Codman estate. It is probably more ornate than the one Phoebe used to prepare John's breakfast chocolate, but it no doubt shares the basic form. Phoebe would have removed the finial on the top of the cover in order to froth the chocolate with a wooden stirrer. Courtesy of Historic Deerfield.

What drove Phoebe, Phillis, and Mark to murder? The testimonies re-corded in the court and printed records of Massachusetts differ on some of the particulars, but they make one thing clear: The three sought to poison their enslaver because he violently trampled upon their intimate lives. It was Mark who appears to have hatched the plan. According to Phillis, Mark had told her and Phoebe that he "had read the Bible through, and that it was no sin to kill him if they did not lay violent Hands on him so as to shed Blood." And it was Mark who initiated the execution of the plan, procuring poison from bondspeople in Boston not once but on three separate occa-sions. The sources that survive suggest that Mark was driven to desperation by John's constant attacks on his familial and community relationships. Mark's cherished connections differ in certain respects from those investi-gated thus far. Not one of Mark's relationships adhered to Anglo-American family norms: No liaisons were sanctioned by justices of the peace, no chil-dren were claimed before congregations, no notices were sent to town clerks. As a result, not a single archival trace of these intimate ties would exist today had Mark not committed his deadly deed. But the words put to paper as the result of John's death allow us to make out the contours of Mark's bonds of affection.[2]

Mark had, to begin with, a nuclear family. He maintained a relationship with a Boston woman whom he called his "wife"—though he appears never to have formalized this relationship—and he parented a child, likely with this woman. Anglo-Americans would have discussed this family using terms such as fornication or bastardy, but, from Mark's perspective, no matter; these in-formal relationships were life-giving. And Mark placed himself in a second circle of belonging sanctioned by neither church nor state. He associated with a rowdy group of Black folks who took to the streets and made merry in tav-erns after dark. This community, which was based in Boston, enabled the enslaved to socialize with friends under conditions of their choosing, away from the oversight of their enslavers and the watch of the province's order keepers. Finally, archival fragments suggest that Mark valued a third form of belonging. Mark, Phoebe, Phillis, and the other people bound by John in Charlestown were, in some sense, a family unto themselves. They slept together and ate together, they shared dreams and frustrations, they pooled resources, they provided one another with medical care, and they sought to protect each other from harm. All of these networks of meaning sustained Mark, from the unsanctioned nuclear family, to the kinship of the streets, to the intimacy born of shared experiences in a slaveholding household. And John put each of these communities at risk.

The extraordinary means to which Mark, Phoebe, and Phillis resorted were unusual in early New England, where the enslaved rarely physically harmed those who claimed ownership of them. In fact, John's bondspeople would be the only ones convicted of murdering their enslaver in Massachusetts during the entire eighteenth century.[3] However, aspects of the grievances motivating the trio's desperate violence were widespread. Other enslaved people—including, for that matter, Phoebe and Phillis—built circles of connection similar to Mark's, whether they pursued unsanctioned sexual relationships, raised out-of-wedlock children, cultivated cross-town friendships, caroused with underground drinking partners, or cared for fellow sufferers in the homes of their enslavers. And other enslavers cut off such connections, circumscribing the intimate lives of the bondspeople in their households. They did not necessarily do so with a brutality and malevolence that matched John's, but the harm they inflicted was nonetheless profound.

In this chapter, I explore Mark's spheres of belonging, and, to a lesser extent, the intimate worlds of Phoebe and Phillis. After considering clues to Mark's early life in Barbados and his forced transition to Massachusetts, I turn to the man's relentless attempt to gain proximity to his family in Boston. Mark tried to sabotage John's business by arson, he attempted to recruit a Bostonian to buy him, and he arranged to hire himself out to a master who lived in Boston. Mark's wife appears to have made attempts to access him as well. The two seem to have been committed to one another, and determined to overcome the distance that separated them, even though they had never officially married. That the situation of Phoebe and her husband was much the same serves as an important reminder: Despite the unusual embrace of province-sanctioned marriages among the enslaved in the region, most bound couples probably had informal marriages, like Mark and his wife, and Phoebe and her husband, rather than formal unions, like Jane and Sebastian. Family is a crucial component of this story, but at this point I pivot to Boston's other main draw for Mark: The town simply brimmed with possibilities for people in bondage who wished to belong. A wide array of historical records shows Black Bostonians traversing just about every inch of the port, day and night, with all sorts of companions. The social lives of the enslaved could become so robust, in fact, that enslavers and those who kept order in Boston sometimes felt it necessary to remove certain bondspeople from the town. Mark was one so removed—and it was upon his return to Charlestown that he began plotting to kill John. Murdering his enslaver, he hoped, would provide him proximity to both his family and his community on the streets. And it would do something else as well: It would protect Phillis and Phoebe. Here we turn to the sexual abuse of women in New England's slaveholding households and, finally, to the protective, kin-like connections forged by Mark, Phillis, Phoebe, and the other bondspeople enslaved by John. Imperiled by John's life, these intimacies, in the end, would be destroyed by the man's death.

*   *   *

Mark was separated from his birth family at a young age. The narrative he gave in prison while awaiting execution began thus: "I was Born in *Barbados* some-time in the Year 1725, in a reputable family." But, Mark continued, "leaving my native Place very Young, [I] came to *Boston*." The narration opens by positioning Mark as a free actor moving through the Atlantic: He was born in an upstanding family, he left Barbados, he came to Boston. But the tone of the piece is misleading. Being "Born . . . in a reputable family" meant merely that Mark was born to an African woman owned by white people who had grown wealthy from the commerce in sugar and slavery that drove the Atlantic system. And Mark did not set out to explore the world, and thereby choose of his own accord to leave Barbados for Boston. Rather, his "reputable" enslaver decided to sell him, apparently to a New England merchant, and that merchant brought the boy to Boston for resale.

How old was Mark when he was sent away from his "native Place," from the only world that he knew? He described himself as "very Young." But he was no toddling child. The boy was old enough to have formed memories: Bits of Barbados stayed with him in Boston. For example, when asked during his interrogation if he knew about a plan to poison John using cashew nuts, he denied knowledge of it by declaring, "I have not seen a Cushoe nut since I have been in this country."[4] And some of Mark's memories of Barbados required sophisticated reasoning, which suggests that the boy had developed the ability to analyze and interpret his surroundings before he was sold from the tiny Caribbean island. For instance, it is doubtful that Mark would have been able to make a judgment on the social standing of the family that owned him if he had been younger than seven or eight. This age makes sense in light of the market for enslaved workers in New England. Infants, toddlers, and children too young to engage in productive labor were not attractive bondspeople; they *required* toil rather than provided it. But a seven-year-old could be useful. The man who ultimately bought Mark in Boston, a merchant named Henry Caswell, no doubt wanted a boy who could stock his warehouse and run errands in the busy port.[5] Apparently Mark fit the bill.

Mark stayed with Henry in Boston for "some Time," he recalled. But then Henry sold the boy to a Boston brazier named John Salter. According to Mark's narrative, John "learn'd me to read, and educated me as tenderly as one of his own Children."[6] Before long, however, John sold Mark to Joseph Thomas, a man of rank who lived in the town of Plympton, south of Boston. Mark's confession stated that Joseph "treated me with the same Kindness that Mr. *Salter* did." But when Joseph died in 1743, he left a large estate deeply indebted, and Mark, the most valuable of his five bondspeople, was sold to John Codman, a man who was decidedly *not* kind. Mark's statement provides no happy description of the enslaver; it simply states, "Then Mr. *John Codman* of *Charlestown* bought me."[7]

Only three sentences in Mark's "*Last & Dying Words*" narrate the man's life in Massachusetts prior to taking up residence at John's Charlestown estate, but this short account points to important realities for those enslaved in the region. Bondspeople could be subjected to tremendous instability: Four people laid claim to Mark in three Massachusetts towns during a period of time spanning just over a decade.[8] And the region's enslavers differed tremendously in temperament. John Codman would become known for his harshness to his bondspeople, while Mark's confession recalled John Salter teaching him "tenderly." The account of John Salter might well have been embellished by the "subscribers" who witnessed Mark's dying words, but it contained a grain of truth: Mark was indeed literate, as he signed his testimony with his own hand and, according to Phillis's deposition in court, he had read the entire Bible.[9] The confession's authenticity is also bolstered by the fact that it described two enslavers as "kind" and remained silent on the disposition of the other two. If Mark's statement was invented wholesale by the white men who visited Mark in jail, why did it not contrast the goodness of *all* slaveholders with the depravity of their murderous bondspeople? Why not eulogize the murdered John in print by including a single sympathetic statement on his behalf?

From Henry Caswell to John Salter to Joseph Thomas to John Codman. From an enslaver given no favorable description, to two whom Mark deemed "kind," to one who was decidedly cruel. From Boston to Plympton to Charles-

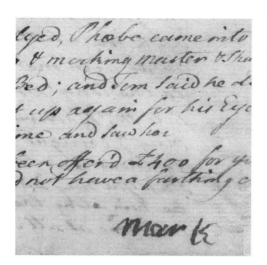

Figure 10. Mark's signature. Mark signed his examination twice, with a clear and strong hand. Courtesy of the Massachusetts State Archives.

town. At some point after Mark had navigated all these transitions, he entered into a relationship with a Boston woman he would later describe as his "wife," and he fathered a child.[10] Taken far from his own kin decades before, Mark began to rebuild fragile bonds of blood and affection. But maintaining family ties was difficult from a distance. Charlestown was separated from Boston by a body of water: the churning convergence of the Charles River, the Mystic River, and Boston Harbor. Getting back and forth could be tricky. Mark did not own a boat, so he was forced to rely on others to transport him across the channel; he had to either ride the ferry or take another vessel. This was not only inconvenient, but it was public. There was no sneaking back and forth to his relatives unnoticed. Mark's inability to connect with his kin at will appears to have angered him. The man, as Phillis put it, "wanted to get to Boston." He was so upset by the distance separating him from his family, in fact, that he told the bondsman who supplied him with poison that the plot to murder John was "about his Child."[11] The fact that Mark's predicament was extraordinarily common for enslaved fathers in the region made it no less vexing.

Mark was frustrated by a problem that shaped the family lives of most bondspeople with spouses and children in Massachusetts: the problem of proximity. Only a small fraction of enslaved people had marital partners who belonged to the same person they did. Most could not wed within their enslaver's household because the great majority of those who claimed human property owned only one or two bondspeople. The preponderance of enslaved families therefore spanned multiple Anglo-American homes. This problem was not as acute for some as it was for others. Bound laborers like Jane and Sebastian, who lived in the same neighborhood and had the advantage of enslavers, neighbors, and brethren in the church who supported their marriage, chafed less at the limitations imposed by geography than Mark, who had to take a ferry from Charlestown to Boston in order to see his family, was owned by a particularly vicious and unbending man, and appears to have had no white allies. Nonetheless, the intimate relationships of most bondspeople in eighteenth-century New England were shaped in some way by the problem of distance. The dispersal of Black people in relatively small numbers across the landscape meant that Afro-New Englanders faced challenges that differed from those faced by many of their enslaved counterparts in the British American colonies.

Mark's story provides us with a window into how one enslaved man sought to deal with the problem of a nuclear family separated by distance. In 1749, in what seems to have been his first attempt to get out of Charlestown, Mark orchestrated the burning of John's "Work House" and "Shop." Phillis, evidently, was the one who actually set the blaze—she "threw a Coal of Fire into some Shavings between the Blacksmith's Shop & the Work House"—but she claimed that the burning "was thro' Mark's means." He "gave me no rest 'till I did it," she declared.[12] Supposedly the arson was Mark's idea. "Mark first proposed it, to Phoebe and I," Phillis claimed. Why? He wished to get off the estate, "and if all was burnt down, he did not know what Master could do without selling us."

Mark's purported assessment was accurate. If he could destroy the estate's outbuildings, John would indeed be forced to sell him—unless, of course, the enslaver was able to rebuild. Mark labored in those very buildings, after all. He was a man of great skill in metalworking, a craft he likely learned when he belonged to John Salter, the brazier, his second enslaver in Massachusetts. Mark's third enslaver, Joseph Thomas, had used him as a blacksmith. And after Joseph's death, John Codman had bought Mark, a youth on the verge of manhood, for his skill in the forge. John was a chaisemaker, or one who made carriages.[13] From the Charlestown estate came a constant stream of skillfully forged handiwork: John supplied *chaises, chairs,* [and] *refined iron* to well-to-do buyers throughout the region. This was an operation in which Mark was crucial. So crucial, in fact, that the men who interrogated him following John's death referred to the blacksmith shop on the Charlestown estate not as *John's* blacksmith shop, nor as *the* blacksmith shop, but instead as *Mark's* blacksmith shop: "Had you and Phoebe any Conversation together about your master in or near your Blacksmith's Shop . . . ?"[14]

The 1749 fire inflicted serious damage. A local newspaper reported that "several Shops and other Buildings belonging to Capt. Codman were consumed," adding that a whopping forty barrels of flour had become tinder for the expanding blaze. All told, John's loss was "reckoned to be 3 or 4000 Pounds."[15] The *New-York Evening Post* picked up the story the following week, providing additional details about the blaze and putting the damages at 6,000 pounds.[16] But the fire did not achieve what Mark had hoped. John was not forced to dispose of his enslaved laborers out of financial duress. Nor did he opt to divest himself of the bondspeople who worked in his outbuildings. Apparently, he rebuilt his holdings, and the work at the Charlestown estate continued apace. Not a single enslaved laborer was sold. Nobody got to Boston.

At some point, Mark tried a new strategy: finding a buyer for himself. He seems to have recruited somebody—no doubt a Bostonian who lived close to his family—to offer John the colossal sum of 400 pounds.[17] But John turned it down. So Mark attempted another approach. If John would not sell him, perhaps he would hire him out to a person who lived closer to his family. Such arrangements were common in eighteenth-century New England. By renting their bondspeople to others or by allowing them to find work themselves, whether as a sailor at sea, a cooper in a Boston workshop, or a hand on a Roxbury farm, enslavers could profit from those who might otherwise be idle.[18] For Mark, this strategy worked. He got to go to Boston, apparently with John's blessing. According to Mark's confession, "My Master let me live in *Boston* with my Wife, and go out to work."[19]

The persistent man got his way. Burning a shop. Attempting a sale. Devising an employment arrangement. Mark was unrelenting in his attempt to get to Boston. But he was not unusual in his refusal to accept a living situation he found intolerable.[20] Other Black people in the region worked exceedingly hard to obtain proximity to their family members. The most reliable way they could ensure themselves access to their kin was by extricating them from slavery. Scipio, for instance, purchased Margaret, whom he wished to wed, so he could "Enjoy the said Margaret without any Interuption." Likewise, Titus paid twenty pounds to liberate Dinah so that he "might ffreely Live with her."[21] And consider the persistence of Lancaster Hill, who bought his children from the man who owned his wife, redeeming them, one after another, following their births. First came Mingo, but the child must have died, because two years later Lancaster purchased another infant named Mingo. Next, Lancaster liberated baby Margaret. A child named Lancaster was also born, later another Lancaster, then a child named Patience, and finally a third Lancaster.[22] It was a costly endeavor, obtaining legal title to those babies. As well as a troubling one. What if the enslaver decided *not* to sell a child at some point? Or what if his prospects turned sour and he had to sell Lancaster's wife away? From the repeated appearance of given names, it was a bleak endeavor as well, this buying of children from slavery only to watch them succumb to disease or hunger and die.

Not all Black fathers who worked to liberate their children shared Lancaster's even limited success. The case of Scipio Gunney makes this devastatingly clear. Scipio, a Boston mariner, was "moved by Humanity & parental affection" to free his daughter, Eunice, from "the Bonds of Slavery." However, he did not have enough cash on hand to purchase Eunice from her Plymouth enslaver, so he had to borrow from a middleman. A fellow Boston mariner named Estes How, "pretending to befriend" Scipio, lent him the twelve pounds he needed in order to free Eunice from obligation to her enslaver. In return, Scipio gave Estes Eunice's bill of sale for a year: This would repay the twelve pounds as well as any interest. But the results of Scipio's careful calculations were devastating. Instead of subjecting Eunice to servitude for the single agreed-upon year, Estes sold her out of the province, sending her, according to the lawsuit Scipio would file, "to parts" of the world "unknown." Scipio won fifty pounds in damages from the court, but the victory no doubt rang hollow; Eunice, who had once lived just a county away, was now lost in the Atlantic, condemned to slavery in the Caribbean, perhaps, or the southern mainland.[23] Short of an extraordinary stroke of good fortune, father and daughter were now separated for life.

Scipio's thoughtful plan might have come to naught, but it is worth noting that Black men tended to be more successful than Black women when it came to buying the freedom of their family members. Nearly all the manumissions by purchase in Massachusetts during the eighteenth century for which documentation survives were accomplished by men, not women. This reality stemmed in large part from simple economics. Men's labor was valued more highly than women's, particularly when many enslavers counted the reproductive potential of women in bondage—elsewhere so valuable—as a cost. Because of the value of men's work, fathers and husbands stood a better chance of earning enough to purchase themselves and their family members than did mothers and wives. But this should not be taken to mean that women of African descent were idle when it came to maintaining kin ties across geographic distance and, when possible, uniting families severed by the obligations of slavery. Their efforts were merely more likely to be obliterated by the centuries. Without the financial means to procure the freedom of their kin, Black women's attempts at building and sustaining their enslaved families were less likely to be preserved by the Anglo-Americans who rendered their world in written form for posterity.

One wonders about Mark's wife. Was she as determined to get to Mark as he was to her? It is impossible to know with certainty, as she is entirely invisible in the saga. Unlike Phoebe's husband, she was not called as a witness in court.[24] Indeed, despite the extensive evidence documenting her husband's crime, no eighteenth-century source so much as mentions her name. But a curious incident recorded in the court records of Suffolk County provides what may be a telling clue. In August of 1752, an enslaved woman named Cloe turned up on John's Charlestown estate. She belonged to a Boston merchant named Jacob Holyoke, who later sued John. The Charlestown "Gent[leman]," Jacob claimed, had known that Cloe belonged to him, but he had refused to return her. Instead, he "corrupted & disposed of her to his own use." In the language of the law, Jacob had "lost" Cloe, and John had "found" her.[25]

But Cloe had most certainly *not* been lost. Lawsuits over "lost" and "found" bondspeople recur in the court records of the region, and the people in question regularly knew where they were and where by law they should have been.[26] The people in these cases appear to have *chosen* to leave their enslavers in favor of another master, and the legal contest over Cloe was no doubt the same.[27] Cloe was no newcomer to the region; she had resided in Boston with Jacob for nearly ten months prior to leaving for Charlestown, and she had lived in Boston with Joseph Goldthwait, another of the port's merchants, before her purchase by Jacob. Therefore, Cloe had not ended up on John's estate because of geographic disorientation. She had decided on her own accord to go to Charlestown.

Why, we might ask, would Cloe have done this? By all accounts, John was a cruel enslaver. According to Phillis's testimony, those he bound had longed for "good masters," and John had so abused one of them, a man named Tom, that he inflicted serious damage on his eye. Even Mark's *Last & Dying Words*, which spoke warmly of some enslavers, had nothing good to say about John. By going to Charlestown, then, Cloe was willingly choosing to serve an enslaver whose bondspeople found him intolerable. She was thirty at the time she went to John's; Mark was twenty-seven.[28] And, like the woman whom Mark called his wife, Cloe hailed from Boston. Could it be that Cloe was willing to get "lost" on John's oppressive estate because she was, indeed, Mark's wife—the one he tried so hard to reach? It certainly seems plausible. The tattered evidence of that long-ago lawsuit recorded for future generations what appears to have been Cloe's own attempt at family unification.[29]

Phoebe's spouse never got "lost" in Charlestown, but he, too, sought to bridge the distance that separated him from his chosen partner. Phoebe's husband, like Mark's wife, lived in Boston. And Phoebe's marriage, again like Mark's, existed entirely beyond the purview of the state. It was not preceded by the posting of banns, nor was it brought into being by the declaration of a local official, nor was it followed by the delivery of notices to the town clerk. But the informality of the matter was of no consequence to those involved. Phoebe and her husband, Quacoe, appear to have valued their union deeply and, much like Mark and his wife, they intensely desired to live close to one another. According to Mark, Quacoe had been "contriving all he could to get her over to *Boston* to live with him."[30] To Quacoe, geographic proximity was worth more than what must have seemed to him an extravagant sum. The man had once told Mark that "he would not value *Forty Pounds*" if he could arrange for Phoebe's relocation.

The fact that neither Mark's nor Phoebe's families engaged with the Anglo-American institutions that shaped life and recordkeeping in eighteenth-century Massachusetts serves as an important caution. We must not assume that the unusual marriage culture among the enslaved in Boston, explored in Chapter 2, applied universally to people in bondage who wished for intimacy.[31] It did not. Certainly, many Black people thought it important to obtain a formal marriage, at least in part because certain white people gave more credence to province-sanctioned marriages formalized before ministers and justices of the peace than they did to unofficial unions formed independently of Anglo-American institutions. This devaluing of informal marriages is evident even in the records of the trial of John's bondspeople. When justice of the peace William Stoddard discussed Phoebe and Quacoe's relationship, he did not call Phoebe "Quacoe's wife." Instead, William referred to Phoebe as the "negro woman whom he [Quacoe] Called his Wife." Compare this to the way Mark referenced the relationship: Twice when discussing Phoebe in his *Last & Dying Words*, he called Quacoe "her Husband."[32] To Mark, the unrecognized liaison meant what any marriage did—that the two were husband and wife—but to William the arrangement worked out among bondspeople, independent of the province, had no real validity.

It is not clear if Phoebe and Quacoe wanted a formal marriage, like so many of their fellow bondspeople—the sort of union that a man like William would be more apt to recognize. Likewise, we cannot know if Mark wished to wed his wife before a minister or justice of the peace. Extant evidence does not provide answers. Perhaps Mark and his wife, perhaps Phoebe and Quacoe, preferred to negotiate their relationships away from the oversight of the Massachusetts government and local ministers. Some of their enslaved neighbors no doubt did.[33] Or maybe these people indeed wished to marry officially but were prevented from doing so by their controlling enslaver. While it is certainly possible that "lawful" marriage mattered as much to Mark and Phoebe as it did to some of their enslaved neighbors, none of the testimony preserved by the courts mentioned the bondspeople's inability to marry as a grievance underlying the plot to kill John. What was important, for Mark and Phoebe, seems to have been their ability to access their spouses, not their ability to formalize their unions.

*   *   *

It is clear that Mark and Phoebe sought proximity to their family members—and yet, at least for Mark, getting to Boston meant more than seeing his wife and child every day. Boston opened up an entire world of belonging to the man: a belonging that was often discouraged, and sometimes outright illicit, but no less meaningful on account of being, in theory, off limits to the enslaved. The disparaging way Mark's on-the-streets community was discussed by record keepers tempts those of us lured by the loudest voices of the past to find in it nothing more than crime and disorder. When the *Boston Gazette* reported John's death, it described Mark as a man "well known for his Roguery."[34] And Mark conceded, at least to some degree, to this vision. In his *Last & Dying Words*, he confessed to "resorting to private Places with my wicked Companions in drinking and Carousing" after church on Sabbath days.[35] Crime and disorder were indeed part of Mark's Boston community, but moving beyond labels such as "Roguery" and descriptors such as "wicked," and delving deep into the archive of Boston's streets and taverns allows us to see more. Bondspeople in Boston and its surrounds were constantly "out of doors," as they would have put it, and their movements on the roads, in the markets, and along the docks had relational meaning. People like Mark found

"Companions" far from their enslavers' homes, and with these companions they built durable forms of community. What was "roguery" to one Bostonian may have been sociability—even a form of kinship—to another.

Of course, much of the movement of the enslaved in and around Boston was at an enslaver's bidding. Bound people trod every inch of the town on errand. A man of African descent named August carried biscuits all over Boston for his enslaver, a baker named James Thwing. A Black printer named Peter Fleet delivered newspapers for his enslaver, John Fleet. And when Bostonian James Collison needed someone to vend his wares in the town, it was clear that a bound person would be best: James sought to purchase a "Negro Man" who "speaks plain English, and has a good Voice for Crying Things to Sell in Streets."[36] People like August, Peter, and whomever ended up selling James's goods remind us that we ought to imagine the streets of eighteenth-century Boston as filled with Black bodies and ringing with the voices of the enslaved.[37]

Record keepers, of course, rarely remarked on aspects of life so ordinary that they found them unremarkable, but the diversity of people out of doors shows up inadvertently in the archive time and again. For example, we know that an unnamed man of African descent stood up in the heart of the city to hear a proclamation that was read aloud to the beat of a drum; we learn that two Black men had a conversation on the street in Boston's North End; and we can be confident that John Cuffee walked through the port on a day in mid-June. None of these things were considered important in and of themselves to those who noted them, but unexpected turns of event made them worth reporting.[38] The man who heard the proclamation had the gall to question its veracity, one of those conversing in the North End dropped dead even as he spoke, and a cart laden with grain ran over poor John's leg. Thus, the archive was made: Incidental everyday occurrences were preserved on paper for future generations. Most glimpses of Black people out and about have long since been lost, but signs of bondspeople's presence on Boston's byways nonetheless are ubiquitous in the partial and patchy historical record that remains.

One clue to the mobility of the enslaved in the region lies in what they found around town. The surviving evidence generated by Boston's system of lost and found suggests that enslaved people were very much on the move. In the mid-eighteenth century, town crier Arthur Hill collected items found by residents and then, for a fee, he walked the streets in search of their owners. Enslaved people fill Arthur's records. Bostonians in bondage, for instance, happened upon gold buttons—over and over and over again. Folks of African descent found other luxury goods as well, like rings, silver buckles, and silk stockings. And they handed over a profusion of additional items: pocket books and beaver hats; iron bars and a handsaw; thread, cloth, sheep, wood, oars—even a whale boat. A number of enslaved folks simply turned in sums of money.[39] These finders were female as well as male. One woman in bondage stumbled upon bedding, another came across a silver spoon, and a third discovered "a Pocket Case w[i]th a Gold Earring in it."[40] Local newspapers can flesh out Arthur's records, as some Black Bostonians turned to print to advertise their around-town finds rather than relying on the town crier. One posted an advertisement describing a gold ring with a floral pattern that he had "pickt up . . . in one of the Streets in this Town." Another, who called himself an "Honest Negro," informed readers that he had discovered a "plain Gold Ring" on the Boston Common. His advertisement shows how people of African descent could profit from keeping their eyes open as they made their way around town. The finder offered to return the ring, but only after the owner gave him a "suitable Reward" and reimbursed him for placing the advertisement.[41]

Lists of lost items allow us to envision bound Bostonians stooping to pick up unexpected treasures glinting in the sun. We can also visualize Black folk in broad daylight, whether they trod Boston's alleys or hurried past its wharves, by reading the regulations passed by the town. Local officials tried continually over the course of the eighteenth century to restrict the daytime movements of enslaved Bostonians. The perceived problem was particularly acute on Sundays, when, free from toil, many bondspeople did what they wished rather than attending services at local meetinghouses. Recall that Mark "resort[ed] to private Places" with "wicked Companions" on Sabbath days. Enough bondspeople did likewise that, as early as 1712, town officials ordered eight men to guard the road connecting Boston to its hinterland.[42] These men were to "restraine" passersby from "Idle walking, or unnecessary Travel." Repeated over and over throughout the decades to come, this regulation was enacted annually by the selectmen toward the middle of the century, around the time Mark would have been in town.[43] And Sabbath movements were not the only concern. To prevent funerals from facilitating prolonged assemblies of the enslaved, town selectmen ordered that non-white people who died in Boston were to be carried "the nearest way to their Graves." Bondspeople were prohibited from raising hogs in part because it gave them "an opportunity of Meeting and conferring together." And the enslaved, along with servants and youths, were instructed to stop gambling in the "Streets,

Lands or alleys, wharfs yards or Back Sides within the Town of Boston."⁴⁴ A
picture emerges of bondspeople passing daylight hours just about everywhere.

White people sought to regulate the movements of the enslaved during
the daytime, but they put even more effort into curtailing nighttime mobility. In 1703, the Massachusetts General Court passed an "Act to Prevent
Disorders in the Night," which was intended to put an end to the "great disorders, Insolencies, and burglaries" that were supposedly committed under
cover of darkness by the enslaved. The Court established a 9 P.M. curfew for
such persons and "Impowered" citizens to "take up and apprehend" those
who failed to heed it.⁴⁵ This was the beginning of a long and unsuccessful
struggle to circumscribe bondspeople's nocturnal movements. Two years
later, the province's lower-level criminal court ordered constables and citizens "frequently to walk the Streets" in search of bound people of African or
Indigenous ancestry who were out at night.⁴⁶ The province-wide statutes
must not have had their desired effect, though, for in 1723 Boston's selectmen
formulated their own policy, which limited the movement of the enslaved
according to the setting of the sun and its rising.⁴⁷

The perceived problem continued. In 1736, a committee appointed to
resolve the issue reiterated the need for watchmen to "Walk the Streets,
Lanes &c" in order to round up enslaved people out past curfew. Soon after,
newspapers quoted the original 1703 "Act to Prevent Disorders in the Night"
and assured the populace that "some Gentlemen in Authority" had decided to "put in Execution" the law. But two years later, town selectmen
found themselves urging local officials yet again to "restrain the Disorders
among the Negroes" out at night. No lasting success resulted. In 1743, the selectmen once more had to remind Boston's watchmen to take up nocturnal
wanderers "as the Law directs." Indicating that a half-century of work on
the issue was all for naught, Boston's citizens were urged in 1750 to convene
in Faneuil Hall to discuss, among other things, "Whether any more effec-
tual Method, than is already prescrib'd by Law, can be taken to prevent the
Disorders that are frequently committed by Negro Servants in the night."⁴⁸

In 1755, the year Mark went looking for poison "in the Evening after Candle Light," Boston's selectmen ordered that the original "Act to Prevent Disorders in the Night" be printed in the town's newspapers.⁴⁹ Soon after, citizens
tried a new approach, voting to fine those who broke curfew rather than inflict corporal punishment. Nighttime wanderers—or those who enslaved
them—would now be required to pay five shillings per offense. But the economic sanction seemed to have little effect; the selectmen had to continue

giving orders about bondspeople out after 9 P.M.[50] By 1761, the task of curtailing the mobility of bondspeople was incorporated into the boilerplate instructions given to constables of the night watch upon appointment: These men were to "take up all Negroes Indian & Molotta Slaves, that may be absent from their Masters Houses, after 9 o'Clock at Night."[51] And the town clerk, acting upon the order of the selectmen, flooded newspapers year after year with reminders to both watchmen and townsmen of their joint duty to keep bondspeople in according to curfew.[52] However, there is no evidence that these printed warnings had any effect: Bostonians continued to ask the selectmen to put a stop to nighttime wanderings, and the selectmen continued to give "strict Orders" to those in charge of policing the streets. The quest in Boston for "good Order" to be "observ'd in the Night" was elusive. People like Mark were regularly out, as Mark himself put it, "after Sunset"—and many seem to have had little inclination to turn in at curfew.[53]

The frenzy of local regulations is not the only barometer of the nocturnal movements of Black folks. Plenty of other evidence shows bound Bostonians on the go after dark. Reports filed by the watchmen—those keepers of the street harried incessantly by the town selectmen—provide us with yet more glimpses of nighttime occurrences. One member of the watch described investigating a light shining in the harbor to find three bondsmen of African descent on a fishing boat with an "Indian Woman who s[ai]d she was free." Another watchman found "8 or 9 negros playing on a vialend and flute," who scattered after he reminded them of the time. A nighttime patroller of Boston's South End apprehended an enslaved man from Roxbury but released him when he gave "a Good Acc[oun]t of himself." And when a watchman found Cuff, a local chimney sweeper, out under cover of darkness, he "carr[i]ed [him] hom to his master."[54]

Newspaper advertisements posted by those wishing to buy or sell enslaved people provide additional clues to nighttime mobility. Bondspeople's nocturnal habits influenced how enslavers valued them. Being "addicted to be out of Nights," as one enslaver described a man in his household, could make an otherwise useful bound laborer unappealing. Conversely, a bondsperson who "will not go out a Nights" was considered an asset.[55] And nighttime movements show up in court records as well as newspaper advertisements. Indeed, the archive generated by criminal prosecutions in Suffolk County's courts presents a veritable who's who of after-dark perambulating. Peter was convicted of being out at an "unseasonable time of night"; Ceesar of assault "at night, between ten & eleven a Clock"; Tom of breaking into a Boston home at "2 aClock in the Morning"; Caesar of theft "in the night time"; and Nello of attempted burglary at "one of the clock in the night."[56] Examples abound.

Clues to the doings of the enslaved after dark can be found in other places as well. A significant body of evidence relates to the "houses of entertainment" that sprang up in town despite the best efforts of authorities to quash them. Bostonians periodically were rounded up and charged in the county's lower criminal court with the crime of "Entertaining Negro's" in these "disorderly" dwellings.[57] This began in the seventeenth century. In 1694, the neighbors of Thomas Atkins, whose wife, Zipporah Atkins, was a free Black property holder, complained that "Negroes have resorted to the house" and disturbed them with "revellings & routs in the night seasons." A dozen years later, a Boston woman of African descent named Mariah was convicted of several crimes, including "Entertaining of Negros."[58] In 1723, a Boston widow named Alice Oliver, doubtless white given her lack of racial identifier, was charged with "keeping . . . bad Company in her House . . . at unseasonable time[s] of Night." Alice catered to a mixed-race clientele—her patrons were "White & black," the indictment read—and she apparently sold them liquor without a proper license.[59] Rachel Hubbard, another white widow, was convicted later in the eighteenth century of maintaining an "ill govern'd" house visited in the nighttime by "negro Slaves." And an Anglo-American victualler named Thomas Simmons was punished in 1770 for allowing enslaved people in his home and permitting "quarrelling, fighting, & tipling, & drinking to Excess." Enabling bondspeople to cavort in places where alcohol flowed freely and where the eyes and ears of their enslavers could not track them was a serious offense, one that the court investigated with care. In 1772, when a white man named Patrick Carrel was brought before the bar for "maintaining . . . an ill governed and disorderly House," the jury found him guilty as charged, "except [of the charge of] Harboring Negroes."[60]

As this partial list of those accused of "entertaining Negroes" suggests, white people served bound patrons after dark, but free Black folks facilitated the nighttime recreation of the enslaved as well.[61] An unnamed woman of African descent, said to live "in this Town at her own hand," made ends meet the way Thomas Atkins and Mariah had: by "disorderly entertaining Negroes." Similarly, a Black laborer named John Bachus welcomed people described as "of ill fame" into his house in the nighttime.[62] Black householders like John provided valuable places for connection after dark. Though few had title to the homes in which they lived—meaning that deeds can do little to help us locate them—squabbles over rental agreements allow us to see certain free people living on their own in town. Basthen Morret and Mingo inhabited a house on the road leading from Boston to Roxbury. A porter named Jemmy occupied a "Dwelling House Coach house & garden" in Boston's South End. Robert Cummens, a laborer, leased a place near the wharves on Boston's southern flank. John Freeman dwelled in the North End near the Charlestown Ferry. A widow named Elizabeth Morsimore lived near the Common on Frogg Lane. Peter Milroe leased a "Tenement" on Newbury Street. James Lancaster lived near Summer Street, the lane to Boston's southernmost wharves. And Tully Saul rented a place on the road heading to Roxbury.[63] We do not know that any of these people operated households considered "disorderly." But there was a link in the minds of many white observers between the nighttime gatherings of the enslaved and the homes of free people of African descent. As one townsperson rued in print, enslaved nightwalkers thought it "reasonable" to filch food and drink in order to "raise a Bounty for the Ethiopian Housholder, under whose Roof they meet."[64]

Whether their nighttime gatherings were held in the homes of "Ethiopian Housholders," white folks, or elsewhere, bondspeople appear to have had a rollicking good time. Their revelry tended to involve both drink and song. One Bostonian described stumbling upon a "Nocturnal Frolick" in a tavern: A dozen "black Gentry" were singing in "very merry Humour" accompanied by a violin and plenty of alcohol. Another inhabitant discussed a "merry Frolick" in which people of African descent, well supplied with rum, "Regale[d] themselves" in the wee hours of the morning in a warehouse on Wentworth's Wharf. And a report circulated about "half a score" of bondspeople, who gathered at the home of a free person of African descent with a "large Bowl of Punch, and other necessary Inducements to Rudeness and Disorder." The problem was grave enough that the selectmen voted to punish those who should "forward, sell or deliver" alcohol to Black people in bondage or allow such persons to "sit tipling in their Houses."[65] But the ban was not always respected, so sometimes enslavers took things into their own hands, reminding taverners and retailers not to allow bondspeople access to drink. We can see this in Mark's story. Mark treated Robbin, his supplier of poison, to a toddy, which they shared as they stood in the lane leading to Charlestown's wharf. But Mark's enjoyment of the sweetened rum came abruptly to an end when his enslaver found him. John "drove him away," and then he told the woman who sold Mark the toddy never again to "sell any Drink to any of his Servants."[66]

Bondspeople drank at their "Nocturnal Frolicks," they made music with violins and flutes and their spirited voices, and they pursued their pleasure in other ways as well. Some of these nighttime gatherings appear to have presented the enslaved with opportunities for erotic encounters. These were clearly sites of mixed-gender sociability. One report described "He's and She's" together with a "Store of Wine and Punch before them." Another described "Negro Servants of both Sexes" at a "very unseasonable Hour." And the repetition of the term "lewd" when discussing visitors to these "ill govern'd" houses suggests that record keepers understood such places to permit sexual intimacy.[67] An occasional piece of stray evidence confirms such a reading. For instance, a white man named William Cox did not just "entertain" people in bondage and sell alcohol without a proper license; he also allowed a "Molatto" woman named Bettey to live in his home, and he permitted her, to the dismay of authorities, to "ly in the Same Bed with him s[ai]d Cox & Wife."[68] That a multiracial group of both men and women was called before the bar to testify to William's behavior reinforces once again the diversity of many of these nighttime gatherings. Unfortunately, not a single word of Bettey's survives, so it is impossible to decipher what she made of her nocturnal proximity to William. Was she simply grateful for a place on which to lay her weary body? Or did that time in bed with William and his wife mean something more? We cannot know. Nonetheless, it seems clear that the enslaved left home both day and night in an attempt to fulfill relational needs, whether they were searching for sexual intimacy or wishing for companionship. Consider the words of one wandering bondsman, who was asked "what bisnis" he had in town. He had come, he stated unequivocally, "to se my frinds."[69] Similarly, an enslaved woman of African descent announced that she was "going . . . amongst her friends" before walking to the next town over.[70] Some friendships were made at the meetinghouse or in the kitchen garden or, like Jane and Sebastian's, by the water pump. But not all relationships were forged in settings considered reputable by those who sought to keep order in the port. The around-town connections of Mark and many like him were formed instead in places and with people deemed "disorderly."

When enslavers became uncomfortable with the social circles their bondspeople built, some reacted by seeking to disrupt those circles. Removal from town was the easiest way to accomplish this. Slave-for-sale advertisements show that many sought to send bondspeople away, requiring that they be "Shipt off," "sold over Sea," "Sold out of Town," "Sold out of the Country," or "carried away from this Town."[71] Sometimes these advertisements stated explicitly that the requested relocation was motivated by a bondsperson's social interactions. One Boston man was to be "carried out of the Province" because he had been "enticed into the Company of a Rascally Club of Negros." Another had likewise been "intic'd," and had allegedly become, as a result, "taken to Lying and Thieving." A third had, according to the advertisement, grown "impudent and saucy" by "keeping bad Company." And one man had made such a "great Acquaintance" in Boston that he would only become "valuable" if he was taken out of the town.[72] In the eyes of enslavers, the relationships that bondspeople forged on the streets could become a serious problem. They certainly did for Mark. In the end, Mark's days in Boston were numbered by the so-called "wicked Companions" with whom he spent so much time: The Boston selectmen decided that Mark was a troublemaker and ordered that the man leave town.[73] Then, as Phillis recalled, "my master brought him home from Boston." Back in Charlestown, severed from his community on the streets, the man started plotting.

*   *   *

According to Phillis, a week or two after John brought his roving bondsman "home," Mark persuaded Phillis and Phoebe to help him poison their enslaver. Mark "was uneasy," Phillis said, "and wanted to have another Master." The women became willing accomplices to the frustrated bondsman. In the testimony recorded by the province's highest court, Phillis disclosed that she and Phoebe had taken turns pouring a white powder from a vial into their enslaver's victuals. They put this powder, perhaps arsenic, in John's breakfast "Chocolate," his "watergruel," and his "Infusion." Again and again the women poisoned their enslaver's meals, which they watched him devour in the kitchen. And then, according to Phillis, Mark delivered the final dose: "Potter's Lead" in the medicinal sago that the bondspeople were ordered to prepare in hopes of John's recovery.[74] Toward the end, John was in "great Misery," according to Mark's confession. The man began convulsing in bed. Finally, on the last day of June in 1755, the enslaver died.

In July, Mark and Phillis were ordered to the Middlesex County courthouse in Cambridge. There, perspiring perhaps in the midsummer heat and under the pressure of his interrogators, Mark described his around-town search for poison. To the same men, Phillis narrated the course of events that led to John's death: a tale of powders and vials and feasting and wasting.

In August, both pled not guilty, despite having admitted to obtaining the poison and administering it to their unsuspecting enslaver. The jury

convicted Phillis of murder and Mark of assisting her in the act, and it decided that the two must "Suffer the pains of death."[75]

In September, Mark and Phillis were secured to a sleigh outside the
Middlesex County jail. At the sheriff's order, the vehicle lurched forward,
sending sprays of dust into air made fetid and pungent by the nearby tan-
nery. After passing the tan yard, with its soaking vats and line-hung hides
and animal flesh in decomposition, the sleigh heaved to the right. Turning a
corner, it continued in the direction of the Blue Anchor Tavern, an important local gathering place. The county courthouse loomed across the street.
Perhaps, as they clattered down this road to death, Mark and Phillis had
flashbacks of their time in that very building. The question must have hung
in the foul air: If they had said something else, might they somehow have
avoided the fate they now faced? A few moments later, the sleigh came upon
Harvard College, which stood facing the southern tip of the Cambridge
Common. Students in the lofty brick dormitories likely quit their studies to
join the masses that made for the northern boundary of the grassy meadow.[76]
The gallows, atop what had come to be called "Gallows Hill," were now in
sight. They were meant for Mark. A stake about ten yards away was intended
for Phillis. She would burn.[77]

Phoebe was not there. In fact, she was curiously absent from the entire
saga of trial and execution. If she provided testimony to the court, it does not
survive. None of the verdicts mention her. And yet, from the statements attributed to her partners in crime, she was at least as culpable as they.

What happened?

According to Mark's *Last & Dying Words*, Phoebe became "Evidence in
Behalf of the King" in the trial. This seems to have been the story that circulated throughout the region following John's death. Indeed, it was still being
passed from resident to resident more than fifty years later, when one of
Charlestown's first historians, Josiah Bartlett, was collecting evidence to write
an account of the town. Phoebe, he wrote, "was said to have been the most
culpable" in John's murder, and she "became evidence against the others" in
the trial. Josiah's *Historical Sketch of Charlestown* provides the only surviving clue to Phoebe's final fate. The woman, he wrote, "was transported to the
West Indies."[78]

It is possible that Phoebe *was* used as evidence against the others in the
trial. But she was hardly necessary; Mark and Phillis effectively incriminated
each other in their statements. And, if Phoebe's testimony had indeed been
crucial to the final judgment, it is odd that the court did not bother to file

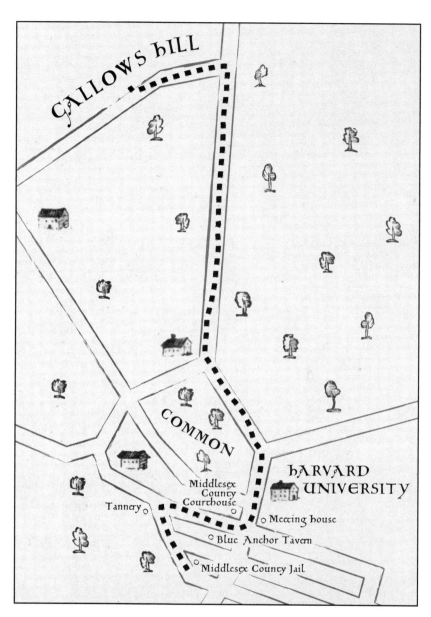

Map 2. Map of Cambridge, Massachusetts. This map shows the likely path of
the sleigh that transported Mark and Phillis from the Middlesex County Jail to
Gallows Hill, the site of their execution. Map drawn by Vanessa Knoppke-
Wetzel.

whatever she said with the papers relating to the trial. What is more, if Phoebe was truly the "most" culpable—which Mark's and Phillis's statements both suggest and Josiah heard more than half a century later—why was she given the lightest sentence? Transportation to the Caribbean was a death sentence of a kind, but the men who decided Phoebe's fate likely considered it less horrifying then hanging from the gallows or burning at the stake. Further, if Phoebe *was* exiled to the West Indies as punishment, why was her sentence not recorded by the court? Her name appears nowhere: There is no mittimus ordering her to prison, no summons requesting her presence in court. She was not mentioned in the indictment. She made no appearance in the record of the case. She was disregarded by the writ of execution.

It is as if the woman simply disappeared at the dawn of the prosecution. But she did not disappear. She was at the old estate in Charlestown on the thirteenth of August, when three men inspected her deceased enslaver's "Mansion House," "Front Shop," "Work Shop," and "Yard" to inventory his possessions. From "Shoe Buckells" to "Spectacles," from "Wine Glasses" to "Wheels," the men methodically tabulated all that John had accumulated in his fifty-eight years of life. A "Parcell of Buttons" valued at five shillings. Three "Broad Axes" valued at four pounds. A "Scarlett Coat & Breetches" valued at sixteen pounds. A "Negro" named "Phoebe" valued at two hundred pounds. There she was. Mark and Phillis were not included on the inventory, as their deaths were imminent; John's heirs would not benefit from their value. But Phoebe was alive and well and still reckoned of worth.[79] Phoebe was not headed to the gallows for murder.

Only one explanation can account for Phoebe's apparent complicity in John's death and her invisibility in the court proceedings. *She was silenced.* The court seems to have left Phoebe out of the proceedings altogether, then stealthily shipped her away from the province.

But why?

To protect John's name, perhaps. Shards of evidence suggest that the old enslaver sexually exploited Phoebe in the years leading up to his murder. As the record stands, no explicit statement links Phoebe and John sexually, which doubtless is what the men who controlled the court's record making would have wanted. However, the clues that remain all point in that direction.[80]

After John's wife, Parnel, died in 1752, the embittered widower had chosen not to remarry, dwelling alone on his estate with his youngest children (now reaching the age of majority) and his bondspeople.[81] Phoebe seems to have played an intimate role in caring for him. The night before John died,

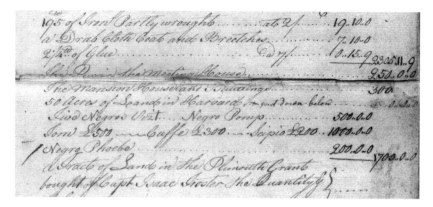

Figure 11. Appraisal of Phoebe. Mark and Phillis were not mentioned in John's inventory, as their deaths were imminent, but Phoebe was appraised alongside the others bound on the Codman estate. Note the slash next to the woman's name. Though her value was not stricken through, Phoebe seems to have been set aside from the rest of the people and objects in the inventory. The maker of this mark likely knew of the plan to sell Phoebe away. Courtesy of the Massachusetts State Archives.

for instance, it was Phoebe rather than his own daughters who stayed by his side, "watch[ing] with him." And John appears to have been kinder to Phoebe than to his other bound laborers. According to Mark, John "treated her better than any of us Servants," and the hard-hearted enslaver evidently was somewhat concerned about Phoebe's welfare, at least on certain occasions. For instance, after Phoebe stayed up all night with the dying man, Mark remembered John asking her "how she did after Watching."[82] Nonetheless, Phoebe, even more than her accomplices, appears to have delighted in John's suffering and death. "The Day before master dyed," Mark testified, "Phoebe . . . got to dancing & mocking master & shaking herself & acting as Master did in the Bed."[83] And Mark's *Last & Dying Words* attributes to Phoebe a bitter, sexually charged statement: "the *old Dog* was just [about] gone," Phoebe had apparently said when Mark asked her how the man was doing on the day before his death, "and she would stick as close to him as his Shirt to his Back, and not only so, but she would cut down the *Old Tree*, and then would hew off the Branches."[84]

John's sexual advances did not just cripple Phoebe's already beleaguered intimate life; they troubled her fellow bondspeople, too. Mark wished to poison John so that he could "have another Master," but he also wanted to kill the man because, as Phillis put it, "he was concerned for Phoebe and I." Mark did not seem to have special fear for his enslaver's other bound laborers, all of whom were male: Pompey, Cuffe, Scipio, and Tom. This despite the fact that John had physically abused Tom to the point of seriously injuring his eye. But Mark recognized, without ever saying so explicitly—at least, without saying so *on record*—the heightened danger of being Black and female in John's household.

Relatively little evidence of the sexual exploitation of New England bondswomen survives. It may be that coercive sexual encounters between enslavers and the women they bound happened less frequently in New England than they did in colonies in the southern mainland and the Caribbean, where such behavior came to be expected.[85] This, at least, is what some legislators seem to have hoped for; there was a real effort in Massachusetts to prevent sexual encounters across the color line. In the early eighteenth century, the province passed an unusually comprehensive law outlawing sex between all Black and white inhabitants. This legislation, which meted out nearly identical punishments for white women and white men who had sex across the color line, contrasts with comparable legislation in other North American colonies, which focused on eliminating sex between white women and Black men but winked at sexual relationships between white men and Black women.[86] Virginia, for instance, developed legislation that policed the interracial fornication of white women but not white men.[87] North Carolina punished white women who gave birth to mixed-race children but showed no legislative interest in the interracial sex pursued by white men.[88] And a Maryland legal code devoted more than a thousand words to penalizing the sexual intimacy of white women with Black men but included only a single sentence censuring white men who married or impregnated Black women.[89] From a legislative perspective, then, Massachusetts was unusual in the degree to which it formally prohibited the access of white men to the women of African descent who labored in their homes.

If men in Massachusetts who held women in bondage lacked the legislative loopholes that many of their counterparts in the South enjoyed, they were potentially restrained in another way, as well. Massachusetts allowed people of African descent—including the enslaved—to testify in court against white people. What is more, the province's bondspeople had the right to judicial recourse if wronged, and court records show that at least some exercised this right.[90] The access of the enslaved to the court of law, and the ability of the enslaved, once there, to testify against the powerful, meant that women could, in principle, bear witness against those who wronged them. Perhaps not surprisingly in light of these circumstances, Black women in Massachusetts managed, more than just about anywhere else in the British-American colonies, to charge their abusers in court.[91] Consider the case of an unnamed "Ethiopian woman" who accused a white man named Zebulon Thorp of "Ravishing her" in 1717. Race and enslaved status notwithstanding, the court took the woman's accusation seriously and ordered the relevant parties to come before the bar. But Zebulon never made it to the trial. Upon declaring that "if he were guilty he wish[ed] he might never get alive to Plimouth," the man was, quite fittingly, struck down en route: He rode his horse aggressively while drinking and fell to his death before the sun rose on the day of his prosecution. Though justice in this case appeared to have come from the hand of God himself, the Massachusetts judicial system might well have had a reckoning with Zebulon had the man not denied it that opportunity. A Massachusetts Superior Court justice scorned the defendant as a "very debauch'd man" when, upon news of his death, the trial was called off.[92]

Courts in Massachusetts might have shown more willingness to hear Black women's stories than courts in many other British-American regions, but this does not mean that they listened well or often. Indeed, there is reason to believe that the "Ethiopian woman" whom Zebulon violated was highly unusual in her ability to obtain justice—and not simply because few sexual predators were thrown from their horses in drunken stupors. Despite the province's legal prohibition of sex between white men and Black women, as well as the nominal access of enslaved people to Massachusetts courts, many white people in the province took for granted the sexual violation of bound women in their households, just as white folks did elsewhere.[93] A collection of depositions produced in eastern Massachusetts during the middle of the eighteenth century vividly confirms this. When a Black woman named Nanny became visibly pregnant, the town of Barnstable came alive with gossip. Isaac Hinkley, the son of Nanny's enslaver, apparently spread the rumor that Nanny was impregnated by Joseph Otis, the son of a leading local family.[94] Underage Joseph was defended vigorously by his father, a Harvard-educated lawyer who filed suit against Isaac for slander. In the process, local residents were compelled to testify in court, which resulted in details of the case being put on paper.[95]

The talk around town reveals a predatory connection between enslavers' sons and the women bound in their households. Townspeople remembered

Isaac worrying time and again that people would suspect him of fathering the child. A woman who lived "Down Street" from the tempestuous household recalled the young man expressing concern that "People" might think he was responsible for Nanny's baby. He was "Especially" anxious about "strangers," who did not, presumably, know his character. When the sympathetic neighbor reassured Isaac that "No: Body Could think so," he told her that "there had been some such Instances abroad & they most Commonly Laid them to their masters Sons." At the time Isaac spoke, the term "abroad" was not necessarily associated with foreign countries or with places overseas; it could simply mean "away from home" or "far off."[96] Therefore, these "Instances abroad," in which the sons of enslavers were believed to have fathered the children born to bondswomen in their houses, might not have been too distant. The cases Isaac had in mind almost surely took place no farther away than in other New England colonies, and they may well have occurred elsewhere in Massachusetts, or even in towns neighboring Barnstable.

Isaac worried aloud to other folks at other times that people might believe him culpable. One witness remembered a conversation in which Isaac indicated that Joseph was responsible for Nanny's child and then "farther added" that "he did not know but that some *folks would think that the s[ai]d Negro Child was his* [own]."[97] The local miller remembered Isaac telling him that "Down in Town" people said that "it was his Child." Isaac apparently sensed that establishing his innocence would be an uphill battle; he told the man that "he was obliged to get him self Clear" of the charges because there had been "Instances" elsewhere of enslavers' sons pursuing the women bound in their households. Still another neighbor recalled Isaac expressing "some uneasiness" because people were "Apt" in such situations to attribute the unexplained pregnancies of bondswomen to "Masters Sons."[98]

For Isaac, and for those with whom he spoke, the idea that enslavers' sons might target bondswomen in their households was hardly surprising. Though Isaac claimed that this was not, in the case of Nanny, what had happened, his assertions paraded against a backdrop of assumption that his impregnating Nanny was a real possibility—perhaps even a probability. And the words of others in Isaac's orbit reveal with even greater clarity the extent to which women like Nanny were victimized. Some of those who testified spoke with a candid vulgarity that appears seldom in the archive of the region but is telling. Joseph's aunt, apparently "very much Disturbed" by the rumors circulating about her nephew, did not find the gossip credible. After all, "if Joseph Otis wanted a Negro," she was quoted as saying, he "had one at home & [she]

wondered [why] he should go after Capt[ain] Hinckleys Negroes."[99] The statement is unambiguous and unapologetic—unnervingly so—and it aligns the
relationships between enslavers and the women they bound in Massachusetts
with those in other parts of the Anglo-Atlantic world.[100] As Joseph's aunt saw
it, Joseph would not have bothered pursuing Nanny because the woman
bound in his home was available to satisfy his sexual urges. There was no recognition that this unnamed woman should have had a say in the matter—no
sense at all that she ought to have been able to decide whom could penetrate
her body.

Another witness put the same idea in even crasser language. She asked
why Joseph would have gone looking for sex at the Hinkley house when at
home the Otises already had "a Poison Whore," by which she meant, she explained, "their own Negro." As these two witnesses saw it, Joseph had no
reason to pursue Nanny because he could simply have forced himself on the
bondswoman in his own household. The ugly language with which this
assumption was voiced—"Poison Whore"—reinforces yet more starkly
the wholesale disregard of enslaved women's bodies and sexuality in this
little Massachusetts town. Isaac's language was soiled with similar expressions; he used slurs like "Nasty Durty whore" on more than one occasion.
The repetition of the term "whore" to describe Black women, and the use of
descriptors such as "Nasty," "Durty," and "Poison," indicate that women in
slavery were seen as sullied, foul, and sexually promiscuous: ready prey, that
is, to abusers. And Black women were not the only battered women in bondage. There was also discussion among townspeople as to whether "Squaws"
were "as good as negros," which shows that women of Indian descent as well
as women of African ancestry were vulnerable to sexual exploitation.[101]

The gossip that swirled in Barnstable serves as an important reminder that
the sexual well-being and personal autonomy of enslaved women could be
of no importance at all to the white people in their homes and neighborhoods.
After all, the packet of depositions from Barnstable was not produced because
Nanny had sued a sexual violator and the court found itself charged with responding to her accusation. Rather, the concern of the court was whether
Isaac had slandered Joseph in his desperate attempt to frame him for impregnating Nanny. Likewise, the story of Phoebe, her troubled intimacies, and
her final reckoning with the man who caused her pain compels us to acknowledge that enslaved people were abused sexually—and courts were willing to
look the other way—in New England as well as in the South. Archival fragments suggest that women like Phoebe, Nanny, and the unnamed "Ethiopian

woman" who endured abuse at the hands of a drunkard were vulnerable to gross violation.

∗   ∗   ∗

Mark, Phillis told her interrogators, "was concerned for Phoebe and I."[102] Was it that Mark could not bear to watch his enslaver's leering eyes trail the women in the kitchen? That he could not abide the man's roving hands? That he could not stomach the thought of John's heavy frame pressed into Phoebe's behind closed doors? Clearly, from Mark's perspective, the man had to be stopped, and poisoning him would accomplish that. Phillis's statement about Mark's "concern" for the bondswomen with whom he lived, together with Mark's decision to murder his enslaver, suggest that Mark saw himself as a protector of Phillis and Phoebe. The bonds of care linking Mark to the women with whom he lived, born of shared experiences and joint suffering, ran deep. Indeed, the evidence even suggests a kind of kin connection between them: Those John enslaved, separated from the families of their choosing, formed family-like relationships over the years right there in the old house in Charlestown.

The testimonies that Mark and Phillis submitted to the court provide us with windows onto the bondspeople's daily interactions on the Codman estate. In the summer of 1755, when John was killed by degrees at the breakfast table, there were seven enslaved people living in the household: Mark, Phillis, and Phoebe, as well as Tom, Cuffe, Pompey, and Scipio. Based on their names and assessed values in John's inventory, these latter four bondspeople were able-bodied grown men. Mark and Phillis's depositions make it clear that the two women and five men bound in John's household talked together— seemingly constantly. They started in the morning, or, as they sometimes put it, in the "Forenoon." They continued in the afternoon. They kept on "after dark." And they were still at it in the dead of night. Their words drifted through every corner of the estate: the backyard, where Phillis and Phoebe did the laundry; the blacksmith shop, where Mark hammered red-hot bars of iron; the garret, where they all slept after long days of work; the kitchen, where Phillis and Phoebe prepared meals for the dozen or so members of the household; the "closet" off the kitchen, where the enslaved supped together; the cellar, where they drew their cider; and even the outhouse, where, in addition to doing the business one would expect, they exchanged furtive messages and hidden goods.

The Charlestown estate positively vibrated with the voices of the enslaved. In groups of all sizes, they conversed for all purposes. Phoebe shared
the latest news with Phillis. Mark deliberated next steps with Phoebe. Tom
and Mark came to a disagreement. Phillis and Phoebe placed bets with each
other. Mark asked Phoebe questions. Mark, Phoebe, Tom, and Scipio chatted
to pass the time. Mark pressured Phillis and Phoebe to concede to his vision
for the future. Phoebe gave Mark instructions. Mark admitted his fears to
Phillis. Phillis and Phoebe discussed recent happenings. Mark conferred
with Pompey. Phillis updated Mark on the day's events. Mark passed information from other bondspeople on to Phillis. Phoebe gave Phillis advice. Mark
disclosed his treasured hopes to Phillis. And Phoebe and Phillis told Mark
secrets.[103] In groups large and small, the enslaved on John's estate processed
life together. Their conversations, laced with both care and coercion, piled
one upon another in a complicated but comforting network of belonging.

Though the words of the enslaved ricocheted off every beam in the house
and each stone in the yard, some of their conversations—including their most
intimate ones—were reserved for what Mark called "our Garret."[104] All seven
of those enslaved in John's household slept in the one-room garret of the
Charlestown home. This was both unusual and utterly common at the same
time. Seven bondspeople bedding down in the attic of an enslaver's home was
rare insofar as this was quite a large number for a Massachusetts slaveholding. Probate records suggest that the average enslaver in the region held fewer
than two people in bondage during the mid-eighteenth century. Indeed, of
every hundred decedents whose estates claimed bondspeople in probate
court, only one had seven or more bound laborers at this time.[105] Few enslaved
people in the region, therefore, had as many others in bondage with whom
to sleep as Mark, Phillis, and Phoebe.

The nighttime configuration on the Codman estate was common, however, in that enslavers seemed partial to housing bondspeople in the upper
reaches of their homes. Time and again, estate inventories locate enslaved
New Englanders in the garrets of dwellings. For instance, we know that Tom
slept on the uppermost floor of a Boston home because an appraiser found
the "Negros Bedding" when he climbed up to the garret. A boy named Jemey slept in the "Kitchin Garret" of a Boston home, while one named Sharper
slept in the "Back Garret" of a dwelling in the same town. And Will was
housed in one of "the several rooms in the upper storys" of a large Boston
residence.[106] The records rarely allow us to place more than one or two
bondspeople physically in the homes of enslavers, which makes sense given

the small size of slaveholdings in the region. However, bedding for "6 Ne-groes" was found in the upper reaches of one home; beds for three were found in another; and two men and a woman—Harry, Robert, and Tamus—slept together in the garret of a third home.[107]

These examples suggest, as does the case of John's bondspeople in Charles-town, that most enslaved people who lived in households with others in bond-age slept alongside those people. Of course, not all enslavers thrust every bound member of the household into a single room. Sharper and Nancy each had their own bedrooms in Arthur Savage's household, Sharper sleeping in the "Westermost Garret" and Nancy in the "Meal Garret" (which the ap-praiser called "nancy's Chamber"). Bedding and bondspeople appear to have been divided between a "Back Garret" and a "Front Garret" in the home of Josiah Langdon. And Phillis and Cato were housed in "Garrets"—rendered in the plural—in William Lambert's house.[108] But these are exceptions. En-slavers did not ordinarily bother to separate their bondspeople one from another. And why would they? Masters themselves, at least those of modest means, such as yeomen and artisans, often slept in the same rooms as others, such as their children. In households with two or more bondspeople, then, the enslaved almost always shared sleeping spaces with others in bondage.

What were these shared quarters like? The upper reaches of houses in eighteenth-century New England were hardly desirable living spaces: They were bitterly cold during the winter, suffocatingly hot on sultry summer days, and probably damp in inclement weather. They were also cramped and clut-tered. The inventory of John's estate shows that the garret floor was spread with beds. There were five beds made of straw as well as one feather bed, which was far costlier, and which would have been much more comfortable. Per-haps the feather bed was reserved for Phoebe. If so, it would sometimes have been shared by her husband, Quacoe, whom Phoebe at least occasionally hosted on weekends. Phoebe and Quacoe would not have been the only ones to bed down with a mate in the garret, as six beds could not have slept John's seven bondspeople without a little sharing.[109] On these six beds, the appraiser counted ten bed rugs, or heavy coverlets, to keep bodies warm and, one hopes, to keep abrasive straw at bay. And the garret of John's house contained more than beds and bedding, as was typical; attic areas housing bondspeople often had a jumble of unwanted or rarely used items. Mark, Phillis, and Phoebe slept alongside pieces of broken windows, some missing their glass, others with panes preserved. In Boston, Toney and Tom slumbered in gar-rets hemmed in by an array of bottles, corks, rakes, tea chests, old chairs, and other miscellanea. Pompey slept in a kitchen garret with "Lumbering things." And a man named Boston spent his nights on an upper story of his enslaver's house alongside a boat, a pistol, a chest, tools, and more.[110]

The very undesirability of these spaces, cluttered and given to extremes in temperature, afforded their inhabitants a degree of seclusion. Other members of enslavers' households chose to sleep in the more spacious "lower chambers" or "lower rooms" of their homes, which were heated during the winter and had better air circulation in the summer.[111] Those who were not bound preferentially passed their waking hours in these areas as well. Mark and Phillis's testimony indicates that John and his children spent time in the kitchen, the yard, and even the lower levels of neighbors' houses, but there is no indication that they climbed the ladder to "our Garret," as Mark put it. Perhaps that is why Mark used the possessive when he referred to the space: This part of John's home seemed to belong to the enslaved. And as a place that belonged to them—as their private alcove—the garret must have been an important site of connection. Together, night after night, Mark, Phillis, Phoebe, and the others bedded down, exchanging final words in the shifting shadows of candlelight. Together, morning after morning, they peeled their bodies off the prickly straw, greeting one another in the glimmer of dawn. Nearly all of what they said is beyond recovery, but the fact remains that they were there, and they were out from under their enslaver's gaze, both at the setting of the sun and at its rising. It is hardly a flight of fancy to imagine that the garret became a site of intimate interaction as the passing nights became weeks, the weeks turned to months, and the months stretched to years.

We do know, because the court had interest in this, that the garret was a crucial location for the exchange of classified information and forbidden goods. Mark first gave Phoebe the poison "In our Garret." Phoebe later passed the poison on to Phillis in the same place. And, still later in the garret, Phoebe gave Phillis the iron tool that Mark had made for measuring the poison, along with an earful of instructions on how to use it. The garret, though, was not the only place that Mark, Phoebe, and Phillis claimed on the estate, nor was it the only location in which noxious powders changed hands. Phillis received poison from Mark in what she called "our" privy, which leaves open the interpretation that John's bondspeople relieved themselves in a different outhouse from that of the rest of the family. And there was, of course, the blacksmith shop where Mark worked, which was recognized on some level as the man's own. Intimacies were forged in the shop alongside iron goods. It was here, for instance, that Phoebe compassionately cared for Tom's eye, which

John, in a fit of rage or an act of cold calculation, had grievously injured. From the perspective of the shop, the privy, and the garret, it seems clear that the murder was about more than Mark's wife and more than Phoebe's husband, that it was about more than Mark's child and more than the mobile man's community on the streets. It was about more, even, than the town of Boston, which seemed to offer so many forms of belonging. The plan to kill John was, at least in part, an attempt to exact vengeance on the man who had exposed a cherished, kin-like community of fellow bondspeople to harm.

Enslaved people conceived of a host of devices aimed at safeguarding their circles of belonging. For instance, Mark—husband and father, around-town friend, and companion in bondage—plotted arson, recruited a buyer for himself, hired himself out, and ultimately masterminded a murder. Mark's wife might have deserted her enslaver to take up residence alongside her husband on John's estate. Phoebe poured arsenic into her enslaver's morning chocolate in an attempt to escape his clutches and access her husband. Quacoe dreamed of purchasing his wife. Phillis joined the effort to poison her enslaver, hoping, no doubt, to rid herself and her comrades of a menace. All to no avail. The relationships of blood, commitment, and shared experience that these people forged, imperiled by John while he lived, were permanently broken as a result of the enslaver's death.

By all accounts, the blaze on Gallows Hill was ghastly. The dreadful sight of Phillis being burned at the stake was, according to one onlooker, "shocking to behold" and "dismal to our Eyes."[112] She was *burnt to death*," Harvard professor John Winthrop wrote in horror, calling the display of power on Cambridge Common a "terrible spectacle."[113] Not far away, Mark met his end by hanging. His body was then brought to Charlestown, where, according to a local newspaper, it was suspended "in Chains on a Gibbet erected there for that Purpose." Mark was, in death, a macabre warning to all enslaved people who might elect to take justice into their own hands, who might resolve to make plans "about [their] child[ren]," who might decide to fracture their enslavers' families in an attempt to bind up their own communities of intimacy.[114] Of Mark's wife and child, of his companions on the street, of the others with whom he had lived in John's household—Phoebe, Tom, Cuffe, Pompey, Scipio—we have only questions. Were they there that day among the "great" number of "Spectators" who turned out for the execution? Did they later pay homage to the remains of the man who had refused to let his enslaver snatch away his intimacies? And would Mark's child come of age in the busy port, shadowed by his father's body?

CHAPTER 6

The Vassalls

Black Families and the End of Slavery in Revolutionary Massachusetts

The Petition of a Grate Number of Blackes of this Province
who . . . are . . . deprived of every thing that hath a tendency
to make life even tolerable, the endearing ties of husband
and wife we are strangers to for we are no longer man and
wife then our masters or Mestreses thinkes proper marred
or onmarred Our Children are also taken from us by force
and sent maney miles from us wear we seldom or ever see
them again there to be made slaves of fore Life which
sumtimes is verey short by Reson of Being dragged from
their mothers Breest Thus our Lives are imbittered to us on
these accounts By our deplorable situation we are rendered
incapable of shewing our obedience to Almighty God how
can a Slave perform the duties of a husband to a wife or
parent to his child How can a husband leave master and
work and Cleave to his wife How can the wife submit
themselves to there Husbands in all things. How can the
child obey thear parents in all things.
   —Petition to the Massachusetts Governor, his Council,
      and the Province's House of Representatives, 1774

The house was quiet. Half holding his breath, for the stale air seemed meant
not to move, six-year-old Darby might have watched adults padding from one

room to another, carrying a powder of white willow bark, or an Indian tea thought effective for fevers, or a sour citrus cocktail hoped to deliver relief. Perhaps Darby was tasked with drawing water from the pump to cool a feverish brow, or maybe he was sent to pluck healing herbs from the kitchen garden. No matter: Nothing helped the patient. Skin flushed, often confused, and weaker by the day, the bedridden man was now never left alone. Someone always was watching, ready to alert the others should he suddenly worsen. Did Darby take a turn? It would have been uncomfortable work. The room was likely stifling due to the heat of early summer and the warmth of the bodies filing through, and fresh air was elusive; propping open doors and windows seemed only to invite the presence of flies and their vibrating buzz. The white noise of death. It might have lulled the little boy to sleep had he not been jolted intermittently by blasts of cannon and volleys of gunshots, close enough, according to a neighbor, to be "very plainly heard." Listening to the cacophony in the sickroom, Darby would have been well aware that the man on the bed drawing his final breaths was but one of many.[1]

George Reed Jr. was laid to rest on June 26, 1775. An early victim of the fight for liberty waged by Massachusetts colonists against the British, he died from a fever, which, according to a local minister, was "occasioned by a surfeit or heat he got in the Charlestown fight." That is, by joining the patriot forces in the Battle of Bunker Hill, George overexerted himself and somehow contracted the illness that would claim his life. The freedom fighter came home from combat to convalesce in the presence of Darby, the little boy of African descent whom he held in bondage. Darby had spent most of his short life under George's authority. Born on May 15, 1769, he had been given at a "tender" age to George, who lived in Woburn, three towns north of his family in Cambridge.[2] But Darby never forgot the members of his birth family. Somehow he knew them and somehow he knew where they lived, despite having been sent some ten miles distant as a young child. And when George died of his revolution-induced illness, Darby left: He simply walked home.

The journey on which Darby set out was a prodigiously long one for a six-year-old, and it took him through perilous terrain. The child would have begun by walking south from Woburn into Medford, where the gunshots undoubtedly became louder and the toll of the conflict more evident. On his way, he likely crossed paths with refugees fortunate enough to have escaped from British-occupied Boston, whether secreted in fishing boats or rowed on rafts after dark: wanderers who brought with them nothing more than the clothes on their backs and tales of deprivation. Many fled Boston, but Darby headed toward it. Continuing his southward journey, the boy would have passed homes plundered by the British, tree limbs blasted by stray bullets, and stone walls toppled by colonial snipers.[3] Fortunately, the dead had by now been hauled away—at least, the dead who had lost their lives in the recent skirmishes. In Charlestown's common, Mark's sun-bleached bones still stood sentinel nearly two decades after the man's execution. Darby might have gazed at them in horror, but those who regularly passed by were little bothered; Mark's remains had become a neighborhood landmark, a means by which the area's inhabitants could locate themselves in the landscape. Two months earlier, Paul Revere had happened upon them on his famous "midnight ride" to warn the countryside of the British troops' advance. "I saw two men on horseback," Paul would recall, "nearly opposite where Mark was hung in chains."[4]

From Woburn to Medford. From Medford to Charlestown. From Charlestown to Cambridge. Here the gunshots rang out still louder. The boy was now not far from the narrow strip of land connecting Boston to Roxbury, on which rebel Americans clashed continually with British soldiers guarding the way into the occupied town. With the relative safety of the farms and forests of Woburn now far behind him, Darby must have been afraid. He must also have been hot. "95° in the shade," a local diarist recorded in the second week of July. And then: "Rained . . . as fast as I ever saw." Not long after came a "Great shower of hail."[5] We do not know precisely when Darby left George's home or when, for that matter, he arrived in Cambridge, and even if we did we could not reconstruct with precision the boy's passage: It is impossible for us to make out whether Darby sought shelter from the heat and hail, or wondered at the sight of Boston's escapees, or stared back in terror at Mark's ghastly grimace. But there can be little doubt that the six-year-old, by now accustomed to the sound of heavy artillery, was relieved to reach his destination. The proud Georgian mansion built by John Vassall, a loyalist who had recently fled to the British, not only offered a roof over Darby's head, but it also offered what the boy seems really to have sought: his kin.

What kind of reunion united Darby with his family of origin? Was it joyous? Tearful? Hesitant? No sources speak of the moment in which Darby reentered the household of his birth, but stories later passed down suggest that the boy was embraced by his kin and quickly became comfortable around the Vassall estate. Darby supposedly was at play, "swinging on the gate" that

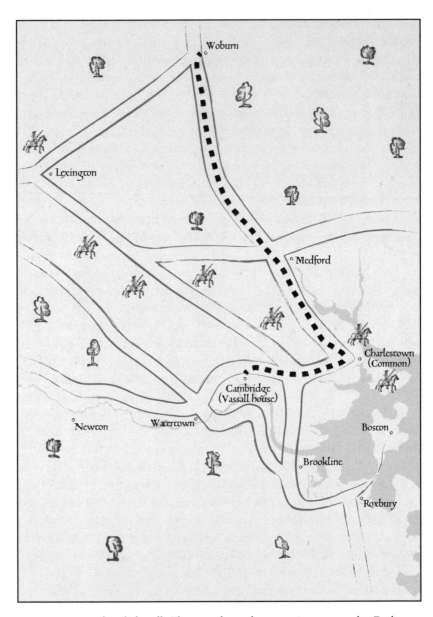

Map 3. Map of Darby's walk. This map shows the approximate route that Darby would have walked from his enslaver's home in Woburn to his family members in Cambridge. The horse-mounted soldiers mark the sites of recent skirmishes between the Americans and the British in the Battles of Lexington and Concord and the Battle of Bunker Hill. Map drawn by Vanessa Knoppke-Wetzel.

guarded the way to the stately home, when he first met its new master, a Virginia colonel who had traveled north to lead the Continental Army: George Washington. Watching Darby on that gate, the towering enslaver saw a child who needed a task with which to occupy himself. George therefore promptly instructed the boy to go inside, where "they would tell him what to do and give him something to eat." But Darby did not follow the general's orders. Instead, the child asked what his wages would be. The commander in chief was taken aback. How could the boy be "so unreasonable at such a time as to expect to be paid"?[6]

This snippet of a story connecting Darby and George is one of countless bits of antiquarian lore surrounding the wartime experiences of the first president of the United States. There are plenty of reasons to discount it. Its teller remains anonymous, for instance, and it was not put to paper until 1871, nearly a century after it allegedly took place. Even the man who finally entered the account into the written record felt compelled to caution readers that it was merely "an anecdote" that "is related"—by whom he said not—of the boy and the general.[7] Nevertheless, this tale, apocryphal though it might be, points to a larger truth. Darby answered the towering enslaver with such boldness because, in the storyteller's words, he was "Feeling the value of his freedom." Indeed. Darby had deserted the household of the man who had long enslaved him, walked ten miles across a war-torn region, and settled into the home in which he wished to live. That is, there is every indication that Darby understood his freedom, and its value, at this time. And Darby was not alone. A great deal of evidence indicates that others of African descent in the region understood themselves to be free at this moment in a way that an outsider like George could not possibly have comprehended—and in a way that historians peering back from the future have long struggled to make out.[8]

In this chapter, I tell the story of Darby and his kin, examining through their experiences how Black families managed first to weaken the institution of slavery in revolutionary Massachusetts and then to navigate the transition from bondage to freedom.[9] After tracing the paths that Darby's parents took to Massachusetts, I chart the growth of the family that they built together. Then I turn to the unusual situation in which they found themselves at the outbreak of the Revolution. By the time Darby walked home from Woburn, his family's loyalist enslavers had fled to quieter corners of the British Empire, and his parents and siblings were living cheek by jowl with George and other leaders of the patriot war effort in the Vassall mansion. Pointing to sources that reveal the withering of slavery early on in the war, I argue that

Figure 12. Vassall home. The gate on which Darby swung does not survive, but the façade of the Vassall home has changed little in the centuries since Darby mounted its steps in 1775. Courtesy of the National Park Service.

slavery in the region ended earlier and differently than scholars have long believed. This transformation resulted in large part from the work of Black activists, who shifted white people's thinking about the institution by arguing repeatedly in widely circulated sources that slavery was illegitimate because of how it harmed Black families. Bondspeople like Darby also voted with their feet by simply leaving—sometimes to pursue family reunification. But not everybody walked away from slavery in the revolutionary moment. Darby's family members, unlike many of their neighbors, chose to stay put. Shrewdly reasoning that his kin could profit by remaining where they were, Darby's father managed to obtain compensation from his erstwhile enslaver's estate for supporting his wife and children. This and other strategies that made much of his provision bore fruit: The man netted a handsome sum for his efforts. Other Black families looked to patriarchal household heads in their fight against the poverty and discrimination that plagued them in freedom. In the end, though, patriarchy was a feeble defense against intractable social ills. Darby, despite his father's revolutionary-era financial successes, would die a poor man. Still, even as his strength ebbed, the man who had marched out of slavery as a little boy would seek to provide in meaningful ways for his kin.

*   *   *

Darby's story does not begin with the American Revolution; its genesis, at least in part, lies in another violent bid for independence. The life of Darby's mother, Cuba, had been turned upside-down four decades earlier by people in pursuit of freedom. When Cuba was a child on Antigua, the island's enslavers had become petrified that their bondspeople intended to rise up and seize their liberty.[10] The plan of the bound revolutionaries, as best their enslavers could make it out, was to blow up the island's elite inhabitants as they danced at a ball just four miles from Cuba's home, and then overrun the island, executing any white people they could find. The ultimate aim was to set up an independent Black nation. However, all did not go according to plan. The plot was discovered before it could loose a single rebel's bonds, and forty-eight of the accused conspirators were banished from Antigua. Another eighty-eight were executed. Some of these people Cuba knew. Quaco, who labored on the same plantation as she, was exiled, perhaps to St. Croix, perhaps to Hispaniola. Hector, who likewise lived alongside the girl, was burned at the stake.[11] And the man who wielded the power of life and death over Cuba and her kin decided that enough was enough. Antigua was no longer worth the risk.

A wealthy merchant with Massachusetts roots, Isaac Royall gathered his family, ordered their belongings packed, and selected the bondspeople he wished to take from the island, to rend from all that they knew. Then he returned home. Isaac would rebuild his life on a sprawling estate in Medford, about five miles northwest of Boston, where the labor of enslaved people—both those who remained in Antigua and those he took to Massachusetts—allowed him to live as a gentleman. For her part, Cuba would adjust to bondage in New England, to the unforgiving soil and the bitter winters and the sense of being outnumbered by those who enslaved. But Cuba did not stay in Medford for long. The old enslaver died a few years after his Massachusetts homecoming, deeding Cuba, her siblings, and her mother to his daughter, Penelope, who soon left home to marry. Penelope's new husband, Henry Vassall, a recent emigrant from Jamaica, lived in Cambridge with his coachman, Anthony, an enslaved man of Spanish origin.[12] And so Cuba, a girl of African ancestry born into bondage in Antigua and transported first to Medford and then to Cambridge, found herself in the same household as Anthony, a young man of African descent bound in a Spanish region, hauled to Jamaica, and brought to Cambridge. Living on the same estate overlooking the salt marshes in a quiet corner of Massachusetts, these two seasoned Atlantic travelers would marry and start a family.[13]

Cuba began bearing children in the middle of the eighteenth century. A son named James arrived sometime before 1758, when expenses for the boy appeared in his enslaver's account book. And Cuba appears to have given birth to two daughters, Flora and Dorrenda, by the middle of the 1760s.[14] But then, circumstances beyond Anthony and Cuba's control threatened to upend all that they knew. Their enslaver's lavish spending and crippling addiction to gambling caught up with him in the final years of his life. By the time Flora and Dorrenda were born, Henry was plagued by the demands of his creditors, and he had no place to turn; he had already spent his wife's inheritance—that wealth generated by sweat and tears and the lash in Antigua—and he had borrowed from his daughter as well.[15] Cuba and Anthony must have watched in terror as merchants, lawyers, and other men of prominence descended on Henry's home in early 1765. The visitors spoke with members of the extended Vassall clan in hushed tones about debts and deeds and mortgages and sales. A parcel of "Negroes" in Antigua changed hands. A plot of land near Henry's Cambridge estate, already mortgaged, was sold.

Henry's home was mortgaged still further.[16] But still Henry could not meet his obligations. In time, he was forced to sell personal property in an attempt to obtain cash to survive. Anthony and Cuba no doubt knew they could be next.

Who to sell? And to whom? The decisions of the dissipated enslaver would shape indelibly the lives of those he bound. Would the Vassall children live with their mother or their father? With both? Or with neither? Would the siblings be separated? Would Anthony and Cuba be sold to distant towns— or out of the province altogether? Until this time, the family had enjoyed good fortune, if the lot of any family bound by slavery can be described that way: Unlike most enslaved families in Massachusetts, Anthony, Cuba, and their children had always lived together in the same home.[17] Well aware of Henry's financial instability, and aware as well that the decisions he made had the potential to safeguard—or destroy—their family, Anthony and Cuba probably did what they could to influence the decision-making of their insolvent enslaver. Could they persuade him not to sell? Likely not. But could they persuade him to sell them in a way that would preserve the integrity of their family? Perhaps.

A "lingering illness" took Henry's life in March of 1769. Around this time, title to the children, as well as to pregnant Cuba, transferred to John Vassall, Henry's nephew. The owner of booming Jamaican sugar plantations, John lived across the street from Henry. Soon after he took possession of the children and Cuba, Darby was born. But John apparently did not want a baby to occupy the time of his newly acquired bondswoman. The infant, therefore, was promptly delivered to George Reed Jr., an acquaintance who lived in Woburn.[18] Little Darby, out of easy reach by foot, would be raised by others. We do not know how Darby's parents responded to this loss, but they undoubtedly realized that the damage could have been worse: The Black Vassalls could have been scattered across the region upon the death of their bankrupt enslaver. As it was, most of the family members lived on the same two estates, and these estates were exceedingly close to one another. Young James could still work with his father in Penelope's stables, and Anthony could pay frequent visits to Cuba, who now toiled in John's mansion. Routines would need to be remade, but the Black Vassalls could maintain much of their familial life.

None of the Vassalls at this juncture—Black or white—could have anticipated the political avalanche that was to come. In just a few short years, Penelope, John, and their kin would be caught on the wrong side of the American Revolution, and they would pay dearly for their allegiance to England.[19] The danger would become unmistakable in September of 1774. On the second day of that month, thousands of angry farmers would march past the Vassall estates on their way to the home of Thomas Oliver, John's brother-in-law. Anthony and Cuba would have heard their hollers, their feet on the street, their musket fire. The farmers were keenly aware that they had been "deprived of their Rights and Priviledges" by British legislation that took power from the people and placed it in the hands of the royal governor, and they had come to demand that Thomas, who had been appointed by the governor to the upper house of the legislature, resign from his position. "The Populace," John's besieged brother-in-law would recall, "began to press up to my windows, calling for vengeance against the Foes of their Liberty."[20] It was too much for the extended white Vassall family to take. Thomas fled to Boston the following morning. John followed him, taking refuge temporarily with the British before relocating permanently to England. Penelope apparently decided that the dangers that had chased her father out of Antigua were less worrisome than those posed by American farmers, and she sailed to the Caribbean with her family. What of Anthony, Cuba, and their children? Neither Penelope nor John took them along when they fled Cambridge. Nor did the enslavers appear to have made any effort to sell them before they skipped town. Perhaps the Black Vassalls resisted both departure and sale, and Penelope and John were too hurried to bother with them. Or maybe the white Vassalls hoped that their erstwhile bondspeople would maintain the Cambridge estates in their absence. Whatever the reason, Anthony, Cuba, and their children stayed put and began to learn the rhythms of a new life: a life without enslavers.

As 1774 turned to 1775, mobs on the street turned to armed conflict between British soldiers and local militias. The province mobilized quickly, filling churches and Harvard dormitories and abandoned mansions with soldiers. Soon, Anthony and Cuba were no longer alone on the estate with their children. Three military companies, numbering some 150 men, descended on John's home in May. In June, part of the mansion was set aside to serve as a hospital. And in July, around the time Darby walked home, the soldiers—both sick and well—were sent elsewhere in order to make room for the mansion's new master: George Washington.[21] By midsummer 1775, Anthony, Cuba, and all of their children found themselves living in a militarized town in a rebel province, sharing an estate with the patriot army's commander in chief. As they watched the pageant of American war and resistance play out on the very property on which they resided, the Black Vassalls did the most ordinary thing imaginable. They worked. They "improved a little spot of land" on John's estate: digging, planting, hoeing, weeding, watering, and harvesting. While George met with dignitaries in John's parlor, Anthony and Cuba engaged in what they would call "the most careful cultivation" of the absentee's acreage.[22] Perhaps George found it reassuring to gaze out the windows of John's home upon a familiar scene: Black bodies, stooped, hard at work tending crops. At a time when change was proceeding at revolutionary pace, it might have gladdened the general to gaze on the holdings that John had built up and consider how things were not really as different as they seemed.

*   *   *

But things were indeed different—markedly so. Darby's freedom march provides a crucial clue. The boy walked from Woburn to Cambridge, and from bondage to liberty, in 1775. This was five years before the Massachusetts constitution declared all men "free and equal" and eight years before the Supreme Judicial Court supposedly enacted abolition in the state by granting a man named Quock Walker his freedom on the basis of the state's liberatory constitution. That is, Darby walked away from bondage well before the dates to which historians have ascribed the end of slavery in the region.[23] Darby's ability to leave cannot be attributed to the fact that George Reed died because, for Black New Englanders, the death of an enslaver meant a change in ownership rather than the end of bondage. Heirs or creditors would now lay claim to bondspeople's lives and labors. This was a reality of life in slavery that even a child would have understood. Nevertheless, Darby did not have to return to George Reed's estate, nor, to George Washington's alleged chagrin, did the boy have to work without wages, for slavery was crumbling in Massachusetts at precisely the time that the boy decided to go home. At the outbreak of revolution, people of African descent like Darby—young, old, and in their prime—simply walked away from their enslavers' homes, shops, and farms. The state's constitution and its courts would not initiate this Black exodus; they would take their cue from it.

Measuring the unlegislated end of slaveholding practices in the region is difficult. Status changes at this time very rarely generated a paper trail, and the issue is confused further by the reality that many newly free people remained in the homes of their former enslavers, working in similar capacities as they always had. Though these people might have begun to receive some form of compensation in return for their labor, and though they might have enjoyed new freedom of movement—including the liberty to leave the homes in question—the documentation produced in this era tends to make invisible the sorts of transformations that formerly enslaved people would have considered significant indeed. In fact, the very language used to refer to free people who labored for white households obscures entirely their embrace of liberty: These people were regularly called "negroes," "servants," and "negro servants," which had long been the terms used to refer to the enslaved. The example of a free person named Dick Frost makes the difficulty clear. A stack of papers generated in Boston during the year 1777 references Dick over and over because he had casual contact with a suspected traitor to the American cause. Dick was described by different record keepers twenty times, called variously a "negro," a "servant," and a "negro boy." Only twice, though, did informants include a clarification that would have been very important to Dick: that he was, in fact, "free." Dick was unusual at this time—but not because of his free status. Dick was unusual, rather, because he was so amply described. Most African-descended people do not repeatedly show up in revolutionary-era archives, and the spare extant acknowledgments of their existence rarely shed light on their status. Historians therefore have little to work with when trying to assess when and how the bound population in the region seized, like Dick, the status of "Free Negroes."[24]

Still, Darby's snippet of a story suggests that something was afoot in 1775. The start of the Revolution marked a decisive turning point in the relationships of enslaved residents of eastern Massachusetts with those who bound them. Careful analysis of probate records—one of the few sources to illuminate patterns of slave ownership at this time—shows that Darby marched in step with the times when he walked from his deceased enslaver's home in 1775.[25] Before the onset of war, these records suggest, the system of slavery in the region was relatively robust.[26] From 1775 on, however, wills bequeathing human property all but disappeared, and bound laborers of African descent nearly vanished from the inventories of estates that they had populated in Massachusetts since the seventeenth century. What is more, the inventories that *did* catalog people of African descent tended to treat them differently in this period. The scant but suggestive surviving evidence portrays these people as fixtures in white households who were at least quasi-free: Some executors considered them worth reporting on inventories, but they largely went unvalued, as their value apparently did not by right belong to the decedents in question.

This was true of Anthony and Cuba. A few years after Darby's homecoming, committees were appointed to appraise the deserted estates of both John and Penelope. Those who had extended credit to the loyalists prior to their hasty departures had begun to demand reimbursement for their outlays, so assessors traipsed through the abandoned grounds by the Charles River, tabulating the valuable—houses and land—and the commonplace: "Dung forks" and "Old Buckets." As they peered and measured, they encountered the human beings whom the white Vassalls had once enslaved. "One negro woman of about 40 years of age," the appraisers of John's estate scrawled; "one negro boy about 8 years." And "another negro child about 3 months." This last record they struck out with a thick line of ink. The other two they let stand, but without assessed values. And they totaled John's "Articles of moveable Estate" *prior* to listing the three people. The valueless human "moveables"—Cuba, no doubt, along with Cyrus and baby Catherine— were included below, almost as an afterthought, perhaps because they were present on the estate being assessed. The appraisers of Penelope's estate did the same thing. They recorded "one negro man named toney" on the list of her possessions, last. The industrious coachman, like his wife and children, had no value.[27] The Black Vassalls might have lived on and worked the white Vassalls' land, but, as the appraisers saw it, they were no longer part of the white Vassalls' holdings.

Anthony and Cuba are examples of a new and unprecedented category of persons to emerge in the region: able-bodied but value-less people in slavery. For more than 130 years, people of African descent in eastern Massachusetts had been assigned monetary values in probate unless they truly were incapable of laboring. During the Revolution, however, people who might otherwise have contributed to the value of estate appraisals were included on inventories with zeroes next to their names.[28] And this phenomenon was not limited to probate records. Residents of eastern Massachusetts began in the revolutionary era to advertise able-bodied laborers for the taking in the newspapers that circulated the region. Boston's weeklies had long offered young children "to be given away," of course, but people of full strength had always been advertised for sale rather than given for free. Consider, though, the "HEARTY NEGRO MAN" whose enslaver was eager enough to send him off that he promised to pay whomever would take him. Or the "Negro Man" capable of "most any Kind of Work" offered gratis with "his Cloathes" and a "Sum of Money." Or the "NEGRO MAN" who, though able to "labour enough for his living," nonetheless was to be given away along with his bed and a monetary incentive. These were able-bodied enslaved people for whom, in the revolutionary moment, there was no market; enslavers were even willing to pay potential masters—preferably some ways off ("in the Country," one advertisement read)—to take them in. The practice of slaveholding was faltering in ways that it had not in the past.[29]

The newspapers that passed from hand to hand on Boston's streets, in Cambridge's taverns, or outside Woburn's meetinghouses offer other clues to changes in ideas about bondage and freedom during the war. While some household heads tried to dispose of able-bodied laborers, others began to buy and sell people of African descent for *terms* rather than for *life*. Consider, for instance, the woman and two men who were advertised for sale for a term of seven years, after which, the notice specified, they were "to be Free'd by the Purchaser." Or the would-be master who sought to buy a "Negro Man or Boy" but anticipated owning the laborer for only "a few Years." Another notice offered a "likely Negro Boy," clarifying that he was to be sold "For seven Years only."[30] Likewise, a "stout likely Negro Man" was advertised for "a small term of years" and a prospective master who announced his need for a "Negro Boy" clarified that he expected the child to serve only until the age of 21.[31] Other notices sought a Black youngster "'till of age," requested such a child's "time," and offered to sell for a "term of years" a girl of African descent.[32] The increasingly finite nature of bondage in the period is reflected as well in advertisements describing African-descended freedom seekers, such as Pomp, who was described by his erstwhile master as "an indented Servant for six Years," and James, who was "not a Slave" but "bound for a Number of Years."[33]

Related changes were gaining momentum in this historical moment. Newspapers suggest that New Englanders living through the Revolution were increasingly willing to think of Black and white laborers in the same frame: Sometimes labor-seekers posted notices equating one with the other. For instance, one household head sought a "WHITE or BLACK" servant for his family, promising the laborer "very large Wages." Another wanted either a "Man Servant"—by implication white—or a "Negro" to work for "good Wages."[34] Postings such as these, in which Black servants were conceived of not only as comparable to white ones but also as deserving of compensation for their toil, suggest a growing demand for waged laborers of African descent. Black people were coming to be seen as participants in the labor market who could make decisions about how and for whom they would labor, and, without remuneration, they were bound to turn elsewhere. These new genres of advertising—the white or Black laborer sought for "good Wages," the Black servant to be sold for a term, the able-bodied bondsperson to be given away—did not overtake the traditional ways in which advertisers referenced people of African descent during the revolutionary era, but their presence nonetheless marks a stark break from how Black New Englanders were described in print during earlier decades.[35]

Other archival sources confirm the changes evident in probate records and newspaper advertisements. For instance, petitions submitted to Massachusetts authorities in the early years of the Revolution illuminate how people thought about slavery at the time. Most valuable are the rare entreaties filed by people of African descent, which provide unparalleled insight into the ways in which Black people understood bondage and freedom in wartime Massachusetts. Consider the case of a man named Joseph Johnson, who wrote in 1778 to the Massachusetts Council, which in the early years of the Revolution acted in the stead of the recalled royalist Massachusetts governor.[36] Joseph had been captured at sea and was living as a "free" man in Boston, but he understood his autonomy to be vulnerable. He was not worried about being reduced to bondage in Boston and forced to labor locally, however; Joseph feared enslavement elsewhere. He had been, as he put it, "threatned to be Sold (and sent to Albany) as a Slave."[37] A different petition elaborates on the point. Cuba, a twenty-five-year-old woman of African descent, was captured by an American warship and brought to Boston in 1777. Once there, she "rejoiced" that she had been brought to "this Land of Liberty"—a place where she expected to "spend her life in Comfort and freedom"—but she, like Joseph, feared being sent away. She claimed that an officer on board the ship that captured her planned to have her "sold as a slave and sent to Jamaica," and he seemed determined to stop at nothing, pledging to carry out his scheme "in Spite of all Courts and Persons whatsoever."[38] The officer's purported words, reported by Cuba to the person who wrote her petition, suggest the depth of the resistance that he faced in selling an African-descended war captive as a slave. By stating that he was ready to act "in Spite of all Courts and Persons whatsoever," the officer revealed his expectation that he would need to counter both the local justice system and the local populace: The region's courts and its inhabitants, he suspected, were on Cuba's side.

The officer threatening Cuba was right. Surviving evidence suggests that local inhabitants and lawmakers looked askance at attempts to ship Black captives off to places where slavery stood on firmer practical and ideological grounds. In September of 1776, when confronted with this practice, the Massachusetts General Court hastily put forth a resolve aimed at keeping sea captains and navy officers from engaging in it. The legislation, titled a "RESOLVE FORBIDDING THE SALE OF NEGRO CAPTIVES," declared to be "null and void" any financial transaction involving African-descended people taken from the enemy. The statute provided a baseline standard to which those who found themselves with authority over prisoners were required by law to adhere. Whoever might be dealing with Black captives, whether the Massachusetts Council, or the state's commissary of prisoners, or the captain of an American warship, had to treat those captives just as they would white prisoners, who could be kept in confinement but could not be sold for a profit.[39] Interestingly, though, the Massachusetts Council sometimes seemed inclined not to treat Black prisoners in a color-blind fashion. The Council, which was the governing body to which most petitions in this era were addressed, treated such captives at least on certain occasions with special sympathy.

The Council's thrice-edited response to the 1777 petition filed by a captured traveler named Hugh Munro shows an impulse toward liberty for Black captives. Hugh had been taken prisoner by American forces on his way to England, and he wished to be allowed to leave Massachusetts, bringing with him his wife and child, a young female relative, and two enslaved people of African descent. According to the committee charged with responding to Hugh's request, Hugh and his three white family members were to be allowed safe passage, and, in return for the generosity shown them by Massachusetts officials, Hugh was to seek the release of four American captives held by the British. However, the committee determined that Hugh would not be allowed to take "the negros" mentioned in his petition; these people, the committee wrote, would instead "be free'd" according to the General Court's legislation pertaining to "negroes that are Captivated."[40] The members of the committee then reconsidered; the Court's resolve had not required that Black captives be set *free*, after all. They therefore scratched out the word "free'd" and substituted "Treated" in its place: The two bondspeople would be *treated* according to the legislation—that is, presumably, they would be kept as prisoners of war with the rest of the state's captives. The following day, however, when the committee presented the matter to the entire Council, the Council's desire to procure additional American prisoners outweighed the committee's desire to retain the enslaved people, whether freed or imprisoned. A hastily scrawled note granted permission for Hugh's family to depart—a household consisting now of *six* people rather than four—and pressed upon Hugh the importance of "procur[ing] the release of as many Persons belonging to this state . . . as his said Family upon their arrival may Consist of." In the end, by shipping off the two bondspeople with Hugh, the Massachusetts Council used them as so many bargaining chips in the contest between the colonies and Great Britain, but the committee's early impulses, first to free the two, and then to retain them along with other prisoners of war, suggest that the decision to protect enslavers' property by keeping bondspeople with those who claimed them was, by this point, certainly not automatic.[41]

Other petitions filed at the time, and the Massachusetts Council's rulings on them, suggest that some people of African descent fared better than the two unnamed bondspeople sent to England with Hugh. Take the case of an anonymous "Negro Man" captured at sea. When the Massachusetts commissary of prisoners of war asked the Council what to do with the hostage, the Council directed him to let the man "go at large" in Boston as long as he behaved himself in an "orderly" fashion.[42] Another Black man obtained at sea, identified in records as David Mitchell, appealed directly to the law governing the treatment of Black captives, seeking, as he put it, the "Benefit of the Act of the Great & General Court of this State relative to Negroes being taken Prisoners and brought into this State." The Massachusetts Council declared in response that the man was "now admitted to his Freedom."[43] And when John Greenwood asked the commissary of prisoners for his sometime bondsman, Neptune, who had recently been recovered from a British ship, Neptune was set free from his "Confinement" as a prisoner of war according to John's request. However, he was not required to remain in slavery. John was told that Neptune would return to serve in his household "only if he chooses."[44]

Neptune, crucially, was given a choice. So, too, were other bondspeople. Though not necessarily set at liberty by the Council, some captives of African descent nonetheless were given the opportunity to make decisions for themselves. For instance, when Bostonian Richard Gridley requested that a young Black prisoner named Sarah be sent from the barracks to live with his family for a time—a common arrangement that the commissary of prisoners pursued to house a diverse array of prisoners—the Council did not approve the petition on the spot. Richard was told by the Council that he could bring Sarah to his home only if "she consent[ed]."[45] Likewise, when Betty Pote sought to leave Massachusetts, bringing her bondswoman with her, lawmakers stipulated that the "said Negro woman" must "consent" to be taken out of the state. Without the woman's agreement, Betty could not remove her from Massachusetts.[46]

Still other bodies of evidence, beyond petitions, newspapers, and probate records, contain clues to the withering of slavery in the region during the early years of the Revolution. There are, to start with, manumission papers stashed in area archives, some of which suggest that this moment was particularly ripe for envisioning freedom. Take the case of Cuff, who was freed in 1776 in the town of Lincoln, about a dozen miles west of Boston. In the document drawn up by his enslaver, John Hoar, Cuff was liberated because he was "now desiring to be made free."[47] *Now?* It is difficult to imagine that Cuff would ever have preferred bondage to freedom, but something about "now"—that is, spring of 1776—made it possible for Cuff to articulate his desire for liberty to his enslaver. It was not until this revolutionary moment that Cuff, John, or perhaps both could finally conceive of freedom as a real possibility.

Cuff, and others like him, were given deeds of manumission, but there are many mentions of enslaved people who left their places of bondage in the early years of the Revolution who probably lacked written permission to do so. The unnamed "Negro Man" enslaved by Benjamin Pemberton of Roxbury had been by Benjamin's side in April of 1775 at the Battles of Lexington and Concord, but by 1779 had "long since gone from him." Asel and Eber, two young men claimed by Elisha Allis, had "lived quietly" with Elisha's family, "having never deserted their service," until 1775, when they "went from him." In 1775, Caesar was believed by his erstwhile enslaver to be "strolling about in some of the neighbouring Towns" around Boston and reportedly "talk[ing] much of being free." Prince discreetly "left" Elisha Jones's household in May of 1775. A woman named Nane departed from the home of Francis Perkins in late 1775 "under a Pretence of a Visit," never to return. Two unnamed "Negro Men" who had lived "quietly & Peaceably" with Joseph Prout walked away in midsummer 1777, but they did not skip town; at least one of the men was still working locally months later. Likewise, Roger and Peg, husband and wife, deserted in 1776 "the house & service" of Bostonian Thomas Walker in order to work in the town on their own.[48] The archives are filled with such examples.

We know that Roger and Peg walked down the street and out of Thomas's life because their foiled enslaver sued, unsuccessfully, for their return.

The details of the suit provide still more confirmation of the degree to which slavery in Boston was faltering at the time. Rather than trying to obtain the return of *enslaved* laborers, Thomas based his case on Roger and Peg's supposed status as *indentured* ones. He need not have bothered: The case was tossed out of court.[49] Other court records provide evidence that local people were questioning slavery in the early years of the Revolution—and that white inhabitants were realizing they might not be able to claim the lives and labors of Black people much longer. For example, in 1777, Cato, described as "an African by birth," arranged for a Boston man named Samuel Conant to be hauled into court. The charge? Samuel had "attempted to sell him the s[ai]d Cato as a slave & to transport him to foreign parts."[50] Curiously, the arrest warrant, which details Cato's grievances, does not describe Cato as "free," as it almost certainly would have had the man formally obtained his liberty: The case seemingly hinged on Cato's freedom, after all. But it does not describe Cato as enslaved, either, as one would expect had the man been known as a person in bondage. Cato's status seems to have been in limbo. Was he, perhaps, a long-enslaved person living at a moment in which a society that had accepted slavery as a social fact—indeed, a social necessity—was coming to see the institution as illegitimate? That Cato and Samuel shared both a location (Boston) and an occupation (each was a baker) as well as seem to have been familiar with one another makes it possible that Cato had been enslaved by Samuel, but that, at the present juncture, he glimpsed an opportunity to make a break from bondage and avoid being sent to a location where slavery's grip on African-descended people was tighter. The arrest warrant does not spell out all the details, but it suggests that local white people were looking to profit by selling the enslaved or those nominally in bondage to places with more robust systems of slavery, and it suggests as well that the Massachusetts justice system took seriously the claims of Black inhabitants who found themselves victimized in the process. Cato, who feared "foreign parts," like Cuba, who was terrified of Jamaica, and Joseph, who dreaded passage to Albany, appealed to local authorities in an attempt to keep himself in a place where the system of slavery was caving in around him.

Yet slavery did not end in this moment for everyone in Massachusetts. Some people remained in bondage long after the institution began breaking down at the Revolution's outbreak. Even the 1780 constitution declaring all men "free and equal" and the abolitionist 1783 judicial ruling failed to end slavery completely. Neither, after all, convinced John Fisher, a Franklin yeoman, that his "Negro boy" ought to be allowed to go free. John's estate appraisers listed the boy, whom they valued at ten pounds in the fall of 1784, on the inventory of John's possessions between his "household furniture" and his "one Cow."[51] Nor did the constitution or resultant judicial decisions fully stop Suffolk County decedents from including freedom provisions in their wills, which suggests that neither had convinced the white populace as a whole that slaveholding had been abolished. Even Ellis Gray, a Boston merchant who served as a delegate to the state's constitutional convention, stipulated in his will, written *after* the passage of the constitution, that his bondsman was to be freed. "If my Negro Cato is not free by the Laws of the Land," he wrote, "it is my Will that he shall be so." Ellis had played a role in drafting the constitution, but he still did not know whether its stipulation that all men are "free and equal" had actually outlawed slavery.[52] And evidence of slavery in Massachusetts exists through the 1790s and beyond.[53] But this should be expected, as one would anticipate that an unlegislated end to a longstanding institution would proceed piecemeal. Certain outliers, resisting the new beliefs gaining traction in the region, insisted on retaining their bondspeople and could not easily be forced into compliance without clear legislative mandates. However, the evidence from eastern Massachusetts makes clear that the most significant changes in slaveholding practices of the long revolutionary era took place in the first years of revolutionary conflict, well before the passage of the constitution that supposedly laid the legal groundwork for the court cases in the early 1780s, which have long been understood to have ended slavery in the state.

*   *   *

The ability of Darby to walk away from bondage in 1775, leaving one village on the outskirts of Boston for another, makes sense given the changes taking place in the region. Likewise, the zeroes marked down as the putative values of Anthony and Cuba are hardly surprising when one considers the widescale breakdown of slavery at the time of the pair's appraisal. But an important question remains. If the historical record makes clear that the institution of slavery collapsed in the Boston area during the 1770s, then *how did this come to be*? What were the historical forces driving the revolutionary changes that allowed Darby to set one foot in front of the other, entirely unimpeded and apparently without risk of recapture and punishment, all the way back to his place of birth?

To begin with, it is worth noting the economic context of this transformation. Boston found itself on unstable economic footing in the mideighteenth century, so much so that even the boom in British spending during the Seven Years' War—which paid for the construction of barracks, the building of ships, the provisioning of troops, and more—could not pull the town fully from recession. And when the fighting in North America ceased in 1760 and the British army sent its resources elsewhere, Boston descended into the throes of depression, its citizens facing uncertain employment and burdensome taxes levied in support of the expanding ranks of the poor. Some evidence suggests that the importation of bondspeople to Massachusetts slowed at this time. Various would-be enslavers no longer had the resources to buy into the market, and others probably decided that hiring laborers when needed was more prudent than supporting permanent bondspeople. This economic malaise provides an important backdrop for our story: When it came to dependence on slavery in the 1760s, Boston, Massachusetts, was no Charleston, South Carolina, or Bridgetown, Barbados. Yet material factors are insufficient to explain the collapse of slavery in eastern Massachusetts during the 1770s. Boston, for one, was not alone in its economic troubles. Other northern seaports, such as New York, suffered from serious postwar economic downturns starting in 1760 but did not turn from slavery at the Revolution's outbreak the way Boston and its surrounds did. What is more, the sources pointing to the crumbling of the institution of slavery in eastern Massachusetts—such as the sudden absence of the enslaved from probate records, the advertising of able-bodied bondspeople to be given for "free," and the equation of Black laborers with white ones—post-date the onset of economic crisis by well over a decade. Economic malaise may well have made white people in Massachusetts more willing to consider parting with those they bound, but it cannot explain the sudden ability of Darby and others to walk out of slavery. More was at work.[54]

One thing is abundantly clear. If most Black people in the area obtained their liberty *before* the great political and legal developments that supposedly eradicated slavery in the state, the emancipatory process must have been a bottom-up rather than a top-down revolution in social relations. Our attention should therefore shift from the political and legal changes enacted by prominent citizens—delegates to the constitutional convention, lawyers, court justices, and juries—to the internal dynamics of slaveholding households.[55] We must center the actions of ordinary people around the time

of the Revolution's outbreak: white people who chose to manumit bound laborers and Black people who managed to extricate themselves from bondage. Many enslavers did not wait until they were compelled by an external
force, such as a constitution that presumably outlawed slavery, to release their
bondspeople. And those in bondage did not wait until the state constitution
declared them "free and equal" to make their bids for freedom. Instead, they
left their enslavers in large numbers at a time when no framing documents
espoused universal liberty for residents of Massachusetts and when no ju-
ries had found Black people free on the basis of the "Laws of the Land."[56]

Conceiving of the end of slavery in Massachusetts as a bottom-up revolution in social relations runs counter to much of the past century of historical scholarship on the matter, but this interpretive thrust is not altogether
new. It echoes arguments made more than 200 years ago by Jeremy Belknap,
the first historian to study the end of slavery in Massachusetts. Jeremy re-
searched the issue in 1795 at the behest of St. George Tucker, a Virginia
judge eager to understand the history of slavery and abolition in Massachusetts. Circulating a series of queries to some forty people whom he
thought knowledgeable (both Black and white), and consulting as well what
he elliptically referred to as "other sources of information," Jeremy came to
a firm conclusion regarding the process by which slavery ended in the
state.[57] Slavery had been abolished not by the constitution, nor by the courts,
but by "*publick opinion*." He repeated this—always emphasizing the two key
words—throughout his missive to the curious Virginian. In the prerevolutionary moment, Jeremy argued, "both slavery and the slave-trade began
to be discountenanced. The principal cause," he wrote, "was *publick opinion*." At another juncture, Jeremy declared that "slavery hath been abolished
here by *publick opinion*." And he later went on to state, once again, that "the
publick opinion was . . . strongly in favour of the abolition of slavery" during
the Revolution.[58]

According to Jeremy, early signs of this shift in popular sentiment were
visible in public debates that took place nearly a decade before the outbreak
of war. In the mid-1760s, as conflict between Massachusetts and Britain heated
up, Jeremy observed that inhabitants of the region who despised slavery took
the "occasion publickly to remonstrate against the inconsistency of contending for our own liberty, and at the same time depriving other people of
theirs." According to Jeremy, the controversy between proslavery and antislavery factions intensified in 1773; at that point, as he put it, the debate was
"very warmly agitated."[59]

Surviving sources bear out Jeremy's claims that a cluster of antislavery voices emerged in the printed material that emanated from Boston in the 1760s and that arguments over slavery became particularly vocal in 1773. These sources reveal something else as well: the active participation of Black people in public discourse. People of African descent—including the enslaved—did not sit idly by while white citizens debated the meaning and proper extent of liberty. They put forth great effort to shape the thinking of their neighbors and to give form to the conversations that rang through the port's busy streets. As the debate over slavery reached fever pitch, Black activists raised their voices, launching a powerful petition campaign aimed ostensibly at lawmakers but intended every bit as much to sway the minds and hearts of their neighbors.

A series of printed appeals written by both enslaved and free people of African descent made their way through prerevolutionary Boston and the surrounding villages. The first, written in the opening days of 1773, begged the Massachusetts General Court to abolish slavery. Such a law would be to the enslaved "as Life from the dead," the petition proclaimed.[60] Though the petitioners directed the appeal to the legislature, they sought the widest possible readership for their complaint and managed to get it printed with the help of an anonymous Bostonian who called himself a "lover of constitutional liberty." This person penned an antislavery tract to accompany the appeal, and together the tract and the petition circulated throughout the region. Other media furthered the reach of the Black activists' message. The *Massachusetts Spy*, one of Boston's prominent newspapers, informed the public on several occasions that one could obtain the petition at Ezekiel Russell's print shop on Union Street for a mere seven pennies.[61] The *Spy* also published an opinion piece written by an unnamed "customer" of the paper, who begged the members of the General Court to receive the petition favorably. But the lawmakers were not the sole intended audience of this piece. The essayist wrote as well to pull the public to the activists' side, calling attention to the hypocrisy of "the protestations of liberty which [white citizens] daily make, when at the same time these blacks are kept in the utmost slavery."[62]

Three months later, an expanded group of bound men composed another petition and sent it to the House of Representatives. Once again, Massachusetts lawmakers were not the only targets of their activism. They persuaded a local minister named John Allen to include their petition in the fourth edition of his tract, *An Oration on the Beauties of Liberty*. The tract made a case for the colonists' right to political liberty, and John appended to it the Black Bostonians' call for liberty from slavery. "These distressed people," he wrote, "are unjustly held in bondage."[63] At least four different newspapers advertised the printing of this petition and the pamphlet to which it was annexed, and the enormously popular tract sold out quickly, bringing the demands of the enslaved to audiences throughout New England.[64] The activists must have been pleased with their work. Scoring a place in John's *Oration* was strategic not simply because of the tract's broad popularity but also because of its attractiveness to common people; the *Oration* appealed especially to non-literate audiences, for, unlike most political treatises of the era, it was intended primarily to be heard rather than read.[65] Such a publication enabled antislavery advocates of African descent to expand the reach of their protest considerably. And the activists went still further by printing their appeal as a broadside and directing it to various towns in the province. Hoping to encourage town representatives to stand against slavery when the legislature sat in May, they directed "instructions" to these representatives and styled themselves spokespersons for a "Committee" of enslaved people in Massachusetts. These strategies display impressive insight into the politics of the time; town representatives in the province regularly received instructions from their constituents as to how they should vote, and committees of correspondence had recently started to form all across Massachusetts in opposition to British policies.[66]

It was not enough, however, for the words of these activists to be read aloud at town meetings, to join the din of mealtime chatter in taverns, or to ring out on street corners by printing houses. The matter was urgent and the legislature had not yet bent to their demand, so the Black activists reconvened. Two months later, in June of 1773, enslaved Bostonians again petitioned the Massachusetts governor, his Council, and the House of Representatives, asking once more for the abolition of slavery. A local newspaper printed the full text of their request the following month. Splashed across the first page, the petition declared that people of African descent had "a natural right to be free."[67] Three weeks later, an unidentified bondsman, perhaps inspired by the recent surge in antislavery protests, sent a condemnation of slavery to the *Boston Gazette*. Though he had "hardly learnt to Read and Write," this complainant "appeal[ed] to the Conscience of all who Inslave us Negroes." A similar statement, written by a "SON of AFRICA," was printed in Boston's *Massachusetts Spy*. And a third such appeal, this signed by a free Black man named Caesar Sarter, who lived north of Boston in Newburyport, Massachusetts, occupied nearly all of the cover page of the *Essex Journal*.[68]

The region's Black activists did not let up. In January of 1774, enslaved Bostonians sent yet another petition to their lawmakers. Once again, local newspapers picked up the story, bringing the petitioners' words into public houses and meetinghouses, courtrooms and bedrooms. In May of that year, the petitioners addressed the governor, his Council, and the House of Representatives again.[69] The following month, June, they sent yet another plea to Massachusetts lawmakers and, once more, made sure that the text of their complaint was broadcast in print to their community. Placed in the first column on the front page of the *Massachusetts Spy*, the entreaty could not be missed.[70] The appeals simply kept coming during these prerevolutionary years. The printers kept printing. The public, presumably, kept reading. The legislature never acquiesced to the petitioners' demands, at least in part because the governor dissolved the General Court in the midst of the petition drive, but the petitioners won their broader point.[71] Black protest and activism, together with the revolutionary ideology that swept the region, appear to have helped convince white inhabitants that their claims to human property were not legitimate.[72] But how? On what grounds did the enslaved community render illegitimate long-held beliefs and long-practiced customs?

Black abolitionists in eastern Massachusetts pursued a variety of strategies to convince their white legislators, neighbors, coreligionists, and enslavers that slavery was unjust. They appealed, not surprisingly, to natural law, proclaiming, "your Petitioners apprehend we have in common With all other men a naturel right to our freedoms." They drew attention to the hypocrisy of white residents of Massachusetts who sought freedom from Britain while continuing to enslave the Africans in their households, declaring with sarcasm, "We expect great things from men who have made such a noble stand against the designs of their *fellow-men* to enslave them." They used the Bible to discredit slaveholding, calling on the teachings of Jesus, the "indiscriminate Saviour of Jew and Gentile, of White and Black" who "Commanded that all Men do unto others as they would have others do to them."[73] And they seized upon the problem of family.

Family figures prominently in this body of appeals, which moved through the region in newspapers, tracts, manuscripts, circular letters, oral recitations, and rumors.[74] Black activists consistently and with vigor depicted slavery as a crime not merely against the individual but also against the *family*. For those captured in Africa, the instance of enslavement nearly always severed intimate relationships, and for that it was damnable. "We were dragged by the cruel hand of power," one petition reads, "some of us . . . stolen from the bosoms of tender parents and brought hither to be enslaved."[75] The petitioners repeated this line of reasoning over and over, even recycling the very words they used to express it. A later appeal echoed almost verbatim: "we were unjustly dragged by the cruel hand of power . . . sum of us stolen from the bosoms of our tender Parents . . . and Brought hither to be made slaves for Life in a Christian land."[76] Another petition used essentially the same words.[77] And a fourth entreaty elaborated on the theme, bemoaning that the enslaved "were unjustly dragged, by the cruel hand of Power . . . some of them even torn from the Embraces of their tender Parents—From a populous, pleasant, & plentiful Country—& in violation of the Laws of Nature & of Nation & in defiance of all the tender feelings of humanity, brought hither to be sold like Beasts of Burthen, & like them condemned to slavery for Life."[78] Black activists altered other aspects of their requests from petition to petition, which makes this continuity of language and argument striking; the supplicants must have recognized that doubling down on the destruction of African families by the Atlantic trade was crucial to delegitimizing slavery.

If the instance of enslavement severed intimate ties, so too did the long grind of slavery as experienced over the course of a lifetime. "[W]e are deprived of every thing that has a tendency to make life even tolerable," the petitioners wrote. "The endearing ties of husband, wife, parent, child and friend, we are generally strangers to: And whenever any of those connections are formed among us, the pleasures are imbittered by the cruel consideration of our slavery."[79] Once again, the petitioners used repetition strategically to hammer home their point. The following appeal reiterated: "we [are] deprived of every thing that hath a tendency to make life even tolerable, the endearing ties of husband and wife we are strangers to." It went on to provide specific examples of familial destruction wrought by practices of slaveholding in Massachusetts. Slavery broke conjugal bonds: "we are no longer man and wife then our masters or Mestreses thinkes proper marred or onmarred." And slavery broke parental bonds as well: "Our Children are also taken from us by force and sent maney miles from us wear we seldom or ever see them again there to be made slaves of fore Life which sumtimes is verey short by Reson of Being dragged from their mothers Breest."[80] Another petition laid out the same scenarios. "[W]e [are] deprived of every thing that has a tendency to make life even tolerable," it echoed. "The endearing ties of husband, wife, parent, children, friend; children did we say? Alas! no sooner are they born, but they are either sold or given away helpless without our consent, whereby we are rendered ignorant of them and they of us." Slavery compromised family integrity in a host of disturbing ways, and bound activists highlighted in petition after petition the damage caused by these disruptions to their intimate lives.[81]

By making the case that slavery was wrong because it destroyed family ties, Black abolitionists claimed for themselves the right to family integrity. That much is clear. What is less clear is why this strategy helped convince white people in revolutionary Boston and its hinterland that slavery was unethical. Part of the answer is tied up in the rhetorical strategies of these antislavery writings. The activists worked hard to elicit emotions on the part of their white audience, and for good reason: That audience was primed to respond on a sentimental register to family-related appeals. Two broad historical changes can account for this. First, as new ideas about the universality of human emotion emerged in the years before the Revolution, many of the activists' white neighbors came to believe that people of African descent experienced the same sorts of feelings that their enslavers experienced.[82] And, second, colonists over the course of the eighteenth century came to think about families as affective units more than economic ones. Putting these changes together, if Black people had the same sorts of sentiments that white people had, and if white people believed that families were (or ought to be) knit together by love and affection, it follows that many of the activists' white neighbors could be convinced that the enslaved were deeply invested on an emotional level in their familial relationships. The long-standing Christian ethos in Massachusetts served only to amplify the importance of family feeling among kin—and the authors of these antislavery pieces clearly understood this. They used sentiment-laden language to describe the "shocking Inhumanities" that enslaved families suffered in Massachusetts. And with passion they reminded listeners of their complicity: In the course of their daily lives, after all, white readers and hearers "beh[e]ld our Wives and Children taken from us, bought and sold like dumb Beasts, and often with less Regard." The language of these entreaties was sometimes personal. As one antislavery advocate implored his audience, "Let me, who have now no less than eleven relatives suffering in bondage, beseech you, good people."[83]

Activists also forced white audiences to imagine familial destruction that they could not see in Massachusetts, to feel their way through elaborately described scenes of emotional wreckage brought about by enslavement in

Africa. One Black writer set the stage thus: "Though the thought be shocking—for a few minutes, suppose that you were trepanned away." He urged his audience to envision "The husband [seized] from the dear wife of his bosom—the wife from her affectionate husband—children from their fond parents—or parents from their tender and beloved offspring, whom, not an hour before, perhaps, they were fondling in their arms, and in whom they were promising themselves much future happiness." He then brought home these disturbing examples of family disintegration. "Suppose, I say that you were thus ravished from such a blissful situation, and plunged into miserable slavery, in a distant quarter of the globe: Or suppose you were accompanied by your wife and children, parents and brethren manacled by your side—harrowing thought!" Apparently, this was not enough. He continued, describing loved ones "clinging," family members "dreading," tears "droping."[84] Other antislavery writers used similar language to evoke emotional responses to the annihilation of families in Africa. "Who would not shudder at viewing the tender parent weeping for the loss of a favorite son!" one asked rhetorically. And white audiences were presented with the child's point of view as well, asked to feel the "irretrievable misfortune" of "Dutiful children" mourning the loss of "affectionate, tender, and loving father[s]." Of a montage of such scenes, one writer commanded his audience: "Think! O think of this!"[85]

This emotional language was carefully calculated to employ the sentimental idioms that pulsed through prerevolutionary Boston and its surrounds, but activists also used a second strategy that was less of the moment. Taking their cue from a playbook as old as the institution of slavery in New England, antislavery writers emphasized the spiritual ramifications of splintered families. As one petition put it, the distortions of family life under slavery rendered bondspeople "incapable of shewing our obedience to Almighty God." How, the petition asked, "can a Slave perform the duties of a husband to a wife or parent to his child?" "How can a husband leave master and work and Cleave to his wife?" "How can the wife submit themselves to there Husbands in all things?" "How can the child obey thear parents in all things?"[86] The answers were self-evident; enslaved husbands, wives, and children living in Massachusetts could not live out their intimate lives according to the commands of God. Another petition asked the same questions, appending to them the obvious conclusion: "We are often under the necessity of obeying *man*, not only in omission of, but frequently in opposition to the laws of *God*."[87] Still another petition echoed, "how can a slave perform the duties of husband or parent, wife or child? We are often under the cruel necessity of obeying man, not only in omission of, but frequently in opposition to the laws of GOD, so inimical is slavery to religion!"[88] Thus, activists in the 1770s seized upon the very line of reasoning that had persuaded Dorcas's Dorchester congregation to free her some five generations prior.

Dorcas had made the case in 1652 that she needed to be liberated in order to engage in family building the way God intended it. That is, she had demonstrated to the brethren, to use the words of the revolutionary petitioners, "how inimical is slavery to religion." Dorcas's cross-status, cross-ethnic claims on her free white brethren were successful because she, in quite stunning form, acculturated herself to a highly religious community, a community that allowed itself to feel discomfort at the degree to which slavery compromised one member's ability to adhere to its family norms. Central to Dorcas's feat was the intensity of her intimate interactions with the other people in that little hamlet outside of Boston who believed themselves chosen by God. There was the joyous confession, which established that Dorcas was one of them. There was, as well, the psalm singing, in which Dorcas's descant mingled with the melodies of the saints around her. And, of course, there were the long services in the meetinghouse, which Dorcas attended with the brethren whether rivulets of sweat ran down her temple or water froze in the baptismal.

Some 120 years after Dorcas's redemption, Black activists in the Boston area made the same cross-status, cross-ethnic claims on their free white community, and they justified their claims at least in part the very way Dorcas had. But they appealed not to a confined congregation of saints; their demands rang out across a much greater geographic space and reached a much larger—and much more religiously diverse—audience. Therefore, the intimate encounters that moved the brethren to redeem Dorcas could not aid the revolutionary-era activists, whose audiences ordinarily did not know them and had no way of judging their religiosity.[89] While Dorcas was redeemed because of her personal piety, then, Black protesters in the revolutionary moment did not—could not—base their claims to freedom on themselves and their accomplishments. Nonetheless, they had a powerful foundation on which to build, for the Black community in Boston and its surrounds had a lengthy track record of maintaining faithful families against all odds.

Here one has to be careful. It would be a mistake to take too literally what these petitions proclaim. "We have no Property! We have no wives! No children!" one petition reads, while another declares, "The endearing ties of husband, wife, parent, child and friend, we are generally strangers to."[90]

Each of these claims contains a kernel of truth. Time and again, enslaved people faced major challenges when it came to building intimate ties with one another in New England. Most crippling was the demography of the region, which ensured that the families built by people in slavery nearly always bridged multiple Anglo-American households. Some scholars have noted this and other challenges, and they have concluded that the enslaved could not form families in New England.[91] This is, indeed, what one has to conclude if one simply takes the petitions at their word. "We have no wives! No children!"

We must, however, remain sensitive to the rhetorical world in which these petitions were conceived. In this historical moment, the British-American colonists were experts when it came to hyperbole, and Boston was the epicenter of their outrage, which means that the town's inhabitants—white and Black—encountered inflated grievances everywhere they turned. Taxes equated to enslavement; tea was a "poisonous draught."[92] We would expect Black activists to have spoken the melodramatic idiom of the streets when laying out their complaints. And, indeed, they did. One can see clearly their dramatic flourishes when one reconstructs the context in which they wrote. Evidence of the family ties of bondspeople was everywhere in eighteenth-century Massachusetts. In just the town of Boston, for instance, more than a thousand Black people were married by ministers and justices of the peace over the course of the eighteenth century.[93] These Bostonians went to great effort to establish their marital ties in public and to wed in an official capacity: The process of obtaining legal marriage involved town clerks, ministers, justices of the peace, and the broader community, which vetted the relationships of both Black people and white people and had the potential to forbid from marrying couples deemed unsuitable. If enslaved people married in large numbers, so, too, did they bear children. The fragmented records of Boston's churches indicate that hundreds of enslaved and free Black children were baptized before Boston's congregations over the course of the eighteenth century, a ritual that ordinarily was carried out by the minister with the aid of the child's father. Baptisms were performed in the same place where marriages were announced: in Boston's local meetinghouses, which stood at the center of Boston's social life, and which residents of all races were required by law to attend.

Because enslaved people engaged in family-building so actively and because they often chose to do it in public, through the institutions white people set up to govern marriage and family, Black families were visible in Massachusetts in a way they were not in much of the rest of the Anglo-Atlantic world. It is inconceivable that any white person reading the antislavery appeals could have believed that Black men in Boston had no wives or that Black parents in the town had no children. Everyone in Boston knew Black people—many of them—who had built and sustained kin ties despite the challenges of slavery. Indeed, these words were so powerful because, as the region's white community read or heard them, they did not just think of abstract and theoretical struggles that could be faced by people in bondage; they must have thought of actual *Black families facing those struggles*. Families they knew. Intact families. Enslaved people in their churches who had built bonds of blood and contract with one another. The claim that bound people should have a right to family autonomy would have made sense to white Bostonians because they had long watched Black people construct family ties under the constraints of slavery. Husbands and wives ordinarily lived in separate households. Children could be given away. Any family member could be sold out of town. And yet, enslaved people continued to broadcast their bids for family unity to their communities. They stood before their congregations. They asked their ministers to announce their marriage intentions. They approached local justices of the peace and other officials. They sought advocates in their community. They tried to purchase their children's freedom. They sued for their wives' liberty in the courts.

Jeremy Belknap, the early historian who in 1795 sought to grasp how slavery had ended in Massachusetts, concluded that, by the time of the Revolution, "the *publick opinion* was . . . strongly in favor of the abolition of slavery." This came on the heels of an aggressive campaign waged by the enslaved to impugn slavery for the handicaps it placed on the intimate lives of those in bondage. And it was accompanied by a mass exodus. Black people were well aware of the transformations taking place in the minds of their white neighbors and enslavers: Jeremy stated explicitly that "many . . . t[oo]k . . . advantage of the *publick opinion*" to seize their freedom, some by asking for it, others by simply leaving.[94] At precisely the time that Black activists submitted a barrage of petitions to the legislature demanding freedom in order to right their family lives, the enslaved acted on the sentiment by voting with their feet: walking out of bondage. The young woman who slipped off to join the "Company" of a free man of African descent. The twenty-seven-year-old man who seized the opportunity to live at liberty in Boston with the woman "whom he calls his Wife." The Black woman who "carried off" a five-year-old child (her daughter?) from an enslaver's home.[95]

The six-year-old boy—little Darby—who deserted the household of the man who bound him to rejoin his birth family three towns away. Some people doubtless left bondage for reasons unrelated to intimate ties, but all bound people benefited from the changing tide of public opinion: the recognition on the part of many white people that slavery was no longer defensible in large part because it encroached on the right of bondspeople to family integrity. Slavery fell in Massachusetts at least in part because of the problems it caused for Black families.[96]

*   *   *

The overwhelming impetus in the region's Black community during the opening acts of the revolutionary drama was toward seizing freedom, and freedom for many people meant family reunification. Darby strode away from his enslaver's household for the purpose of returning to his parents and siblings. But we need to remain sensitive to the complexity of this historical moment and take care not to flatten the actions and aspirations of the Black inhabitants of Massachusetts by assuming that all were animated by a single-minded search for personal liberty. The Black Vassalls, Darby excepted, had different aims than their neighbors. They were, by this time, a family of bondspeople with no local enslavers living in the chaos of war, and they could simply have walked away from the white Vassalls' estates, taking hold of their independence. It would have been easy: All across eastern Massachusetts, laborers were leaving those who had long held them in bondage, and the white Vassalls certainly could not, from a distance, have forced the Black Vassalls to remain. But Anthony and Cuba chose to keep their family where it was. Apparently, they reasoned that there was more to be gained by staying on John Vassall's estate than by leaving.

While George Washington formulated a plan of action for the patriot war effort in John's parlor, Anthony and Cuba formulated a plan of action for their family's provision in John's garden. The pair's strategy was surprising. It was brilliant. And, most important, it was effective. Central to the scheme was Anthony and Cuba's reasoning that the white Vassalls' property—the estates left by John and Penelope—was not confined to land and houses and horses in barns. The white Vassalls' property included *people*: the Black Vassalls. Massachusetts had assumed responsibility for the upkeep of loyalists' confiscated estates, so the state therefore ought rightly to assume responsibility for the welfare of the people belonging to those estates. The enslaved were everywhere deserting their enslavers, but no law actually declared them to be liberated—which, for the Black Vassalls, was key. They would exploit their uncertain status to accomplish the opposite of what their Black neighbors sought to achieve: Rather than contending that Cuba and the children were free, the Vassalls would claim that they remained enslaved. At precisely the same time that Black people across the state were walking out of slavery into lives and identities as freed people, then, the patriarch of the Black Vassall family would insist that his wife and children remain where they had long toiled in slavery, and he would make much of their bound status: In Anthony's formulation, Cuba and her children "belonged to the Estate of [the] s[ai]d [John] Vassall."[97]

Anthony had a great deal to gain by wedging his subordinates firmly into bondage during the Revolutionary War. By drawing attention to their status as John's property, he managed to persuade the town official charged with maintaining the white Vassalls' confiscated estates to compensate him for feeding and clothing his own family. This official, a Cambridge resident named Thomas Farrington, left accounts showing that he paid Anthony the extraordinary sum of 222 pounds for "supporting a Negro woman & two Children [for] 3 years." Technically, Anthony was every bit as enslaved—or every bit as free, depending on how you look at it—as his wife and children. They shared precisely the same status, whatever it was. But Anthony did not claim for himself enslaved status as he did for his wife and children. He demanded only that his household subordinates be maintained by the estate, not that he be so maintained, and he postured himself as a caretaker rather than as a person in need of care.

Anthony surely chose to identify himself as an emancipated man, but to identify his wife and children as bondspeople, because he understood the power of gendered norms with regard to familial provision. By positioning himself as a free household head and simultaneously portraying his family members as enslaved dependents, Anthony assumed a patriarchal role familiar to the people who held the purse strings of the confiscated Vassall estates. He became a provider for the powerless, a custodian of dependents. Had Cuba postured herself this way, Thomas and those of his ilk would hardly have rewarded her with hundreds of pounds sterling. Only Anthony, as household head, could stand before authorities and claim for himself inflated compensation for his efforts to feed and clothe his family.

Anthony turned out to be a provider extraordinaire for his family.[98] After obtaining support through the town of Cambridge via Thomas Farrington, he petitioned the Massachusetts legislature multiple times for title to the land on which he worked. In September of 1780, he recruited a sponsor to write out a request. Anthony and his "little family," the petition read, had "since the commencement of the present war . . . occupied a small tenement, with three quarters of an acre of land . . . [on] John Vassall's estate in Cambridge." But the land was "not sufficient to supply them with such vegetables as [we]re necessary for their family use," so the petition asked that the legislature add more land to it. And would the "Hon[ora]ble Court" be so good as to promise this land to the Black Vassall family "for life"?[99] Their present title was "precarious," and they felt "an anxious concern for the future support of themselves & children." The petition, signed in the hand of whomever wrote it by both Anthony and Cuba, was referred to a committee, where it seems to have been buried by other correspondence related to the Revolution.

But the committee's lack of action did not dissuade Anthony. The following year, he presented another appeal. This entreaty made more of the crushing burdens facing Anthony as household head, and it was signed only by him, marked with a confident and carefully rendered "T" for Tony. In the 1780 petition, Anthony had been "considerably advanced in life"; by the 1781 rendition, he was an "old man." In 1780, Anthony had been responsible for a "little family"; by 1781, he had a "large family of children to maintain." And in 1780, Anthony's wife was a co-supplicant, presumably a partner; by 1781, however, she had become "sick," a dependent whose welfare hinged on her husband's capacity to obtain "a sufficiency of bread." Anthony now "fear[ed] that if his house should be taken from him, and he be denied . . . the little spot of land" he currently farmed, his family would be forced to "adopt the hard necessity of begging for a little bread." Why, according to the plea, was Anthony in such a precarious financial position? And why might his dependents be "throw[n] . . . upon the charity of others"? Ordinarily such a situation would be considered evidence of a failure of patriarchal leadership. Perhaps the household head did not work hard enough, or was not prudent enough with his spending, or simply did not plan well for the future. But this was not the case with Anthony: "Your memorialist begs leave to observe that though dwelling in a land of freedom, both himself and his wife have spent almost sixty years of their lives in slavery." Would they now be "denied the sweets of freedom the remainder of their days by being reduced to the painful necessity of begging for bread"? Anthony's inability to provide properly for his family stemmed from the injustice of slavery, not from fault of his own. The court, however, had the ability to restore the household to

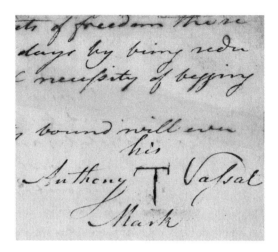

Figure 13. Anthony's mark. Anthony signed his 1781 petition to the Massachusetts legislature with a bold and well-formed "T" for "Tony." Courtesy of the Massachusetts State Archives.

proper order if it would only grant his request for the house and land he had long occupied.[100]

The lawmakers who considered Anthony's second plea found it persuasive. They did not give Anthony the house and land that he asked for, but they passed a resolution to pay Anthony twelve pounds out of the proceeds of John Vassall's estate that year and to allocate twelve pounds to Anthony each year to come from the state's coffers.[101] And so, the African-descended man of indeterminate status, head of a Black household of equally ambiguous rank, managed to manipulate his revolutionary circumstances to safeguard his family and bolster his position as its patriarch.[102] Between his public pension—which he was still receiving when he died twenty years later—and the impressive sum he netted from caring for his supposedly enslaved dependents during the war years, Anthony emerged from the Revolution with a significant nest egg.[103] He lost the home he had long occupied when the Vassall estate was sold in 1781, but he purchased within a decade a house less than a mile from John Vassall's old mansion. Four years later, he expanded his holdings by procuring an adjacent plot of land. And two years after that, in 1793, he bought five acres across the street.[104] The 152 pounds he paid for these acquisitions, which far exceeded what most laboring people—Black or white—could afford for housing, provided him with a comfortable home and enough land to set himself up as a farrier. The former coachman shoed his neighbors' horses, groomed them, housed them, and grew hay to feed them. Anthony appears to have earned enough money through this trade to support his family comfortably and to establish himself in the eyes of his neighbors as a respectable independent farmer and tradesman. Some documents even called the aging former bondsman a "yeoman," an appellation indicating a social status several notches higher than that of a common laborer.[105]

Anthony and Cuba's story illuminates how gender could work in this historical moment among Black people who were embarking on lives as free people. In the Vassalls' experience, freedom appears to have brought with it a real commitment to patriarchal gender relations. Anthony took the lead in petitioning for land, pleading for housing, and demanding reimbursement for living expenses. He went to great lengths to do this, cultivating relationships with various literate allies and negotiating with the town official in charge of maintaining the Vassall estates. Perhaps most revealing in this entire process is not that Anthony spearheaded the task of providing for the family in freedom but rather the irony that in his efforts to do so he went so far as to insist that his wife and children, who shared his status as effectively autonomous, were in fact firmly ensconced in slavery. By positioning himself as the caretaker of enslaved dependents, Anthony managed to net for himself a tremendous gain, which made a real difference in his ability to safeguard his family in freedom. But this gain came only when Anthony made much of his own independent initiative and financial outlay—and much of his wife and children's reliance on his provision. The Black Vassalls prospered in the revolutionary and postrevolutionary era by developing a male-dominated family unit. And the patriarchal skew in gender relations, at least insofar as it related to financial provision, does not appear to have been an illusion, crafted only for the benefit of onlookers; no evidence indicates that Cuba ever worked outside the home, but the evidence of Anthony's enterprising public-facing endeavors is abundant.

Of course, Anthony and Cuba were unusual in many ways. Their experience points to the upper limit of what was possible for people who extricated themselves from slavery in revolutionary New England; most Black families could not afford to depend solely on the income of their male breadwinners. Nonetheless, other families in the region experienced aspects of the transition from slavery to freedom in similar ways, building households that were dominated by men in the postrevolutionary years. Striking evidence of this dynamic can be seen in the returns of the first federal census, which, taken in 1790, sheds light on the structure of Black households in the region. These records make clear that the process by which formerly enslaved people moved out of white homes and set up households of their own was very piecemeal. For all intents and purposes, Anthony and Cuba were free—and had their own autonomous household—in 1774, when the white Vassalls fled Cambridge for the safety of the British army in Boston. But not all people of African descent obtained independent living quarters so quickly. A sizable minority of Black people—39 percent—still lived in white-headed households when census takers walked the streets of eastern Massachusetts in 1790. They might have been "free"—indeed, according to the census records, all of them were, as no enslaved people were recorded in the state—but they nonetheless lived as dependents in Anglo-American homes.[106] Not surprisingly, people of African descent who remained embedded in white families appear to have suffered stunted family lives of their own. Most were the only non-white people in their respective households, though some lived with one other Black person, and a very small number lived with more than one other person of African descent. On average, white-headed households with Black residents had merely 1.3 Black inhabitants, while Black-headed households across the region had 3.7 Black inhabitants. So Black people who lived in Black households cohabited with nearly three times more people of African descent than those who lived in white households.

What did these Black households look like? Unfortunately, census returns do not provide details on the people who lived in Black households; census takers logged neither age nor gender of Black-household residents, and they neglected to note Black people's names unless they were household heads.[107] But the scant information is nonetheless illuminating. Census records reveal that Black households were overwhelmingly male-dominated: 551 of the Black people enumerated in Cambridge and the surrounding towns lived in Black-headed households, and only 10 of these 551 people lived in families governed by female heads—that is, less than 2 percent of people in Black households lived in families that were headed by Black women.[108] The ten Black people living in families headed by Black women were divided into six households. Three of these households were composed simply of one woman: Dinah Jenkins, Deb Sewall, and Lucy Payne governed nobody besides themselves. And three of these households were composed of multiple people: Mrs. Underwood and Molly Reed headed households of two people (that is, themselves and one dependent), and Rose Morris headed a household of three people (herself and two dependents). Of the 551 Black people living in Black-headed households, then, merely four were subordinate to female family heads. Black female household leadership was all but nonexistent; it was more common, in fact, to find *white people* who lived as dependents in households run by *Black men* than it was to find *Black people* who lived as dependents in households governed by *Black women*.[109]

Two questions follow naturally the observation that Black households were uniformly patrifocal in structure during the postrevolutionary era. First, were these households *actually* headed by men, or is the apparent skew toward male leadership the result of biases encoded in the census data? The answer, the sources suggest, is that these households were indeed headed by men: The officials who canvassed the region operated from a worldview that allowed for women-run households, as they recorded white female household heads with regularity. The patrifocal tendency apparent in Black families, then, does not seem to have been an artifact of census takers' ideas about proper gender norms but appears instead to have been a reflection of the reality for people of African descent on the ground in postrevolutionary New England. This brings us to the second question: *Why* were Black households so consistently headed by men? Why, that is, were the families of people emerging from slavery more patrifocal in form than were the families of the white residents who lived in their neighborhoods? The question becomes particularly perplexing given that enslaved families in New England were unusually matrifocal in structure—more matrifocal than enslaved families just about anywhere else in the Atlantic world, and far more matrifocal than white families in New England.[110] With the advent of freedom, though, the mother-centered trend among Black families rapidly reversed. Why did this happen?

Anthony and Cuba's story offers clues. Left behind by their enslavers in 1774, Anthony and Cuba countenanced—perhaps for the first time—a life of freedom. The first thing they did was cohabit: Anthony left Penelope's place and moved in with his wife and children on John's estate. He assumed the role of household head; the census taker for Cambridge would scrawl "Anthony Vassall" in the column reserved for the "Names of heads of families." Anthony assumed as well the role of public advocate. It is not clear how this came to be. Did Cuba persuade Anthony to appeal on their family's behalf to the authorities—to Thomas Farrington, to the educated men who helped him pen petitions, to the members of the Massachusetts General Court? It is certainly possible. Or did Anthony insist that he take on these responsibilities himself? We do not know. One way or another, however, Anthony assumed publicly the task of promoting, protecting, and providing for his family.

The decision on the part of the Black Vassall family—whoever made it—to have Anthony perform the role of male provider was strategic. Anthony played deftly on his family's ambiguous status and his society's patriarchal presumptions to net a handsome profit for himself and his dependents. Other Black people in revolutionary New England no doubt understood the power of patriarchy in the region and disbursed authority within their households accordingly: Black men could make arguments for their family's welfare in ways that Black women could not. The intensity with which newly liberated people appear to have embraced patrifocal households is remarkable. Anthony and Cuba's Black neighbors, so long denied the right to build father-centered households in slavery, seem to have seized with particular passion the patrifocal family form in freedom. Unfortunately, many would learn over the course of the ensuing decades that their male household heads could do little to protect them from the ravages of poverty and discrimination. Patriarchy, they would find, was a feeble defense against racism. Indeed, even the Black Vassall family, whose transition to freedom had every mark of success, would falter in the years to come.

* * *

Darby came of age in his parents' Cambridge home, shoeing horses for his father, heaving hay in the barn, and tilling the acres across the street. There he enjoyed simple pleasures that eluded people in poverty: sleeping on a feather bed, sitting at a mahogany table, gazing into the looking glass. Upon reaching adulthood, however, Darby seems to have lost little time in leaving the town to which he had journeyed as a six-year-old. The young man, together with his siblings, went to Boston. Perhaps it seemed a more auspicious place to conduct business than their parents' sleepy Cambridge. It was certainly a better place to find a spouse. Despite the disruptions of revolution, Boston had more Black people than any other town in New England.[111]

In the spring of 1802, Darby married a woman named Lucy Holland.[112] It was a match that harkened back to Darby's early life. Lucy was born of free Black parents who had settled in Woburn during the years Darby lived in George Reed's household. Had the little boy known them there? It seems likely. But he had not at that time known his future wife, for Lucy had been born just after the six-year-old had set out, through heat and hail and the hammering of artillery, for Cambridge.[113] Grown now and master of his own household, Darby soon had a throng of little ones to provide for. In the first five years of their marriage, Lucy would give birth to five children. The year of the fifth birth marked a special milestone: It was that year that Darby moved his family into their own home. The magnitude of his accomplishment no doubt seared the date into his mind. "I built my present house in the year Eighteen hundred and six," the man would recall nearly three decades after the fact.[114] It was a time of great expansion for the Vassall family. Lucy would soon bear another child. And Darby's sister, Flora, and brothers, James and Cyrus, all of whom were married in Boston, had children of their own. By 1810, all but one of Anthony and Cuba's living children had married, and the aging couple, pensioners on the estate Anthony had built in Cambridge, had welcomed at least twelve grandchildren.[115]

The future looked bright for the Black Vassalls, and Darby seems to have operated with a spirit of optimism—a sense that what was not right about the present could be changed in the future. He worked closely with both white people and Black people, cultivating relationships with several predominately white churches in Boston while engaging in activism with and on behalf of Boston's Black residents.[116] Various clues point to Darby's leadership in Boston's Black community. The man would help found Boston's "African Society," pledging to behave as a "true and faithful Citizen" of Massachusetts and purchasing for himself, through monthly subscription, care in case of sickness. He would petition legislators to better fund schools for children of African descent. And he was one of three Black Bostonians to "preside" over a celebration of Haiti's independence in 1825, when, more than two decades after the fact, France finally acknowledged its former colony as an independent nation. At this moment of great hope and enormous pride for people of African descent, Darby, who had been declared the "*2d Vice President . . . of the Day*," had raised his glass to "Freedom": "May the freedom of Hayti be a glorious harbinger of the time when the color of man shall no longer be a pretext for depriving him of his liberty."[117]

It was a magnificent hope, but it was a hope that would go unrealized. In the final months of his life, on the eve of the Civil War, Darby would make yet another stand for freedom alongside Boston's Black community, joining other "Colored Citizens" of Boston in urging Massachusetts to oppose the Fugitive Slave Act. As they put it, they keenly felt the "danger" posed by the Act, though they were "free & citizens of Massachusetts." They were "bound," after all, "by ties closer in many instances than those of race to fugitives from slavery."[118] Intimate bonds united those, like Darby's descendants, who had been born free in Massachusetts, with those who had fled slavery in the South

Figure 14. Darby's tomb. Darby's remains rest in the Vassall family tomb, which lies beneath Christ Church in Cambridge. Courtesy of Nicole Piepenbrink and Christ Church Cambridge.

for liberty in Boston: Ties of kin and camaraderie crossed divisions of status and geographic origin. Allowing residents of Boston to be hauled back to slavery in the South was not just a strike against liberty but also a strike against family. Darby, who had become known endearingly to Boston's Black community as "Daddy Vassal," would stand with the oppressed.[119] Along with his daughter, Frances, and his son-in-law, Jonas, the ninety-one-year-old man who had walked out of slavery a lifetime ago would seize the petition and boldly ink his name in support of liberty: Darbe Vassell.

Darby had, by this time, suffered a lifetime of loss. Six of his seven children appear to have died young.[120] And his large extended family had all but vanished a generation ago; there was a stretch in the early eighteenth century when, in less than a decade, death had claimed his mother and his father, his wife's parents, his two brothers and their wives, his sister and her husband, and his nephew. And Darby had also lost, along with his kin, all of his material possessions: the land he had purchased with his earnings, the home he had built with his hands, the inheritance he had collected after his father's passing. By the end of his life, Darby was sustained by the charity of Boston's Brattle Street Church, and he lived with his sole surviving daughter and her husband, who also appear to have been impoverished.[121] And yet, even as the man became dependent for survival on the charity of others, he sought to practice the lesson that he had learned growing up in his father's household: the lesson that patriarchs must provide. By now, Darby could no longer shelter his heirs in life, but perhaps he was cheered that he could still impart to them safe haven in death. The man had managed to acquire from Catherine Russell, the granddaughter of Henry and Penelope Vassall, a document promising that he and his family could be buried in the tomb of her grandfather. Darby must have asked Catherine to list his family members in order to ensure that each would be given access to Henry's resting place, for the woman stipulated that "Darby Vassal's family consists of two grandchildren and one daughter." In death, Darby's descendants would be housed in the chamber of their ancestors' enslavers.[122]

This arrangement apparently meant a great deal to Darby. Those who knew the former bondsman would later say that he had thought with care and at length about the prospect of being buried alongside the Black Vassalls' former enslavers. Famed abolitionist William Cooper Nell put it this way: "The idea of this tomb being his last resting-place was often the subject of his meditation, and he was eloquent in grateful expressions towards [Catherine,] whom he had always regarded as a considerate, rare, and valued friend."[123] Catherine's written promise was, as Darby put it, his "pass." For generations under slavery, passes written by enslavers allowed bondspeople access to places denied, but Darby understood that a pass could have power for a free man as well. For Darby, this pass served as a leveling mechanism, as a ticket to ultimate equality with those who had once bound his family. Darby's body would be laid alongside the remains of Henry and Penelope, of their daughter and their granddaughter.[124] It was a fitting end for the little boy who had marched out of slavery through the war-torn countryside in search of his family, for the grown man who had become a beloved leader of Boston's Black community, for the aging patriarch who had advocated for the oppressed even as his strength ebbed. Darby managed to obtain parity in death with those whose prospects had differed so drastically in life. All would return to dust together among the broken coffins and mouse-gnawed "cherry stones" of Darby's final resting place.[125]

CONCLUSION

Massachusetts was a forerunner. In 1641, when Bay colonists deemed Dorcas a "stranger," Massachusetts became the first English colony in the Americas to set in law a comprehensive set of conditions under which slavery was legal.[1] In so doing, the colony's inhabitants inadvertently introduced the central conflict with which *Belonging* has grappled: the problem, for the enslaved, of building families in bondage. For Black inhabitants of Massachusetts, the mandates of slavery ran contrary to those of family. The smallholding pattern of ownership in the region meant that wives and husbands—Dorcas and Menenie, Jane and Sebastian—ordinarily could not live together. Families stretched across multiple households, even across towns, far more than they centered on a single home, a common hearth, or a shared garret. Consider Mark's and Phoebe's Boston kin, separated from Charlestown by the watery depths of the Charles River and Boston Harbor. Husbands and fathers in bondage rarely could provide materially for their families the way Thomas Bedunah could because the benefits of their productive labor were appropriated by those who bound them. Wives and children were forced to answer to enslavers rather than to the heads of their bound families. Women in bondage, like Phoebe, could fall victim to the sexual appetites of those who enslaved them. Children were separated from their fathers with frequency because those who claimed ownership of mothers also laid claim to their children. And youngsters in slavery, such as Sue Black and her sons, regularly were taken from their mothers as well. Boys and girls beyond number grew up like Darby Vassall, entirely alone in Anglo-American households. Of course, enslaved people in the southern mainland colonies or in the British Caribbean faced many of these challenges as well—the lack of familial control, the sale of children, the sexual predation—but racial and familial isolation defined enslavement in New England, even among those who belonged to families of their own making. The frequency with which families were divided across households, and the extent to which Black people were outnumbered in the white worlds they navigated, shaped the intimate experiences of slavery in New England. Living more with white people than with Black ones presented a certain set of obstacles to inhabitants of African descent trying to make their way in the region.[2]

Still, despite all these constraints, bondspeople showed remarkable tenacity when it came to forging intimate ties and seeking protections for those ties. They seized upon a diversity of means by which to do so. Dorcas performed an astonishing act of spiritual integration, incorporating herself into Dorchester's Christian community with a finesse that eluded many of her white neighbors. Then, by making clear to her congregation that slavery compromised her ability to engage in family-building the way God had intended it, she managed to persuade the brethren to pool their resources and redeem her from bondage. Jane and Sebastian cultivated white allies in their neighborhood to help them negotiate their marriage and make plans for the care of their children. They also did what they could to register their family in the bureaucratic apparatus of provincial Massachusetts, thereby legitimizing it in the eyes of their neighbors: They posted banns prior to marriage; they wed one another in a formal capacity, with a justice of the peace presiding; and they baptized their children in the local church. Mark valued a series of intimate ties—ties binding him to his wife and child, to his community on the streets of Boston, and to the bondspeople who labored alongside him in his enslaver's household. Attempting to protect these kin-like connections, Mark first tried to arrange his sale, then plotted to burn his enslaver's workshop, next hired himself out to work for a Bostonian, and ultimately orchestrated the murder of the man who thwarted him at every turn. Mark's wife, for her part, appears to have gotten "lost" on the estate on which Mark labored, no doubt hoping to gain proximity to her spouse. Phoebe measured arsenic into her enslaver's breakfast chocolate in an effort to free herself of his abusive grasp and to unite with her husband. And little Darby voted with his feet, walking out of slavery and away from the isolation of a white household through the war-torn countryside to the home in which he had been born.

The enslaved were not alone in making ingenious plans to safeguard their families; people of African descent in freedom, or in quasi-freedom, did so as well. By marrying white wives, Thomas Bedunah and his male heirs embedded their children in the protective webs of white kin networks to the point that their descendants played the role of white people in the community and became nearly indistinguishable from their Anglo-American neighbors. When it was strategic to do so, however, Thomas's son, Joseph, chose to exploit his Blackness as a useful identity. Joseph sued a local militiaman for impressing him into the army because, as a person of African descent, he was not legally bound to serve. It was a surprising but effective move; by rejecting the status of a white man, Joseph managed to stay with his family in lieu of traveling to fight a distant war, and he was reimbursed for the heavy monetary penalty that had resulted from his refusal to march. Joseph's strategy for maintaining family integrity and protecting family economy echoes in the story of the Vassalls. Anthony Vassall managed to convince local authorities that his wife and children were enslaved at precisely the moment that their Black neighbors everywhere were walking away from bondage. The economic advantages that Anthony netted for his family by pursuing this line of reasoning were impressive. Freedom and whiteness brought benefits to early New Englanders in almost every situation, but people of African descent kept their ears to the ground and when, on rare occasions, it was in their favor to make much of their Blackness or enslaved status, they acted accordingly. They were too strategic, and their resources were too limited, to turn down opportunities for the betterment of their families.

If Massachusetts was a forerunner in legalizing slavery, thereby presenting enslaved people with the difficulties chronicled in this book, its Black and white population also led the way in abolishing the institution. A deep dive into the archive of revolutionary Massachusetts shows clues to the breakdown of slavery just about everywhere. At the outset of the Revolution, wills bequeathing enslaved laborers in Boston and the surrounding towns all but disappeared, and people of African descent essentially ceased to be valued in decedents' inventories. If racial slavery in British America had been premised on an assumption that the enslaved were chattel property, this foundation of the institution seems at this time to have begun to dissolve. Newspapers printed in eastern Massachusetts inaugurated new genres of advertisements, such as notices selling bondspeople for terms rather than for life and postings equating Black workers with white ones (and seeking the labor of either). Other archival sources—from the petitions sent to the revolutionary government to the records filed in the region's courts—display the local breakdown of slavery as well. And they give voice to the fears that Black people harbored of being taken from a place where slavery was crumbling to one where the institution was robust. A careful assessment of the evidence suggests that slavery had all but disintegrated in the Boston region prior to the passage of the state's constitution, which declared all men "free and equal."

This silent collapse of slavery in eastern Massachusetts has long been over-looked in part because events elsewhere in the state tell such a different story. In 1781, a western Massachusetts woman named Elizabeth (Bett) Free-man sued for her liberty on the basis of the state's 1780 constitution, and two years later the state's Supreme Judicial Court ruled that a central Massachu-setts man named Quock Walker was free, presumably because of the impli-cations of the "free and equal" language of the constitution. The archive of slavery and freedom plumbed by *Belonging* suggests that these lawsuits, long thought to be the sharp edge of the movement to end slavery in Massachu-setts, actually came toward the end of that undertaking. Freedom in eastern Massachusetts preceded rather than followed the liberatory constitution to which Bett and Quock appealed, and this freedom was seized by the enslaved rather than conferred by members of constitutional conventions or court ju-ries. People like Bett and Quock, who were bound in parts of Massachusetts that did not as quickly experience the changes that marked the state's urban center, later had to appeal to the constitution in order to enact abolition for themselves. Slavery first dissolved in Massachusetts, then, in the area where it was most prevalent, and it persisted in the more remote, less populous areas of the state where fewer bondspeople toiled. The divergent experi-ences of enslaved people in various parts of Massachusetts serve as an important reminder of how different the terrain of slavery and freedom could look in geographic locales of relative proximity. The Boston area's un-heralded emancipation was the inaugural act of abolition in the region.

How did this unlegislated emancipation come to pass? It certainly helped that Boston had never been as dependent on slavery as most urban centers to its south, and that the town found itself in economic malaise during the prerevolutionary period. But economic circumstances on their own cannot explain Boston's early turn from slavery; other northern port towns, like New York, emerged from serious downturns with slavery intact. What is more, Boston's turn from slavery came well after the onset of depression, which sug-gests that an adverse economic climate alone was not sufficient to bring about abolition. Political realities were relevant as well. New Englanders in general, and Bostonians in particular, were especially vocal in their outrage during the years prior to the outbreak of revolution. The revolutionary rhe-toric that coursed through the arteries of eastern Massachusetts in the form of pamphlets, newspapers, sermons, and more employed a vitriol rarely equaled elsewhere at the time. Bostonians and their neighbors were insistent on their rights, defiant in the face of British forms of "slavery," and obsessed with ideas of liberty: It was for good reason that the British saw New England—and, above all, Boston—as the revolutionary lynchpin. Cultural transformations also helped create the context for abolition in eastern Massachusetts; consider, for instance, the rise of the companionate marriage ideal, which ran starkly counter to the realities of life in bondage. Boston's turn from slavery, though, was no knee-jerk reaction to the new conceptions of family life that suffused the Anglo-Atlantic world. If the proliferation of sentimental family literature could have effected such transformations on its own, abolition would have swept many other places at this time. These cultural changes, then, did not have the power to call slavery into question unaided. In the Boston context, however, new understandings of family were particularly useful for fighting slavery because Black families were so visible and, in certain ways, so integrated into white community life. These families were, as well, often legitimate from the perspective of white society, with marriages registered in the administrative apparatus of the province. And they were almost always divided across geographic space.[3]

By the revolutionary era, people enslaved in eastern Massachusetts had for generations made arguments in support of family integrity. Bondspeople's claims to family life, along with the desperation they expressed at the ruin of their kin ties, were therefore ubiquitous in the port. Consider the newspaper account that circulated in Boston, detailing the deaths of a man from Boston's North End and a woman from the town's South End. The two had "contracted an intimate and strict Friendship," the *Boston Evening-Post* informed its readers. It was a relationship more precious than life itself: When the couple learned of the woman's impending sale, they "resolved to put an End to their Lives, rather than be parted." This was a "Tragedy," the printer opined.[4] Or consider the report of an enslaved girl's death sentence. When Boston's newspapers informed the public that the girl had been found guilty of murder, all four publications included something else as well: a commentary on how the girl's sentence had affected her mother. "The Mother of said Girl Died with Excess of Grief last Saturday Night," they reported.[5] Or consider the epitaph published in a Boston newspaper, purportedly penned by a bondsman named Sambo upon the passing of his wife, Dinah. "Heere lie Dinah, Sambo Wife, Sambo lub [her] like he Life. Dinah die sic Week ago, Sambo Maser tell him so." The source is difficult to interpret. On the one hand, it could have served as a mockery of African American speech. On the other hand, however, the epitaph's criticism of slavery's effect on Black unions is pointed. Dinah and Sambo, husband and "Wife," had deep affective ties:

Sambo loved Dinah "like h[is] Life."[6] But when Dinah died, not only was Sambo unable to tend to her at her deathbed, but he did not even learn of her passing until six weeks later—and the news came to him through, of all people, his enslaver. Slavery interrupted those ties that should have been most intimate, and the claims of bondspeople reverberated through the region as hopeless lovers' lifeless bodies, the mother who succumbed to "Excess of Grief," and Sambo's effort to memorialize his wife.

White people, of course, did not need to read newspaper reports to learn about Black families. In the eighteenth century, eastern Massachusetts was filled with white folks who had intimate familiarity with families in slavery. The great bulk of the population would have known bondspeople who hashed out family arrangements with their enslavers prior to marriage, who solicited ministers to proclaim from the pulpit their intention to marry, who wed before local justices of the peace, who dashed across town as dusk fell so that they could spend the night with their spouses, and who stood before their congregations and held up their infants for baptism. Everyone living in Boston had enslaved neighbors with spouses and children, and many living outside the port town did as well. Crucially, all of these onlookers would have been able to see that Black families were caught up in a bundle of contradictions. These families were, on one level, shattered—husbands, wives, and children were scattered throughout Boston and the surrounding villages, living apart as often as together. But that shattering, that scattering, did not necessarily translate into full rupture; families in countless instances navigated intimacy at a geographic remove. Likewise, bondspeople were at once utterly isolated, living most frequently in ones and twos in Anglo-American households, and at the same time they were valued members of kin communities that were starkly visible to neighbors because they so often existed out of doors. Unlike bondspeople in other times and places who lived together in large groups on rural plantations, set apart from their enslavers and removed from white neighbors, Boston's enslaved community navigated intimate ties in public. Fathers, mothers, children, lovers, and friends hurried down Boston's crooked lanes, chatted on its wharves, worshipped at its meetinghouses, passed through its common, rendezvoused in its kitchen gardens, and dallied at its water pumps.

Because enslaved families were so visible in Boston, so enmeshed in the institutions of church and government, and so frequently divided across geographic space, people of African origin in eastern Massachusetts were able to lay claim to family in unusual ways. They were able as well to lodge convincing grievances about the ways in which slavery compromised their family lives. Arguments for the right to family integrity on the part of the enslaved thundered both in word and action through the streets, and these arguments were crucial to the early breakdown of slavery in eastern Massachusetts. The impossibility of maintaining familial integrity in bondage featured prominently in the case that Black activists made against slavery. As one petition that circulated through Boston proclaimed, "Alas! no sooner are [our children] born, but they are either sold or given away helpless without our consent, whereby we are rendered ignorant of them and they of us."[7] Or, as another petition declared, "We have no Wives! No Children!"[8] According to yet another, "The endearing ties of husband, wife, parent, child and friend, we are generally strangers to: And whenever any of those connections are formed among us, the pleasures are imbittered by the cruel consideration of our slavery."[9] So, as one petition asked, "How can a husband leave master and work and Cleave to his wife?" And "How can the wife submit themselves to there Husbands in all things?" And "How can the child obey thear parents in all things?"[10] These were questions, claims, and lines of reasoning that would not remain confined to revolutionary Massachusetts. If Massachusetts was a forerunner in establishing slavery in the English Americas and Massachusetts was a forerunner in eradicating it, Massachusetts was also a forerunner in outlining the rhetorical and ideological strategies that would define and bring success to the abolition movement more broadly. Black activists in revolutionary Massachusetts honed arguments that would reverberate over the generations and throughout the country, arguments that would provide antislavery advocates with their greatest ammunition in the fight to end the odious system of oppression that had plagued North America since Dorcas was deemed a stranger.

In the nineteenth century, as Darby Vassall would live to see, Massachusetts would become famous for its commitment to ending slavery. The sentimental abolitionism that emanated from antebellum New England was fixated on the family; antislavery activists, both Black and white, railed against the abuses that slavery heaped on intimate kin. Writing from Lynn, Massachusetts, Frederick Douglass bemoaned the "sundering of husbands and wives, parents and children, sisters and brothers." He described "scatter[ed]" families, "crying children," and offspring divided "like so many sheep."[11] More than anything else, Frederick argued, slavery was marked by the loss of family ties: "There is not, beneath the sky, an enemy to filial affection so destructive as slavery."[12] Harriet Jacobs railed against slavery in her searing tale of sexual predation. Her narrative, which was published in Boston, excoriated enslavers who "seemed to think that slaves had no right to any family ties of their own."[13] Writing from Boston, William Wells Brown damned slavery for similar offenses. He punctuated his narrative with a series of heartrending separations: the woman who drowned herself because she had "no desire to live" without her kin; the man who "wept like a child" when faced with separation from his family; the woman who mourned "piteously" after her infant was given away.[14] And Harriet Beecher Stowe's *Uncle Tom's Cabin* explored, more than anything else, slavery's devastating effect on Black kin. The entire plot of this work of sentimental fiction—first printed in book form in Boston—is set in motion by the decision of an enslaver to sell his bondspeople, thereby ravaging their families. In defending her depiction of slavery, Harriet would later declare that the "worst abuse of the system of slavery is its outrage upon the family."[15]

Scholars have long understood those who wrote abolitionist sermons, tracts, narratives, and fiction in the North to have composed their searing indictments of slavery's effects on the family in reaction to the horrors of southern slavery. And they are absolutely right to make such a connection. The impassioned autobiographical accounts written by Frederick Douglass, Harriet Jacobs, William Wells Brown, and others who made their way from slavery to freedom drew directly on the horrors their authors witnessed in the South. And for writers of sentimental abolitionist fiction, like Harriet Beecher Stowe, it made all the sense in the world to look for source material in the ugly stories of life in the southern states; southern slavery, after all, was the target of their criticism.[16] Without a doubt, then, New England's abolitionist literature was written in response to the brutality of slavery as practiced in the antebellum South. But the archives of slavery and family in seventeenth- and eighteenth-century New England show that the concern for family integrity so central to northern abolitionism built upon lines of argumentation that had long been established in the region. In nineteenth-century Massachusetts, now an antislavery stronghold, abolitionists constructed a case against slavery that had many decades earlier been assembled by Black activists determined to obtain freedom for the province's own people in bondage. These continuities are important. The argument that slavery was objectionable because it destroyed Black families resonated so powerfully in antebellum Boston—and antebellum New England more broadly—because by then Black activism in favor of family integrity had shaped white people's understandings of Black families for generations. That certain standards and ideals of family integrity had come, over time, to transcend race in the region made abolitionist arguments centered on the family persuasive. By paying close attention to the intersection of intimacy and slavery in early New England, *Belonging* unearths the colonial and revolutionary-era roots of the concern for Black family integrity—a concern that was vital to the sentimental abolitionism for which Massachusetts would later become famous. The argument made over and over by Afro-New Englanders prior to American independence would come to full flower in the nineteenth-century fight to end American slavery, when northerners in droves—both white and Black—would damn southern slavery for its depredations on the family.

For people of African descent enslaved in seventeenth- and eighteenth-century New England, the search for family was a search for meaning. It was a quest for belonging. It was an attempt to affix fragile threads of connection to others in a place where people of African ancestry found themselves surrounded by European settlers. Bondspeople likely could not have foreseen that pursuing familial intimacy—and advocating for it when it was denied—would help bring about the end of slavery in their region, although on occasion family ties were clearly bound up in efforts to end the enslavement of individuals. They certainly could not have envisioned that such activism would be linked to the freedom of people who lived in faraway places and inhabited a future in which Massachusetts would be perceived as a land of liberty. That by claiming family in this early moment bondspeople in the province pried open the door to claim freedom as well is to their great and lasting credit. In early New England, as in so many other times and places, the enslaved were the first, the fiercest, and the most effective advocates of their own emancipation. Fighting through the generations to embed themselves in community, time and again they etched their humanity—and slavery's devastation—in bold relief. Eventually, belonging to one another would help the enslaved to convince those who shared their world that they ought not belong to enslavers.

NOTE ON SOURCES

Probate Records Database

The probate records database contains information about people in bondage, and those who claimed ownership of them, in Suffolk County. It is based on a page-by-page reading of Suffolk County's Probate Records beginning in 1639, when the Massachusetts General Court first ordered that probate documents be filed in court, and continuing through the end of the year 1790, by which time people in bondage had virtually disappeared from the probate documents of white decedents.[1] Over the course of this century and a half, the Suffolk County Probate Court produced 131 volumes of records. Of these volumes, 89 are from the First Series of the Suffolk County Probate Records (SCPR, FS), created by court clerks in the seventeenth and eighteenth centuries, and 42 are from the New Series (SCPR, NS), created in 1907 by archivists working from unrecorded documents originally produced in the seventeenth and eighteenth centuries. The two sets of volumes contain transcriptions of a wide variety of documents written by ordinary people who worked to settle the estates of the deceased: wills, estate inventories, accounts of administration, deeds, affidavits, petitions, appraisals, lists of debts, agreements between heirs, statements of objection, and more. Adding the 89 original volumes to the 42 latter volumes makes for a remarkably complete run of records through more than 150 years of the county's history; there were no prolonged breaks in record making or recordkeeping during this time.[2]

The probate records database is therefore based on analysis of a sizable collection of estates. The court numbered 19,659 of the estates it probated between 1639 and 1790, but the volumes from those years have many unnumbered estates, so the total processed by the court during this time period—and the total under consideration here—likely exceeds 20,000.[3] Most of these estates did not mention people in bondage, but many of them did: I collected in the probate records database evidence pertaining to 2,691 bondspeople. Building this database required discretion. Often the same bound people showed up multiple times in the records—say, in both the will and the inventory of a given decedent. In all cases, I cross-checked documents related to the same decedent to ensure that I did not double count any people in servitude. Also, because this book seeks to understand the dynamics of slavery in New England, I excluded from the database all bondspeople who resided outside New England, had never been to the region, and, as far as I could tell from the records, were not headed to New England. It is worth noting that occasionally I was compelled to round when counting enslaved people; probate documents ordinarily make clear how many bondspeople were claimed by a given decedent, but from time to time the records are ambiguous. In all such cases, I was as conservative as possible. Finally, on the rare occasion in which decedents claimed to own a fraction of a laborer, I counted the whole person.

The vast majority of the 2,691 people included in the probate records database were described in the records in a way that makes it possible to deduce their racial identity. Some were identified as "Scotch," "Irish," or "White"; some were labeled "negro"; some were called "Indian" or "Spanish Indian"; some were recorded as "molatto."[4] From very early on, however, most of the bondspeople mentioned in probate records were identified as of African descent.[5] For the purposes of my analysis in this book, I have not usually separated those few white, Native, and mixed-race people in servitude from the much larger body of bondspeople of African ancestry. Therefore, for instance, when I use this database in Chapter 2 to chart the atomized living situations of those bound in turn-of-the-eighteenth-century Massachusetts, I include non-Black people in my count. Were I to consider only people of African descent, the racial isolation of bondspeople in Anglo-American households would appear starker—though only very slightly. The probate records database allows me to do more than map the distribution of bondspeople throughout white households. Probate records usually make clear the approximate ages of people in servitude, so I am able to trace the relative rarity with which enslaved children cohabited with bound adults. Probate records also tend to specify the gender of those in bondage, so I am able to glimpse the distribution through space of bondspeople who might have chosen to couple with one another. The probate records database does other work as well, from allowing me to locate bondspeople spatially within enslavers' homes to enabling me to chart the crumbling of slavery in the region. In my sustained engagement with these records, I have found their capacity for illuminating the demography of people in bondage—and for shedding light on the institution of slavery itself—every bit as impressive as Gloria L. Main posited on the pages of the *William and Mary Quarterly* nearly half a century ago.[6]

Vital Records Database

The vital records database contains the births, baptisms, marriages, and deaths of people of African descent in Boston (and, in the case of inter-town marriages, of neighboring towns). This database is based on both church and municipal records. Massachusetts ministers and justices of the peace were required to report marriages to civil authorities, which meant, in Boston, reporting to the town clerk. However, a researcher who relies solely on the records of the clerk will obtain an incomplete picture of the marriage patterns of enslaved people in Boston because many of the city's eighteenth-century marriage records have been lost—and some seem never to have been delivered to the clerk. Therefore, I have incorporated marriages recorded in Boston's churches into my database alongside the clerk's data, which helps fill out the record. I have likewise supplemented town records with notations of baptisms and deaths gleaned from church records. This compilation is a work in progress: I am still in the process of incorporating some of the records of three of Boston's many churches—First Church, Old South Church, and Trinity Church—which will increase both the marriage counts and the total number of people in the database.

To construct the vital records database, I drew on the following printed and manuscript sources: *BBMD*; *Boston Births*; *Boston Marriages*, 1; *Boston Marriages*, 2; Robert J. Dunkle and Ann S. Lainhart, eds., *Deaths in Boston: 1700–1799* (Boston: New England Historic Genealogical Society, 1999); *First Church Records*, 1; *First Church Records*, 2; Church in Brattle Square, *The Manifesto Church: Records of the Church in Brattle Square, Boston: With Lists of Communicants, Baptisms, Marriages, and Funerals, 1699–1872* (Boston: Benevolent Fraternity of Churches, 1902); Andrew Oliver and James Bishop Peabody, eds. *Publications of the Colonial Society of Massachusetts*, vol. 56: *The Records of Trinity Church, Boston, 1728–1830*, vol. 2 (Boston: Colonial Society of Massachusetts, 1982); Second Church (Boston, Massachusetts) Records, MHS, specifically "Baptisms and admissions, 1689–1716," vol. 4, "Baptisms and admissions, 1717–1741," vol. 5, "Record Book, 1741–1816," vol. 6, and "Record Book, 1768–1815," vol. 7; First Baptist Church of Boston Records, ANTS Special Collections and Archives, specifically "Minutes of Church Meetings, 1665–1799" and "Samuel Stillman . . . marriage record book"; Old South Church Records, CLA, specifically "Baptisms, 1669–1875" (microfilm: reel 4), "Admission [to full church membership] of Old South, 1669–1855," "owners of the baptismal covenant, 1669–1814," and "Marriages [solemnized by] Joseph Eckley, pastor, 1780–1882"; King's Chapel (Boston, Massachusetts) Records, MHS, specifically "King's Chapel vestry records, 1787–1867," vol. 38, "Register of baptisms, 1703–1843," vol. 39, "Register of burials, 1714–1843," vol. 40, and "Register of marriages, 1718–1841," vol. 41; New North Church Record Book, BPL; New South Church Records, BPL, "Baptisms, marriages, deaths, and persons admitted to communion," vol. 1; New Brick Church Records, BPL, "Records of those who own'd the Covenant With the Names of those Baptised &c"; Old North Church (Christ Church in the City of Boston) Records, MHS, "Clark's register, 1723–1851," vol. 34; Arlington Street Church (Boston, Massachusetts) Records, 1730–1979, AHTL, "Records of baptisms and marriages, 1730–1863," and "Records of baptisms and marriages, 1730–1772"; Boston West Church Records, BPL, "Record book, 1736–1854"; Hollis Street Church Records, BPL, "Records of membership, 1732–1739"; Second Baptist Church of Boston Records, BPL, "Libro Secundo"; and Second Baptist Church (Boston, Massachusetts) Records, ANTS, "Church Record Book, 1787–1793."

NOTE ON IMAGES

In order to keep the focus in this book on the people at its center, I have chosen to label and caption all images in relation to my historical actors and the worlds they inhabited. *Belonging* is not concerned with the Anglo-American makers of communion silver or of embroideries. Rather, *Belonging* is concerned with the Black people who interacted with the communion silver or whose experiences might have been depicted by said embroidery. Some of my images are therefore under-described according to the conventions of historical citation. For images found in repositories that require fuller information in order to be tracked down by curious readers, I have included the needed details here.

For the communion cup, see Beaker by John Hull, American (born in England), 1624–1683, and Robert Sanderson Sr., American (born in England), 1608–1693, 1659, Boston, Massachusetts, accession number 1999.90, Museum of Fine Arts, Boston. This silver vessel measures 9.9 × 9.3 cm, 0.19 kg (3 7/8 × 3 11/16 in., 0.42 lb.) and was purchased with funds donated anonymously in honor of Jonathan L. Fairbanks.

For the map of Jane and Sebastian's neighborhood, see *The Town of Boston in New England by Capt. John Bonner, 1722*, facsimile map engraved by George G. Smith, 1835, Massachusetts Historical Society, Boston.

For the advertisement of the enslaved girl, see B. Greene, *A Negro Infant Girl About Six Weeks Old, to Be Given for the Bringing Up: Inquire of John Campbell, Post-master . . .* advertisement from the *Boston News-Letter*, September 30, 1706, page 2, Newspaper Collection, New-York Historical Society.

For the embroidery showing a bound child, see *The First, Second, and Last Scene of Mortality*, embroidery by Prudence Punderson, Preston, Connecticut, 1776–1783, Gift of Newton C. Brainard, accession number 1962.28.4, the Connecticut Historical Society.

For the chocolate pot, see Chocolate Pot, Zachariah Brigden, Boston, Massachusetts, ca. 1760, accession number HD 75.463, Historic Deerfield.

ABBREVIATIONS

AHTL   Andover-Harvard Theological Library. This library was renamed the Harvard Divinity School Library in 2021.

ANTS   Andover Newton Theological School. I accessed material in the school archives, which were then located in Newton, Massachusetts. The school has since formally affiliated with Yale Divinity School and moved to New Haven, Connecticut.

BBMD   Boston Record Commissioners, *A Report of the Record Commissioners Containing Boston Births, Baptisms, Marriages, and Deaths, 1630–1699* (Boston: Municipal Printing Office, 1883).

BOSTON BIRTHS   Boston Record Commissioners, *A Report of the Record Commissioners of the City of Boston, Containing Boston Births from A.D. 1700 to A.D. 1800* (Boston: Rockwell and Churchill, 1894).

BOSTON MARRIAGES, 1   Boston Record Commissioners, *A Report of the Record Commissioners Containing Boston Marriages from 1700 to 1751* (Boston: Municipal Printing Office, 1898).

BOSTON MARRIAGES, 2   Boston Record Commissioners, *A Volume of Records Relating to the Early History of Boston, Containing Boston Marriages from 1752 to 1809* (Boston: Municipal Printing Office, 1903).

BPL   Boston Public Library.

CLA	Congregational Library and Archives, Boston.
FIRST CHURCH RECORDS, 1	Richard D. Pierce, ed., "Records of the First Church of Boston, vol. 1" in *Publications of the Colonial Society of Massachusetts, vol. 39* (Boston: Colonial Society of Massachusetts, 1961).
FIRST CHURCH RECORDS, 2	Richard D. Pierce, ed., "Records of the First Church of Boston, vol. 2" in *Publications of the Colonial Society of Massachusetts, vol. 40* (Boston: Colonial Society of Massachusetts, 1961).
HUA	Harvard University Archives.
JAH	*Journal of American History.*
KJV	King James Version of the Bible.
MA ARCHIVES	Massachusetts State Archives, Boston.
MAC	Massachusetts Archives Collection (also known as the "Felt Collection"), microfilm, MA Archives. Much of this collection is now available digitally on familysearch.org under two titles: "Massachusetts State Archives collection, colonial period, 1622–1788" and "Massachusetts State Archives collection, colonial and post colonial period 1626–1806."
MASSACHUSETTS SCJ RECORDS	Superior Court of Judicature Records, Judicial Archives, MA Archives. These records are now available digitally on familysearch.org under the title "Court records, 1686–1799."
MATHER DIARY, 1	Cotton Mather, "Diary of Cotton Mather, 1681–1724, vol. 1," in *Collections of the Massachusetts Historical Society, vol. 7, 7th series* (Boston: Massachusetts Historical Society, 1911).
MATHER DIARY, 2	Cotton Mather, "Diary of Cotton Mather, 1681–1724, vol. 1," in *Collections of the Massachusetts Historical Society, vol. 8, 7th series* (Boston: Massachusetts Historical Society, 1912).

MHS	Massachusetts Historical Society, Boston.
NYHS	New-York Historical Society, New York.
SCPR, FS	First Series of the Suffolk County Probate Records, microfilm, Judicial Archives, MA Archives. These volumes are now available digitally on familysearch.org under the title "Suffolk County (Massachusetts) probate records, 1636–1899."
SCPR, NS	New Series of the Suffolk County Probate Records, microfilm, Judicial Archives, MA Archives. These volumes are now available digitally on familysearch.org under the title "Suffolk County (Massachusetts) probate records, 1636–1899."
SEWALL DIARY, 1	Samuel Sewall, "Diary of Samuel Sewall, 1674–1729, vol. 1," in *Collections of the Massachusetts Historical Society, Vol. 5, 5th Series* (Boston: Massachusetts Historical Society, 1878).
SEWALL DIARY, 2	Samuel Sewall, "Diary of Samuel Sewall, 1674–1729, vol. 2," in *Collections of the Massachusetts Historical Society, Vol. 6, 5th Series* (Boston: Massachusetts Historical Society, 1879).
SEWALL DIARY, 3	Samuel Sewall, "Diary of Samuel Sewall, 1674–1729, vol. 3," in *Collections of the Massachusetts Historical Society, Vol. 7, 5th Series* (Boston: Massachusetts Historical Society, 1882).
SF	Suffolk Files Collection, microfilm, Judicial Archives, MA Archives. These records are now available digitally on familysearch.org under the title "Suffolk County (Mass.) court files, 1629–1797."
SUFFOLK COUNTY CCP RECORDS	Suffolk County Court of Common Pleas Records, microfilm, Judicial Archives, MA Archives. These volumes are now available digitally on familysearch.org under the title "Court Records, 1701–1855."

SUFFOLK COUNTY GSP   Suffolk County General Sessions of the Peace
RECORDS   Records, microfilm, Judicial Archives, MA Ar-
                       chives. These volumes are now available digitally
                       on familysearch.org under the title "Court Rec-
                       ords, 1702–1780."

WMQ   *William and Mary Quarterly*, 3rd series.

NOTES

On Names and More

1. Others before me have decided to rely exclusively on first names. See, for instance, Amrita Chakrabarti Myers, *Forging Freedom: Black Women and the Pursuit of Liberty in Antebellum Charleston* (Chapel Hill: University of North Carolina Press, 2011), 15. I will occasionally make exception to this method and refer to historical actors by both first and last name when it seems necessary for the sake of clarity.

2. For guides to the language of slavery, see P. Gabrielle Foreman et al., "Writing About Slavery? Teaching About Slavery?: This Might Help" community-sourced document, https://naacpculpeper.org/resources/writing-about-slavery-this-might-help/; "The Afterlife of Slavery: Language and Ethics," Wakelet compiled by LaTanya S. Autry https://wakelet.com/wake/f589cdc4-7512-43ff-a489-5ed48062179f; and Katy Waldman, "Slave or Enslaved Person? It's not just an academic debate for historians of American slavery," *Slate*, May 19, 2015, https://slate.com/human-interest/2015/05/historians-debate-whether-to-use-the-term-slave-or-enslaved-person.html. The archives of seventeenth- and eighteenth-century New England are filled with white dependent laborers under the command of people referred to as "masters." For just two examples, both from Massachusetts, consider William Everton, a white indentured servant who deserted his "Masters Service," and Thomas Bennett, a white apprentice who was "Enticed" from his "master." See Phillips v. Everton, Suffolk County CCP Records, vol. 1739, 314; Bennett v. Winslow, Suffolk County CCP Records, vol. 1742–1743, 9.

Introduction

1. Deposition of Penelope Hadlock, SF case 22148.

2. *Sewall Diary*, 2, 46, see November 2, 1701.

3. For intimacy and race in the making of empire, see Ann Laura Stoler, "Tense and Tender Ties: The Politics of Comparison in North American History and (Post) Colonial Studies," *JAH* 88, no. 3 (December 2001): 829–865.

4. See E. Franklin Frazier, *The Negro Family in the United States* (Chicago: University of Chicago Press, 1939); Kenneth M. Stampp, *The Peculiar Institution: Slavery in the Antebellum South* (New York: Knopf, 1956); Stanley M. Elkins, *Slavery: A Problem in American Institutional and Intellectual Life* (Chicago: University of Chicago Press, 1959); Herbert G. Gutman, *The Black Family in Slavery and Freedom, 1750–1925* (New York: Vintage Books, 1977); John W. Blassingame, *The Slave Community: Plantation Life in the Antebellum South* (New York: Oxford University Press, 1972); Deborah Gray White, *Ar'n't I a Woman? Female Slaves in the Plantation South* (New York: Norton, 1985); Ann Patton Malone, *Sweet Chariot: Slave Family and Household Structure in Nineteenth-Century Louisiana* (Chapel Hill: University of North Carolina

Press, 1996); Brenda E. Stevenson, *Life in Black and White: Family and Community in the Slave South* (New York: Oxford University Press, 1997); Philip D. Morgan, *Slave Counterpoint: Black Culture in the Eighteenth-Century Chesapeake and Lowcountry* (Chapel Hill: University of North Carolina Press, 1998); Larry E. Hudson Jr., *To Have and to Hold: Slave Work and Family Life in Antebellum South Carolina* (Athens: University of Georgia Press, 1997); Wilma A. Dunaway, *The African-American Family in Slavery and Emancipation* (New York: Cambridge University Press, 2003); Emily West, *Chains of Love: Slave Couples in Antebellum South Carolina* (Champaign: University of Illinois Press, 2004); Annette Gordon-Reed, *The Hemingses of Monticello: An American Family* (New York: Norton, 2008); Heather Andrea Williams, *Help Me to Find My People: The African American Search for Family Lost in Slavery* (Chapel Hill: University of North Carolina Press, 2016); and Tera W. Hunter, *Bound in Wedlock: Slave and Free Black Marriage in the Nineteenth Century* (Cambridge: Harvard University Press, 2017).

5. It is worth noting that even studies of southern regions where comparatively smaller holdings predominated examine enslaved people who lived in significantly more sizable groups than those in most of New England. See, for example, Stevenson, *Life in Black and White*, and Dunaway, *The African-American Family in Slavery and Emancipation*. The same is true of Diane Mutti Burke's analysis of enslaved families in the Lower Midwest. See *On Slavery's Border: Missouri's Small Slaveholding Households, 1815–1865* (Athens: University of Georgia Press, 2010).

6. Cecilia A. Green, "'A Civil Inconvenience'? The Vexed Question of Slave Marriage in the British West Indies," *Law and History Review* 25, no. 1 (Spring 2007): 26. Green argued that "marriage among slaves had not been the subject of law or of slave codes because, slaves being legal non-entities, the possibility had no conception in law." According to legal historian Margaret Burnham, though "no statutes forbidding slaves to marry" existed in mainland North America, "the prohibition [of marriage to the enslaved] was judicially defined." See Margaret A. Burnham, "An Impossible Marriage: Slave Law and Family Law," *Minnesota Journal of Law and Inequality* 5, no. 2 (June 1987): 207. A host of scholars concur that bondspeople were denied legal marriage. See, for example, Norma Basch, *Framing American Divorce: From the Revolutionary Generation to the Victorians* (Berkeley: University of California Press, 1999), 48–49; Stevenson, *Life in Black and White*, 226; Malone, *Sweet Chariot*, 224; Lorri Glover, *Southern Sons: Becoming Men in the New Nation* (Baltimore: Johns Hopkins University Press, 2007), 127; Morgan, *Slave Counterpoint*, 499; Michael Grossberg, *Governing the Hearth: Law and the Family in Nineteenth-Century America* (Chapel Hill: University of North Carolina Press, 1985), 130–132; and Nancy Cott, *Public Vows: A History of Marriage and the Nation* (Cambridge: Harvard University Press, 2002), 32–35. Tera Hunter mentions puritan practices regarding marriages of enslaved people in early Massachusetts, but she does not get the story right because the existing scholarship does not treat the issue satisfactorily. See Hunter, *Bound in Wedlock*, 66–67.

7. For recent work on slavery in New England, see Joanne Pope Melish, *Disowning Slavery: Gradual Emancipation and "Race" in New England, 1780–1860* (Ithaca: Cornell University Press, 1998); Robert K. Fitts, *Inventing New England's Slave Paradise: Master/Slave Relations in Eighteenth-Century Narragansett, Rhode Island* (New York: Garland Publishing, 1998); James Oliver Horton and Lois E. Horton, *In Hope of Liberty: Culture, Community, and Northern Free Blacks, 1700–1860* (New York: Oxford University Press, 1998); John Wood Sweet, *Bodies Politic: Negotiating Race in the American North, 1730–1830* (Baltimore: Johns Hopkins University

Press, 2003); Alexandra A. Chan, *Slavery in the Age of Reason: Archaeology at a New England Farm* (Knoxville: University of Tennessee Press, 2007); Gretchen Holbrook Gerzina, *Mr. and Mrs. Prince: How an Extraordinary Eighteenth-Century Family Moved Out of Slavery and into Legend* (New York: Amistad, 2008); Elise Lemire, *Black Walden: Slavery and Its Aftermath in Concord, Massachusetts* (Philadelphia: University of Pennsylvania Press, 2009); Joyce Lee Malcolm, *Peter's War: A New England Slave Boy and the American Revolution* (New Haven: Yale University Press, 2009); C. S. Manegold, *Ten Hills Farm: The Forgotten History of Slavery in the North* (Princeton: Princeton University Press, 2010); Catherine Adams and Elizabeth H. Pleck, *Love of Freedom: Black Women in Colonial and Revolutionary New England* (New York: Oxford University Press, 2010); Margot Minardi, *Making Slavery History: Abolitionism and the Politics of Memory in Massachusetts* (New York: Oxford University Press, 2010); Richard A. Bailey, *Race and Redemption in Puritan New England* (New York: Oxford University Press, 2011); Allegra Di Bonaventura, *For Adam's Sake: A Family Saga in Colonial New England* (New York: Norton, 2013); Emily Blanck, *Tyrannicide: Forging an American Law of Slavery in Revolutionary South Carolina and Massachusetts* (Athens: University of Georgia Press, 2014); Margaret Ellen Newell, *Brethren By Nature: New England Indians, Colonists, and the Origins of American Slavery* (New York: Cornell University Press, 2015); Christy Clark-Pujara, *Dark Work: The Business of Slavery in Rhode Island* (New York: New York University Press, 2016); Jared Ross Hardesty, *Unfreedom: Slavery and Dependence in Eighteenth-Century Boston* (New York: New York University Press, 2016); Wendy Anne Warren, *New England Bound: Slavery and Colonization in Early America* (New York: Norton, 2016); Erica Armstrong Dunbar, *Never Caught: The Washingtons' Relentless Pursuit of Their Runaway Slave, Ona Judge* (New York: 37 Ink/Atria, 2017); Jared Ross Hardesty, *Black Lives, Native Lands, White Worlds: A History of Slavery in New England* (Boston: University of Massachusetts Press, 2019); and Richard Boles, *Dividing the Faith: The Rise of Segregated Churches in the Early American North* (New York: New York University Press, 2000).

8. See, for instance, W. E. B. Dubois, *Black Reconstruction in America, 1860–1880* (New York: Free Press, 1998, originally 1935); C. L. R. James, *The Black Jacobins: Toussaint L'Ouverture and the San Domingo Revolution* (New York: Vintage Books, 1989, originally 1963); Vincent Harding, *There Is a River: The Black Struggle for Freedom in America* (New York: Harcourt Brace Jovanovich, 1981); Ira Berlin, Barbara J. Fields, Steven F. Miller, Joseph P. Reidy, and Leslie S. Rowland, *Slaves No More: Three Essays on Emancipation and the Civil War* (New York: Cambridge University Press, 1992); David Williams, *I Freed Myself: African American Self-Emancipation in the Civil War Era* (New York: Cambridge University Press, 2014); David Roediger, *Seizing Freedom: Slave Emancipation and Liberty for All* (New York: Verso, 2014); Manisha Sinha, *The Slave's Cause: A History of Abolition* (New Haven: Yale University Press, 2016); and Kelly Carter Jackson, *Force and Freedom: Black Abolitionists and the Politics of Violence* (Philadelphia: University of Pennsylvania Press, 2019).

9. Arthur Zilversmit, "Quock Walker, Mumbet and the Abolition of Slavery in Massachusetts," *WMQ* 25, no. 4 (October 1968): 614–624; Arthur Zilversmit, *The First Emancipation: The Abolition of Slavery in the North* (Chicago: University of Chicago Press, 1967); A. Leon Higginbotham, "Racism and the American Legal Process," *Annals of the American Academy of Political and Social Science* 407 (May 1973): 13; John D. Cushing, "The Cushing Court and the Abolition of Slavery in Massachusetts: More Notes on the 'Quock Walker Case,'" *American Journal of Legal History* 5, no. 2 (April 1961): 119; James T. Allegro, "'Increasing and Strengthening the Country': Law, Politics, and the Antislavery Movement in

Early-Eighteenth-Century Massachusetts Bay," *New England Quarterly* 75, no. 1 (March 2002): 7; Emily Blanck, "Seventeen-Eighty-Three: The Turning Point in the Law of Slavery and Freedom in Massachusetts," *New England Quarterly* 75, no. 1 (March 2002): 24, 31; Loren Schweninger, "Freedom Suits, African American Women, and the Genealogy of Slavery," *WMQ* 71, no. 1 (January 2014): 37.

10. Mary Beth Norton, *Founding Mothers and Fathers: Gendered Power and the Forming of American Society* (New York: Knopf, 1996), 17. This definition of family seems to have emerged in the mid-fifteenth century. According to the *Oxford English Dictionary, family* was used to mean "a group of people living as a household, traditionally consisting of parents and their children, and also . . . any servants, boarders, etc." as early as 1452 (*Oxford English Dictionary,* December 2013, s.v. "Family, n. and adj," available at OED Online). Scholars have long been in agreement that puritan families included a host of non-kin workers who were bound to the family unit not by affection but by obligation to contribute to the family economy. See Edmund S. Morgan, *The Puritan Family: Essays on Religion and Domestic Relations in Seventeenth-Century New England* (Boston: Trustees of the Public Library, 1944); John Demos, *A Little Commonwealth: Family Life in Plymouth Colony* (New York: Oxford University Press, 1970); and M. Michelle Jarrett Morris, *Under Household Government: Sex and Family in Puritan Massachusetts* (Cambridge: Harvard University Press, 2013). In his extensive compilation of early American census data, Robert Wells found that colonial census takers used the words "household" and "family" interchangeably to mean "an independent, economic unit, the members of which lived in . . . close proximity . . . under the control of the 'master of the family.'" See Robert V. Wells, *Population of the British Colonies in America Before 1776: A Survey of Census Data* (Princeton: Princeton University Press, 2015), 42. For the importance of property over emotion even in marriage settlements, see Steven Mintz and Susan Kellogg, *Domestic Revolutions: A Social History of American Family Life* (New York: Free Press, 1988), 3, 10–11, 19–20. As for the relationship between blood ties and the meaning of *family* in early America, Mary Beth Norton affirms that "kinship ties were not essential to the definition of *family*" in early America. Norton, *Founding Mothers and Fathers,* 17.

11. See, for instance, Sarah M. S. Pearsall, *Atlantic Families: Lives and Letters in the Later Eighteenth Century* (New York: Oxford University Press, 2008), 6–16; Mintz and Kellogg, *Domestic Revolutions,* 17–23, 43–46; Sarah Maza, "Only Connect: Family Values in the Age of Sentiment: Introduction," *Eighteenth-Century Studies* 30, no. 3 (Spring 1997): 207–212. The classic formulation of this transformation in England, which has been critiqued but not discarded, is Lawrence Stone, *The Family, Sex, and Marriage in England, 1500–1800* (New York: Harper and Row, 1977). For the manifestation of these changes in English visual culture, see Kate Retford, *The Art of Domestic Life: Family Portraiture in Eighteenth-Century England* (New Haven: Yale University Press, 2006). For the diminished authority of fathers over their grown children in New England, see Philip J. Greven, *Four Generations: Population, Land, and Family in Colonial Andover, Massachusetts* (Ithaca: Cornell University Press, 1970), chap. 8, and Daniel Scott Smith, "Parental Power and Marriage Patterns: An Analysis of Historical Trends in Hingham, Massachusetts," *Journal of Marriage and Family* 35, no. 3 (August 1973): 419–428. For the history of emotion and the language of sensibility in eighteenth-century North America, see Sarah Knott, *Sensibility and the American Revolution* (Chapel Hill: University of North Carolina Press, 2009), and Nicole Eustace, *Passion Is the Gale: Emotion, Power, and the Coming of the American Revolution* (Chapel Hill: University of North Carolina Press, 2008).

12. Petition for freedom to Massachusetts Governor Thomas Gage, His Majesty's Council, and the House of Representatives, May 25, 1774, 1–2, Jeremy Belknap Papers, MHS ("endearing"); *Massachusetts Spy*, July 29, 1773, 1 ("bosoms"); Gunney v. How, Writ of Attachment, December 11, 1769, Suffolk County Court of Common Pleas File Papers, Docket no. 187, MA Archives ("parental"); *Essex Journal*, August 17, 1774, 1 ("affectionate"); and Peggy's Habeas Corpus, SF case 102787 ("comfort").

13. This paragraph draws on Gloria McCahon Whiting, "Power, Patriarchy, and Provision: African Families Negotiate Gender and Slavery in New England," *JAH* 103, no. 3 (December 2016): 601–605. For the man who purchased his wife-to-be, see "Bill of Sale of a Negro Servant in Boston, 1724," *New England Historical and Genealogical Register*, 18 (Albany: J. Munsell, 1864), 78–79.

14. See, for instance, Hardesty, *Unfreedom*, 11, 13; William Pierson, *Black Yankees: The Development of an Afro-American Subculture in Eighteenth-Century New England* (Amherst: University of Massachusetts Press, 1988), 37–43, 145–146; and Horton and Horton, *In Hope of Liberty*, 16–21.

15. For an example of the influence of a geographically distant uncle who was nonetheless valued by his kin, see Record Book, 1736–1854, 290, West Church of Boston, Ms.f Bos.Z3 (1) Boston, BPL. For a son-in-law, see page 283 of the above volume. For a boy and his grandfather, see Baptismal Records, 1669–1875, Old South Church in Boston, November 22, 1772 (no page number), CLA.

16. James H. Sweet points to polygyny, childbirth, adoption, pawnship, and slavery as strategies used by household heads to expand their kin networks in precolonial West Africa. See Sweet, "Defying Social Death: The Multiple Configurations of African Slave Family in the Atlantic World," *WMQ* 70, no. 2 (April 2013): 255. For the importance in West Africa of acquiring wealth in people, see John Thornton, *Africa and Africans in the Making of the Atlantic World, 1400–1800* (New York: Cambridge University Press, 1998), 72–97. For the argument that enslaved people in African societies were incorporated into kinship groups, see Suzanne Miers and Igor Kopytoff, "African 'Slavery' as an Institution of Marginality," in *Slavery in Africa: Historical and Anthropological Perspectives*, ed. Miers and Kopytoff (Madison: University of Wisconsin Press, 1977), 3–81.

17. For a penetrating account of the freedom conferred by kinship and the capacity of Black women to "belong to themselves and each other" in the context of the French Atlantic, see Jessica Marie Johnson, *Wicked Flesh: Black Women, Intimacy, and Freedom in the Atlantic World* (Philadelphia: University of Pennsylvania Press, 2020).

18. See, for instance, Newell, *Brethren By Nature*, and Warren, *New England Bound*. Newell argues that the English in New England bound local Native peoples almost exclusively before the eighteenth century, while Warren argues that African slavery dominated seventeenth-century New England. It is possible that each is correct for certain regions of New England, but the wide lenses of their studies make it difficult for readers to make sense of the conflicting claims. For the argument that Africans made up most of the bound labor force in Suffolk County from early on in New England's history, see Gloria McCahon Whiting, "Race, Slavery, and the Problem of Numbers in Early New England: A View from Probate Court," *WMQ* 77, no. 3 (July 2020): 405–440.

19. Population numbers for the seventeenth century are hard to come by, but one estimate put the Black population of Massachusetts at 200 in 1676, most of which would have been clustered in the Boston area, as that was the center of gravity for the white population as well. See

Lorenzo Johnston Greene, *The Negro in Colonial New England* (New York: Athenaeum, 1969), 79–80. For the comparison between Boston's Black population and that of the province, consider the 400 estimated Black Bostonians in 1708 versus the 1,310 estimated Black inhabitants of Massachusetts in 1710 (31 percent); the 1,374 enumerated Black Bostonians in 1742 versus the 3,035 estimated Black inhabitants of Massachusetts in 1740 (45 percent); and the 1,541 enumerated Black Bostonians in 1752 versus the 4,075 estimated Black inhabitants of Massachusetts in 1750 (38 percent). See *Historical Statistics of the United States Colonial Times to 1970*, vol. 2 (Washington, DC: Bureau of the Census, 1975), Z 1–23. See also Greene, *The Negro in Colonial New England*, 84.

20. For 15 percent, see Jared Hardesty, "Disappearing from Abolitionism's Heartland: The Legacy of Slavery and Emancipation in Boston," *International Review of Social History* 65 (April 2020): 149. Various factors can help explain the lower census numbers from the later eighteenth century. For instance, a 1755 census suggested a drastic reduction (552 people) in Boston's Black population from a census taken only three years before. However, the 1752 census counted the entire Black population, while the 1755 census counted only adults in slavery. That is, free Black people and enslaved children were both excluded from the latter accounting. See George A. Levesque, *Black Boston: African American Life and Culture in Urban America, 1750–1860.* (New York: Routledge, 2018), 31; Greene *The Negro in Colonial New England*, Appendix C. For more on the inaccuracy of later censuses, see Hardesty, "Disappearing from Abolition's Heartland," 162–163. For the population of Boston compared to other towns in New England, see Greene, *The Negro in Colonial New England*, chap. 3.

21. The individual stories told in *Belonging* are crucial, but so too is the body of evidence—thousands of clues culled from court, church, town, private, and print records—that allows one to explore the contexts of those stories. In the rare instances in which scholars have profiled particular African-descended New England families in depth, it can be difficult to distill broader trends from the evocative particularities of the narrative in question, and *Belonging* seeks to capture both. For two beautifully crafted narratives of Afro-New England families, see Gerzina, *Mr. and Mrs. Prince*, and Di Bonaventura, *For Adam's Sake*.

22. The asymmetries of the historical record are so great that some historians of the Black Atlantic have begun to call for a move beyond archival empiricism in their effort to depict individual lives; the clues to the enslaved are just too sparse. See, for instance, Stephanie E. Smallwood, *Saltwater Slavery: A Middle Passage from Africa to American Diaspora* (Cambridge: Harvard University Press, 2007); Saidiya Hartman, *Lose Your Mother: A Journey Along the Atlantic Slave Route* (New York: Farrar, Straus and Giroux, 2007); Saidiya Hartman, "Venus in Two Acts," *Small Axe* 12, no. 2 (June 2008): 1–14; Marisa J. Fuentes, *Dispossessed Lives: Enslaved Women, Violence, and the Archive* (Philadelphia: University of Pennsylvania Press, 2016); the special issue of *Social Text* titled "The Question of Recovery: Slavery, Freedom and the Archive," *Social Text* 33, no. 4 (December 2015); and the special issue of *History of the Present: A Journal of Critical History* 6, no. 2 (Fall 2016), on the violence of the archives of slavery. A number of scholars have theorized the processes by which they explore what the archive of slavery leaves unknowable. Saidiya Hartman has laid out the method of "critical fabulation"; Marisa J. Fuentes has written of "stretch[ing] archival fragments by reading *along the bias grain*"; Jennifer L. Morgan has called for a "methodological capaciousness" that will allow us to hear, as she quoted Hartman, "the 'mutters and oaths and cries of the commodity.'" I share the concerns of these scholars; I want my readers to hear the people whose lives this book explores and to envision the worlds these people navigated. I desire, as Saidiya Hartman so

powerfully put it, to "paint as full a picture of the lives of the captives as possible." I therefore occasionally engage in imaginative reconstruction. Each chapter of *Belonging* begins with a scene in the life of the main character(s) of that chapter. Sometimes a wealth of direct evidence undergirds my narration of these moments; sometimes I rely more on oblique archival clues. For those who wish to distinguish between what is made clear in the archive and what is inferred, my language provides the crucial clue. Where my prose is halting, clothed in the uncertainty conveyed by words such as "perhaps," the evidence from which I am working is indirect. When my language is forthright, the historical record provides direct evidence on the matter at hand. It is important to note that nothing in this book is invented: When, for instance, I write in the opening of Chapter 5 about a black jug that was placed in the corner of a closet, the jug, which was indeed described in the record as black, was in fact specified as occupying the corner of the closet. See Hartman, "Venus in Two Acts," 11; Fuentes, *Dispossessed Lives*, 7; Jennifer L. Morgan, *Reckoning with Slavery: Gender, Kinship, and Capitalism in the Early Black Atlantic* (Durham: Duke University Press, 2021), 169.

23. In this, I echo the calls of others. For instance, Jessica Marie Johnson has drawn attention to the "additional labor" demanded of historians who search the archive for clues to the lives of enslaved and free Black people in the Atlantic regions that practiced slavery. See Johnson, *Wicked Flesh*, 5.

Chapter 1

Epigraph: "A Coppie of the Liberties of the Massachusets Colonie in New England" (1641) in *Collections of the Massachusetts Historical Society*, vol. 8, 3rd series (Boston: Massachusetts Historical Society, 1843), 231.

1. This chapter opens with an imaginative reconstruction of Dorcas's narrative of God's work in her life. No relations of faith survive from the Dorchester congregation that Dorcas joined, so we lack direct evidence of what Dorcas said before the brethren. However, many such narratives from mid-seventeenth-century Massachusetts are extant. The narratives exhibit marked similarities—scholars have drawn attention to the "basic structure" or "pattern" that they follow—and we can be confident that Dorcas's confession would have met her audience's expectations. To evoke this experience in Dorcas's life, I examined more than a hundred confessions, culling statements with language that Dorcas might have used in her own. Of course, Dorcas might not have uttered these words at all, which is why my prose is laden in hesitancy. Nonetheless, this body of confessions provides us with an idiom and period locution with which to express, haltingly, of course, some of the ways in which people in slavery might have articulated their experiences to the puritans around them. For the "structure" of relations of faith, see Lori Stokes-Rogers, "Making Sense of the Shepard Conversion Narratives, *New England Quarterly* 89, no. 1 (March 2016): 117. For the "pattern" common to such narratives, see Edmund S. Morgan, *Visible Saints: The History of a Puritan Idea* (Ithaca: Cornell University Press, 1965), 91. For a description of the building in which the early Dorchester saints worshipped, see Dorchester Antiquarian and Historical Society, *History of the Town of Dorchester, Massachusetts* (Boston: Ebenezer Clapp Jr., 1859), 33. For an episode that suggests that expectant silence was routine among audiences of confessions, see Michael P. Clark, ed., *The Eliot Tracts: With Letters from John Eliot to Thomas Thorowgood and Richard Baxter* (Westport: Praeger, 2003), 279.

2. Confession of Goodman With (Nicholas Wyeth) in George Selement and Bruce C. Woolley, eds. *Thomas Shepard's Confessions* (Boston: Colonial Society of Massachusetts,

1981), 194. For the likelihood that Dorcas originated in West Central Africa, see David Wheat, *Atlantic Africa and the Spanish Caribbean, 1570–1640* (Chapel Hill: University of North Carolina Press, 2016), 72–102; also David Wheat, "The First Great Waves: African Provenance Zones for the Transatlantic Slave Trade to Cartagena de Indias, 1570–1640," *Journal of African History* 52, no. 1 (March 2011): 4, 7.

3. For "sad," see Confession of old Goodwife Cutter (Elizabeth Cutter), Selement and Woolley, eds., *Thomas Shepard's Confessions*, 144. I have silently substituted first-person singular ("me") for first-person plural ("us") in this quotation. For "sick," see Confession of Monequassun, Clark, ed., *Eliot Tracts*, 278. For "kindred," see Confession of Ponampiam, Clark, ed., *Eliot Tracts*, 385.

4. Data culled from slightly after Dorcas's voyage (1652–1700) show that 16.7 percent of captured Africans taken from West Central Africa died prior to arriving in the Caribbean, and they indicate that the average voyage lasted 75.4 days. A ship carrying 250 enslaved Africans with this mortality rate would lose at least one captive every other day. Dorcas's earlier and longer voyage would likely have been yet more deadly. See David Eltis and David Richardson, *Atlas of the Transatlantic Slave Trade* (New Haven: Yale University Press, 2010), 169. See also Confession of Richard Cutter, Selement and Woolley, eds., *Thomas Shepard's Confessions*, 179. Stokes-Rogers, "Making Sense," 124.

5. For "straits," see Confession of Goodwife Champney (probably Jane Champney), Selement and Woolley, eds., *Thomas Shepard's Confessions*, 191; for "affliction," see Confession of John Sill his wife (Joanna Sill), Selement and Woolley, eds., *Thomas Shepard's Confessions*, 50; for "sad trials," see Confession of Goodman Manning (William Manning), Selement and Woolley, eds., *Thomas Shepard's Confessions*, 97. For hypocrisy, see Andy Dorsey, "A Rhetoric of American Experience: Thomas Shepard's Cambridge Confessions and the Discourse of Spiritual Hypocrisy," *Early American Literature* 49, no. 3 (2014): 631.

6. For "prayed," see Confession of John Speen, Clark, ed., *Eliot Tracts*, 387. For the relative harmony enjoyed by church members and the ethics of equity they fostered, see David D. Hall, *A Reforming People: Puritanism and the Transformation of Public Life in New England* (New York: Knopf, 2011), 159–190.

7. For "freeness," see Confession of Sister Moulton in Robert G. Pope, ed., *The Notebook of the Reverend John Fiske, 1644–1675* (Boston: Colonial Society of Massachusetts, 1974), 9. For "closing," see Confession of Mr. Eaton (Nathaniel Eaton), Selement and Woolley, eds., *Thomas Shepard's Confessions*, 56. For "weeping," see Confession of Mr. Sparhawk (Nathaniel Sparrowhawk), Selement and Woolley, eds., *Thomas Shepard's Confessions*, 63. For "love," see Confession of Goodman Luxford his wife (Elizabeth Olbon), Selement and Woolley, eds., *Thomas Shepard's Confessions*, 41. I silently substituted first person for third in this quotation; the original read, "He let her feel his love."

8. *New Englands First Fruits; In Respect, First of the Conversion of Some, Conviction of Divers, Preparation of Sundry of the Indians . . .* (London: Printed by R.O. and G.D. for Henry Overton, 1643), 10.

9. See Charles Lloyd Cohen, *God's Caress: The Psychology of Puritan Religious Experience* (New York: Oxford University Press, 1986), 207.

10. Confession of Richard Eagle (or Richard Eccles), Selement and Woolley, eds., *Thomas Shepard's Confessions*, 116.

11. Note that Deborah Colleen McNally has carefully reconstructed aspects of Dorcas's life. See McNally, "To Secure Her Freedom: 'Dorcas ye blackmore,' Race, Redemption, and the Dorchester First Church," *New England Quarterly* 89, no. 4 (December 2016): 533–555.

12. In 1641, when Dorcas was baptized in Dorchester's church, she was referred to as a "maid." Neither a girl nor a spinster, the designation suggests that she was close to twenty. Dorcas would have a child in 1652, so she was clearly of child-bearing age at that time, and she would have another within two years. She must have been fairly young—probably no older than her early thirties—in order to conceive and bear two children so close together. Assuming she was thirty in 1652 when she bore her first child, she would have been nineteen when she was baptized in 1641, which would give her a hypothetical birth year of 1622. For "maid," see Richard S. Dunn, James Savage, and Laetitia Yeandle, eds., *The Journal of John Winthrop, 1630–1649* (Cambridge: Harvard University Press, 1996), 347.

13. See Dorchester First Church, *Records of the First Church at Dorchester, in New England, 1636–1734* (Boston: G. H. Ellis, 1891), 5.

14. James H. Sweet, *Recreating Africa: Culture, Kinship, and Religion in the African-Portuguese World, 1441–1770* (Chapel Hill: University of North Carolina Press, 2003), chap. 5; also, John K. Thornton, "Afro-Christian Syncretism in the Kingdom of Kongo," *Journal of African History* 54, no. 1 (March 2013): 53–77.

15. Linda M. Heywood, "Slavery and Its Transformation in the Kingdom of Kongo: 1491–1800," *Journal of African History* 50, no. 1 (March 2009): 10–16.

16. On Kongo sending captives to merchants in Angola, see John K. Thornton, "The African Experience of the '20. and Odd Negroes' Arriving in Virginia in 1619," *WMQ* 55, no. 3 (July 1998): 421–422. On the Portuguese and Afro-Portuguese traders in Angola, see Wheat, *Atlantic Africa and the Spanish Caribbean*, 81–92.

17. John K. Thornton, "Religious and Ceremonial Life in the Kongo and Mbundu Areas," in *Central Africans and Cultural Transformations in the American Diaspora*, ed. Linda Heywood (New York: Cambridge University Press, 2002), 71–90.

18. For detailed treatment of the ways in which war and civil unrest in Central Africa fed the Atlantic slave market in the first half of the seventeenth century, see John K. Thornton and Linda M. Heywood, *Central Africans, Atlantic Creoles, and the Foundation of the Americas, 1585–1660* (New York: Cambridge University Press, 2007), chap. 3; also, Wheat, *Atlantic Africa and the Spanish Caribbean*, 78–79.

19. For the experience of Ndongo captives in Portuguese slaving campaigns of 1618, 1619, and 1620, see Linda M. Heywood and John K. Thornton, "In Search of the 1619 African Arrivals," *Virginia Magazine of History and Biography* 127, no. 3 (2019): 208.

20. For "S Juan Bautista," see #29591, for "Espírito Santo," see #29775, and for "Buen Jesus" see #29388, all recorded in Slave Voyages, the Trans-Atlantic Slave Trade Database, https://www.slavevoyages.org/.

21. Eltis and Richardson, *Atlas of the Transatlantic Slave Trade*, 21–22.

22. Between 1626 and 1640, 70 percent of vessels known to have conveyed bound Africans to either Cartagena or Veracruz hailed from Angola. See Wheat, "The First Great Waves," 20. Enslaved people arriving in South Atlantic ports skewed even more heavily from West Central Africa during this era.

23. Engel Sluiter, "New Light on the '20. and Odd Negroes' Arriving in Virginia, August 1619," *WMQ* 54, no. 2 (April 1997): 395–398.

24. See Karen Ordahl Kupperman, *Providence Island, 1630–1641: The Other Puritan Colony* (New York: Cambridge University Press, 1993), chaps. 4 and 9.

25. It is worth noting that a small number of enslaved Africans were brought to New England prior to the arrival of this group. See Lorenzo Johnston Greene, *The Negro in Colonial New England* (New York: Athenaeum, 1969), 16. For firsthand accounts of African-descended prisoners taken from the Spanish mainland to Providence Island, see David Wheat, "A Spanish Caribbean Captivity Narrative: African Sailors and Puritan Slavers, 1635," in *Afro-Latino Voices: Narratives from the Early Modern Ibero-Atlantic World, 1550–1812*, ed. Kathryn Joy McKnight and Leo J. Garofalo (Indianapolis: Hackett Publishers, 2009), 195–213. Deborah Colleen McNally has argued that Dorcas likely was brought to Boston aboard the *Desire* in 1638. See McNally, "To Secure Her Freedom," 537. See also Margaret E. Newell, *Brethren By Nature: New England Indians, Colonists, and the Origins of American Slavery* (Ithaca: Cornell University Press, 2015), 93–94, and Wendy Anne Warren, *New England Bound: Slavery and Colonization in Early America* (New York: Norton, 2016), 139–141.

26. Dunn et al., eds., *Journal of John Winthrop*, 246.

27. Though no surviving records list the names of the bound Africans aboard the *Desire*, it is likely that Dorcas was one of the Africans conveyed on the vessel to Boston. The *Desire* not only brought the only known shipment of bound Africans to the region prior to Dorcas's 1641 baptism, but the timing of her voyage aligns with clues to Dorcas's origins in the colony. When Dorcas stood before Dorchester's First Church in April of 1641 and proclaimed her faith in Christ, she was not a new arrival to Massachusetts. She had been learning scripture (and English) for some time—"divers years," as the colony's governor, John Winthrop, had put it. Had the *Desire* carried Dorcas on its February 1638 homecoming, the African woman's arrival in Massachusetts would have predated her April 1641 baptism by just over three years, a period of time that corresponds with Winthrop's statement. The timing of the *Desire*'s voyage works well on another account: The man who ultimately purchased Dorcas, an influential colonist named Israel Stoughton, was actively seeking an enslaved woman for his household at the very time the *Desire* embarked on her Atlantic passage. It is hardly farfetched, then, to imagine that he bought one of the African captives on the *Desire* when the ship returned to port. See Dunn et al., eds., *Journal of John Winthrop*, 347, and Letter from Israel Stoughton to John Winthrop, ca. June 28, 1637, in John Winthrop, *Winthrop Papers, vol. 3, 1631–1637*, ed. Allyn Bailey Forbes (Boston: Massachusetts Historical Society, 1943), 435.

28. Map of the Town of Boston 1648, Drawer 9 (XL), Folder 1, Samuel Chester Clough research materials toward a topographical history of Boston, MHS.

29. Regarding Israel's children, the man bestowed upon his "Eldest sonne Israell," born in England, a "double portion" in his will. See Israel Stoughton's will, 1644, SCPR, FS, vol. 1, 63. For evidence relating to the existence of an eldest daughter, likely named Susanna, who was born in England and therefore not mentioned in New England records, see William R. Newman, *Gehennical Fire: The Lives of George Starkey, an American Alchemist in the Scientific Revolution* (Chicago: University of Chicago Press, 2003), 51–52. Hannah Stoughton's birth date was not noted by Dorchester's First Church when it occurred, nor does it appear in surviving records created by Dorchester's early town clerks (which are fragmentary for the 1630s), but it was listed after the fact on the back flyleaf of the Dorchester church's book of records, possibly by a town clerk, in the early 1700s: "2nd m[onth] 1637." William Stoughton's birth date is given on the same page: "30[th day] 7th m[onth] 1631." Dorchester First Church, *Records of the First Church at Dorchester*, 148.

30. On October 21, 1637, John was whipped by the court for "divers miscarriages" toward both Elizabeth and Israel, as well as for running away. Elizabeth's status as a widow and Israel's involvement in disciplining her dependent suggest that the woman had joined Israel's household prior to this time. See Dunn et al., eds., *Journal of John Winthrop*, 755.

31. For references to Alexander, John, and Robert, see Nathaniel B. Shurtleff, ed., *Records of the Governor & Company of the Massachusetts Bay in New England, vol. 1* (Boston: William White, 1853–1854), 100, 163–164. As for the Indigenous woman, Israel asked that the colony's governor, John Winthrop, allow him to keep a captive whom his military company had seized in present-day Rhode Island. See Letter from Israel Stoughton to John Winthrop, ca. June 28, 1637, in Winthrop, *Winthrop Papers, vol. 3*, 435.

32. Geographic intimacy did not necessarily breed relational harmony. For the argument that sharing an enslaver's home led to a milder form of slavery, see William Pierson, *Black Yankees: The Development of an Afro-American Subculture in Eighteenth-Century New England* (Amherst: University of Massachusetts Press, 1988). For the counterargument that quartering bondspeople in enslavers' homes led to monitoring and the incessant implementation of racial segregation, see Robert K. Fitts, "The Landscapes of Northern Bondage," *Historical Archaeology* 30, no. 2 (1996): 54–73.

33. According to Israel's inventory, he owned a barn in addition to his "dwelling house," but it is unlikely that people inhabited it; Bay colonists did not develop a pattern of building separate quarters to house those they enslaved. There are, of course, a few exceptions to this, such as the case of the Royalls in eighteenth-century Medford, Massachusetts. See Israel's inventory, 1650, SCPR, NS, vol. 3, 261–262, and Alexandra A. Chan, *Slavery in the Age of Reason: Archaeology at a New England Farm* (Knoxville: University of Tennessee Press, 2007).

34. Abbott Lowell Cummings, *The Framed Houses of Massachusetts Bay, 1625–1725* (Cambridge: Harvard University Press, 1979), 22–25; Israel's inventory, 263.

35. See John Demos, *A Little Commonwealth: Family Life in Plymouth Colony* (New York: Oxford University Press, 1970), 39, 46–51.

36. "A morning prayer to be used in private families," in Arthur Dent, *The Plaine Mans Path-way to Heaven* (London: Imprinted by R. Bradock for Robert Dexter, 1607), Dd.

37. Glenda Goodman, "'The Tears I Shed at the Songs of Thy Church': Seventeenth-Century Musical Piety in the English Atlantic World," *Journal of the American Musicological Society* 65, no. 3 (Fall 2012): 691–725.

38. For "hunger," see Richard Rogers, William Perkins, Richard Greenham, Miles Mosse, and George Webb, "A thanks-giving before meate," in *A Garden of spirituall Flowers. PLANTED BY Ri. Ro. Will. Per. Ri. Gree. M. M. and Geo. Web.* (London: Printed by W. White for T. Pavier, 1610). For "fed," see Rogers et al., "A thanks-giving after meate," in *A Garden of spirituall Flowers.*

39. "Evening Prayer for a Family" in Lewis Bayly, *The Practice of Piety: Directing a Christian how to walke that he may please God* (London: Printed by F. Kingston for Robert Allot, 1635), 315–316. This section is based on Charles E. Hambrick-Stowe's discussion of the family devotions practiced by seventeenth-century New England puritans. See Charles E. Hambrick-Stowe, *The Practice of Piety: Puritan Devotional Disciplines in Seventeenth-Century New England* (Chapel Hill: University of North Carolina Press, 1982), 143–150.

40. Rogers et al., "A godly Meditation to be had in minde at our going to bedde," in *A Garden of spirituall Flowers.*

41. Hambrick-Stowe, *The Practice of Piety*, 96–103.

42. For books, see Israel's will, 65–66. For Israel's leadership, see Dorchester First Church, *Records of the First Church at Dorchester*, xiv; Boston Record Commissioners, *Dorchester Town Records* (Boston: Rockwell and Churchill, 1896), 44.

43. Roger Clap, *Memoirs of Captain Roger Clap: Relating Some of God's Remarkable Providences to Him, in Bringing Him into New England, and Some of the Straits and Afflictions the Good People Met with Here in Their Beginnings* (Boston: Printed for William Tileston Clap by David Carlisle, 1807), 13.

44. See Dunn et al., eds., *Journal of John Winthrop*, 604–605.

45. If she arrived on the *Desire* in 1638 and was received into the church in 1641, Dorcas must have come to faith in that narrow window of time.

46. John Saltmarsh, *Sparkles of Glory, or Some Beams of the Morning-Star* (London: Printed for Giles Calvert, 1647), 144.

47. *New Englands First Fruits*, 10.

48. Quoted in Francis J. Bremer, "'To Tell What God Hath Done for Thy Soul': Puritan Spiritual Testimonies as Admission Tests and Means of Edification," *New England Quarterly* 87, no. 4 (December 2014): 634.

49. *New Englands First Fruits*, 10. For the steps required for admission to puritan congregations in early New England, see Morgan, *Visible Saints*, 88–89.

50. No extant New England church records document the baptism or membership of an identifiably African person prior to 1641. Dorcas's admission to the First Church was unusually early; the Dorchester congregation would not receive another Black member until 1700, and, when Dorcas ultimately transferred her membership to Boston's First Church in 1677, she would be the first person of African descent to covenant with that congregation as well. For the Dorchester church's second Black member, see Dorchester First Church, *Records of the First Church at Dorchester*, 211. For the quotation, see Richard Mather, *An Answer of the Elders of the Severall Churches in New-England unto Nine Positions, Sent Over to Them, (by Divers Reverend and Godly Ministers in England) to Declare Their Judgments Therein* (London: Printed by T. P. and M. S. for Benjamin Allen, 1643), 51.

51. William Bradford, *Bradford's History "Of Plimoth Plantation" from the Original Manuscript* (Boston: Wright & Potter Printing Co., 1898), 95.

52. For the religious motivations of the migration, see Virginia Dejohn Anderson, *New England's Generation: The Great Migration and the Formation of Society and Culture in the Seventeenth Century* (New York: Cambridge University Press, 1991), 37–46; for the kin connections of the migrants, see 21–26; and for their relative prosperity, see 31–36. For the extent to which literacy of migrants to New England outpaced literacy in England itself, see David Hackett Fischer, *Albion's Seed: Four British Folkways in America* (New York: Oxford University Press, 1989), 29–31.

53. Virginia Dejohn Anderson emphasized the "comparative economic equality" that characterized New England, but, as her work makes clear, *comparative* economic equality is not the same as full-scale equivalence: Townspeople were well aware of their own social ranks and of those of their neighbors. See Anderson, *New England's Generation*, 1 ("comparative"), 160–172. For the greater equality of wealth distribution in colonial New England as opposed to the Chesapeake, see Gloria L. Main, "Inequality in Early America: The Evidence from Probate Records of Massachusetts and Maryland," *Journal of Interdisciplinary History* 7, no. 4 (Spring 1977): 559–581. For "Equall" and "Equallitie," see Hall, *A Reforming People*, 64; for

"equity," see 67; for the division of land, see 64–66; for taxes, see 66–70; for legal justice, see 147–154.

54. Thomas Shepard spoke of the members of his Cambridge, Massachusetts, church as "already in heaven." See Hall, *A Reforming People*, 160.

55. Newell, *Brethren By Nature*, chaps. 1 and 2.

56. Michael Guasco, *Slaves and Englishmen: Human Bondage in the Early Modern Atlantic World* (Philadelphia: University of Pennsylvania Press, 2014), chap. 5.

57. For John's report of the *Desire*'s journey to Providence Island, see Dunn et al., eds., *Journal of John Winthrop*, 246.

58. M. I. Finley, "Slavery," in *International Encyclopedia of the Social Sciences, vol. 14*, ed. David Sills (New York: Macmillan, 1968), 308, and Suzanne Miers and Igor Kopytoff, "African 'Slavery' as an Institution of Marginality," in *Slavery in Africa: Historical and Anthropological Perspectives*, ed. Suzanne Miers and Igor Kopytoff (Madison: University of Wisconsin Press, 1977), 3–81.

59. Michael L. Fickes, "'They Could Not Endure That Yoke': The Captivity of Pequot Women and Children After the War of 1637," *New England Quarterly* 73, no. 1 (March 2000): 73. See also Warren, *New England Bound*, 106.

60. For Israel's interpretation of this process, see Israel Stoughton, "A relation concerning some occurences in New England" (1635), *Proceedings of the Massachusetts Historical Society* 5 (January 1861): 137. For a historian's account of this process, see Edmund S. Morgan, *The Puritan Dilemma: The Story of John Winthrop* (Boston: Little, Brown, 1958), 112.

61. David Hall has concisely distinguished between two kinds of freedom: "doorways to personal freedom" and "protections against unauthorized and unjust actions of the civil state." The "liberties" that Stoughton sought to protect were of the latter category, not the former. See Hall, *A Reforming People*, xii. *Records of the Massachusetts Bay Colony, vol. 1*, 279.

62. For "published" and "satisfy," see Dunn et al., eds., *Journal of John Winthrop*, 315. For "democratical," see John Winthrop, *Winthrop Papers, vol. 4, 1638–1644*, ed. Allyn Bailey Forbes (Boston: Massachusetts Historical Society, 1944), 162–163.

63. Dunn et al., eds., *Journal of John Winthrop*, 347.

64. Had John regularly attended the meetings at which area churches admitted new members, his journal—at least early on, when it recorded his daily activities—would have indicated this, but it does not do so. As he casually mentioned in 1639, he "did very seldom go from his own congregation upon the Lord's day." See Dunn et al., eds., *Journal of John Winthrop*, 297.

65. Puritans baptized adults if they had not been baptized in infancy but made a profession of faith when grown. For John's references, see Dunn et al., eds., *Journal of John Winthrop*, 79, 96, 158.

66. I use the page count of Winthrop's published journal here rather than that of the manuscript edition.

67. Dunn et al., eds., *Journal of John Winthrop*, xiii and xv–xvi. John's first book, begun in 1630, had no title.

68. For "published," see Dunn et al., eds., 367. For "recorded," see Dunn et al., eds., 425. For "left out," see Dunn et al., eds., 442.

69. Dunn et al., eds., 315, 380.

70. Shurtleff, ed., *Records of the Governor & Company of the Massachusetts Bay, vol. 1*, 346.

71. Dunn et al., eds., *Journal of John Winthrop*, 380.

72. "A Coppie of the Liberties," 231. These "liberties," numbered 89 and 90, are found in the section called "Liberties of Forreiners and Strangers."

73. "A Coppie of the Liberties," 231.

74. See, for example, Robert M. Spector, "The Quock Walker Cases (1781–83): Slavery, Its Abolition, and Negro Citizenship in Early Massachusetts," *Journal of Negro History* 53 (January 1968): 19.

75. See Jonathan A. Bush, "The British Constitution and the Creation of American Slavery," in *Slavery and the Law*, ed. Paul Finkelman (Lanham, MD: Rowman & Littlefield, 2002), 382.

76. "A Coppie of the Liberties," 231.

77. Exod. 21:2, KJV.

78. Deut. 15:12–14, KJV; Jer. 34, KJV.

79. Lev. 25:44–46, KJV.

80. Lev. 25:46, KJV.

81. Dorcas's story exemplifies the paradox described by Richard A. Bailey. The freemen's redemptive theology enabled them to see Dorcas as a spiritual equal, worthy of the church membership that lay beyond the grasp of most English people, but brutal inequality condemned so many people of African and Indigenous descent in the region to bondage. See Bailey, *Race and Redemption in Puritan New England* (New York: Oxford University Press, 2011).

82. These were words spoken in the conversion narratives of Jane Holmes and Roger Haynes. See Confession of Goodwife Holmes (Jane Holmes), Selement and Woolley, eds., *Thomas Shepard's Confessions*, 80, and Confession of Mr. Haynes (probably Roger Haynes), Selement and Woolley, eds., *Thomas Shepard's Confessions*, 167.

83. See, for example, Richard Archer, *Fissures in the Rock: New England in the Seventeenth Century* (Hanover: University Press of New England, 2001), 69, and Robert G. Pope, *The Half-way Covenant: Church Membership in Puritan New England* (Princeton: Princeton University Press, 1969), 279–286.

84. *New Englands First Fruits*, 10–11. According to Raymond P. Stearns, the tract was published in London during the winter of 1642–1643 by Thomas Weld and Hugh Peter, presumably using materials they obtained from Henry Dunster and John Eliot. These four men were all ministers, but because I cannot discern who wrote which part of the tract, I refer simply to reports of "a minister" when citing the tract in this chapter. See Raymond P. Stearns, *The Strenuous Puritan: Hugh Peter, 1598–1660* (Urbana: University of Illinois, 1954), 167.

85. Richard W. Cogley, *John Eliot's Mission to the Indians Before King Philip's War* (Cambridge: Harvard University Press, 1999), 20.

86. *New Englands First Fruits*, 4.

87. No extant sources provide evidence that newcomers of African descent had joined the colony's bound labor force since the *Desire* docked in 1638, but we do know that New England ships were engaged in the slave trade during this time. In 1645, John Winthrop mentioned the return of "One of our shipps," which had brought pipe staves—that is, wooden barrels—to the Canary Islands and purchased "Africoes" from the Cape Verde Islands, whom she traded for "wine & Sugar & salt, & some tobacco" in Barbados. Dunn et al., eds., *Journal of John Winthrop*, 573. Later that year, the Bay Colony's court ordered the return of Africans "stolen" from Guinea by Captain James Smith and his mate, Thomas Keyser. See Shurtleff, ed., *Records of the Governor & Company of the Massachusetts Bay, vol. 2*, 136, 168.

88. *First Church Records*, 1, 323.

89. The importance of spousal cohabitation was ubiquitous in puritan thought. For a representative example, see the sermon titled "The mutual Duties of Husbands and Wives towards each other," by Richard Baxter, a seventeenth-century English puritan church leader and theologian. See William Orme, *The Practical Works of Richard Baxter: With a Life of the Author, and a Critical Evaluation of His Writings, vol. 4* (London: J. Duncan, 1830), 119.

90. For instance, the minister of Hollis Street Church noted in the early eighteenth century that John Vingus was "Baptised in his own Countrey by a *Romish* priest." See Hollis Street Church Records, BPL, "Records of Membership 1732–1739," no page number.

91. Henry Russell's will, 1640, SCPR, FS, vol. 1, 24; William Brimsmead's will, 1647, SCPR, FS, vol. 1, 54.

92. I infer Dorcas's request from the subsequent actions of her congregation. It seems far more likely that the congregation would have intervened in a radical way to assist one of its members if requested to do so than if the member in need had simply gone about her business in silence. This is also a way to recognize Dorcas as an actor rather than as someone acted upon, as a self-advocate rather than as someone rescued by others' benevolence.

93. Dorchester First Church, *Records of the First Church at Dorchester*, 2.

94. Matt. 7:16–17, KJV.

95. Most of the judgments pertaining to emancipation petitions of servants and masters are found in the Court of Assistants, also called the Quarter Court. Only magistrates (the governor, deputy governor, and their assistants) sat on the Court of Assistants (as opposed to magistrates *and* deputies), so usually magistrates ruled on these freedom suits. My language here reflects this tendency. Occasionally, though, freedom petitions were brought before the General Court, on which both magistrates and—after 1634—deputies sat. In these instances, both magistrates and deputies influenced the outcome of the cases in question.

96. Shurtleff, ed., *Records of the Governor & Company of the Massachusetts Bay, vol. 1,* 91, 105, 121.

97. Shurtleff, ed., 186.

98. Shurtleff, ed., 193.

99. Shurtleff, ed., 267, 282. Israel was discharged from his 40-shilling fine because the court determined that "hee could not hould his servant, having no covenant." In Israel's case, then, the servant's early freedom seems to have had legal grounding; as the servant never indentured—or "covenanted"—himself to Israel, then it was legal for him to leave Israel's service at any time. The other emancipations referenced in this section did not hinge on this matter. The court in those cases seems to have been ruling on servants who sought release from their indentures before having served their time.

100. Shurtleff, ed., 286.

101. Shurtleff, ed., 306, 307, 315, 317.

102. Shurtleff, ed., *Records of the Governor & Company of the Massachusetts Bay, vol. 2,* 12, 32, 67.

103. See Bailey, *Race and Redemption in Puritan New England*, chap. 5.

104. Luke 10:41–42, KJV.

105. *BBMD*, 47. Martha lived in Boston, which suggests that Dorcas had relocated sometime between the 1652 baptism of her son in Dorchester and the 1654 death of her daughter in Boston—timing that makes sense in light of her 1653 emancipation.

106. Menenie's inventory, 1675, SCPR, FS, vol. 5, 266.

107. Evidence is spotty, but, according to the best demographic data available, the population of Black people was small in Boston at the time of Menenie's death. In 1680, Simon Bradstreet, the governor of Massachusetts, reported to England that there were between 100 and 120 people of African descent in the colony, forty to fifty of whom had been brought on a ship from Madagascar two years earlier. According to this estimate, there could have been as few as fifty people of African descent in Massachusetts in 1675 when Dorcas Menenie appeared in probate court, which means that the number in Boston would have been even lower: perhaps between thirty-five and forty, assuming (generously) that around three-quarters of the colony's Africans were clustered in its principal port. Another, higher, contemporary estimate of the colony's African population exists. In 1676, Edward Randolph, an English colonial administrator, reported that "there are not above 200 slaves in the colony." Edward's number might be inflated. The man has been described as "always extravagant in his statistics relating to Massachusetts," and the way he phrased his estimation as "not above 200" suggests that he might have been approximating the ceiling of the African population. Assuming that Edward's figure was accurate, though, the population of Afro-Bostonians would come in at around 150. So somewhere between forty and 150 Black people resided in the port at the time Dorcas presented her husband's estate in court. At most, half of them were female, as evidence from probate records indicates that male bondspeople slightly outnumbered female bondspeople at this time. This means that only twenty to seventy-five females of African descent lived in Boston, and some of these were undoubtedly children: Simon estimated that "five or six blacks [were] born a year." Simon's and Edward's two estimates, then, one low and one perhaps high, leave us with between a dozen and fifty or so African women in Boston. Simon is quoted in Joshua Griffin, *An account of some of the principal slave insurrections: and others, which have occurred, or been attempted, in the United States and elsewhere, during the last two centuries* (New York: American Antislavery Society, 1860), 9; also Warren, *New England Bound*, 46. For Edward's statement, see Charles Deane, *The Connection of Massachusetts with Slavery and the Slave-Trade* (Worcester: Charles Hamilton, 1886), 28 n2.

108. *Munene* stems from the proto-Bantu root "-nene." For links between Kongo and the Kasai region, see David Birmingham, *Central Africa to 1870: Zambezia, Zaire, and the South Atlantic* (New York: Cambridge University Press, 1981), 94 and 89, and Thornton and Heywood, *Central Africans, Atlantic Creoles*, 54. According to Jan Vansina, "*Ngongo munene*" was "a compound of *ngongo* (world, country, bush) and *munene* (big)." See Jan Vansina, "Government in the Kasai Before the Lunda," *International Journal of African Historical Studies* 31, no. 1 (1998): 10, 13. Joseph H. Greenberg has argued that "*munene*" meant "tall" among the Ciluba speakers of the Kasai. See Joseph H. Greenberg, "Linguistic Evidence Regarding Bantu Origins," *Journal of African History* 13, no. 2 (April 1972): 198.

109. Dorchester First Church, *Records of the First Church of Dorchester*, 12. Contemporaneous dismissals noted in the church's record book dismiss "members," not those who were "formerly" members, as most leaving the church had been regular attenders until the time it dismissed them to another congregation.

110. *First Church Records*, 1, 74.

111. For Charles Meneno, also referred to as Charles Menino, see Boston Record Commissioners, *A Report of the Record Commissioners of the City of Boston, Containing the Records of Boston Selectmen, 1701 to 1715* (Boston: Rockwell and Churchill, 1884), 60 ("Highwayes"), 74, 76, 116, 137, 166, and 210; Boston Record Commissioners, *A Report of the Record Com-*

missioners of the City of Boston Containing the Records of the Boston Selectmen, 1716 to 1736 (Boston: Rockwell and Churchill, 1885), 83 and possibly 145.

112. In Suffolk County, enslaved Africans made up a minority of the bound labor force recorded in probate records during the 1640s, 1650s, and 1660s; however, by the first decade of the eighteenth century, 88 percent of bound laborers listed in probate documents were of African descent. Over the same period of time, the records shifted from mostly enumerating term servants to primarily cataloging enslaved people. Therefore, in the interval between Dorcas Menenie's emancipation and the time Charles Meneno labored in Boston, probate records suggest that the region's bound labor force had shifted primarily from white to Black and from term servitude to lifelong enslavement. See Gloria McCahon Whiting, "Race, Slavery, and the Problem of Numbers in Early New England," *WMQ* 77, no. 3 (July 2020) 425–426.

Chapter 2

Epigraph: Samuel Sewall, *The Selling of Joseph: A Memorial* (Boston: Bartholomew Green and John Allen, 1700), 1.

1. I reconstructed Jane's walk using period maps of Boston along with Karen J. Friedmann, "Victualling Colonial Boston," *Agricultural History* 43, no. 3 (July 1973): 189–205; David B. Landon, "Feeding Colonial Boston: A Zooarchaeological Study," *Historical Archaeology* 30, no. 1 (1996): 15–18; and Bruce C. Daniels, *Puritans at Play: Leisure and Recreation in Colonial New England* (New York: St. Martin's Press, 1995), 188.

2. We know that Jane's household used the pump at the neighboring home of Samuel Sewall because Samuel mentioned that Jane's enslaver was "at our pump for water" on the morning of the day she died. Jane was not the only person in the household who fetched water, as Samuel's notation shows, but, as the household's sole bondsperson, she doubtless performed the task regularly. *Sewall Diary*, 2, 28, January 4, 1701. For the location of Samuel's home, see Estes Howe, "Communication from Dr. Estes Howe, of Cambridge, in Regard to the Abode of John Hull and Samuel Sewall," *Proceedings of the Massachusetts Historical Society*, ser. 2, vol. 1 (1884–1885): 312–326. The Thayer home was located on the north side of Marlborough Street, just to the east of the Sewalls' home, near Winter Street in the direction of School Street. See Henry F. Waters, *Notes on the Townsend Family* (Salem: Essex Institute, 1883), 2. For the importance of fetching water to facilitating relationships between enslaved people in another urban northern context, see Jill Lepore, *New York Burning: Liberty, Slavery, and Conspiracy in Eighteenth-Century Manhattan* (New York: Knopf, 2005), 129–136, 144–149, 152–154, 166, 168–169.

3. *First Church Records*, 1, 91. My rendering of Jane and Sebastian's story responds to Richard J. Boles's call to "treat churches as influential social institutions, not just religious ones." See Boles, *Dividing the Faith: The Rise of Segregated Churches in the Early American North* (New York: New York University Press, 2020), 7–8. For seating in the galleries, see Vestry Records, July 23, 1733, and June 11, 1760, box 45, folder 35, Old North Church Records, MHS and Records of the Old South Church and Congregation, August 4, 1732, box 1, vol. 1, 72, Old South Church Records, CLA. See also Boles, 26.

4. *Mather Diary*, 1, 176–177, October 10, 1693; *Mather Diary*, 2, 364, August 6, 1716, and 532, May 5, 1718. For another example of such a group, see Jeremy Belknap, 1770 Ames almanac, January 21 and April 1, MHS.

5. For the mobility of bondspeople in Boston, see Jared Ross Hardesty, *Unfreedom: Slavery and Dependence in Eighteenth-Century Boston* (New York: New York University Press, 2016), 72, 93–102.

6. Cary v. Penelope Sungo, SF case 6876.

7. Cotton Mather, *The Diary of Cotton Mather for the Year 1712* (Charlottesville: University Press of Virginia, 1964), 83. See October 12, 1712.

8. *Sewall Diary*, 3, 9, July 13, 1714. Richard A. Bailey has argued that New England's enslavers sought to select marriage partners for those they bound, but the examples he provides show enslavers attempting (unsuccessfully) to prevent bondswomen from marrying rather than compelling those they enslaved to enter unwanted marriages. See Bailey, *Race and Redemption in Puritan New England* (New York: Oxford University Press, 2011), 104, 113.

9. John Waite's inventory, 1702, SCPR, FS, vol. 15, 179; Deborah Thayer's account, 1703, SCPR, FS, vol. 15, 149.

10. For a detailed explanation of the probate records database upon which this analysis rests, see the Note on Sources.

11. Thomas Selby's inventory, 1727, SCPR, FS, vol. 25, 535. Only 47 of these 408 households (12 percent) had bound men, women, *and* children—and therefore potential co-resident nuclear families. I derived this data from the probate records database. The vital records database (see Note on Sources) currently contains 229 unions between bound individuals that were solemnized by marriage or intended to be so. (I have included marriage intentions to help compensate for spotty marriage records.) In 36 of these unions, the bondspeople were claimed as property by the same person. But in 193 of these marriages or intended marriages, the parties had different enslavers and therefore did not live in the same household unless they managed to work out an unusual arrangement. This means that a mere 15.7 percent of enslaved people who married others in bondage actually lived with their spouse. Note that this statistic does not take into account the living patterns of enslaved people who married freed persons, as it is more difficult to ascertain whether those individuals lived together or apart. Nor does it take into account the living patterns of Black Bostonians whose enslaved status is not made clear in the records.

12. David D. Hall, *The Faithful Shepherd: A History of the New England Ministry in the Seventeenth Century* (Chapel Hill: University of North Carolina Press, 1972), 99, 100; Richard Archer, *Fissures in the Rock: New England in the Seventeenth Century* (Hanover: University Press of New England, 2001), 69; and David D. Hall, "On Common Ground: The Coherence of American Puritan Studies," *WMQ* 44, no. 2 (April 1987): 223.

13. Heb. 13:4, KJV, and 1 Cor. 7:3, KJV. *First Church Records*, 1, 10.

14. I seek here to build on Richard J. Boles's research on African-descended participants in northern churches and what might have motivated their participation in Christian worship. See Boles, *Dividing the Faith*, 20.

15. Map of the Town of Boston, 1676, Samuel Chester Clough Research Materials Toward a Topographical History of Boston, MHS. *Sewall Diary*, 1, 210, April 13, 1688.

16. See, for instance, *Sewall Diary*, 1, 389, April 2, 1694, and 397, February 15, 1695.

17. *Sewall Diary*, 1, 495, April 1, 1699, and April 8, 1699. According to the arrangement, the Waites would end up paying two and a half times Sebastian's assessed value (twenty pounds in 1702) during the first decade of his marriage. This suggests that Eunice's claim about the marriage being to their family's "prejudice" was warranted.

18. Though Samuel never said so explicitly, all clues suggest that Deborah was the person who stalled Jane and Sebastian's wedding. The Waites approached Samuel three times, imploring him to endorse the marriage, but Samuel never recorded an interaction with Deborah in which she spoke favorably of the match. At one point in the bargaining process, Samuel mentioned needing to "persuade" Deborah. And after Deborah's death, the long-delayed marriage was solemnized with all possible speed. *Sewall Diary*, 1, 495, April 1, 1699, and 495, April 8, 1699. See also *Sewall Diary*, 2, 22, September 26, 1700; 29, January 10, 1701; and 29 January 4, 1701. And see *Boston Marriages*, 1, 2.

19. *Sewall Diary*, 1, 497, May 8, 1699; 497, June 5, 1699; and 500, July 24, 1699. *Sewall Diary*, 2, 14, May 20, 1700, and 15, June 16, 1700.

20. *Sewall Diary*, 1, 455, June 12, 1697. For an extraordinary analysis of Samuel and his diary, see David D. Hall, *Worlds of Wonder, Days of Judgment: Popular Religious Belief in Early New England* (New York: Knopf, 1989), 213–238.

21. Samuel Sewall, *The Selling of Joseph*, 1. *Sewall Diary*, 2, 16, June 19, 1700.

22. Lawrence W. Towner, "The Sewall-Saffin Dialogue on Slavery," *WMQ* 21, no. 1 (January 1964): 46–52. The first English-language protest against slavery printed in the Americas was *An Exhortation and Caution to Friends Concerning Buying or Keeping of Negroes*, supposedly authored by George Keith and printed by William Bradford in New York in 1693. See Richard Newman, "The First Printed Protest Against Slavery," *AB Bookman's Weekly* 93, no. 6 (1994): 545–554, and Katharine Gerbner, "Anti-Slavery in Print: The Germantown Protest, the "Exhortation," and the Seventeenth-Century Quaker Debate on Slavery," *Early American Studies* 9, no. 3 (Fall 2011): 552–575.

23. Scholars have rooted Samuel's prescience in his "peculiar habits of mind," as Mark A. Peterson summed up the historical consensus on Samuel's authorship of *The Selling of Joseph*, and, more recently, in his international network of forward-thinking Protestants. Both explanations have some purchase, but I would like to suggest that neither gets at the heart of *The Selling of Joseph*. See Mark A. Peterson, "*The Selling of Joseph*: Bostonians, Anti-slavery, and the Protestant International, 1689–1733," *Massachusetts Historical Review* 4 (2002): 1–22, esp. 4 (quotation), and Mark Peterson, *The City-State of Boston: The Rise and Fall of an Atlantic Empire, 1630–1865* (Princeton: Princeton University Press, 2019), 196.

24. Cotton Mather, *The Negro Christianized: An Essay to Excite and Assist That Good Work, The Instruction of Negro-Servants in Christianity* (Boston: B. Green, 1706). Boston Record Commissioners, *A Report of the Record Commissioners of the City of Boston Containing the Records of Boston Selectmen, 1701–1715* (Boston: Rockwell and Churchill, 1884), 5. The court imposed the recommended duty in 1705. See "An Act for the Better Preventing of a Spurious and Mixt Issue" in *Massachusetts Acts and Resolves, vol. 1* (Boston: Wright and Potter, 1869), 578–579.

25. Samuel was reading Paul Baynes, *An entire commentary upon the whole epistle of the Apostle Paul to the Ephesians Wherein the Text Is learnedly and fruitfully opened . . .* (London: M. F. for R. Milbourne and I. Bartlet, 1643), 694–699. Samuel wrote about Joseph Belknap's petition on June 19, 1700, but his account does not specify whether Joseph came to his house on June 19 or on a previous day. *Sewall Diary*, 2, 16, June 19, 1700.

26. For instance, the case of Nathanael Foarce and Daniel Foarce, two men described as "Negroe" and "sold . . . as slaves" in Boston, made its way through the Massachusetts court system in the late seventeenth century. The men, who claimed to be unjustly bound, appear to have obtained their freedom. See Welsh v. Robinson, Suffolk County CCP Records, vol. 1692–1698,

2 (quotation); Clarke v. Fowler, Suffolk County Court, photostat copy, vol. 1680–1692, no page number (dated November 19, 1689) MA Archives; Backway v. Fowler, Suffolk County Court, photostat copy, vol. 1680–1692, no page number (dated April 2, 1691) MA Archives; John Noble, *Records of the Court of Assistants of the Colony of the Massachusetts Bay, 1630–1692, vol. 1* (Boston: County of Suffolk, 1901): 350; MAC, vol. 9, 119–131.

27. Benjamin Wadsworth, *The Well-Ordered Family* (Boston: B. Green for Nicholas Buttolph, 1712), 23 ("cohabit"), 29 ("indeavour").

28. Sewall, *The Selling of Joseph*, 1.

29. Sewall, *The Selling of Joseph*, 2. It is important to note that while some of Samuel's arguments about the incompatibility of slavery and family show that the man was genuinely concerned about the welfare of his Black neighbors, Samuel used racist claims in his arguments as well. He contended, for instance, that emancipated Africans "seldom use their freedom well," and that "they can never embody with us, and grow up into orderly Families to the peopling of the land" because "there is such a disparity in their Conditions, Color & Hair." For Samuel, the idea of an interracial commonwealth was unfathomable; people of African descent "remain in our Body Politic as a kind of extra-vasat blood." See Sewall, *The Selling of Joseph*, 2.

30. For recent examples of the importance of Black activism in antislavery agitation, see David Williams, *I Freed Myself: African American Self-Emancipation in the Civil War Era* (New York: Cambridge University Press, 2014); David Roediger, *Seizing Freedom: Slave Emancipation and Liberty for All* (New York: Verso, 2014); Manisha Sinha, *The Slave's Cause: A History of Abolition* (New Haven: Yale University Press, 2016); Kelly Carter Jackson, *Force and Freedom: Black Abolitionists and the Politics of Violence* (Philadelphia: University of Pennsylvania Press, 2019); and Van Gosse, *The First Reconstruction: Black Politics in America from the Revolution to the Civil War* (Chapel Hill: University of North Carolina Press, 2021).

31. *Sewall Diary*, 2, 22, September 26, 1700, and 29, January 10, 1701.

32. For the case of the nineteenth-century South, see Patrick W. O'Neil, "Bosses and Broomsticks: Ritual and Authority in Antebellum Slave Weddings," *Journal of Southern History* 75, no. 1 (February 2009): 29–48; Thomas E. Will, "Weddings on Contested Grounds: Slave Marriage in the Antebellum South," *Historian* 62, no. 1 (Fall 1999): 99–117; and Tera W. Hunter, *Bound in Wedlock: Slave and Free Black Marriage in the Nineteenth Century* (Cambridge: Harvard University Press, 2017), 45–50.

33. *Sewall Diary*, 2, 22, September 26, 1700. For legislation on asking banns, see Joseph Dudley, *A Proclamation by the President and Council For the Orderly Solemnization of Marriage* (Boston: Richard Pierce, 1686), and "An Act for the Orderly Consummating of Marriages," November 3, 1692, *Acts and Resolves of the Province of the Massachusetts Bay, vol. 1*, 61.

34. For the interpretation that the occasional Black couple who chose to publish banns prior to marrying in Jamaica might have been doing so for strategic reasons linked to the "memories of the parish community," see Nicholas M. Beasley, "Domestic Rituals: Marriage and Baptism in the British Plantation Colonies, 1650–1780," *Anglican and Episcopal History* 76, no. 3 (September 2007): 327–357, quotation 337.

35. For "Jane Lake," see *Boston Marriages*, 1, 2. For "Jane Basteen," see *First Church Records*, 2, 372. Sebastian's name, which appears in town, church, and private records, was corrupted progressively over the course of the early eighteenth century. Sebastian originally surfaces in the historical record as "Sebastian" or "Bastian" in the 1690s. By 1710, he was regularly called "Bastian," "Bastion," or "Basteen," as well as, occasionally, "Boston"; in the second

two decades of the eighteenth century he became simply "Boston." Jane's and the children's last name went through parallel transformations, moving from "Basteen" to "Boston." For the reference to "Jane Boston," see *Sewall Diary*, 2, 319, July 12, 1711.

36. Much literature demonstrates the extent to which slaveholding communities attempted to undermine the authority of men in bondage. For diverse ways in which bound men opposed this, see David Stefan Doddington, *Contesting Slave Masculinity in the American South* (New York: Cambridge University Press, 2018), and Christopher H. Bouton, *Setting Slavery's Limits: Physical Confrontations in Antebellum Virginia, 1801–1860* (New York: Lexington Books, 2020). *Boston Marriages*, 1, 2.

37. For Katherine Cornwall, see *Boston Marriages*, 1, 214; Cornwall's will, 1748, SCPR, NS, vol. 26, 304; *Boston Marriages*, 2, 12. For Margaret Sash, see Order for Sale, Massachusetts SCJ Records, vol. 1730–1733, 142. For Dorcas Menenie, see inventory of Menenie, 1675, SCPR, FS, vol. 5, 266.

38. For a reference to the "African practice of adopting the father's first name as a surname," see Catherine Adams and Elizabeth H. Pleck, *Love of Freedom: Black Women in Colonial and Revolutionary New England* (New York: Oxford University Press, 2010), 87. Africanists have produced helpful scholarship related to this issue. See, for example, John Thornton, "Central African Names and African-American Naming Patterns," *WMQ* 50, no. 4 (October 1993): 736–737, and Anne Hilton, "Family and Kinship Among the Kongo South of the Zaïre River from the Sixteenth to the Nineteenth Centuries," *Journal of African History* 24, no. 2 (1983): 192. On the African-origin given names doubling as surnames listed here, see David DeCamp, "African Day-Names in Jamaica," *Language* 43, no. 1 (March 1967): 139–149. The list of surnames referenced in the text derives from the vital records database; see Note on Sources. For an example of Sebastian's children receiving their father's given name as a surname, see Samuel Sewall's reference to "little Mary Bastian." *Sewall Diary*, 2, 183, March 5, 1707.

39. *Sewall Diary*, 2, 46, November 1, 1701. Contextual evidence supports Samuel's statement; Anglo-American men had the privilege of naming children in early New England, and men in many of the African regions that fed the Atlantic slave trade appear to have named their children as well. On Anglo-American practices, see Robert M. Taylor Jr. and Ralph J. Crandall, eds., *Generations and Change: Genealogical Perspectives in Social History* (Macon: Mercer, 1986), 223. For examples of African practices, see Jean Allman, "Fathering, Mothering, and Making Sense of *Ntamoba*: Reflections on the Economy of Child-Rearing in Colonial Asante," *Africa: Journal of the International African Institute* 67, no. 2 (1997): 300–301; Philip F. W. Bartle, "The Universe Has Three Souls: Notes on Translating Akan Culture," *Journal of Religion in Africa* 14, no. 2 (1982): 94; H. A. Wieschhoff, "The Social Significance of Names Among the Ibo of Nigeria," *American Anthropologist* 43, no. 2, part 1 (April–June 1941): 213; and William Russell Bascom, *The Yoruba of Southwestern Nigeria* (New York: Holt, Rinehart and Winston, 1969), 56.

40. *Sewall Diary*, 2, 46, November 2, 1701; *Sewall Diary*, 1, 383, September 13, 1693.

41. Samuel Willard, *Compleat Body of Divinity* (Boston: B. Green and S. Kneeland for B. Eliot and D. Henchman, 1726), 610.

42. See, for instance, Margaret A. Burnham, "An Impossible Marriage: Slave Law and Family Law," *Minnesota Journal of Law and Inequality* 5, no. 2 (June 1987): 207–208. *Sewall Diary*, 2, 22, September 26, 1700.

43. Sentence of Cesar and Goslin, court session beginning October 2, 1705, Suffolk County GSP Records, vol. 1702–1712, 116.

44. Sentences of Abigail Trott and Andrew and Anne Johnson, Suffolk County GSP, vol. 1702–1712, 116.

45. Across the South in the mid-nineteenth century, women were more likely to be manumitted than men and they therefore outnumbered their male counterparts in the free Black population, especially in urban areas. See, for example, Loren Schweninger, "The Fragile Nature of Freedom: Free Women of Color in the U.S. South," in *Beyond Bondage: Free Women of Color in the Americas*, ed. David Barry Gaspar and Darlene Clark Hine (Chicago: University of Illinois Press, 2004), 107. This was also the case in the French, Portuguese, Spanish, and Dutch Atlantic. See Jennifer L. Palmer, *Intimate Bonds: Family and Slavery in the French Atlantic* (Philadelphia: University of Pennsylvania Press, 2016), 102; Douglas Cole Libby, "Notarized and Baptismal Manumissions in the Parish of São José do Rio das Mortes, Minas Gerais (c. 1750–1850)," *Americas* 66, no. 2 (October 2009): 222–225, 233; Lyman L. Johnson, "Manumission in Colonial Buenos Aires, 1776–1810," *Hispanic American Historical Review* 59, no. 2 (May 1979): 263; and Rosemary Brana-Shute, "Sex and Gender in Surinamese Manumissions," in *Paths to Freedom: Manumission in the Atlantic World*, ed. Rosemary Brana-Shute and Randy J. Sparks (Columbia: University of South Carolina Press, 2009), 179–198. In North America, communities affected by gradual emancipation in the nineteenth century appear to have been similar to eighteenth-century Boston and its surroundings when it came to favoring the manumission of men, but for very different reasons. Whereas women in the Boston area appear to have obtained their freedom less frequently than men because of their inferior earning power, women were at a disadvantage under gradual emancipation because of the heightened significance of their reproduction, which was crucial to maintaining an unfree labor force. For the manumission of women in gradual emancipation New Jersey, see James J. Gigantino II, *The Ragged Road to Abolition: Slavery and Freedom in New Jersey, 1775–1865* (Philadelphia: University of Pennsylvania Press, 2014), 134.

46. Of the fifty-four bondspeople liberated by will in Suffolk County during the first half of the eighteenth century, thirty-five (65 percent) were men. If one could find a reliable way to assess the manumission of the enslaved who bought their liberty (as opposed to those manumitted by will), the gendering of freedom would skew even more male, as more African men had the financial wherewithal to purchase their freedom than did African women. Unfortunately, the freedom papers or bills of sale generated when bondspeople bought their liberty were not systematically filed with the probate court—or anywhere else—and therefore have largely been lost. In my research, I have found evidence of fathers, sons, husbands, and prospective husbands arranging to free their relatives, but I have found very little evidence of African-descended women freeing their enslaved family members; the process of manumission seems to have moved almost exclusively in the opposite direction (and it did so throughout the entire provincial period). The fifty-four manumissions by will can be found in SCPR, FS, and SCPR, NS.

47. For the extent to which mothers and children were grouped in households apart from husbands and fathers, see Gloria McCahon Whiting, "Power, Patriarchy, and Provision: African Families Negotiate Gender and Slavery in New England," *JAH* 103, no. 3 (December 2016): 586–588. See Chapter 3 for more on the assumption that the enslavers of women retained rights to the offspring of those women. For racialized dispossession and heritability throughout the English Atlantic world, see Jennifer L. Morgan, "*Partus sequitur ventrem*: Law, Race, and Reproduction in Colonial Slavery," *Small Axe* 22, no. 1 (March 2018): 1–17. The analysis of owner-

ship patterns of married bondspeople derives from the vital records database (see Note on Sources).

48. That these families were matrifocal and nonetheless appear to have adopted elements of patriarchy is unusual in light of scholarship on gender, family, and slavery in North America, which has overwhelmingly emphasized enslaved families in plantation contexts. The atomized experiences of bondspeople within the deeply religious context of early Boston suggests that families could assume very different forms under slavery. For more on the supposition that the form that enslaved families assumed inevitably shaped their normative values, see Whiting, "Power, Patriarchy, and Provision," 590–592. For relevant scholarship, see Ann Patton Malone, *Sweet Chariot: Slave Family and Household Structure in Nineteenth-Century Louisiana* (Chapel Hill: University of North Carolina Press, 1992); Brenda E. Stevenson, *Life in Black and White: Family and Community in the Slave South* (New York: Oxford University Press, 1996); and Wilma A. Dunaway, *The African-American Family in Slavery and Emancipation* (New York: Cambridge University Press, 2003).

49. Samuel Sewall's diary noted that Sebastian was "at the Castle" at the time of little Jane's birth. See *Sewall Diary*, 2, 46, November 1, 1701. For payments to the Waite household in return for Sebastian's labor in October, November, and December of 1701, see Fortifications on Castle Island, MAC, vol. 244, 21–22.

50. In August of 1703, Eunice received further payment from the province in return for "Boston's work." See Fortifications on Castle Island, MAC, vol. 244, 39.

51. The chronological proximity of John Waite's death (1702), Sebastian's manumission (between 1703 and 1708), and the naming of little John (1703) makes it plausible that John asked Eunice to free Sebastian after a period of faithful service and that Sebastian therefore named his son in honor of the deceased enslaver. Unfortunately, John died intestate, so we cannot know his final wishes, but delayed manumissions were fairly common among enslavers who wished to free their bondspeople but left surviving wives. Moreover, Sebastian seems to have had a more amicable relationship with the family that bound him than many people in slavery had with their enslavers; he stayed in communication with the Waite family long after his manumission and was still conveying news of the household to Samuel as late as 1716. *Sewall Diary*, 3, 99, August 21, 1716. A variety of sources allows the dating of these disparate events in Sebastian's life. According to Samuel, John died on February 21, 1702; his estate was inventoried by the probate court on April 28, 1702. See *Sewall Diary*, 2, 53, February 21, 1702, and John Waite's inventory, 1702, SCPR, FS, vol. 15, 179. Regarding the 1703 to 1708 timeframe for Sebastian's manumission, Sebastian was still laboring for Eunice in 1703, but he was declared a "Free Negro" in town records in 1708. See Fortifications on Castle Island, MAC, vol. 244, 39, and Boston Record Commissioners, *Records of Boston Selectmen, 1701–1715*, 73. For little John's 1703 birth, see his baptism record in *First Church Records*, 2, 374, and his birth record in *Boston Births*, 1, 20.

52. For Mary, Jane, Joseph, and Elizabeth's baptisms, see *First Church Records*, 2, 375, 377, 381, and 383. Jane and Sebastian bore children at the same rate as free white New Englanders, that is, approximately every two years. See John Demos, *A Little Commonwealth: Family Life in Plymouth Colony* (New York: Oxford University Press, 1970), 68, 133, and Philip J. Greven Jr., *Four Generations: Population, Land, and Family in Colonial Andover, Massachusetts* (Ithaca: Cornell University Press, 1970), 30, 112.

53. James Mills's conviction, Suffolk County Court, photostat copy, vol. 1680–1692, no page number (dated December 18, 1684), MA Archives. The fifteen stripes punishment was for going

to Thomas's house at night and "receiving money and other stol[e]n goods" from the woman in addition to spending time with her.

54. "An Act for the Orderly Consummating of Marriages," November 3, 1692, *Acts and Resolves of the Province of the Massachusetts Bay, vol. 1*, 61. On the punishments given to Massachusetts children for marrying without parental permission, see David Hackett Fischer, *Albion's Seed: Four British Folkways in America* (New York: Oxford University Press, 1989), 78. See also the stipulation in Plymouth Colony's laws that "none be allowed to marry that are under the covert of parents but by their consent & approbacon." David Pulsifer, ed., *Records of the Colony of New Plymouth, vol. 11: Laws. 1623–1682* (Boston: W. White, 1861), 13. On the legal prohibition of servant marriage, see Steven Mintz and Susan Kellogg, *Domestic Revolutions: A Social History of American Family Life* (New York: Free Press, 1988), 8; Pulsifer, ed., *Records of the Colony of New Plymouth, vol. 11*, 29; and William H. Whitmore, ed., *Colonial Laws of Massachusetts: Reprinted from the Edition of 1672, with the Supplements Through 1686* (Boston: Rockwell and Churchill, 1887), 101.

55. "An Act for the Better Preventing of a Spurious and Mixt Issue" in *Massachusetts Acts and Resolves, vol. 1*, 578. The marriage clause set the Massachusetts act apart from its southern antecedents, which did *not* provide the enslaved with the right to marry. See Chapter 4 for more on this act.

56. Sewall, *The Selling of Joseph*, 1.

57. Thomas Shepard, *The Works of Thomas Shepard, First Pastor of the First Church, Cambridge, Mass.: With a Memoir of His Life and Character, vol. 3* (Boston: Doctrinal Tract and Book Society, 1853), 263. On the risk to households, see, for instance, *Mather Diary*, 2, 139, December 9, 1711.

58. In 1717, Toney, bound by a man referred to as Mr. Pratt, and Ginney, bound by a woman referred to as Mrs. Brick, were "forbid[den]" from marrying by Mrs. Brick. It is not clear whether Mrs. Brick forbade them from marrying because she did not wish Ginney to marry or because she was aware of some moral shortcoming that should rightly have prevented the union—say, if Toney was already married to another woman. See *Boston Marriages*, 1, 96.

59. Records of the New North Church in North St., Boston, 1714–1870, vol. 1, 261, BPL.

60. See Gary Nash, *The Urban Crucible: The Northern Seaports and the Origins of the American Revolution* (Cambridge: Harvard University Press, 1986), and Douglas L. Winiarski, *Darkness Falls on the Land of Light: Experiencing Religious Awakenings in Eighteenth-Century New England* (Chapel Hill: University of North Carolina Press, 2017).

61. For Samuel Phillips's vows, see George Elliott Howard, *A History of Matrimonial Institutions*, vol. 2 (London: T. Fisher Unwin, 1904), 225–226. The story of Robert Hubbard and Roger Newton is recorded in a town history of Greenfield, Massachusetts, compiled in the early twentieth century. Antiquarian collections of town lore, which rarely provide sources for their stories, are not particularly reliable historical sources, but the nature of this particular tale suggests that it may well have been based on an actual exchange. See Francis McGee Thompson, *History of Greenfield: Shire Town of Franklin County, Massachusetts*, vol. 2 (Greenfield: Press of T. Morey & Son, 1904), 1002–1003.

62. John Graham's testimony, see Exeter v. Hanchet, SF case 158594. For Flora and Exeter, see Kirsten Sword, *Wives Not Slaves: Patriarchy and Modernity in the Age of Revolutions* (Chicago: University of Chicago Press, 2021), 234–240.

63. Petition for freedom to Massachusetts Governor Thomas Gage, His Majesty's Council, and the House of Representatives, May 25, 1774, 1–2, Jeremy Belknap Papers, Massachusetts Historical Society, Boston.

64. Petition, Series VII: Legal Documents, 1709–1858, box 6, folder 1 and undated, Slavery Collection, NYHS.

65. Petition of Jack, Suffolk County GSP Records, vol. 1702–1712, 203. *Boston Marriages*, 1, 29.

66. In the end, Henry did sell Toney to Thomas, but not until nearly six months had passed, and the selling price was 80 pounds rather than the 90 pounds Thomas had originally considered paying. There is no explanation in the diary of either the delay or the lower price point. Perhaps Thomas still had reservations about Toney's liaison with the unnamed woman and therefore insisted on paying a smaller sum. Perhaps Thomas felt he needed to purchase the bondswoman from his brother in anticipation of the marriage and consequently had less cash with which to pay for Toney. The records of Braintree, Massachusetts, indicate that Toney married a woman named Peggy, who also belonged to Thomas, a few weeks after his sale. Was Peggy the bondswoman once claimed by Thomas's brother, whom Toney purportedly wished to marry? Or was Toney compelled by Thomas to marry a different woman in bondage, perhaps to quash Toney's previous liaison? While the answers are not forthcoming, the fact remains that the possibility of a marriage between Toney and his hoped-for bride complicated Toney's sale. For the diary entries, see Diary of Henry Flynt, 1723–1747, November 24, 1737, and May 2, 1738, HUG 1399.18, HUA; see https://iiif.lib.harvard.edu/manifests/view/drs:46676980$263i (Sequences 246 and 263). For the marriage, see Samuel A. Bates, ed., *Records of the Town of Braintree* (Randolph: D. H. Huxford, 1886), 752.

67. Diary of Reverend Stephen Williams, vol. 3, 114, November 25, 1736; 168, October 28, 1737; 181, January 10, 1738; 192, January 16, 1738; and 181, January 10, 1738, Richard S. Storrs Memorial Library. Records of First Church of Christ, Longmeadow, MA, from Rev. Stephen Williams books, no. 1, 58, May 22, 1744, Richard S. Storrs Memorial Library.

68. Letter from Samuel Sewall to Benjamin Colman, March 22, 1718, Benjamin Colman Papers, MHS.

69. It is probable that Ezer and Dinah were married; otherwise, Cotton would not have been so enthusiastic to endorse their children's baptism, but the marriage records of the Second Church are very sparse and those of the Old South Church do not exist for the period before 1780. For the baptisms, see Baptismal Records, 1669–1875, Old South Church in Boston, Massachusetts, February 25, 1722 (no page number), CLA.

70. Testimony of John Gyles, MAC, vol. 9, 249, and Testimony of Thomas Saunders, MAC, vol. 9, 250.

71. *Boston News-Letter*, June 27, 1745, 2.

72. *Boston Gazette*, July 18, 1737, 3; *Boston Evening-Post*, May 24, 1742, 2; *Boston Post-Boy*, May 14, 1759, 3; and *Boston Gazette*, May 17, 1736, 4.

73. *Boston News-Letter*, June 29, 1749, 2; *Independent Chronicle*, August 6, 1778, 4.

74. Robert Keayne's will, 1653, SCPR, FS, vol. 1, 207; Richard Smith's will, 1691, SCPR, FS, vol. 13, 30; Jacob Eliott's inventory, 1694, SCPR, FS, vol. 13, 457; William Burnet's inventory, 1729, SCPR, FS, vol. 27, 345; Leonard Vassall's will, 1737, SCPR, FS, vol. 33, 217; Edmund Quincy's will, 1737, SCPR, FS, vol. 33, 466; Jonathan Furnass's inventory, 1745, SCPR, FS, vol. 40, 75.

75. Samuel Niles's will, 1762, SCPR, FS, vol. 60, 372–373.

76. John Barns's will, 1769, SCPR, FS, vol. 56, 424.

77. Briggs v. Tony and Maria, SF case 12282; Lancashire v. Kingsland, Suffolk County CCP Records, vol. 1720–1721, 70; Jo Sentenced, Massachusetts SCJ Records, vol. 1715–1721, 355; Titus v. Bill, Suffolk County CCP Records, vol. 1727–1728, 286; Case of Quaco, SF case 83313; Seymour v. Goold, SF case 86670; The King v. Geoffs, Massachusetts SCJ Records, vol. 1771, 35; Habeas Corpus of Peggy, SF, case 102787; Lewis and Martha Dismissed, Suffolk County GSP Records, vol. 1702–1712, 230; Exeter Turner and Luce Sentenced, Suffolk County GSP Records, vol. 1719–1725, 114; Stone v. Jackson, Massachusetts SCJ Records, vol. 1715–1721, 198; Betty Sentenced, Suffolk County GSP Records, vol. 1702–1712, 232; Packard v. Freeman, Massachusetts SCJ Records, vol. 1771, 50.

78. The vital records database counts 1,176 people who were married in an official capacity at least once. But the number of Black people who married over the course of the century is probably significantly higher, as not all marriage records survive.

79. *Boston Marriages*, 1, 181 and 256. New North Church Records, vol. 1, 50 and 57, BPL. Many other bondspeople remarried in the region's churches after their spouses passed away. For example, over the course of a long life in bondage, a woman named Clarinda wed three Black men, all in province-sanctioned marriages: first Dick, then Joseph, and finally Caesar. See *Boston Marriages*, 1, 256, and 2, 325, also Church in Brattle Square, *The Manifesto Church: Records of the Church in Brattle Square, Boston: With Lists of Communicants, Baptisms, Marriages, and Funerals, 1699–1872* (Boston: Benevolent Fraternity of Churches, 1902), 254.

80. According to Lorenzo Johnston Greene's dated but nonetheless useful analysis of slavery in New England, the enslaved were "compelled" to follow Anglo-American marriage customs, and marriage for the enslaved "did little more than legalize sexual intimacy." See Lorenzo Johnston Greene, *The Negro in Colonial New England* (New York: Atheneum, 1969), 192, 211. However, enslaved people almost never were punished by the courts in Massachusetts for engaging in sexual relationships outside of marriage. Reading page by page through the lower criminal court (General Sessions of the Peace) for Suffolk County, the province's most populous county, as well as the Superior Court of the Judicature for the entire province yielded no criminal actions against enslaved people in the eighteenth century for having sex outside of marriage. Lewis and Martha, one couple of African descent (who were probably free), were "presented for fornication before Marriage" in 1711, but the court dismissed the case. See Lewis and Martha Dismissed, Suffolk County GSP Records, vol. 1702–1712, 230. The courts' failure to prosecute people of African descent who had sex outside of marriage cannot be attributed to enslaved people's commitment to refraining from extramarital sex, as fragments from church and court records nonetheless show that people in bondage engaged in the same types of sexual behavior outside of marriage that white people did. For instance, Richard, an African man baptized in Boston's Second Church was censured for fornication in 1704. See Second Church (Boston, MA) Records, vol. 4, entry for July 16, 1704, MHS.

81. Often associated with enslaved people in the South, jumping the broom was a ritual in which a man and woman stepped hand in hand over a broomstick when they married. This ritual was ordinarily used by people whose marriages were endorsed by neither church nor state—hence the contrast to the government-sanctioned marriages of Afro–New Englanders like Jane and Sebastian. See Tyler D. Parry, *Jumping the Broom: The Surprising Multicultural Origins of a Black Wedding Ritual* (Chapel Hill: University of North Carolina Press, 2020), 1–5.

82. Hannah and Bostan lived in Scarborough, which is now in Maine but was then part of Massachusetts. The agreement was executed by their enslavers in 1768. See Hannah and Bostan Agreement, Papers of William Scott Southgate, Maine Historical Society.

83. According to Exeter and Leucey's marriage record, they were married by a man referred to as Mr. Woodbridge. Woodbridge married only one other couple in the Boston records, and the clerk's failure to include a first name makes identifying the man challenging. There were no justices of the peace in either Suffolk or Middlesex counties with the last name Woodbridge at the time, so the marriage was most likely performed by Benjamin Woodbridge, pastor of Medford's church. See John H. Hooper, *Proceedings of the Celebration of the Two Hundred and Seventy-Fifth Anniversary of the Settlement of Medford, Massachusetts* (Medford: Executive Committee, 1906), 62. See Letter to Francis Foxcroft dated August 31, 1713, and Letter to Joseph Prout, Town Clerk, dated September 7, 1713, vol. 2, 15, Boston Town Records, BPL. The petition was apparently well-received, as Exeter was for years listed among Boston's free Black inhabitants.

84. Bondspeople were denied legal marriages in the British West Indies, scholars have argued, because marriage was considered a civil contract, and the enslaved, as legal nonentities, could not enter into contracts. See Cecilia A. Green, "'A Civil Inconvenience'? The Vexed Question of Slave Marriage in the British West Indies," *Law and History Review* 25, no. 1 (Spring 2007): 26. A host of scholars assert that the enslaved in North America were denied legal marriage. See, for example, Norma Basch, *Framing American Divorce: From the Revolutionary Generation to the Victorians* (Berkeley: University of California Press, 1999), 48–49; Stevenson, *Life in Black and White*, 226; Malone, *Sweet Chariot*, 224; Lorri Glover, *Southern Sons: Becoming Men in the New Nation* (Baltimore: Johns Hopkins University Press, 2007), 127; Phillip Morgan, *Slave Counterpoint: Black Culture in the Eighteenth-Century Chesapeake and Low Country* (Chapel Hill: University of North Carolina Press, 1998), 499. For an insightful discussion of the lack of legal recognition given to the marriages of enslaved people in the nineteenth-century South, see Hunter, *Bound in Wedlock*, chap. 2.

85. Jethro Boston's Petition for Divorce, MAC, vol. 9, 248.

86. Free Black men were required to contribute a certain number of days of labor each year, usually between two and eight. Boston Record Commissioners, *Records of Boston Selectmen, 1701–1715*, 73, 115, 138, 167, 210, 233; Boston Record Commissioners, *A Report of the Record Commissioners of the City of Boston, Containing the Records of Boston Selectmen, 1716–1736* (Boston: Rockwell and Churchill, 1885), 8, 42, 60, 82, 109. Note that there are no records of labor subscription between 1726 and 1729, so it is unclear if Sebastian worked during those years.

87. For the children's deaths, see *Sewall Diary*, 2, 75, March 20, 1703; *First Church Records*, 2, 375; *Sewall Diary*, 2, 183, March 5, 1707; and Robert J. Dunkle and Ann S. Lainhart, eds. *Deaths in Boston: 1700–1799* (Boston: New England Historic Genealogical Society, 1999), vol. 2, 1033.

88. On the deadliness of Boston, particularly for young people, see Maris A. Vinovskis, "Mortality Rates and Trends in Massachusetts Before 1860," *Journal of Economic History* 31, no. 1 (March 1972): 196, 199–200. For statistics on mortality in the town, see John B. Blake, *Public Health in the Town of Boston, 1630–1822* (Cambridge: Harvard University Press, 1959), 247–250.

89. *Sewall Diary*, 3, 292, September 20, 1721, and 342, August 17, 1724.

90. For "Cottage," see *Sewall Diary*, 2, 264, March 6, 1729. The Bible is filled with metaphors for mortal bodies, such as these two from 2 Cor. 5:1 and 4:16, respectively, KJV. There is slight confusion about the day on which Sebastian died. Sebastian's death was recorded as February 14 in the *New-England Weekly Journal*, February 24, 1729, 2. Samuel's diary, however, suggests that Sebastian's death took place on either February 12 or February 13. (Samuel recorded the death date as February 12, which he called the fifth day of the week, but February 12 that week was actually the *fourth* day of the week according to Samuel's system of reckoning.) Since Samuel produced this diary entry retrospectively—contextual clues suggest that he wrote on February 16—and since the two days he gave for Sebastian's death do not align, I am following the dating provided in the *New-England Weekly Journal*.

91. *New-England Weekly Journal*, February 24, 1729, 2. Although the newspaper does not specify the status of those who attended Sebastian's funeral, the majority of them must have been enslaved because there were nowhere near 150 freedmen in Boston in 1729. The most recent inventory of freed Black men, taken by the selectmen in 1725, listed 26, so probably only about 50 of Sebastian's 150 Black mourners were free. Boston Record Commissioners, *Records of Boston Selectmen, 1716–1736*, 145.

Chapter 3

Epigraph: *Boston News-Letter*, September 30, 1706, 2.

1. I imaginatively reconstructed this birthing scene using Nicholas Culpeper, *Culpeper's Directory of Midwives, or, A Guide for Women: The Second Part* (London: Printed for George Sawbridge, 1676), 186–187; Laurel Thatcher Ulrich, *Good Wives: Image and Reality in the Lives of Women in Northern New England, 1650–1750* (New York: Knopf, 1982), 128–129; William Salmon, *Aristotle's Compleat and Experienc'd Midwife* (London: Printed and Sold by the Booksellers, 1700), 94, 99; Gloria L. Main, *Peoples of a Spacious Land: Families and Cultures in Colonial New England* (Cambridge: Harvard University Press, 2001), 103–104; and Abby Chandler, "From Birthing Chamber to Court Room: The Medical and Legal Communities of the Colonial Essex County Midwife," *Early Modern Women* 9, no. 2 (Spring 2015): 118. To date the birth, see West v. Norton, SF case 20894.

2. West v. Norton, SF case 20894. Elizur's first name was rendered in a variety of ways, including Eleazer and Eleizur, but Elizur seems to have been the most frequent variant, so I have used it here. See Elizur/Eleazer/Eleizur Holyoke in Annie Haven Thwing, comp., *Inhabitants and Estates of the Town of Boston, 1630–1800* (CD-ROM) (Boston: New England Historic Genealogical Society, 2001). For Elizur's father, also Elizur Holyoke, see Stephen Innes, "Land Tenancy and Social Order in Springfield, Massachusetts, 1652–1702," *WMQ* 35, no. 1 (January 1978): 41–42, 54; George Francis Dow, *The Holyoke Diaries, 1709–1856* (Salem: Essex Institute, 1911), xii. For Elizur as a merchant, see Elizur Holyoke's 1711 will, SCPR, FS, vol. 17, 321; William Blake Trask et al., eds., *Suffolk Deeds, vol. 13* (Boston: Rockwell and Churchill, 1903), 13–14. For Elizur's role in local and provincial government, see Theodore E. Stebbins Jr. et al., *American Paintings at Harvard, vol. 1* (Cambridge: Harvard Art Museums, 2008), 492.

3. For the children, see Dow, *The Holyoke Diaries*, xii. For the arrangement of chairs, see Elizur Holyoke's 1711 inventory, SCPR, FS, vol. 17, 408–411. Elizur moved his family in 1705 to a new home, which is described in the 1711 inventory. For Elizur's 1705 home purchase, see Elizur/Eleazer/Eleizur Holyoke in Thwing, comp., *Inhabitants and Estates of the Town of*

Boston. For the garden, cow, orchard, malthouse, and brewhouse, see Elizur Holyoke's 1711 inventory, SCPR, FS, vol. 17, 410–411.

4. *Sewall Diary,* 1, 374, March 9, 1693.

5. No evidence exists to suggest that Elizur Holyoke owned other bondspeople until 1711, nearly twenty years after Samuel's drowning, when the inventory of Elizur's estate valued two men of African descent named Toney and Tom. Toney and Tom's temporal distance from the event makes it less plausible that they were involved than that Sue's mother was, as does their gender; the Holyokes may have been more likely to have left their young son with a female caretaker than a male one. Of course, it is possible that Elizur owned other people of African descent of whom no records survive. See Elizur Holyoke's 1711 inventory, SCPR, FS, vol. 17, 411.

6. For "sell," see West v. Norton, SF case 20894. Susannah Leathers was called both Susannah Leathers and Susannah Leatherer. For references to Susannah Leathers, see Essex Institute, *Vital Records of Manchester, Massachusetts, to the End of the Year 1849* (Salem: Essex Institute, 1903), 76, and Suffolk Deeds vol. 23, 86–87 (January 13, 1707). For references to Susannah Leatherer, see Essex Institute, *Vital Records of Manchester,* 76; Suffolk Deeds vol. 23, 108 (February 5, 1707); and *BBMD,* 175. Susannah Leathers/Leatherer lived with her husband, Richard, in Boston in 1687, where their first child was born, but they had relocated to Manchester by the end of that year. Their next three children were born in Manchester between 1790 and 1792. However, Susannah had returned to Boston prior to January 1706, when she sold a share of a house, land, and wharf she owned in Boston. See *BBMD,* 175; Benj. A. Arrington, ed., *Municipal History of Essex County in Massachusetts, vol. 1* (New York: Lewis Historical Pub. Co., 1922), 137; Essex Institute, *Vital Records of Manchester,* 76; Suffolk Deeds 23, 86–87 (January 13, 1707).

7. West v. Norton, SF case 20894.

8. For the shoes, see Thomas Balhatchett's inventory, 1709, SCPR, FS, vol. 17, 32. For the teapots, see Jeremiah Gibson's inventory, 1709, SCPR, FS, vol. 17, 39. For the skillet, see Richard Lowden's inventory, 1709, SCPR, FS, vol. 17, 51. For the petticoat, see Elizabeth Peck's inventory, 1710, SCPR, FS, vol. 17, 155. For the towels and the wheelbarrow, see Samuel Gray's inventory, 1710, SCPR, FS, vol. 17, 167.

9. For "bargain," see West v. Norton, SF case 20894. For six shillings, see West v. Dodge, SF case 22148.

10. West v. Norton, SF case 20894.

11. Children enslaved in the southern mainland colonies during the eighteenth century were more likely to live with kin than were New England children. See Allan Kulikoff, "The Beginnings of the Afro-American Family in Early Maryland," in *Law, Society, and Politics in Early Maryland,* ed. Aubrey C. Land et al. (Baltimore: Johns Hopkins University Press, 1977), 176–182; Philip D. Morgan, *Slave Counterpoint: Black Culture in the Eighteenth-Century Chesapeake and Low Country* (Chapel Hill: University of North Carolina Press, 1998), 500–501, 507, 540–548; and Jennifer L. Morgan, *Laboring Women: Reproduction and Gender in New World Slavery* (Philadelphia: University of Pennsylvania Press, 2004), 104.

12. Between 1675 and 1725, 432 enslavers probated in Suffolk County claimed a total of 738 bondspeople. Of these 432 enslavers, 184 claimed a total of 223 children. The majority of these 184 households with children (109 households, or 59%) owned *only* children. A bit more on the terms used to identify these children is in order: Usually they were called "boy" or "girl," but sometimes they were referred to as "lad" or "child." Two-hundred-six of these 223 children

were identified racially. Among those whose racial status is deducible from the records, 162, or 79 percent, appear to have been African-descended; they were referred to as "negro." Thirty-one were identified as Indian (a sizable minority of whom were indentured rather than enslaved); five as "mullatto"; and eight as white (a group that appears to be composed of term servants or apprentices). For more on the likely racial composition of the bound labor force in the Boston area, see Gloria McCahon Whiting, "Race, Slavery, and the Problem of Numbers in Early New England: A View from Probate Court," *WMQ* 77, no. 3 (July 2020): 405–440. Note that 24 of the 738 bondspeople probated at the turn of the eighteenth century could not be identified by age. They were therefore excluded from the count of children who lived in proximity to adults. This analysis is derived from my probate records database, described in the Note on Sources.

13. This is similar to slavery in Britain during this period, where most bondspeople were separated from their kin. See Simon P. Newman, "Freedom-Seeking Slaves in England and Scotland, 1700–1780," *English Historical Review* 134, no. 570 (October 2019): 1148. The rate at which children were separated from family members in the Boston area dwarfs the rate at which such separations occurred in various other urban North American places. In Philadelphia, for instance, Jean R. Soderlund found that 20.1 percent of girls and 27.5 percent of boys in Philadelphia lived alone in their enslavers' homes. See Jean R. Soderlund, "Black Women in Colonial Pennsylvania," *Pennsylvania Magazine of History and Biography* 107, no. 1 (January 1983): 59.

14. In the last quarter of the seventeenth century, the average slaveholding household as measured by probate claimed 1.71 bondspeople. This number fell to 1.70 in the first quarter of the eighteenth century before rising to 1.86 in the second quarter of the eighteenth century. In the third quarter of the eighteenth century, the average slaveholding household in Suffolk County claimed 1.83 people. This analysis is derived from my probate records database.

15. Merely 14 enslavers whose estates were probated prior to 1675 claimed to own children, but numbers increased at the end of the seventeenth century. Between 1675 and 1699, 52 of 98 children mentioned in probate lived in households without bound adults; between 1700 and 1724, 63 of 118 children lived in such conditions; between 1725 and 1749, 114 of 244 children lived apart from parental figures; and, finally, between 1750 and 1774, 94 of 194 children did so.

16. On the preferences of southern and Caribbean enslavers, see Gwyn Campbell, "Children and Slavery in the New World: A Review," *Slavery and Abolition* 27, no. 2 (August 2006): 273. On the overrepresentation of children among imported bondspeople in Boston and New England more broadly, see Robert E. Desrochers, "Slave for Sale Advertisements and Slavery in Massachusetts, 1704–1781," *WMQ* 59, no. 3 (July 2002): 649; William D. Piersen, *Black Yankees: The Development of an Afro-American Subculture in Eighteenth-Century New England* (Amherst: University of Massachusetts Press, 1988), 5; and Edgar J. McManus, *Black Bondage in the North* (Syracuse: Syracuse University Press, 1973), 21.

17. *Boston News-Letter*, November 10, 1712, 2 ("Barbadoes"); *Boston News-Letter*, May 14, 1716, 2 ("Country"); *Boston News-Letter*, May 11, 1719, 4 ("several").

18. Mary Auternote v. Tomlin, SF case 14667; Depositions of Jemima Lane and Fedeller Soco, SF case 44242.

19. See Desrochers, "Slave for Sale Advertisements," 659, and Wendy Anne Warren, "'Thrown Upon the World': Valuing Infants in the Eighteenth-Century North American Slave Market," *Slavery & Abolition* 39, no. 4 (2018): 624 n6.

20. *Boston News-Letter*, September 30, 1706, 2.

21. These numbers are derived from keyword searching all newspapers published in Boston archived in the *America's Historical Newspapers* database as of July 2019. Of course, searching this database is an imperfect way to obtain all possible advertisements offering gratis items placed in Boston's papers for multiple reasons: Not all newspaper issues survive, the database's search function is not fully reliable, and some advertisements offering things for free may not have used the formulation "to be given away." However, reading printed weeklies line by line determined that "to be given away" was the phrase most often used by those looking to dispense of items in newspapers, which suggests—notwithstanding missing newspaper issues and missed hits—that searching for that phrase is a useful way to measure trends in advertising.

22. Of 101 advertisements mentioning a "negro child" placed in the first half of the eighteenth century, 95 sought to give the child away. Coincidentally, the number of advertisements touting items "to be given away" in the first half of the eighteenth century (101) and the number of those offering enslaved children (95) are the same.

23. These numbers are derived from keyword searches for the phrase "negro child" in all newspapers published in Boston that were archived in the *America's Historical Newspapers* database as of July 2019. They certainly do not capture every child of African descent mentioned in newspaper advertisements, but they provide a good sample. Other phrases doubtless were used to refer to young children in slavery. "Negro infant," however, returns very few hits. "Negro boy" and "Negro girl" were used with frequency, but these terms appear often to refer to people on the cusp of adulthood, as in the case of the "healthy, strong Negro Girl, about Seventeen Years of Age" advertised in 1724. The market for such people was quite different from the market for the very young. *New-England Courant*, September 28, 1724, 2.

24. For the low values associated with young enslaved children, see Piersen, *Black Yankees*, 27; *Boston News-Letter*, January 11, 1750, 2 ("Girl"); *Boston News-Letter*, December 2, 1756, 2 ("Boy").

25. *New Hampshire Gazette*, February 10, 1764, 2; *Connecticut Courant*, February 15, 1780, 4; *Essex Gazette*, February 14, 1769, 3.

26. *Boston Gazette*, July 9, 1751, 2 ("*likely*"); *Boston Post-Boy*, June 26, 1758, 3 ("Employ"); *Boston Gazette*, June 4, 1770, 4 ("healthy"); *Boston Gazette*, January 29, 1745, 3 ("English"); *Boston Gazette*, March 5, 1745, 4; *Boston Gazette*, May 5, 1755, 2; *Boston News-Letter*, July 15, 1762, 3 ("Family").

27. See Ruth Wallis Herndon, "'A Proper and Instructive Education': Raising Children in Pauper Apprenticeship," in *Children Bound to Labor: The Pauper Apprentice System in Early America*, ed. Ruth Wallis Herndon and John E. Murray (Ithaca: Cornell University Press, 2009), 15.

28. *Boston Gazette*, June 8, 1772, 3 ("too good"); *Boston Gazette*, April 16, 1745, 3 ("poor").

29. *Boston Evening-Post*, March 5, 1744, 2.

30. *Boston News-Letter*, April 5, 1753, 2 ("dispos'd of"); *Boston Gazette*, June 11, 1739, 3 ("few Days"). The child was not quickly spoken for; the *Gazette* published this advertisement through July 2, 1739. *Boston Evening-Post*, December 1, 1760, 4 ("Week").

31. *Boston Gazette*, June 18, 1764, 3 ("Enquire"); *Boston News-Letter*, January 18, 1750, 2 ("10 Days"); *Boston Evening-Post*, March 24, 1746, 2 ("3 Weeks"). For another three-week-old, see the *Boston Gazette*, June 21, 1743, 4.

32. For examples of advertisements offering children a month old, see *Boston Evening-Post*, December 31, 1759, 4, and *Boston Gazette*, July 13, 1761, 3. For the child of five weeks, see *Boston Evening-Post*, September 15, 1740, 2. For those offering children of six weeks, see *Boston Evening-Post*, October 5, 1741, 2, and *Boston Post-Boy*, January 21, 1760, 1.

33. *Boston Evening-Post*, March 17, 1740, 2 (*"healthy"*); *Boston Post-Boy*, April 22, 1765, 2; *Boston Post-Boy*, March 5, 1744, 4.

34. *Boston Evening-Post*, March 3, 1746, 3.

35. *Boston Evening-Post*, February 23, 1747, 2.

36. For examples of "Likely," see *Boston News-Letter*, February 27, 1721, 2, and *New England Weekly Journal*, June 16, 1741, 2. For the use of "Very likely," see *Boston Evening-Post*, February 2, 1747, 2. For examples of "Extraordinary likely," see *Boston Post-Boy*, January 11, 1762, 4, and *Boston Post-Boy*, February 1, 1762, 4. For "lusty," see *Boston Gazette*, June 21, 1743, 4, and *Boston News-Letter*, November 21, 1745, 2. The advertisers used this term to suggest health or vigor. See "lusty, adj." at OED Online, Oxford University Press (accessed August 4, 2022). For examples of "very good," see *Boston Evening-Post*, April 14, 1740, 2, and *Boston Evening-Post*, January 23, 1749, 2. For examples of "excellent," see *Boston Evening-Post*, March 1, 1742, 2, and *Boston News-Letter*, July 1, 1773, 4. For "as fine a Breed as any in America," see *Boston News-Letter*, January 28, 1773, 3. For the use of "well," see *Boston News-Letter*, July 21, 1748, 2. For an example of "in good Health," see *Boston Post-Boy*, February 14, 1763, 4. For a few of many uses of *"healthy,"* see *New England Weekly Journal*, June 6, 1738, 2; *Boston Evening-Post*, March 17, 1740, 2; *Boston Post-Boy*, July 14, 1746, 4; and *Boston News-Letter*, April 30, 1761, 3. For a sampling of instances in which advertisers used *"Fine,"* see *Boston Evening-Post*, September 15, 1740, 2; *Boston Evening-Post*, September 21, 1741, 2; and *Boston Evening-Post*, September 2, 1745, 2. For examples of hearty, see *Boston Gazette*, July 27, 1761, 4, and *Boston News-Letter*, June 24, 1773, 2.

37. *Boston Gazette*, February 6, 1764, 2 ("remote"); *Boston Gazette*, June 15, 1730, 2 (*"Neighbourhood"*).

38. *New-England Courant*, May 18, 1724, 2 ("young"); *Boston News-Letter*, November 21, 1745, 2 ("Necessaries"); *Boston Gazette*, March 18, 1771, 2 ("Money"); *Boston News-Letter*, July 8, 1773, 3 ("Terms").

39. Morgan, *Laboring Women*, 86 ("breeding"), 100 ("issue"). Historians debate the importance of reproduction to enslavers in seventeenth- and eighteenth-century British America. For those who argue for the value of bondswomen's reproduction to their enslavers in the early period, see Morgan, *Laboring Women*, and Jessica Millward, *Finding Charity's Folks: Enslaved and Free Black Women in Maryland* (Athens: University of Georgia Press, 2015), 15. For those who argue that women's reproduction was not valued in certain colonial contexts, see Trevor Burnard, "Toiling in the Fields: Valuing Female Slaves in Jamaica, 1674–1788," in *Sexuality and Slavery*, ed. Daina Ramey Berry and Leslie M. Harris (Athens: University of Georgia Press, 2018), 35, 38; and Kenneth Morgan, "Slave Women and Reproduction in Jamaica, c. 1776–1834," *History* 91, no. 2 (302) (April 2006): 231–253. There is consensus that reproduction became highly valued by enslavers in various locations in the North American South after the abolition of the trans-Atlantic slave trade, however. See Marie Jenkins Schwartz, *Birthing a Slave: Motherhood and Medicine in the Antebellum South* (Cambridge: Harvard University Press, 2006), 13–19; Daina Ramey Berry, *The Price for Their Pound of Flesh: The Value of the Enslaved, from Womb to Grave, in the Building of a Nation* (Boston: Beacon Press, 2017), 12–20; Walter Johnson, *Soul By Soul: Life Inside the Antebellum Slave*

Market (Cambridge: Harvard University Press, 1999), 82–84, 144; and Wilma A. Dunaway, "Diaspora, Death, and Sexual Exploitation: Slave Families at Risk in the Mountain South," *Appalachian Journal* 26, no. 2 (Winter 1999): 143. Reproduction also occupied a central place in the minds of Caribbean enslavers who first feared, and then experienced, the abolition of the trans-Atlantic slave trade. See Hilary McD. Beckles, *Natural Rebels: A Social History of Enslaved Black Women in Barbados* (New Brunswick: Rutgers University Press, 1989), 92; Campbell, "Children and Slavery in the New World," 273; Sasha Turner, *Contested Bodies: Pregnancy, Childrearing, and Slavery in Jamaica* (Philadelphia: University of Pennsylvania Press, 2017), 46; and Colleen A. Vasconcellos, "From Chattel to 'Breeding Wenches': Abolitionism, Girlhood, and Jamaican Slavery," in *Girlhood: A Global History*, ed. Jennifer Helgren and Colleen A. Vasconcellos (New Brunswick: Rutgers University Press, 2010), 328.

40. The clearest statements on the forced reproduction of enslaved women in New England and the economic value of young children in bondage come from the work of Wendy Anne Warren, though they seem to run in opposite directions. Warren emphasized the importance of the procreation of bondswomen in New England in both *New England Bound: Slavery and Colonization in Early America* (New York: Norton, 2016), 7–8, 47, 127, and 166, and "'The Cause of Her Grief': The Rape of a Slave in Early New England," *JAH* 93, no. 4 (March 2007): 1031–1049. More recently, however, Warren has shown that enslavers in New England used local newspapers to give away the bound infants born in their households. See Warren, "Thrown Upon the World," 623–641. The evidence assessed here aligns more closely with Warren's recent article than with her earlier arguments about forced reproduction.

41. This number, derived from my probate records database, fluctuated little over the course of the century stretching from 1675 to 1774. Decedents claimed, in the last quarter of the seventeenth century, an average of 0.8 adults in bondage (150 adults in 185 households); in the first quarter of the eighteenth century, an average of one adult (227 adults in 233 households); in the second quarter of the eighteenth century, an average of one adult (476 adults in 487 households); and, in the third quarter of the eighteenth century, an average of 1.1 adults (534 adults in 472 households). Of course, not all bondspeople mentioned in probate records were identified by age. However, even if we were to assume that all of those people whose age is not recorded were fully grown, adults would still be distributed in very small numbers throughout the region's households. There were 68, 58, 171, and 135 people of unknown age listed, respectively, in the last quarter of the seventeenth century and first three quarters of the eighteenth. If they were all adults—which is unlikely—then the average household would have had 1.2 adults in the last quarter of the seventeenth century, 1.2 in the first quarter of the eighteenth, 1.3 in the second quarter of the eighteenth, and 1.4 in the third quarter of the eighteenth.

42. See Frank Wesley Pitman "The Organization of Slave Labor," *Journal of Negro History* 11, no. 4 (October 1926): 596, 604; Barbara Bush, "African Caribbean Slave Mothers and Children: Traumas of Dislocation and Enslavement Across the Atlantic World," *Caribbean Quarterly* 56, no. 1/2 (March–June 2010): 82; and Jerome Teelucksingh, "The 'Invisible Child' in British West Indian Slavery," *Slavery and Abolition* 27, no. 2 (August 2006): 241, 244.

43. Morgan, *Laboring Women*, 9, 82, 79. Morgan analyzed wills written from 1650 to 1679, finding that 47 of 254 wills mentioning bondswomen, or 19%, used the term "increase."

44. Morgan, *Laboring Women*, 88–92, 98–100, 128–129, 138–140. For the statistical findings, see 100. Morgan analyzed wills written from 1730 to 1749, finding that 67 of 218 wills mentioning bondswomen, or 31%, used the term "increase."

45. Not all of the 329 decedents who composed these wills identified bondspeople by age and sex. But, of those who did, 101 discussed 108 African-descended women and seven Indian women in bondage.

46. The differences between South Carolina and Barbados will writers on the one hand and Massachusetts will writers on the other with regard to the anticipated reproduction of their bondswomen cannot be explained away by other factors, such as a hesitance on the part of Massachusetts enslavers to count on future dividends. Decedents in Massachusetts regularly anticipated what they believed was to come and discussed it in their wills. For instance, they considered future production on the part of bondswomen, as when Sarah Orrock allocated "the Earnings of my said Negro Woman" to the "bringing up of my four youngest Children." See Sarah Orrock's 1747 will, SCPR, FS, vol. 40, 62. Likewise, they planned for children yet to be born, though the focus was on children to be born to themselves or their heirs, not to their bondspeople. Consider Mary Palmer's decision to leave an inheritance to the baby she was "now Pregnant with if born alive." See Mary Palmer's 1745 will, SCPR, FS, vol. 39, 31. The analysis of the discussion of enslaved women in Suffolk County wills is based on my probate records database.

47. I searched all newspapers published in Philadelphia and New York during the first three-quarters of the eighteenth century that were archived in the *America's Historical Newspapers* database as of June 2020. This is not an issue of terminology; Philadelphians and New Yorkers indeed used the term "negro child," sometimes in relation to sale. However, they appear not to have used the term in relation to gifting.

48. The southern colonies appear to have followed the same pattern. Though the surviving eighteenth-century newspaper evidence for these colonies is much less voluminous than it is for the mid-Atlantic and, especially, for New England, the clues from Virginia, Maryland, and South Carolina are suggestive. Comparable searches—for both the phrase "to be given away" and the phrase "negro child"—yield no instances in which enslavers sought recipients willing to take the infants born in their households. These findings accord with those of Patricia Bradley, who observed in a wide-ranging study of newspapers that enslaved babies in Boston were "regularly" given away, but "advertisements for free babies were rare" in other colonies. See Patricia Bradley, *Slavery, Propaganda, and the American Revolution* (Jackson: University Press of Mississippi, 1999), 32.

49. Although enslavers in New York and Philadelphia commanded more labor, on average, than did enslavers in Boston, holdings in the urban mid-Atlantic were nonetheless very small. Census data indicates that in 1703, New York City enslavers owned on average slightly more than two bondspeople (314 enslavers claimed 704 people). See Joyce D. Goodfriend, *Before the Melting Pot: Society and Culture in Colonial New York, 1664–1730* (Princeton: Princeton University Press, 1992), 76. In a study of wills and estate inventories from New York City and its surrounds between 1669 and 1829, Vivienne L. Kruger found an average of 2.4 enslaved people of African descent listed per will and three per inventory—but this slightly underestimates the distribution per household, as Kruger excluded bondspeople from households with multiracial labor forces, which tended to claim more people. See Vivienne L. Kruger, "Born to Run: The Slave Family in Early New York, 1626–1827" (PhD diss., Columbia University, 1985), 148. A 1755 census of bondspeople above the age of fourteen in twenty-one towns in the area around New York City found that households bound an average of 2.2 adults. See Kruger, "Born to Run," 136. As for Philadelphia, 1767 tax records indicate that there were close to three

bondspeople above the age of twelve per slaveholding household in the city; 1,392 were counted among 521 households, but enslaved people over the age of fifty were excluded from the records. See Gary B. Nash, "Slaves and Slaveholders in Colonial Philadelphia," *WMQ* 30, no. 2 (April 1973): 244, 246. Jean R. Soderlund's analysis of probate records suggests that, over the course of the colonial period, enslavers claimed an average of 2.4 bondspeople in Philadelphia. See Soderlund, "Black Women in Colonial Pennsylvania," 53. By the time the first federal census was taken in 1790, the average number of bondspeople per slaveholding household in the state of New York was 2.7, while returns indicated 2.0 bondspeople per slaveholding household in Pennsylvania, where slavery was starting to decline. See S. N. D. North, *A Century of Population Growth: From the First Census of the United States to the Twelfth, 1790–1900* (Washington, DC: Government Printing Office, 1909), 137.

50. It is worth noting that this is not an exclusively New England phenomenon: Daina Ramey Berry found several examples of enslavers selling fertile bondswomen in the mid-Atlantic region during the late eighteenth century. See Berry, *The Price for Their Pound of Flesh*, 20–21.

51. *Boston Evening-Post*, April 23, 1750, 4 ("*breeds*"); *Boston News-Letter*, October 11, 1750, 2 ("disposed"); *Boston Evening-Post*, October 28, 1751, 2 ("Pregnancy").

52. *Boston Evening-Post*, August 9, 1736, 2 ("excellent"); *Boston Gazette*, April 2, 1759, 3 ("notable"); *Boston Gazette*, June 8, 1772, 3 ("too good"); *Boston Evening-Post*, January 25, 1773, 4 ("*too fast*"); *Boston News-Letter*, June 9, 1763, 4 ("considerable").

53. *Boston News-Letter*, July 31, 1766, 2 ("too fast"); *Boston News-Letter*, December 28, 1769, 4 ("only").

54. *New England Weekly Journal*, July 19, 1737, 2 ("careful"); *Boston Gazette*, February 17, 1772, 4 ("Town").

55. *Boston Evening-Post*, February 14, 1757, 4 ("*must go*"); *Boston Evening-Post*, December 28, 1772, 3 ("given").

56. *New England Weekly Journal*, August 19, 1728, 2; *Boston News-Letter*, May 8, 1746, 2 ("10 Months"); *Boston Post-Boy*, July 19, 1742, 3 ("*healthy*"); *Boston Evening-Post*, August 1, 1737, 2 ("*likely*"); *Boston News-Letter*, April 16, 1722, 4 ("Boy"); *Boston Gazette*, November 15, 1736, 4 ("Years *of Age*").

57. *Boston News-Letter*, June 26, 1766, 5. The demand for this pair was not high; the advertisement was still posted nearly a month later; see *Boston News-Letter*, July 25, 1766, 2.

58. Thatcher described one child, "Little Sambo," as "born in my House," which means he was almost surely born to Hagar, as she was the man's sole bound woman. The connection to Hagar of another child, "Little Hagar," is unmistakable. The third child, a boy named Jemmy, is not clearly linked in Thatcher's will to Hagar, but, seeing as the other two children were born to Hagar, it would not be surprising if Jemmy was as well.

59. Peter Thatcher's 1722 will, SCPR, FS, vol. 26, 88. Peter referred to his daughter Theodora as "Gulliver," her married surname.

60. The familial relationships of people in bondage are often difficult to distill from their enslavers' probate records, but the following wills split up groupings that may well have represented nuclear families, freeing some but not others: William Holbrook's 1714 will, SCPR, FS, vol. 18, 410; Sarah Beard's 1719 will, SCPR, FS, vol. 21, 724–725; Elizabeth Pierce's 1723 will, SCPR, NS, vol. 10, 291–292; Francis Holmes's 1726 will, SCPR, FS, vol. 25, 120–121; Jonathan Bill's 1728 will, SCPR, FS, vol. 27, 163–164; Sarah Forland's 1729 will, SCPR, FS, vol.

31, 151; Edmund Quincy's 1737 will, SCPR, FS, vol. 33, 465–466; John Ellery's 1741 will, SCPR, FS, vol. 36, 100; William Waters's 1749 will, SCPR, FS, vol. 52, 482; John Cheever's 1750 will, SCPR, FS, vol. 45, 602–604.

61. John Floyd's 1701 agreement, SCPR, FS, vol. 14, 400–401.

62. West v. Norton, SF case 20894.

63. West v. Norton, SF case 20894.

64. Recent scholarly interpretations suggest that when wet-nursing and slavery intersected, for example, in the United States South, nearly all of the feeding was done by bound nurses for the benefit of white children. See Emily West and R. J. Knight, "Mothers' Milk: Slavery, Wet-Nursing, and Black and White Women in the Antebellum South," *Journal of Southern History* 83, no. 1 (February 2017): 38, and Stephanie E. Jones-Rogers, *They Were Her Property: White Women as Slave Owners in the American South* (New Haven: Yale University Press, 2019), chap. 5.

65. For "malatta," see Inquisition by Ephraim Savage, SF case 5438. For "Nurse," see *Boston Gazette*, June 6, 1749, 2. For additional examples, see the *Boston News-Letter*, September 29, 1768, and the *Continental Journal and Weekly Advertiser*, February 11, 1779, 5.

66. Of the 654 children bound in Suffolk County during the century spanning 1675 to 1774, 389 (59 percent) lived in households without grown women in bondage. This figure fluctuated only slightly over the century. In the last quarter of the seventeenth century, 56 percent (55 of 98) of bound children lived in households without bound women, followed by 65 percent (77 of 118), 57 percent (139 of 244), and 61 percent (118 of 194) in the first three quarters of the eighteenth century, respectively. This analysis is derived from the probate records database. The reality that the majority of children lived in households without bound women sets early New England apart from the nineteenth-century South, where enslavers tended not to separate bound mothers and infants, which Emily West and R. J. Knight suggest can be attributed to "a lack of available wet nurses." See West and Knight, "Mothers' Milk," 41 n12. On young children and family separation in the South, see Michael Tadman, *Speculators and Slaves: Masters, Traders, and Slaves in the Old South* (Madison: University of Wisconsin Press, 1989), 151.

67. West and Knight, "Mothers' Milk," 52.

68. Auternote v. Tomlin, SF case 13991.

69. *New England Weekly Journal*, January 2, 1739, 2. For another such pairing, see the *Boston Evening-Post*, September 18, 1749, 2.

70. These numbers are based on keyword searching through the newspapers archived in the *America's Historical Newspapers* database as of June 2019. All newspapers published in Massachusetts between 1700 and 1750 were searched for the following terms: "nurse," "nursing," "breast," "suckle," and "suck." (Repeat hits of the same advertisement were excluded.) As the database's search function is not foolproof, these searches may have missed relevant notices. However, there is no reason to believe that the relative proportion of advertisements seeking employment for wet nurses and those seeking to hire such nurses would differ meaningfully if the newspapers were all perused word for word.

71. *New England Weekly Journal*, August 9, 1737, 2 ("Breasts"). For married women, see *New England Weekly Journal*, May 8, 1732, 2, and *Boston Evening-Post*, July 30, 1739, 2. For husbands at sea, see *Weekly Rehearsal*, January 7, 1734, 2, and *Boston Evening-Post*, November 14, 1737, 2.

72. *Boston Evening-Post*, March 21, 1737, 2 ("*Reputable*"); *New England Weekly Journal*, July 7, 1741, 2 ("Character"); *Boston Evening-Post*, November 3, 1740, 4 ("*her own House*"); *New*

England Weekly Journal, April 7, 1735, 2 ("her Family"); *Boston Evening-Post,* June 5, 1738, 2 ("*Milk*").

73. *Boston Evening-Post,* April 14, 1746, 5.

74. Marylynn Salmon, "The Cultural Significance of Breastfeeding and Infant Care in Early Modern England and America," *Journal of Social History* 28, no. 2 (Winter 1994): 256; Carla Cevasco, "'Look'd Like Milk': Colonialism and Infant Feeding in the English Atlantic World," *Journal of Early American History* 10, no. 2–3 (December 2020): 154.

75. George Norton's 1717 inventory, Essex County Probate Records, vol. 312, 61, Judicial Archives, MA Archives.

76. West v. Dodge, SF case 22148.

77. Deposition of Samuel Buttman, SF case 164284.

78. It is difficult to make a statement on the extent to which enslaved children in New England were educated, but evidence of the practice crops up—and not just of the famous cases, like those of Phillis Wheatley or Cotton Mather's bondspeople. For instance, one enslaver remarked on how he provided the two bound Africans raised in his house with a Christian education and taught them to read. Another discussed his bondswoman, who had "with Great Pains" acquired literacy and religious knowledge. A third paid considerable sums for "Schooling + Cloathing" a child of African descent, as is evident from the accounts submitted by his executors to the Suffolk County Probate Court. Likewise, an advertisement placed in the *New England Weekly Journal* informed Boston residents that a "certain Person" planned to open a school in April 1728 for the "Instruction of Negro's, in Reading, &c." and encouraged residents to send their bondspeople there. See MAC, vol. 180, 218–219; Nathaniel Byfield's 1732 will, SCPR, FS, vol. 31, 425; Jonathan Draper's 1751 account, SCPR, NS, vol. 25, 487, and Draper's 1751 return, SCPR, NS, vol. 25, 492; *New England Weekly Journal,* April 1, 1728, 2. See also Jennifer E. Monaghan, *Learning to Read and Write in Colonial America* (Boston: University of Massachusetts Press, 2005), 244–245, and Antonio T. Bly, "'Pretends He Can Read': Runaways and Literacy in Colonial America, 1730–1776," *Early American Studies* 6, no. 2 (Fall, 2008): 268–269, 277.

79. On nursing in early New England, see John Demos, *A Little Commonwealth: Family Life in Plymouth Colony* (New York: Oxford University Press, 1970), 133. On babies being held, see Main, *Peoples of a Spacious Land,* 124. On walking, see Karin Calvert, *Children in the House: The Material Culture of Early Childhood, 1600–1900* (Boston: Northeastern University Press, 1994), 31–37.

80. The confusion over Sue's ownership might have stemmed from the fact that she was purchased by a single woman who was living as a dependent in her father's home at the time she made the outlay. Also, as discussed later, Mary moved out of her parents' home not long after acquiring Sue, leaving Sue to be raised by—and to serve—her parents. Of course, because these testimonies were generated as part of a lawsuit over Sue's ownership, they no doubt favored discussions of that ownership. We ought not assume that everyone who met Sue inquired about who owned her. West v. Norton, SF case 20894.

81. West v. Dodge, SF case 22148.

82. For "People," see Deposition of Samuel Buttman, SF case 164284. For "Woman," see West v. Norton, SF case 20894.

83. West v. Norton, SF case 20894.

84. West v. Dodge, SF case 22148.

85. West v. Norton, SF case 20894.

86. The Spanish silver coin called the *peso de ocho reales*, or the "piece of eight," was valued at six shillings of Massachusetts currency. See Joseph B. Felt, *An Historical Account of Massachusetts Currency* (Boston: Perkins & Marvin, 1839), 41; Robert Chalmers, *A History of Currency in the British Colonies* (London: Eyre and Spottiswoode, 1893), 9. There is disagreement among the documents over whether Mary paid a piece of eight for Sue or whether she paid six shillings. As the sums were equivalent, witnesses seem to have been more concerned with reporting the value for which Sue was sold than with communicating the exact coinage. One witness put the price at six shillings, while several others put the price at a piece of eight. See West v. Dodge, SF case 22148; West v. Norton, SF case 20894; West v. Dodge, SF case 164184. For the comment of Mary's mother, see West v. Norton, SF case 20894.

87. West v. Dodge, SF case 22148; George Norton's 1717 inventory, Essex County Probate Records, vol. 312, 61, Judicial Archives, MA Archives. Though we do not have testimony specifying precisely where Sue slept in the Norton home, George's 1717 inventory shows that the household had "Three Bedds & Beddings" at a time when neither children nor any bondspeople besides Sue lived in the home. Moreover, probate evidence from nearby Suffolk County suggests that enslaved people in the region slept in the homes of their enslavers. Finally, the fact that no "negro bedding" was cataloged alongside Sue in George's inventory makes it more than plausible that the woman slept on the Nortons' bedding. For George's dependents, see Sybil Noyes, Charles Thornton Libby, and Walter Goodwin Davis, *Genealogical Dictionary of Maine and New Hampshire* (Portland: Southworth-Anthoensen Press, 1928–1939), 513–514. For an analysis of the physical surroundings of the enslaved in Boston homes, see Peter Benes, "Slavery in Boston Households, 1647–1770," in *Slavery/Antislavery in New England*, ed. Peter Benes and Jane Montague Benes (Boston: Boston University, 2005).

88. Historians have found that African-descended people in the British colonies did not ordinarily live in physical intimacy with those who bound them. See Morgan, *Laboring Women*, 10; Gloria L. Main, *Tobacco Colony: Life in Early Maryland, 1650–1720* (Princeton: Princeton University Press, 1982), 123–124; and Gerald W. Mullin, *Flight and Rebellion: Slave Resistance in Eighteenth-Century Virginia* (New York: Oxford University Press, 1972), 51–52. Scholars studying regions where smallholdings predominated or investigating urban spaces have found greater physical proximity between enslavers and those they bound. See Diane Mutti Burke, *On Slavery's Border: Missouri's Small Slave-Holding Households, 1815–1865* (Athens: University of Georgia Press, 2010), 148, 154, 200, and Marisa J. Fuentes, *Dispossessed Lives: Enslaved Women, Violence, and the Archive* (Philadelphia: University of Pennsylvania Press, 2016), 87.

89. West v. Dodge, SF case 22148.

90. For Mary's marriage, see the *Vital Records of Beverly, Massachusetts, to the End of the Year 1849, vol. 2* (Topsfield: Topsfield Historical Society, 1907), 220. Some court documents suggest that Mary and Samuel married in 1705, but the town's marriage records insist on a January 13, 1702, marriage, and the town's birth records confirm that the two began to have children before the 1705 date: Mary was born on May 16, 1702, and John was born on June 24, 1704. See *Vital Records of Beverly, Massachusetts, to the End of the Year 1849, vol. 1* (Topsfield: Topsfield Historical Society, 1906), 361. For a court document suggesting the 1705 date, see Records of the Massachusetts Superior Court of Judicature, vol. 1725–1730, 117.

91. West v. Norton, SF case 20894.

92. West v. Dodge, SF case 22148.

93. These kinds of skills are mentioned in newspaper advertisements offering bound women and girls for sale, which circulated in the Boston area in the early eighteenth century.

See, for instance, advertisements for a woman "fit for any Dairy Service"; a girl who "uses her Needle pretty well"; a woman who "Washes well, is a very good Cook, [and is] fit for any Houshold Service"; a woman who excelled at "Washing, Scowring, &c."; and a woman who could "Sew, Wash, Brew, Bake, Spin and Milk Cows." *Boston News-Letter*, November 22, 1708, 4; May 5, 1712, 2; September 21, 1713, 2; August 20, 1716, 2; and January 4, 1720, 2. For the example of ironing, see Homans v. Jenkins, SF case 70962. For candle-making, see Demos, *A Little Commonwealth*, 142.

94. West v. Dodge, SF case 164184; West v. Norton, SF case 20894.

95. Essex Institute, *Vital Records of Manchester*, 280.

96. West v. Norton, SF case 20894.

97. West v. Dodge, SF case 22148.

98. No extant evidence dates this pregnancy with certainty, but all clues point to a childbirth in early to middle 1723, soon after Sue's February 1 sale. To begin with, the child, who would be called Jethro, must have been born after the sale rather than before it, as he was understood to belong to Shadrach Norton rather than to old Mrs. Norton. However, records suggest that Jethro's birth followed closely on the heels of this transaction. For example, when Shadrach sold Jethro less than three years after acquiring Sue, the child, described as a "Negro Boye," was worth 30 pounds. This value suggests that Jethro was nearing three years old; one of Jethro's brothers, Abijah, would be sold around the age of three for an equal sum of money. Another clue to the timing of Jethro's birth lies in Sue's subsequent childbirth. Sue bore a son named Matthew in June 1725: two years and four months after her sale. If Sue breastfed Jethro, which she doubtless did, as they lived in the same household and Shadrach would not likely have hired a surrogate nurse, her children probably would have been spaced around two years apart—a spacing that would date Jethro's birth to about four months after Sue's sale. A third clue revolves around Jethro's supposed value in 1726, when Mary sued for possession of the boy: fifty pounds. Inventories compiled by appraisers in nearby Suffolk County can help us interpret this. Seventeen people described as "negro boys" or "negro lads" were inventoried between 1720 and 1730, with listed values ranging from thirty to ninety pounds. In only one case was an age given; the "Negro Boy named Jemey" claimed in Samuel Greenwood's inventory was "aged about 7 years" and valued (with his clothing) at forty pounds. For Jethro's value to reach fifty pounds, he must have been moving from the age of needing care to the age of providing services, which would suggest he was at least nearing five years. This would give Jethro, once again, an early 1722 birth. For Jethro's sale, see Bill of Sale of Jethro Black, SF case 18870. For Abijah's birth, see Deposition of Anne Bennet, SF case 164410. For Abijah's sale, see Bill of Sale of Abijah Black, SF case 21492. For Matthew's birth, see West v. Norton, SF case 20894. For Jethro's value in 1726, see West v. Bennet, SF case 20197. For Jemey's value, see Samuel Greenwood's 1722 inventory, SCPR, FS, vol. 22, 644.

99. In all the testimony related to Sue, to Mary, and to Mary's parents' household, no evidence suggests that either Mary or her parents claimed ownership of other bondspeople.

100. For Jethro, see *Manchester, Mass. First Congregational Church Record Book, 1717–1743*, 53, CLA. For Dille's children, Seser, Mengo, Flowhear, and Dille, all surnamed "Black," see Essex Institute, *Vital Records of Manchester*, 128, 228. For Taff's children, Phillis and Tone, see *Vital Records of Manchester*, 128. For Phillis's baptism, see *First Congregational Church Record Book*, 65.

101. For the birth records, see *Vital Records of Beverly, Massachusetts, vol. 1*, 399. For the marriage records, see *Vital Records of Beverly, Massachusetts, vol. 2*, 361, 359. For the church

records, see William P. Upham and A. A. Galloupe, First Parish Church, *Records of the First Church in Beverly, Massachusetts 1667–1772* (Salem: Essex Institute, 1905), 57, 67–68, 159. For the death records, see *Vital Records of Beverly, Massachusetts, vol. 2*, 623–625.

102. S. N. D. North, *A Century of Population Growth*, 156.

103. Not a single historical source mentions Sue's partner, but the weight of the evidence suggests that he was of African descent. Many dozens of sources mention his children, referring to them, without fail, as "negroes." Though we cannot assume that the racial designations used by record keepers are fail-safe, preliminary evidence suggests that racial labeling in eastern Massachusetts during the early part of the eighteenth century was fairly reliable. Therefore, had Sue's partner been of either European or Indigenous ancestry, the children almost surely would have been referred to as some variant of the term "mulatto"—at least on occasion. As for whether the man hailed from Africa or was born in New England to African parents, demographic evidence suggests that he was brought to the region: The majority of adults in bondage around 1720 hailed from elsewhere. For more on the meaning of "mulatto" in this time period and the usefulness of racial designations in the records, see Whiting, "Race, Slavery, and the Problem of Numbers in Early New England." On the importance of the Atlantic traffic in bound people to New England's enslaved population in the eighteenth century, see Jared Ross Hardesty, *Black Lives, Native Lands, White Worlds: A History of Slavery in New England* (Boston: University of Massachusetts Press, 2019), 33–34.

104. See Laurel Thatcher Ulrich, *A Midwife's Tale: The Life of Martha Ballard, Based on Her Diary, 1785–1812* (New York: Knopf, 1990), 185. Anne Bennet and Elizabeth Whittier were both present at Sue's first birth as well as her third birth. Depositions filed by Mary Peirce and Elizabeth Warring indicate that they attended Sue's third birth, but it is possible they were at her first birth as well. See Deposition of Anne Bennet, SF case 164410; West v. Dodge, SF case 23405; West v. Dodge, SF case 22148; West v. Norton, SF case 20894.

105. In eighteenth-century Jamaica, for instance, enslaved women tended to one another in labor, either in the women's own huts or in plantation birthing houses. The African midwives on plantations practiced African herbalism and folk medicine. See Barbara Bush-Slimani, "Hard Labour: Women, Childbirth and Resistance in British Caribbean Slave Societies," *History Workshop* 36 (Autumn 1993): 92; Morgan, "Slave Women and Reproduction in Jamaica," 250.

106. For Flora, see Deposition of Flora, SF case 78078. For Abigail, see List of Witnesses, SF case 12908. For the woman attended by Hannah, see *Boston Evening-Post*, March 29, 1742, 2. For Nanny, see Otis v. Hinckley, SF case 62026. Nanny's mother, Pegg, was also in attendance both days.

107. Jennifer L. Morgan has argued against "romanticizing" motherhood for the enslaved. Within the context of early Barbadian slavery, for women to feel "ambivalence toward and distance from" their children "would have been as logical" as for them to feel love and the urge to nurture. After all, "[e]motional attachments exposed one to further abuse." Still, Sue's conditions were substantially different from the conditions of the Barbadian women Morgan was researching in terms of labor regimen, dietary sustenance, and disease culture, so Morgan's findings might not describe Sue's vantage on motherhood. See Morgan, *Laboring Women*, 114–115, 200–201. Sasha Turner has emphasized the grief experienced by women in bondage whose children became ill or died, which suggests the power of affective bonds between mother and child in at least some oppressive circumstances. See Sasha Turner, "The Nameless and the

Forgotten: Maternal Grief, Sacred Protection, and the Archive of Slavery," *Slavery and Abolition* 38, no. 2 (2017): 232–250.

108. 1 Kings 15:3, KJV.

109. West v. Norton, SF case 20894.

110. For "carry away," see West v. Dodge, SF case 23405. For "sold," see Deposition of Anne Bennet, SF case 164410. For "Bigah," see Bill of Sale of Abijah Black, SF case 21492.

111. For "Cloaths," see Deposition of William Dodge Jr. and Isaac Dodge, SF case 19836. For the sale to William Dodge Jr., see Bill of Sale of Abijah Black, SF case 21492. He was sold for 40 pounds.

112. Deposition of Moses Morgan, SF case 164417.

113. West v. Dodge, SF case 22148; Bill of Sale for Jethro Black, SF case 18870.

114. Bill of Sale for Jethro Black, SF case 18870. Enslaved people in the English Atlantic were first designated real estate in 1668 by Barbados lawmakers, who sought to ensure that those who inherited land would also inherit the bondspeople needed to work it. Virginians followed suit in 1705. South Carolina law designated enslaved people real property in 1690, but the colony's proprietors overruled this legislation, as well as all other legislation passed during the administration of ousted governor, Seth Sothell. See Thomas D. Morris, *Southern Slavery and the Law, 1619–1860* (Chapel Hill: University of North Carolina Press, 1996), 64, 66; Roy W. Copeland, "The Nomenclature of Enslaved Africans as Real Property or Chattels Personal: Legal Fiction, Judicial Interpretation, Legislative Designation, or Was a Slave a Slave by Any Other Name," *Journal of Black Studies* 40, no. 5 (May 2010): 948; M. Eugene Sirmans, "The Legal Status of the Slave in South Carolina, 1670–1740," *Journal of Southern History* 28, no. 4 (November 1962): 464–465; M. Eugene Sirmans, *Colonial South Carolina: A Political History, 1663–1763* (Chapel Hill: University of North Carolina Press, 1966), 50. That manumissions in New England were sometimes filed with deeds underscores the association of human property with land records.

115. West v. Dodge, SF case 23405; West v. Norton, SF case 20894.

116. West v. Dodge, SF case 22148.

117. Some of the legal reasoning for the case shows up in Mary West's response to Shadrach Norton's arguments for overturning the court's verdict. See West v. Norton, SF case 20894.

118. Deposition of John West, SF case 164417. The testimony of Mary's son, John, provides a rare glimpse into the human interactions inside an enslaver's house in New England. One of William's sons came "out of another Room" and "beed ye Negro boy above s[ai]d [to] Goe a Way," John recalled. Presumably, the boy did not want John to interact with Abijah, as he knew that John's mother claimed ownership of the enslaved child. West v. Dodge, Massachusetts SCJ Records, vol. 1725–1730, 119. Numerous historians have remarked on the tendency of white youth to boss or bully children in bondage. See, for example, Turner, *Contested Bodies*, 240.

119. Curiously, the Superior Court record book does not record a judgment in the case between Mary and Aaron Bennet over the right to Jethro; there is a large blank space left in the book. However, a fragment filed among miscellaneous court papers states that the Superior Court ruled in Mary's favor, and that Mary received Jethro and the costs of the court from Aaron. See Bennet v. West, SF case 20891. Aaron continued to appeal, but the litigation finally stopped when three court-appointed referees ruled in 1731 that Mary rightfully owned Jethro. See Bennet v. Martin, Massachusetts SCJ Records, vol. 1730–1731, 119. As for Matthew, Shadrach lost ownership of the boy in December of 1726, when the Court of Common Pleas ordered that

Mary recover him. See West v. Bennet, SF case 20197. Ultimately, the case was put to rest when the same referees who deemed Mary the legitimate owner of Jethro decided that she also had title to Matthew. See Norton v. Martin, Massachusetts SCJ Records, vol. 1730–1731, 118.

120. By the time Mary died three decades after recovering Jethro and Matthew, she held no human property, but what happened to her bondspeople in the interim is lost to history. Mary Martin's 1762 inventory, Essex County Probate, Old Series, vol. 339, 217, Judicial Archives, MA Archives.

121. West v. Dodge, SF case 22148; Deposition of Anne Bennet, SF case 164410. Scholars have expressed frustration, for good reason, that the archives of Atlantic slavery so often fail to capture the inner worlds of people in bondage. A growing body of literature meditates on the archive, its silences, and its inherent violence. See, for instance, Saidiya Hartman, *Lose Your Mother: A Journey Along the Atlantic Slave Route* (New York: Farrar, Straus and Giroux, 2007); Saidiya Hartman, "Venus in Two Acts," *Small Axe* 12, no. 2 (June 2008): 1–14; Simon Gikandi, "Rethinking the Archive of Enslavement," *Early American Literature* 50, no. 1 (2015), 81–102; Laura Helton, Justin Leroy, Max Mishler, Samantha Seeley, and Shauna Sweeney, eds., "The Question of Recovery: Slavery, Freedom, and the Archive," *Social Text* 33, no. 4 (December 2015); the special issue of *History of the Present* on the violence of the archives of slavery, "Slavery and the Archive," *History of the Present* 6, no. 2 (Fall 2016); and Fuentes, *Dispossessed Lives*. For the argument that even archival sources born of violence can provide important insight into the actions and aspirations of people caught in the snare of bondage, see Whiting, "Race, Slavery, and the Problem of Numbers in Early New England."

122. It is possible that the bound child extracted the promise of her enslaver, as the language here is inconclusive, but it seems more likely that the adult played the active role in negotiating this arrangement. Mary Sergeant's 1705 will, SCPR, FS, vol. 16, 102.

123. Ultimately, Molly "recovered her freedome" and all the costs associated with securing it. See Molly v. Briggs, SF case 14033; also Molly v. Briggs, Massachusetts SCJ Records, vol. 1715–1721, 286.

124. On June 10, 1754, David Burnett "Sett free at the Age of twenty sex years a certain Negroboy named James . . . born of the Body of Lettice a Negrowoman." At the behest of James's mother, Lettice, notary Ezekiel Price "Entered and notarized" the manumission record in his book less than three months later. It is not clear how James obtained the promise of freedom. Lettice, in bondage herself (also to David), likely would not have had the ability to purchase her son's liberty. However, by persuading Ezekiel to record the agreement, Lettice did what she could to force David to keep his word. See Ezekiel Price Notarial Records, Volume I, recorded September 5, 1754, Boston Athenaeum.

Chapter 4

Epigraph: "An Act for the Better Preventing of a Spurious and Mixt Issue" in *Massachusetts Acts and Resolves, vol. 1* (Boston: Wright and Potter, 1869), 578.

1. Sewall Diary, 2, 89, September 29, 1703.

2. William H. Whitmore, *The Massachusetts Civil List for the Colonial and Provincial Periods, 1640–1774* (Albany: J. Munsell, 1870), 126; Augustine Jones, *The Life and Work of Thomas Dudley: The Second Governor of Massachusetts* (Boston: Houghton, Mifflin, 1900), 472; William Richard Cutter, *New England Families Genealogical and Memorial, 3rd ser., vol. 1* (New York: Lewis Historical Publishing Co., 1915), 384.

3. Samuel Sewall, *The Selling of Joseph: A Memorial* (Boston: Bartholomew Green and John Allen, 1700), 1.

4. *Boston Marriages*, 1, 2, 5, and 4.

5. For a description of Thomas and Lydia using these terms, see Sentence of Thomas and Lydia Bedunah, Suffolk County GSP Records, vol. 1702–1712, 32. Extant records provide no evidence that marriages between white and Black people had ever before been solemnized in Boston, which was the town in Massachusetts with the largest concentration of African-descended residents. This suggests that the couple at Samuel's door was asking the justice of the peace to break with tradition. Of course, marriage records were not kept perfectly in this time and place; surely the vows of some inhabitants who stood before ministers or justices of the peace were never recorded by local town clerks. And it is possible that racial identifiers in the records were misplaced or not included. Still, perusing the entire body of seventeenth- and early eighteenth-century marriage records in Boston yields only one Black-white interracial marriage: this one.

6. *Boston Marriages*, 1, 7. The record refers to the two as "Thomas Bedoona" and "Lydia Craft," but I refer to them as Thomas Bedunah and Lydia Crafts because that is how their names were most commonly rendered in the archive.

7. Jacob L. Döhne, *A Zulu-Kafir Dictionary Etymologically Explained, with Copious Illustrations and Examples* (Cape Town: G. J. Pike's Printing Office, 1857), 67; Richard F. Burton, *Wanderings in West Africa from Liverpool to Fernando Po* (London: Tinsley Brothers, 1863), 163–164.

8. For a helpful summary of the economic links between New England and Barbados in the seventeenth century, see Wendy Anne Warren, *New England Bound: Slavery and Colonization in Early America* (New York: Norton, 2016).

9. In 1680, Governors William Leete of Connecticut and Simon Bradstreet of Massachusetts both independently reported that most of the trade in Africans in their respective colonies was with Barbados, from which bondspeople were generally brought in small groups. See Elizabeth Donnan, ed., *Documents Illustrative of the Slave Trade to America* (Washington, DC: Carnegie Institution of Washington, 1932), 3:2 and 3:15.

10. Evidence of self-purchase is occasionally found in probate records, which have survived with much more regularity than the other types of sources that would document the practice, such as diaries, receipts, and account books. See Anthony Haywood's inventory, 1701, SCPR, FS, vol. 14, 281.

11. For a detailed explanation of the probate records database upon which this analysis rests, see the Note on Sources.

12. Ruth Beate's will, 1714, SCPR, FS, vol. 21, 538; Rachel Gatcombe's will, 1752, SCPR, FS, vol. 47, 144; Hannah How's will, 1741, SCPR, FS, vol. 40, 174; Margaret Blackadoor's will, 1755, SCPR, FS, vol. 50, 396.

13. Of course, even those who were to receive their liberty immediately after an enslaver's demise experienced a delay in manumission; they had to wait for their enslavers to die.

14. Rebecca Dudley's will, 1722, SCPR, FS, vol. 22, 701; Hugh Floyd's will, 1730, SCPR, FS, vol. 28, 347; Sarah Beard's will, 1719, SCPR, FS, vol. 21, 724; Joseph Simpson's will, 1709, SCPR, FS, vol. 16, 594; Henry Brightman's will, 1705, SCPR, FS, vol. 16, 57; Elizabeth Mason's will, 1725, SCPR, FS, vol. 24, 191; Francis Holmes's will, 1726, SCPR, FS, vol. 25, 121; John Pim's will, 1719, SCPR, FS, vol. 25, 7; George Lane's will, 1740, SCPR, FS, vol. 35, 383.

15. John Frizell's will, 1720, SCPR, NS, vol. 10, 295; Nicholas and Anna Paige's will, 1703, SCPR, FS, vol. 20, 168; Samuel Wales's will, 1712, SCPR, FS, vol. 18, 57; Mary White's will, 1706, SCPR, NS, vol. 19, 221.

16. Hope Allen's will, 1677, SCPR, FS, vol. 6, 289; Mary Hunt's will, 1723, SCPR, NS, vol. 10, 313; Joseph Rock's will, 1683, SCPR, FS, vol. 6, 712; Henry Brightman's will, 1705, SCPR, FS, vol. 16, 57; Joseph Baxter's will, 1744, SCPR, FS, vol. 37, 518; William Webster's will, 1733, SCPR, FS, vol. 30, 54. For more on the conditional freedom of bondspeople in Boston, see Jared Ross Hardesty, *Unfreedom: Slavery and Dependence in Eighteenth-Century Boston* (New York: New York University Press, 2016), 16, 77, 84.

17. Rebecca Dudley's will, 1722, SCPR, FS, vol. 22, 701; Martha Bridge's will, 1752, SCPR, FS, vol. 46, 178–179. It is possible to read Martha's stipulation in two ways—as an obligation placed on Phillis to live with (and undoubtedly serve) Mary or as an obligation placed on Mary to house (and perhaps provide for) Phillis. When it came to hashing out the "terms" of the arrangement, however, it is hard to imagine that Phillis and Mary had equal power.

18. John Staniford's will, 1750, SCPR, FS, vol. 47, 39–40; John Otis's will, 1751, SCPR, FS, vol. 45, 380; Andrew Lane's will, 1747, SCPR, FS, vol. 42, 327; John Barns's will, 1759, SCPR, FS, vol. 56, 425; Ephraim Bosworth's will, 1760, SCPR, FS, vol. 57, 218; John Larrabee's will, SCPR, 1760, FS, vol. 60, 143.

19. Nathaniel Byfield's will, 1732, SCPR, FS, vol. 31, 425. The town of Bristol belonged to Massachusetts when Nathaniel purchased Rose, but it was transferred to Rhode Island in early 1747.

20. Mary Anderson's codicil, 1690, SCPR, NS, vol. 2, 235; George Lane's will, 1740, SCPR, FS, vol. 35, 383; William Waters's will, 1750, SCPR, FS, vol. 52, 482; John Barns's will, 1759, SCPR, FS, vol. 56, 424; Ephraim Bosworth's will, 1760, SCPR, FS, vol. 57, 218–219; Henry Caswell's will, 1747, SCPR, FS, vol. 40, 247 ("faithfull"); John Fayerweather's will, 1760, SCPR, FS, vol. 57, 254 ("behav[ing] well"); Thomas Palmer's will, 1750, SCPR, FS, vol. 45, 714 ("Fidelity").

21. Joseph West's will, 1691, SCPR, NS, vol. 8, 61.

22. Elizabeth Pierce's will, 1723, SCPR, NS, vol. 10, 292.

23. Ruth Willys's will, 1709, SCPR, FS, vol. 16, 599.

24. Ruth Beate's will, 1714, SCPR, FS, vol. 21, 538.

25. Samuel Read's will, 1725, SCPR, FS, vol. 23, 542.

26. George Raisin's will, 1728, SCPR, FS, vol. 27, 53.

27. Enslaved people were not allowed outside their enslavers' homes after 9 P.M., but no legislation curtailed the movement of free Black people.

28. See John Crafts's inventory, 1685, SCPR, FS, vol. 9, 249–250. John Crafts died intestate, but the Massachusetts General Court ordered that Mary Crafts should have John's personal estate for "her own support and education of her Children" and that John's land would be allocated to "the payment of debts, the widow enjoying her thirds thereof for life according to Law." The "remaining" estate would be "divided amongst the Seven Children of ye deced being one Son and Six daughters." A torn notation indicated that the one son, Ephraim, was to have a double share. See Settlement of John Crafts's Estate, *Records of the Suffolk County Court, 1680–1692*, 247, MA Archives.

29. See Richard Godbeer, *Sexual Revolution in Early America* (Baltimore: Johns Hopkins University Press, 2002), 20–21 and chap. 3, and Cornelia Hughes Dayton, *Women Before the Bar: Gender, Law, and Society in Connecticut, 1639–1789* (Chapel Hill: University of North Carolina Press, 1995), 60.

30. See Henrik Hartog, "The Public Law of a County Court: Judicial Government in Eighteenth-Century Massachusetts," *American Journal of Legal History* 20, no. 4 (October 1976): 300, 303.

31. *Boston Marriages*, 1, 7.

32. Sentence of Thomas and Lydia Bedunah, Suffolk County GSP Records, vol. 1702–1712, 32.

33. *Vital records of Roxbury, Massachusetts, to the end of the year 1849, vol. 1* (Salem: Essex Institute, 1925), 31. The couple married on October 4, and Elizabeth was born on November 12.

34. Sentence of Thomas and Lydia Bedunah, Suffolk County GSP Records, vol. 1702–1712, 32.

35. Sentence of Mary Goslin and Essex, Suffolk County GSP Records, vol. 1702–1712, 6.

36. Sentence of Mary Goslin and Cesar, Suffolk County GSP Records, vol. 1702–1712, 116.

37. "An Act for the Better Preventing of a Spurious and Mixt Issue" in *Massachusetts Acts and Resolves, vol. 1*, 578.

38. The act's provisions regarding whippings were both racialized and gendered; Black men and their white female partners were to be "severely whipped," as were the white male partners of Black women, but Black women were spared physical retribution. The act provides no clues as to why Black women who engaged in sex with white men outside of marriage were to be spared physical punishment, but the uneven punishments called for by this act raise provocative questions about the extent to which legislators recognized the victimization of Black women (most of whom were enslaved) by white men (perhaps their enslavers). Had the lawmakers recognized that Black women were frequently coerced into sexual activity across the color line, they might well have been disposed to excuse those women from corporal punishment as a result of that activity. Nonetheless, Black women, like Black men, were ordered to be shipped out of the province if they engaged in interracial sex. For more on the sexual victimization of Black women in white households, see Chapter 5.

39. Sewall Diary, 2, 143, December 1, 1705.

40. William Waller Hening, *The Statutes at Large: Being a Collection of All the Laws of Virginia from the First Session of the Legislature in the Year 1619, vol. 2* (New York: R. & W. & G. Bartow, 1823), 170.

41. Virginia Bernhard, *Slaves and Slaveholders in Bermuda, 1616–1782* (Columbia: University of Missouri Press, 1999), 92.

42. William Hand Browne, ed., *Archives of Maryland: Proceedings and Acts of the General Assembly of Maryland, January 1637/8–September 1664* (Baltimore: Maryland Historical Society, 1883), 533–534.

43. William Waller Hening, ed., *The Statutes at Large; Being a Collection of All the Laws of Virginia, from the First Session of the Legislature, in the Year 1619, vol. 3* (Philadelphia: Thomas Desilver, 1823), 86–87. For the argument that Anglo-puritan colonies like Massachusetts came late to prohibiting racial mixing and ultimately used less hostile language to ban interracial sex than non-puritan English colonies like Virginia, Maryland, and North Carolina, see Heather Miyano Kopelson, *Faithful Bodies: Performing Religion and Race in the Puritan Atlantic* (New York: New York University Press, 2014), 226.

44. See Hening, ed., *The Statutes at Large, vol. 3*, 454, and "An Act for the Better Preventing of a Spurious and Mixt Issue," *Massachusetts Acts and Resolves, vol. 1*, 578.

45. Boston Record Commissioners, *A Report of the Record Commissioners of the City of Boston, Containing the Records of the Boston Selectmen, 1701 to 1715, vol. 11* (Boston: Rockwell and Churchill, 1884), 5.

46. *Boston News-Letter*, June 10, 1706, 4.

47. Charles Deane, *The Connection of Massachusetts with Slavery and the Slave-Trade: A Paper Read Before the American Antiquarian Society at Worcester, October 21, 1886* (Worcester: Charles Hamilton, 1886), 19.

48. George H. Moore, *Notes on the History of Slavery in Massachusetts* (New York: D. Appleton, 1866), 50.

49. See Lorenzo Johnston Greene, *The Negro in Colonial New England* (New York: Athenaeum, 1969), 207.

50. Sewall Diary, 2, 143, December 1, 1705.

51. Sentence of Bess, Suffolk County GSP Records, vol. 1702–1712, 206.

52. Sentence of Katharine Horton, Suffolk County GSP Records, vol. 1712–1719, 43.

53. Sentence of Bess, Suffolk County GSP Records, vol. 1712–1719, 133.

54. Presentment of John Humphers, Massachusetts SCJ Records, vol. 1715–1721, 356.

55. Discharge of Mary Cuthbert, Massachusetts SCJ Records, vol. 1715–1721, 36.

56. Discharge of Ann Staples, Suffolk County GSP Records, vol. 1712–1719, 14.

57. Sentence of Ann Hardgrove, Suffolk County GSP Records, vol. 1702–1712, 152–153. Savil paid for the child's maintenance in return for two additional years of Ann's labor.

58. Presentment of Chester, Suffolk County GSP Records, vol. 1702–1712, 169.

59. Document labeled "1707-OCT-001," folder 1–4, Box 1 of 3 (1707–1749), Suffolk County General Sessions of the Peace Additional Papers, MA Archives.

60. See "Records: Births, Marriages, Deaths, 1630–1785," 31, 32, 34, 35, 37, 40, and 42. Ancestry.com. See also *Vital Records of Roxbury, vol. 1*, 24, 31.

61. For Thomas Bedunah's real estate purchases, see Suffolk Deeds, vol. 28, 168 (April 3, 1714), and vol. 41, 283–284 (May 10, 1727). For Thomas Bedunah's landholdings and livestock, see his inventory, 1733, SCPR, FS, vol. 30, 230–231. For Thomas Bedunah's cidermaking endeavors, see Bedona v. Odlin, SF case 13297.

62. For Thomas's possessions, see Thomas Bedunah's inventory, 1733, SCPR, FS, vol. 30, 230–231.

63. For the receipt, see Bedona v. Odlin, SF case 13297. Regardless of whether Thomas wrote the document on file, he somehow kept track of the relevant financial information so that it could be drawn up into the form in which it exists in the records. Thomas, therefore, must have kept at least informal notations along the lines of what Sara T. Damiano describes as "chalk scores" in eighteenth-century New England financial recordkeeping. See Damiano, *To Her Credit: Women, Finance, and the Law in Eighteenth-Century New England Cities* (Baltimore: Johns Hopkins University Press, 2021), 65, 67, 127–128. It is unlikely that Lydia kept track of these records on Thomas's behalf, as she could not write her name; she signed with an uncertain mark that changed in appearance from document to document. See Thomas Bedunah's administrative bond, 1733, Suffolk County Probate Records, File Papers of Thomas Bedunah, #6428, MA Archives; Thomas Bedunah's heirs' agreement, 1734, Suffolk County Probate Records, File Papers of Thomas Bedunah, #6428, MA Archives. As for Thomas's books, they were valued at 20 shillings. See Thomas Bedunah's inventory, 1733, SCPR, FS, vol. 30, 231.

64. See Thomas Bedunah's real estate division, 1734, SCPR, FS, vol. 30, 260.

65. See Thomas Bedunah's inventory, 1733, SCPR, FS, vol. 30, 230–231; Thomas Bedunah's real estate division, 1734, SCPR, FS, vol. 30, 260–261; Thomas Bedunah's warrant to appraise, 1734, SCPR, FS, vol. 30, 261; Thomas Bedunah's estate appraisal, 1734, SCPR, FS, vol. 30, 261; Thomas Bedunah's settlement, 1734, SCPR, FS, vol. 30, 261–262; Thomas Bedunah's bond, 1734, SCPR, NS, vol. 17, 412–413; Ebenezer Bedunah's guardian bond, 1734, SCPR, NS, vol. 18,

507; Ebenezer Bedunah's guardian letter, 1734, SCPR, FS, vol. 30, 245; Moses Bedunah's guardian bond, 1734, SCPR, NS, vol. 18, 227; and Moses Bedunah's guardian letter, 1734, SCPR, FS, vol. 30, 254.

66. For two instances in which Thomas was given the status of a yeoman, see Suffolk Deeds, vol. 28, 168 (April 3, 1714), and vol. 41, 283–284 (May 10, 1727).

67. Thomas Bedunah's heirs' agreement, 1734, SCPR, FS, vol. 30, 262.

68. For the documents that racialized Thomas, see Thomas Bedunah's administrative bond, 1733, Suffolk County Probate Records, File Papers of Thomas Bedunah, #6428, MA Archives, and Thomas Bedunah's letter of administration, 1733, Suffolk County Probate Records, File Papers of Thomas Bedunah, #6428, MA Archives.

69. Sentence of Thomas and Lydia Bedunah, Suffolk County GSP Records, vol. 1702–1712, 32; Document labeled "1707-OCT-001," folder 1–4, Box 1 of 3 (1707–1749), Suffolk County General Sessions of the Peace Additional Papers, MA Archives.

70. This is the way Thomas was described when he sued for nonpayment of debt. See Bedona v. Odlin, Suffolk County CCP Records, vol. 1718–1719, 356.

71. The degree to which white communities in eighteenth-century Massachusetts could reject racial impediments imposed on African-descended people might set this place apart from various others. For the emergence of rigid racial hierarchies in Virginia, see T. H. Breen and Stephen Innes, *"Myne Owne Ground": Race and Freedom on Virginia's Eastern Shore, 1640–1676* (New York: Oxford University Press, 1980); Kathleen M. Brown, *Good Wives, Nasty Wenches, and Anxious Patriarchs: Gender, Race, and Power in Colonial Virginia* (Chapel Hill: University of North Carolina Press, 1996); and Rebecca Goetz, *The Baptism of Early Virginia: How Christianity Created Race* (Baltimore: Johns Hopkins University Press, 2012). For Barbados, see Jerome S. Handler, *The Unappropriated People: Freedmen in the Slave Society of Barbados* (Baltimore: Johns Hopkins University Press, 1974).

72. For the reference to Benjamin as laborer, see Thomas Bedunah's heirs' agreement, 1734, Suffolk County Probate Records, File Papers of Thomas Bedunah, #6428, MA Archives. For Benjamin as husbandman, see Thomas Bedunah's bond, 1734, SCPR, NS, vol. 17, 412. The wording in Ebenezer and Moses's guardianships is identical. Ebenezer Bedunah's guardian letter, 1734, SCPR, FS, vol. 30, 245, and Moses Bedunah's guardian letter, 1734, SCPR, FS, vol. 30, 254.

73. For the baptisms of Elizabeth, Benjamin, Joseph, Abigail, and Ebenezer, all children of Samuel Crafts, see Boston Record Commissioners, *A Report of the Record Commissioners, Containing the Roxbury Land and Church Records* (Boston: Rockwell and Churchill, 1884), 126, 138, 128, 132, and 135. I have reconstructed below the Crafts family using Boston Record Commissioners, *Roxbury Land and Church Records*; *Vital Records of Roxbury, vol. 1*; and James M. Crafts and William F. Crafts, *The Crafts Family: A Genealogical and Biographical History of the Descendants of Griffin and Alice Craft* (Northampton: Gazette Printing Company, 1893).

74. Elizabeth (Seaver) Crafts was married to Lydia's uncle, Samuel Crafts, and two of the couple's children, Samuel Crafts and Ebenezer Crafts, married women named Elizabeth: Elizabeth Sharp and Elizabeth Weld. Lydia's half-siblings, Thomas Crafts and Rebecca (Crafts) Turner, both had children named Elizabeth.

75. Ebenezer and Elizabeth's daughter Elizabeth was born on March 7, 1702, while Thomas and Lydia's Elizabeth was born on November 12, 1703. For the birth of Elizabeth Crafts, see *Vital Records of Roxbury, vol. 1*, 78. For the birth of Elizabeth Bedunah (rendered "Bodoona"), see *Vital Records of Roxbury, vol. 1*, 31.

76. Lydia's father, John Crafts, selected Joseph as the name of his final son by his first marriage (to Rebecca Wheelock). Lydia's aunt, Mary (Crafts) Griggs, married a man named Joseph Griggs. And Lydia's aunt, Hannah (Crafts) Wilson, had a son named Joseph.

77. Lydia's aunt, Abigail (Crafts) Ruggles, was her father's sister. Lydia's sister, Abigail, was the first child born to Lydia's mother, Mary (Hudson) Crafts and her father, John Crafts, after the death of John's prior wife, Rebecca (Wheelock) Crafts. Hannah (Crafts) Wilson, John Crafts, Abigail (Crafts) Ruggles, Samuel Crafts, and Moses Crafts all named daughters Abigail. The only child of Griffin Crafts who did not name a daughter Abigail was Mary (Crafts) Griggs, who died childless.

78. Lydia's uncle, Moses Crafts, named his two successive, and apparently sickly, sons Moses.

79. This Samuel Crafts was the son of Lydia's uncle, Samuel Crafts. He died in 1709, and his widow, Elizabeth (Sharp) Crafts, married James Shed in 1718.

80. See Robert E. Wall, *The Membership of the Massachusetts Bay General Court, 1630–1686* (New York: Garland, 1990), 223; James Savage, John Farmer, and Orlando Perry Dexter, *A Genealogical Dictionary of the First Settlers of New England, Showing Three Generations of Those Who Came Before May, 1692, Vol. III* (Boston: Little, Brown, 1861) 586–588; Crafts and Crafts, *The Crafts Family*, 35, 49, 80; *Vital Records of Roxbury, vol. 1*, 301; and John William Linzee, *The History of Peter Parker and Sarah Ruggles of Roxbury, Mass. and Their Ancestors and Descendants* (Boston: S. Usher, 1913), 216–218.

81. Thomas Bedunah's bond, 1734, SCPR, NS, vol. 17, 412–413; Thomas Bedunah's heirs' agreement, 1734, Suffolk County Probate Records, File Papers of Thomas Bedunah, #6428, MA Archives.

82. These men were John, Edward, and Joseph Ruggles; James Shed; Joseph Williams; and Joseph Weld. Joseph Weld's daughter, Elizabeth, had married John Ruggles in 1731. See Linzee, *The History of Peter Parker*, 155.

83. Bedunah v. Turner, Suffolk County CCP Records, vol. 1739, 264; Bedunah v. Turner, SF case 53073.

84. For the description of Mary as "White," see Petition of Francis Brinley and Increase Sumner, MAC, vol. 73, 414. For the marriage record, see James B. Bell, ed., *The Colonial Records of King's Chapel, 1686–1776, vol. 2* (Boston: Colonial Society of Massachusetts, 2019), 680.

85. Boston Record Commissioners, *Roxbury Land and Church Records*, 146. Joseph was the third person in his immediate family to formalize his commitment to the Roxbury church. In 1708, Lydia "Buddoono," then pregnant with Joseph, had "owned the covenant." See Boston Record Commissioners, *Roxbury Land and Church Records*, 143. And in 1745, Joseph's younger brother, Ebenezer, had done the same. See Boston Record Commissioners, *Roxbury Land and Church Records*, 146.

86. Anne A. Brown and David D. Hall, "Family Strategies and Religious Practice: Baptism and the Lord's Supper in Early New England," in *Lived Religion in America: Toward a History of Practice*, ed. David D. Hall (Princeton: Princeton University Press, 1997), 53–54, 60.

87. For Ebenezer Bedunah's baptism, see Boston Record Commissioners, *Roxbury Land and Church Records*, 146. For Benjamin Bedunah's birth, see *Vital Records of Roxbury, vol. 1*, 24.

88. For Lydia's birth, see *Vital Records of Roxbury, vol. 1*, 24.

89. Boston Record Commissioners, *Roxbury Land and Church Records*, 146.

90. Nehemiah Walter had pastored Roxbury's church since 1688. See Walter Eliot Thwing, *History of the First Church in Roxbury, Massachusetts, 1630–1904* (Boston: W. A. Butterfield, 1908), 90.

91. Bedunah v. Turner, Suffolk County CCP Records, vol. 1739, 264.

92. Henry Cheney's account, 1747, SCPR, NS, vol. 20, 29.

93. Boston Record Commissioners, *Roxbury Land and Church Records*, 146.

94. Francis Brinley and Increase Sumner, both of Roxbury, referred to Joseph this way. See Petition of Francis Brinley and Increase Sumner, MAC, vol. 73, 414. For Increase's involvement in the Roxbury Church, see Boston Record Commissioners, *Roxbury Land and Church Records*, 145, 146.

95. Massachusetts did not limit voting rights by race, which meant that free Black and Indigenous men of sufficient property could cast votes alongside their white neighbors. That voting was seen by people like Francis Brinley as an activity undertaken by white men (and therefore proof of Joseph's supposed "white" status) can be attributed to the economic precarity of many non-white men in eighteenth-century Massachusetts. To vote in province-wide elections, Massachusetts inhabitants had to have forty pounds of property. To vote in town elections, inhabitants had to have a twenty-pound "ratable estate." See Robert J. Dinkin, *Voting in Provincial America: A Study of Elections in the Thirteen Colonies, 1689–1776* (Westport: Greenwood Press, 1977), 32; Robert E. Brown, *Middle-Class Democracy and the Revolution in Massachusetts, 1691–1780* (New York: Harper & Row, 1969), 78–99, 80 ("ratable").

96. The 1656 legislation stipulated that "henceforth no Negroes or Indians . . . shall be armed or permitted to train." See Edgar J. McManus, *Black Bondage in the North* (Syracuse: Syracuse University Press, 1973), 69. This reversed a 1652 law, which provided that "Negroes and Indians inhabiting with or servants to the English" could serve in the military.

97. John Hannigan, "King's Men and Continentals: War and Slavery in Eighteenth-Century Massachusetts" (PhD diss.: Brandeis University, 2021).

98. An "Act for Regulating the Militia" passed in 1693 reinforced the 1656 exclusion of nonwhite people from training with the military: "indians and negro's" were listed with "the persons . . . exempted from all trainings." See *Massachusetts Acts and Resolves, vol. 1*, 130. Despite this exemption, the act stated that "all persons exempted by this law from trainings shall, notwithstanding, be provided with arms and ammunition compleat." Free Black men therefore were not allowed to train, but they *were* required to have arms and ammunition. This requirement was intended to protect the province in case of emergency; in situations of crisis—and these situations only—free men of African descent were supposed to join military efforts. As a 1707 law clarified, "all free male negro's or molatto's, of the age of sixteen years and upward" should report for duty in "case of alarm." If they failed to do so, they would be fined twenty shillings or be required to perform eight days of manual labor for their town. See *Massachusetts Acts and Resolves, vol. 1*, 607.

99. Petition of Francis Brinley and Increase Sumner, MAC, vol. 73, 414.

100. See Michael G. Laramie, *The European Invasion of North America: Colonial Conflict Along the Hudson-Champlain Corridor, 1609–1760* (Santa Barbara: Praeger/ABC-CLIO, 2012), 163–164.

101. See *Massachusetts Acts and Resolves, vol. 1*, 606. See also Hannigan, "King's Men and Continentals," 87–88.

102. The forty-pound fine was levied in "Old Tenor" currency. As Joseph put it, he was forced to "pay the sum of Forty pounds in bills of publick credit of the old tenor." Old Tenor

was only one fourth the value of "New Tenor" currency. Hence, the fine was ten pounds in the new currency. For the consequences of evading impressment for white men, see "An Act for the More Easy Levying and Regulating of Souldiers," *Massachusetts Acts and Resolves, vol. 2*, 226. A similar act, assigning the same punishment to those who evaded service, was passed in 1724. See *Massachusetts Acts and Resolves, vol. 2*, 334. For the relation of "Old Tenor" and "New Tenor" in the late 1740s, see Alvin Rabushka, *Taxation in Colonial America* (Princeton: Princeton University Press, 2008), 578, and Andrew McFarland Davis, *Currency and Banking in the Province of the Massachusetts Bay* (New York: Macmillan, 1901), 166.

103. Certification of Work by Joseph Bedunah, SF case 63849.

104. *Massachusetts Acts and Resolves, vol. 1*, 606.

105. No testimony or legal reasoning for this case survives, and the document produced by the Roxbury selectmen does not actually state who requested it or why. That it is associated with this case is undeniable, as it was produced just over a month before Joseph originally sued Francis, and it mentions Joseph (but no other persons of African ancestry) by name. Careful assessment of the case leads to the conclusion that this document was produced on Joseph's behalf rather than on Francis's, as it confirms that Joseph had been performing faithfully the duties assigned by law to him and the other people of African descent in the town since before the war commenced.

106. In 1749, Joseph won the exact amount of money that he had lost in the whole debacle: ten pounds New Tenor (which Francis had fined him) plus the costs that he had accrued in the process of suing for damages. See Bedunah v. Brinley, SF case 65615. See also Brinley v. Bedunah, Massachusetts SCJ Records, vol. 1747–1750, 148 and 212.

107. Documents produced later in Joseph's life and after his death would make no comment on the man's racial status. See, for instance, the birth records of his children, Lydia and Mary: "Records: Births, Marriages, Deaths, 1630–1785," 179 and 181. Ancestry.com. See also the records related to settling his estate: Joseph Bedunah's administrative letter, 1757, SCPR, FS, vol. 52, 145–146; Joseph Bedunah's inventory, 1757, SCPR, FS, vol. 52, 548; and Joseph Bedunah's accounts, SCPR, FS, vol. 55, 143–144.

108. This woman was charged with having had "two white Children contrary to law." See Sentence of Negro Bess, Suffolk County GSP Records, vol. 1712–1719, 133. Curiously, when Bess's supposed white partner was tried (and ultimately acquitted) by the Massachusetts Superior Court of Judicature, the children were referred to as "negro." So, in this case, the court appears to have strategically chosen to emphasize whichever race was more egregious in each of the trials. For the "negro" children, see Presentation of John Barnard, Massachusetts SCJ Records, vol. 1714–1721, 157.

109. "An Act for the Better Preventing of a Spurious and Mixt Issue," *Massachusetts Acts and Resolves, vol. 1*, 578.

110. Sentence of Elinor Waters, Suffolk County GSP Records, vol. 1702–1712, 153.

111. Presentation of Samuel Miles, Suffolk County GSP Records, vol. 1719–1725, 322.

112. See Gloria McCahon Whiting, "Race, Slavery, and the Problem of Numbers in Early New England: A View from Probate Court," *WMQ* 77, no. 3 (July 2020): 411–420.

113. "An Act for the Regulating of Free Negro's," *Massachusetts Acts and Resolves, vol. 1*, 606. Compulsory roadwork was a substitute for militia duty. Although Joseph did not want to perform military service in the particular instance chronicled in this chapter, by excluding people of African (and Indigenous) ancestry from military service and consigning them instead to menial labor, the Massachusetts legislature characterized them as incapable of

protecting Massachusetts citizens. It was another manifestation of the racialization of the Massachusetts legal code.

114. "An Act for the Better Preventing of a Spurious and Mixt Issue," *Massachusetts Acts and Resolves, vol. 1,* 578.

115. The group to whom these regulations applied included Indigenous people as well as African-descended people and those of mixed racial heritage. Boston Record Commissioners, *A Report of the Record Commissioners of the City of Boston, Containing the Boston Records from 1700 to 1728, vol. 8* (Boston: Rockwell and Churchill, 1883), 106. Boston's selectmen voted to request that the Massachusetts House of Representatives adopt these provisions, and Elisha Cooke presented them to the General Court *thirteen times,* but the legislature never adopted them. See Jared Ross Hardesty, *Unfreedom: Slavery and Dependence in Eighteenth-Century Boston* (New York: New York University Press, 2016), 213 n23.

116. See Eric M. Hanson Plass, "'So Succeeded by a Kind Providence': Communities of Color in Eighteenth Century Boston," (master's thesis, University of Massachusetts, Boston, 2014), 47.

117. See MS 7248, Boston (Mass.) Overseers of the Poor Indentures, BPL. The children in question were Thomas, James, Robert, and Ruth Humphreys, children of John and Betty Humphreys. For "poor" and "deceased," see Indenture of Robert Humphreys to Joseph Dyer, October 6, 1756.

118. That bonds of kinship *could* override racial limitations does not mean that they *did* with any sort of frequency. Other evidence suggests the staying power of racial labels in eastern Massachusetts during the early and mid-eighteenth century. See, for instance, Whiting, "Race, Slavery, and the Problem of Numbers."

119. Of the grandchildren I have been able to place, all have been labeled "white" in the records or not labeled racially at all, which suggests they were racialized as white. None have been identified as people of African descent. Below I provide a sampling of the evidence I have obtained from census, military, birth, baptism, court, and death records. In 1800, Moses and Benjamin Bedunah (sons of Thomas's son Ebenezer) were both described in census records as white males aged forty-five or over. See "Moses Budona," United States Census, 1800, New York, Rensselaer County, Stephentown, 105, and "Benjamin Bedunah," United States Census, 1800, Massachusetts, Norfolk County, Roxbury, 106. In 1780, John Waters Bedunah (son of Thomas's son Ebenezer) was described as "light" complected in military records. See "John Waters," Massachusetts Secretary of the Commonwealth, *Massachusetts Soldiers and Sailors of the Revolutionary War: A Compilation from the Archives,* vol. 16 (Boston: Wright and Potter Print Co, 1896–1908), 695. Like the rest of the records pertaining to Thomas Bedunah's grandchildren, birth records do not indicate non-white status. Take, for instance, the children of just one branch of Thomas and Lydia's offspring, those of Ebenezer and Elizabeth Bedunah: Benjamin, Ebenezer, Mary (or Mercy), Moses, Lydia, Elizabeth, and John Waters. Birth records for most of them are found in *Vital Records of Roxbury, vol. 1,* 24, and baptism records for the majority are found in Boston Record Commissioners, *Roxbury Land and Church Records,* 147, 149, 151, and 155. In none of these records are Thomas's grandchildren noted as non-white, though other people labeled "negroes" were baptized in the Roxbury meetinghouse during that era. Probate records also fail to label racially the Bedunah grandchildren. See, for instance, the records related to the guardianship of Mary Bedunah after her father, Joseph, died: Mary Bedunah's guardian bond, 1758, SCPR, NS, vol. 36, 28, and Mary Bedunah's guardian letter, 1758, SCPR, FS, vol. 53, 15. In addition, court records suggest that

the Bedunah grandchildren were considered white. In 1781, Moses Bedunah (son of Thomas's son Ebenezer), who then lived in Albany, New York, sued a Sturbridge "gentleman" named Asa Coburn for nonpayment of debt. A series of records generated by the Worcester County court refer to Moses not as a "Molatto," but, simply, as "Moses Bedunah of Albany, in the County of Albany, in the state of New York, Husbandman." See Bedunah v. Coburn, SF case 153197. Death records of Thomas and Lydia's grandchildren also suggest that they were considered white by their broader community. In 1799, a forty-year-old woman named Elizabeth Beduner died in Roxbury, almost certainly the Elizabeth Bedunah who was born in Roxbury forty-two years earlier to Ebenezer and Elizabeth Bedunah. Though non-white people were typically described racially, she was not. See *Vital Records of Roxbury, Massachusetts, to the end of the year 1849, vol. 2* (Salem: Essex Institute, 1926), 464. And in 1830, an eighty-year-old woman named Mary Bedunah died in Roxbury, almost surely the Mary Bedunah born to Joseph and Mary Bedunah in Roxbury in the year 1750. This Mary's death record did not suggest that she was "colored," as the record keepers of the time would have put it, but it did specify that she died a "pauper." See *Vital Records of Roxbury, vol. 2*, 464.

120. For an insightful caution that terms like "dark" and "light" can be profoundly unreliable for racial identification, see Sharon Block, *Colonial Complexions: Race and Bodies in Eighteenth-Century America* (Philadelphia: University of Pennsylvania Press, 2018). The "complextion" of "Moses Beduner" in "Descriptive lists" produced by military regiments was both "dark" and "light." Moses, the son of Thomas and Lydia's son, Ebenezer, had extensive military service in the American Revolution under a variety of related names. See records for "Moses Badoonah," "Moses Badooner," "Moses Badumah," "Moses Baduner," "Moses Bdeunah," "Moses Beduna," and "Moses Bedunah," Massachusetts Secretary of the Commonwealth, *Massachusetts Soldiers and Sailors, vol. 1*, 438, 439, 837, and 884.

121. Moses Bedunah, son of Ebenezer and Elizabeth, was born June, 6, 1753. See *Vital Records of Roxbury, vol. 1*, 24. For the family's census record, see "Moses Budona," United States Census, 1800, New York, Rensselaer County, Stephentown, 105. The census taker's decision to record Moses as a white man was intentional; he described others in the town as enslaved and noted as well the presence of a free Black man. See "John Godfree (free Negro)," United States Census, 1800, New York, Rensselaer County, Stephentown, 110.

122. *Massachusetts Soldiers and Sailors*, vol. 1, 884. "Moses Beduner," was described in 1781 as twenty-five years old, five feet and five inches tall, with brown hair and blue eyes. He was a farmer by occupation and had by that time moved from Roxbury in eastern Massachusetts to Sturbridge in central Massachusetts. By the time of the 1800 census, he had moved about a hundred miles farther west, to Stephentown, New York.

Chapter 5

Epigraph: *The Last & Dying Words of MARK, Aged about 30 Years, A Negro Man who belonged to the late Captain John Codman, of Charlestown, Who was executed at Cambridge, the 18th of September, 1755, for Poysoning his abovesaid Master* (Boston, 1755), Massachusetts Historical Society Broadsides Collection, MHS.

1. For the details of the poisoning, see Examination of Phillis, SF case 147038.

2. The story of Mark and his co-conspirators, Phoebe and Phillis, is about the destruction wrought by slavery in especially vivid—and violent—ways: rape, murder, execution, and death. One of the central challenges of writing ethically about the brutality of slavery stems from the archive on which historians depend for their understandings of the past—an archive that was,

in this time and place, largely produced by and for people who were invested in the maintenance of an oppressive slave regime. In recent years, an array of scholars, particularly Black
feminist historians, have produced thoughtful reflections on violence, the writing of history, and the archive. For a sampling of relevant scholarship, see Marisa J. Fuentes, *Dispossessed Lives: Enslaved Women, Violence, and the Archive* (Philadelphia: University of
Pennsylvania Press, 2016); Simon Gikandi, "Rethinking the Archive of Enslavement," *Early
American Literature* 50, no. 1 (2015), 81–102; Saidiya Hartman, *Lose Your Mother: A Journey
Along the Atlantic Slave Route* (New York: Farrar, Straus and Giroux, 2007); Saidiya Hart-
man, "Venus in Two Acts," *Small Axe* 12, no. 2 (June 2008): 1–14; Laura Helton et al., "The
Question of Recovery: An Introduction," *Social Text* 33, no. 4 (December 2015): 1–18; Jenni-
fer L. Morgan, *Reckoning with Slavery: Gender, Kinship, and Capitalism in the Early Black At-
lantic* (Durham: Duke University Press, 2021); and Brian Connolly and Marisa Fuentes,
"Introduction: From Archives of Slavery to Liberated Futures?" *History of the Present* 6, no. 2
(Fall 2016): 105–215.

3. Though no other people were convicted by Massachusetts courts of murdering their
enslavers during the eighteenth century, four were found guilty of murdering members of
their enslavers' families. In 1745, Jeffry, enslaved by Thomas Sandford of Mendon, was convicted of killing Thomas's wife, Tabitha, with a hatchet. Phillis, enslaved by John Greenleaf of
Boston, was sentenced in 1751 for poisoning John's son, John Jr. Five years later, Toney, enslaved by Samuel Johnson of Kittery, was found guilty of drowning Samuel's daughter, Mary.
And, in 1763, Bristol, who lived in Taunton, was convicted of killing Elizabeth McKinstry, the
sister of his enslaver, William McKinstry. All these people were sentenced to death. For Jeffry's case, see Dom. Rex v. Jeffry, Massachusetts SCJ Records, vol. 1740–1745, 218; for Phillis's,
see Dom. Rex v. Phillis, Massachusetts SCJ Records, vol. 1750–1751, 180; for Toney's, see Dom.
Rex v. Toney, Massachusetts SCJ Records, vol. 1755–1756, 250; and for Bristol's, see Dom. Rex
v. Bristol, Massachusetts SCJ Records, vol. 1763–1764, 193.

4. Examination of Mark, SF case 147038. There is toxic resin in the shells of cashew nuts,
so cashews that have not been processed with heat can be poisonous.

5. Henry Caswell arrived in Boston in 1716 on a ship named *Eliza*, which hailed from London. He was described in records kept by Boston's Impost Office as a merchant. See Boston
Record Commissioners, *Records Relating to the Early History of Boston, Containing Miscellaneous Papers, vol. 29* (Boston: Rockwell and Churchill, 1900), 234; also, William Richard Cutter, *Genealogical and Personal Memoirs Relating to the Families of Boston and Eastern
Massachusetts, vol. 4* (New York: Lewis Historical Publishing Co., 1908), 2100–2101.

6. Mark did not provide John Salter's name in his confession, referring to him merely as
"Mr. Salter," but John Salter was the only Salter in Boston identified in records of the time
as a brazier, and his estate was sufficient to support an enslaved person. It is therefore reasonable to assume that John was the brazier in question. For references to John as a brazier, see
Suffolk Deeds vol. 42, 63 (April 12, 1728), and vol. 50, 176 (December 5, 1733). For help sift-
ing through the various Salters in the region, I wish to thank Melinde Lutz Byrne, CG,
FASG, FNGS.

7. See statement of insolvency on Joseph Thomas's estate, 1744, Plymouth County Probate
Records, vol. 9, 319, MA Archives. See also Joseph Thomas's inventory, 1744, Plymouth County
Probate Records, vol. 9, 274, MA Archives. For Mark's description of John, see *The Last & Dying
Words of MARK*. This narration undoubtedly reflects some intervention from the men who
served as witnesses.

8. Mark's statement indicates that he was born in Barbados in 1725. If he was brought to Boston at the age of eight, that would have been in the year 1733. Joseph, his third Massachusetts enslaver, died just ten years later, in 1743. Soon after Joseph's death (though no evidence indicates precisely when), he was sold to John, which made John his fourth Massachusetts enslaver in, say, eleven or twelve years.

9. See Examination of Phillis and Examination of Mark.

10. Mark probably met his wife while he was in the possession of John Codman, as the woman lived in Boston, just across the channel from Charlestown. When Mark lived with Joseph Thomas in Plympton, he was more than forty miles south of Boston—far enough that he would doubtless have had limited access to the port. And when Mark had first lived in Boston with Henry Caswell and John Salter, he had been just a youth, not ready to enter a marriage or father a child. It is also possible that he met the girl who would later become his wife at this early point, was separated from her when sold to Plympton, and reconnected with her upon his return to the Boston area.

11. Examination of Phillis.

12. Phillis stated that John's "Work House" burned, while Mark said that his "Shop" burned. The fire likely burned both John's work house and the shop, which he eventually rebuilt, as both are cataloged in his inventory. The testimony of both Phillis and Mark confirm that Phillis was the one who set the building on fire. Mark adamantly denied doing the deed himself, but he did not deny conceiving of the idea. Nor did he deny encouraging the woman to carry it out. See Examination of Phillis; *The Last & Dying Words of MARK*; and John Codman's inventory, 1755, Middlesex County Probate Records, File Papers of John Codman, #4727, MA Archives.

13. For evidence both of Mark's value and of Joseph's blacksmith enterprise, see Joseph Thomas's inventory, 1744, Plymouth County Probate Records, vol. 9, 273–274, MA Archives. As for John's occupation, the man was sometimes referred to as a "captain" because of his position in the local militia. Historians who have referenced John's murder have regularly interpreted the label "captain" to mean that John was a "sea captain," but I have found no evidence that he ever captained a ship. For references to John as a sea captain, see Abner C. Goodell Jr., "The Murder of Captain Codman," *Proceedings of the Massachusetts Historical Society, vol. 20* (1882–1883): 143; Elise Lemire, *Black Walden: Slavery and Its Aftermath in Concord, Massachusetts* (Philadelphia: University of Pennsylvania Press, 2009), 180; John D. Bessler, *Cruel & Unusual: The American Death Penalty and the Founders' Eighth Amendment* (Boston: Northeastern University Press, 2012), 270. For John as a "Chaizemaker," see Warrant Against Mark, SF case 28037.

14. John's son, John Codman Jr., would put a notice in a Boston newspaper just after Mark's execution to assure "*all his father's customers, and other gentlemen, who want chaises, chairs, or refined iron, that they may be supplied as before,*" see *Boston Gazette*, September 1, 1755, 4. He would repeat this advertisement in the *Boston Gazette* on both September 8 and September 22. Mark apparently did not limit his smithwork to his enslaver's business; he manufactured things for his own use in his shop as well. For instance, he hammered out a "narrow Piece of flat Iron" to serve as a tool for dosing John's arsenic. According to Phillis, Mark told her that Robbin, the man who supplied him with arsenic, had given him such a tool, but he had lost it, so he made a similar one. See Examination of Phillis. For Mark's blacksmith shop, see Examination of Mark.

15. *Independent Advertiser*, June 12, 1749, 2.

16. *New-York Evening Post,* June 19, 1749, 3.

17. Word got around to the men who interrogated Mark following John's murder that Mark had smugly announced that John "had been offer'd £400 for [him] but wou'd not take it, and now he shou'd not have a farthing." See Examination of Mark.

18. Many enslavers had more than enough work to fill their bondspeople's waking hours, and they pushed their workers very hard. But some enslavers found it more profitable to have their bondspeople labor for others and earn a wage (which ordinarily went to the enslaver in full, though occasionally bondspeople were given a small share). See Jared Ross Hardesty, *Unfreedom: Slavery and Dependence in Eighteenth-Century Boston* (New York: New York University Press, 2016), 110–113. There are many court cases in the region's records documenting disagreements between enslavers and those who hired their bondspeople. See, for instance, Luce v. Weatherlags, Suffolk County CCP Records, vol. 1739, 315, and Gordon v. Butler, Suffolk County CCP Records, vol. 1740, 144.

19. *The Last & Dying Words of MARK.*

20. Antonio T. Bly has written extensively on the resistance of Black people to the conditions of slavery in New England, dubbing New England "a hotbed of discord" given that New England's newspapers advertised far more freedom seekers in proportion to the region's enslaved population than did southern newspapers during the mid-eighteenth century. See Antonio T. Bly, *Escaping Bondage: A Documentary History of Runaway Slaves in Eighteenth-Century New England, 1700–1789* (New York: Lexington Books, 2012), 7. See also Bly, "Pretty, Sassy, Cool: Slave Resistance, Agency, and Culture in Eighteenth-Century New England," *New England Quarterly* 89, no 3 (September 2016): 457–492, and Bly, "'Indubitable Signs': Reading Silence as *Text* in New England Runaway Slave Advertisements," *Slavery & Abolition* 42, no. 2 (June 2021): 240–268.

21. For Scipio, see "Bill of Sale of a Negro Servant in Boston, 1724," *New England Historical and Genealogical Register* 18, no. 1 (January 1, 1864): 78. As for Titus, he was swindled by Dinah's enslaver but pursued the case through three Massachusetts courts to ultimate victory. See Titus's Petition, Suffolk County GSP Records, vol. 1725–1732, 116; Titus v. Bill, Suffolk County CCP Records, vol. 1727–1728, 286–287; Titus v. Bill, Massachusetts SCJ Records, vol. 1725–1730, 176. For quotation, see Petition of Titus, SF case 164418.

22. For the successive Mingos, see Ezekiel Price Notarial Records, vol. 1, recorded February 5, 1759, Boston Athenaeum; Ezekiel Price Notarial Records, vol. 1, recorded May 22, 1761, Boston Athenaeum. For Margaret, see Ezekiel Price Notarial Records, vol. 2, recorded December 21, 1762, Boston Athenaeum. The baptisms of several of Lancaster's children are found in the records of King's Chapel, vol. 39, which is unpaginated but proceeds chronologically. The first Lancaster was baptized on September 2, 1757; Margaret was baptized on December 24, 1762; Patience was baptized on October 25, 1765; and the third Lancaster was baptized on December 16, 1767. The deaths of two of the children are also recorded in the church's records: The first Lancaster died in 1759, and the second Lancaster died in 1761 (see vol. 40, 19 and 22). As for the Lancaster who died in 1761, it is worth noting that he was actually recorded as "Lancashire," but so was his father. The record reads: "Lancashire of Lancashire & Margaret." Therefore, the supposed name change was evidently a scribal error. See King's Chapel (Boston, MA) records, Ms N–1867, MHS.

23. Gunney v. How, Writ of Attachment, December 11, 1769, Suffolk County Court of Common Pleas File Papers, Docket no. 187, MA Archives.

24. Besides Phillis, only one enslaved woman was called to testify about the case in court: a woman named Dinah who was bound by a man named Richard Foster. But Dinah lived in Charlestown, not Boston; her enslaver was the sheriff of Middlesex County and she is included on a list of residents of Charlestown who were summoned "to give . . . Evidence . . . against Mark a Negro man & Phillis a Negro woman." See Court Summons, SF case 147038.

25. Holyoke v. Codman, Massachusetts SCJ Records, vol. 1752–1753, 234. This language parallels that used by the courts to deal with strayed livestock; cows, pigs, and horses in Massachusetts regularly were "lost" by their owners and "found" by others. See, for instance, Peter Ball's 1771 appeal of a judgment in favor of William Fillis, who had sued Peter for "converting" William's "lost" cow to "his own Use." For this case, see Ball v. Fillis, Massachusetts SCJ Records, vol. 1771, 212. For insight into how writs of trespass such as these—which had long been used only for the recovery of *things*—came to be used in England and its colonies for the recovery of *people*, see Holly Brewer, "Creating a Common Law of Slavery for England and Its New World Empire," *Law and History Review* 39, no. 4 (November 2021): 765–834.

26. Reading the records of the Massachusetts Superior Court of Judicature page by page turned up eleven instances in which enslaved people were "lost" and "found" using this exact formulation. Of these eleven conflicts, nearly all dealt with people who simply could not have been lost. In most instances, the "lost" workers were found laboring in the same towns in which their enslavers lived. And sometimes the "lost" people were working for white people whom they had clearly known for a long while. For instance, Sue Black (see Chapter 3) was "lost" by Mary West, and "found" by Mary's brother, Shadrach Norton. See Norton v. West, Massachusetts SCJ Records, vol. 1725–1730, 117.

27. For an example of a bondswoman declared "lost" who appears to have chosen to leave her enslaver, consider the case of Letitia, who abandoned a man who mistreated her by returning to her previous enslaver. See Wass v. Gordon, Massachusetts SCJ Records, vol. 1739–1740, 166; Wass v. Gordon, SF case 51176; *Boston Gazette*, April 2, 1739, 4.

28. Jacob Holyoke produced as evidence of his ownership of Cloe a bill of sale from October 1751, which stated that he had given Joseph Goldthwait twenty-six pounds, thirteen shillings, and four pence for "a negro woman sold . . . about 30 year old and by name calld Cloe." See Holyoke v. Codman, SF case 100162.

29. The courts' rulings on this case are confusing. Jacob sued John for fifty pounds, but he lost his case in the Suffolk County Court of Common Pleas; the jury awarded John the costs of the lawsuit. When Jacob appealed to the Superior Court, though, he won thirty pounds. This was close to Cloe's value; Jacob had bought her the year before for twenty-six pounds, thirteen shillings, and four pence. The jury's verdict, penned on a fragment included with the court's file papers, assumed two forms. The jury first awarded Jacob "reversion of the former Judgmt, Possession of the Negro Sued for, & Thirty Shillings mony damages & Costs." But somebody scratched out most of that verdict and replaced it with "thirty pounds lawful mony damages & Costs." And that is what John paid; a scrap of paper filed elsewhere indicated that Jacob was "fully satisfied" with John's thirty pounds. It is possible, then, that John ended up keeping Cloe. In that case, if Cloe was indeed Mark's wife, they would have resided in the same place for a period of time. If John ever owned Cloe, though, it was not for long. When he died three years later, the appraisers of his estate tabulated five bondspeople, none of whom were named Cloe. It is worth noting that most of the cases of "lost" and "found" people did not actually record which party got to keep the bondsperson in question. The most reasonable as-

sumption would probably be that the person went to whomever won the case, along with monetary damages (which the records all specify). If the jury in the suit between John and Jacob followed this pattern, Cloe would have been returned to Boston to live with Jacob. For the relevant court case and file papers, see Holyoke v. Codman, Massachusetts SCJ Records, vol. 1752–1753, 234; Holyoke v. Codman, SF case 100162; and Holyoke v. Codman, SF case 71412. See also John Codman's inventory, 1755, Middlesex County Probate Records, File Papers of John Codman, #4727, MA Archives.

30. *The Last & Dying Words of MARK*.

31. Court records refer to Phillis as a "spinster," and no evidence exists of any familial relationships on the woman's part, so it seems likely that she had no spousal-like connection. See Phillis's Indictment, Massachusetts SCJ Records, vol. 1755–1756, 123.

32. Examination of Quacoe, SF case 147038 ("Called"); *The Last & Dying Words of MARK* ("Husband").

33. Enslaved people generally were not punished for fornication in Massachusetts during the eighteenth century, but fragments from church and court records nonetheless show that people of African descent, not surprisingly, engaged in the same types of sexual behavior outside of marriage that white people did. For instance, Thomas of the Old South Church was "Admonished, & Suspended from ye Communion of ye Chh for several Scandalous Offences," and Betty, a married woman of African descent, was convicted by the province's criminal court of being drunk and "in Bedd with another Negro man." For Thomas, see Old South Church Records, box 1, vol. 1, p. 157, CLA; and, for Betty, see Betty's Sentence, Suffolk County GSP Records, vol. 1702–1712, 232.

34. *Boston Gazette*, July 7, 1755, 2.

35. *The Last & Dying Words of MARK*.

36. For August, see *Boston News-Letter*, March 27, 1760, 3. As for Peter, he wrote a will in which he discussed his earnings from delivering newspapers. See "Will of a Boston Slave, 1743," *Publications of the Colonial Society of Massachusetts, vol. 25: Transactions 1922–1924* (Boston: Colonial Society of Massachusetts, 1924), 253. For James's advertisement, see *Boston News-Letter*, April 20, 1732, 2.

37. For an imaginative scholarly act of repopulating streets and public spaces with people of African descent, see Simon P. Newman, "Hidden in Plain Sight: Escaped Slaves in Late Eighteenth-Century and Early Nineteenth-Century Jamaica," *WMQ* (OI Reader app), June 2018, 1–53, https://oieahc.wm.edu/digital-projects/oi-reader/simon-p-newman-hidden-in-plain-sight/. For the challenge of "imagin[ing] the embodied experience of the enslaved" in another urban space—Bridgetown, Barbados—see Fuentes, *Dispossessed Lives*, 29.

38. *New England Courant*, April 22, 1723, 2; *Boston Evening-Post*, July 15, 1771, 3; Cuffee v. Hall, Suffolk County GSP Records, vol. 1724, 11–12.

39. For gold buttons, see Boston Town Papers, Ms.f Bos.7 Collection, BPL, vol. 3, 102, 103, 104, and vol. 4, 6, 120. For other luxury goods, see Boston Town Papers, vol. 3, 150–151, 212, vol. 4, 6. For the miscellanea, see Boston Town Papers, vol. 3, 103, 150, 212, 359, vol. 4, 6–7, 120. For money, see Boston Town Papers, vol. 3, 212, 272, vol. 4, 120.

40. Boston Town Papers, vol. 3, 212, 359, vol. 4, 120.

41. *Boston Gazette*, August 5, 1734, 4 ("Streets"); *Boston Gazette*, September 18, 1738, 4 ("Honest").

42. Boston Record Commissioners, *Reports of the Record Commissioners of the City of Boston, vol. 11* (Boston: Rockwell and Churchill, 1884), 170.

43. Boston Record Commissioners, *Reports of the Record Commissioners, vol. 13* (Boston: Rockwell and Churchill, 1885) 223–224; *vol. 15* (1886), 2, 188, 127–128, 194, 353–355; *vol. 17* (1887), 30–31, 75–76, 116, 141–142, 170–171, 200–201, 225–226, 246–247, 267, and 284–285.

44. For funerals, see *Reports of the Record Commissioners, vol. 8* (Boston: Rockwell and Churchill, 1883), 176–177. This was reinforced in *vol. 13* (1885), 88, and *vol. 15* (1886), 287. For hogs, see *Reports of the Record Commissioners, vol. 14* (1885), 96. For gambling, see *Reports of the Record Commissioners, vol. 8* (1883), 224.

45. MAC, vol. 47, 243–244.

46. *Boston News-Letter*, September 3, 1705, 2.

47. *Reports of the Record Commissioners, vol. 8* (1883), 174.

48. *Reports of the Record Commissioners, vol. 12* (1885), 139 ("Walk"); *Boston Evening-Post*, April 10, 1738, 4 ("Prevent"); *Reports of the Record Commissioners, vol. 15* (1886), 242 ("restrain"); *Reports of the Record Commissioners, vol. 17* (1887), 26 ("Law"); *Reports of the Record Commissioners, vol. 17* (1887), 257 ("Method").

49. In June, the month Mark procured poison, darkness fell after 9 P.M., which means that Mark broke curfew by being out "after Candle Light." See Examination of Mark. See also, for instance, *Boston News-Letter*, January 16, 1755, 2; *Boston Evening-Post*, January 20, 1755, 1.

50. For the fine, see *Reports of the Record Commissioners, vol. 14* (1885), 315. For the continued orders, see *Reports of the Record Commissioners, vol. 19* (1887), 109.

51. *Reports of the Record Commissioners, vol. 19* (1887), 167.

52. These warnings were repeated time and again, sometimes even in the same newspaper. For examples of warnings in the year 1765, see *Boston Gazette*, October 28, 1765, 2; *Boston Post-Boy*, October 28, 1765, 3; *Boston News-Letter*, October 31, 1765, 1; *Boston Evening-Post*, November 4, 1765, 3; *Boston Post-Boy*, November 4, 1765, 4; *Boston Post-Boy*, November 11, 1765, 4; *Boston Evening-Post*, November 18, 1765, 4; *Boston Evening-Post*, November 25, 1765, 4.

53. *Boston Evening-Post*, December 15, 1766, 3 ("strict"); *Boston Gazette*, November 7, 1768, 3 ("good"); Examination of Mark ("Sunset").

54. Boston Town Papers, vol. 6, 237 ("free"); Boston Town Papers, vol. 7, 127 ("flute"); Boston Town Papers, vol. 7, 85 ("Good"); Boston Town Papers, vol. 7, 199 ("master").

55. *Boston News-Letter*, January 5, 1769, 2 ("addicted"); *New England Weekly Journal*, April 14, 1741, 4 ("will not").

56. Peter's Sentence, Suffolk County GSP Records, vol. 1702–1712, 131; Ceesar's Sentence, Suffolk County GSP Records, vol. 1725–1732, 160; Tom's Sentence, Suffolk County GSP Records, vol. 1735–1780, unpaginated but dated January 22, 1738; Dom. Rex v. Fullerton, Massachusetts SCJ Records, vol. 1747–1750, 223; Nello's Sentence, Suffolk County GSP Records, vol. 1702–1712, 9.

57. Case of John Smith, Suffolk County GSP Records, vol. 1712–1719, 76; Case of Nicholas Butler, Suffolk County GSP Records, vol. 1738–1780, unpaginated but dated August 7, 1770.

58. For Thomas, see Testimony of James Stoule, Seth Smith, Mehitable Smith, and Sarah Kallender, SF case 3008; Vivian R. Johnson, "Zipporah Potter Atkins: The Only Seventeenth-Century African Woman to Purchase Land in Boston," *American Ancestors* 11, no. 2 (Spring 2010): 37. For Mariah, see Mariah's Sentence, Suffolk County GSP Records, vol. 1702–1712, 133.

59. Oliver's Acquittal, Suffolk County GSP Records, vol. 1719–1725, 193. Though acquitted, Oliver was hauled back into court soon after with another charge of "keeping a Disorderly house &c." See Oliver's Recognizance, Suffolk County GSP Records, vol. 1719–1725, 199.

60. Indictment of Rachel Hubbard, Suffolk County GSP Records, vol. 1738–1780, unpaginated, but case was heard in the court session beginning February 15, 1766. Indictment of Thomas Simmons, Suffolk County GSP Records, vol. 1738–1780, unpaginated, but case was heard in the court session beginning January 30, 1770. Indictment of Patrick Carrel, Suffolk County GSP Records, vol. 1738–1780, unpaginated, but case was heard in the court session beginning July 14, 1772.

61. Habersham's Fine, Suffolk County GSP Records, vol. 1725–1732, 128.

62. *Reports of the Record Commissioners, vol. 11* (1884), 107 ("Town"); Indictment of John Bachus, Suffolk County GSP Records, vol. 1738–1780, unpaginated, but case was heard in the court session beginning November 14, 1769.

63. For Basthen and Mingo, see Tay v. Ardley, Suffolk County CCP Records, vol. 1706–1710, 94; Bromfield v. Odlin, Suffolk County CCP Records, vol. 1706–1710, 186. For Jemmy, see Dummer v. Jemmy, Suffolk County CCP Records, vol. 1718–1719, 158–159; Dummer v. Jemmy, Suffolk County CCP Records, vol. 1720–1721, 68–69. For Robert, see Marion v. Cummens, Suffolk County CCP Records, vol. 1721, 384–385. For John, see Cutler v. Freeman, Suffolk County CCP Records, vol. 1722, 253. For Elizabeth, see Fagans v. Barthram, Suffolk County CCP Records, vol. 1725, 181–182. For Peter, see Howell v. Milroe, Suffolk County CCP Records, vol. 1729, 161. For James, see Marion v. Lancaster, Suffolk County CCP Records, vol. 1729, 418–419. For Tully, see Phillips v. Saul, Suffolk County CCP Records, vol. 1731, 109.

64. *New England Courant*, November 16, 1724, 1.

65. *Boston Evening-Post*, January 14, 1740, 4 ("Nocturnal"); *Boston Evening-Post*, January 19, 1738, 2 ("Regale[d] themselves"); *New England Courant*, November 16, 1724, 1 ("Punch"); *Reports of the Record Commissioners, vol. 19*, (1887), 156 ("tipling").

66. Examination of Mark; Examination of Phillis.

67. *Boston Evening-Post*, January 14, 1740, 4 ("Wine"); *New England Courant*, November 16, 1724, 1 ("Sexes"). For "lewd," see Indictment of John Timmings, Suffolk County GSP Records, vol. 1738–1780, unpaginated, but case was heard in the court session beginning November 14, 1769; Indictment of Edward Montgomery, Suffolk County GSP Records, vol. 1738–1780, unpaginated, but case was heard in the court session beginning November 14, 1769; Indictment of John Bachus, Suffolk County GSP Records, vol. 1738–1780, unpaginated, but case was heard in the court session beginning November 14, 1769.

68. Summons of Witnesses, MAC, vol. 282, 109; Case of William Cox, SF case 22497.

69. Interrogation of Sesor, Windsor Inferior Court Records, 1719–1753, vol. 2, 4, Connecticut Historical Society, Hartford, CT.

70. Deposition of Joseph Wait, SF case 163475.

71. *Boston Gazette*, January 6, 1735, 4; *Boston Evening-Post*, December 9, 1751, 3; *Boston Gazette*, May 12, 1760, 2; *Boston News-Letter*, October 25, 1764, 3; *Boston News-Letter*, July 1, 1756, 4.

72. *Boston Gazette*, June 17, 1734, 4 ("Rascally"); *Boston Gazette*, July 30, 1770, 3 ("Lying"); *Boston Gazette*, December 3, 1770, 3 ("impudent"); *Boston News-Letter*, July 29, 1773, 3 ("Acquaintance"). Buyers, too, worried about the social connections of Boston bondspeople. One Boston enslaver sought to purchase a young man but only if he was presently living "out of this Town," *Boston Post-Boy*, August 7, 1769, 2.

73. See Warrant against Mark, SF case 28037. The date is only partially legible on this torn document. It was written on the fifth day of an unknown month in the year 1755. A genealogist who examined it in the 1870s believed that it was written in February, which accords seamlessly

with Phillis's rendering of events. Phillis stated that Mark first proposed the plan to poison John "Some time last Winter." This was, she clarified, "before my Master brought him home from Boston." Then, "a Week or a Fortnight after my Master brought him home from Boston" (perhaps later in February 1755), he proposed the plan again. See Examination of Phillis, also Thomas Bellows Wyman, *The Genealogies and Estates of Charlestown in the County of Middlesex and Commonwealth of Massachusetts, 1629–1818, vol. 2* (Boston: D. Clapp, 1879), 1061.

74. Examination of Phillis. The lead Mark acquired from the bondsman of a Charlestown potter; the arsenic from the bondsman of a Boston apothecary. Not all enslaved people wished to play a role in the plot; Mark applied to a man named Carr, bound to a local doctor named Gibbons, for poison, but Carr declined.

75. Warrant, SF case 147038.

76. The "Gallows Lot," or "Place of Execution," was located at the "extreme northwesterly corner" of the Commons. See Lucius Robinson Paige, *History of Cambridge, Massachusetts, 1630–1877* (Boston: Houghton, 1877), 217. The gallows themselves were located at what is now 2 Walnut Avenue. See Christopher Hail, *Cambridge Buildings and Architects,* Harvard/Radcliffe Online Historical Reference Shelf, last modified on January 21, 2003, https://wayback .archive-it.org/5488/20170330145516/http://hul.harvard.edu/lib/archives/refshelf/cba/.

77. *Boston Evening Post*, September 22, 1755, 4. Phillis was prosecuted for the English common-law offense of petit treason, which was reserved for the murder of one's superior. It could be used when a wife killed her husband, when a clergyman killed his prelate, or when a servant or an enslaved person killed his or her master or mistress. The sentence for women who committed this crime was death by burning, and the sentence for male offenders was death by hanging. See Goodell, "The Murder of Captain Codman," 148.

78. Josiah Bartlett, *An Historical Sketch of Charlestown in the County of Middlesex, and Commonwealth of Massachusetts, Read to an Assembly of Citizens at the Opening of Washington Hall, Nov. 16, 1813* (Boston: John Eliot, 1814), 6.

79. It is impossible to know with certainty whether the case had already been heard in the Superior Court because of the court's habit of dating the beginning and the end of a court session but not noting the actual day on which it heard a particular case. The case of Mark and Phillis was heard sometime during the session that began on August 5 and ended on August 19. One way or the other, it was clear to the appraisers by the time of the August 13 inventory that Mark and Phillis would be executed, while Phoebe would be kept on the estate or sold (retaining in either instance her value of two hundred pounds). John Codman's inventory, 1755, Middlesex County Probate Records, File Papers of John Codman, #4727, MA Archives.

80. Linda Kealey suggested that Phoebe was John's enslaved "mistress," and Jared Hardesty contended that John abused Phoebe sexually. See Linda Marie Kealey, "Crime and Society in Massachusetts in the Second Half of the Eighteenth Century" (PhD diss.: University of Toronto, 1982), 82, and Hardesty, *Unfreedom,* 68–69.

81. John faced a good deal of loss early in life; he was orphaned at the age of eleven and suffered the death of a sibling soon after. See Lemire, *Black Walden,* 49.

82. *The Last & Dying Words of MARK.*

83. Examination of Mark.

84. *The Last & Dying Words of MARK.* Curiously, part of this statement is attributed to Phillis in Mark's court testimony, which suggests that either the men interrogating Mark on behalf of the Superior Court or the men recording Mark's final words for circulation through-

out the town made an error. Because the statement is rendered more fully and with more context in *The Last & Dying Words of MARK*, it seems that this account is the more reliable of the two.

85. For the prevalence of mixed-race people in the eighteenth-century South, especially the Chesapeake, and for the "openness" of white men to pursuing sex with Black women in South Carolina, see Philip D. Morgan, *Slave Counterpoint: Black Culture in the Eighteenth-Century Chesapeake and Lowcountry* (Chapel Hill: University of North Carolina Press, 1998), 399, 406. For racial mixing in the British Caribbean, see Morgan, *Slave Counterpoint*, 407, and Daniel Livesay, *Children of Uncertain Future: Mixed-Race Jamaicans in Britain and the At-lantic, 1733–1833* (Chapel Hill: University of North Carolina Press, 2018), 18. In New England, there was less of a demographic foundation for racial mixing than there was in many other parts of the British Atlantic world because the population of Black people in the region was so small: During the mid-eighteenth century, more than thirty white people lived in the region for every New Englander of African descent. Nonetheless, the growth of New England's mixed-race population over the course of the eighteenth century makes the reality of inter-racial sex in the region undeniable. See Robert V. Wells, *The Population of the British Colonies in America Before 1776* (Princeton: Princeton University Press, 1975) 69–109, and Bly, "Pretty, Sassy, Cool," 468.

86. For the Massachusetts law, see "An Act for the Better Preventing of a Spurious and Mixt Issue" in *Massachusetts Acts and Resolves, vol. 1* (Boston: Wright and Potter, 1869), 578. The act stipulated that white offenders—both male and female—were to be whipped and to maintain the children that resulted from their sexual encounter(s). In addition, white male offenders were required to pay a five-pound fine, which means that—in contrast to such leg-islation elsewhere—the penalty for men was stiffer than that for women.

87. According to a 1691 legal code, white women who gave birth to mixed-race children were subject to punishment, but there were no consequences stipulated in the legislation for white men who engaged in sex out of wedlock with Black women. See Peter W. Bardaglio, "'Shameful Matches': The Regulation of Interracial Sex and Marriage in the South Before 1900," in *Sex, Love, Race: Crossing Boundaries in North American History*, ed. Martha Hodes (New York: New York University Press, 1999), 115; also "An Act for Suppressing Outlying Slaves," in *A Documentary History of Slavery in North America*, ed. Willie Lee Rose (Athens: University of Georgia Press, 1999), 21.

88. Kirsten Fischer, *Suspect Relations: Sex, Race, and Resistance in Colonial North Caro-lina* (Ithaca, NY: Cornell University Press, 2002), 123–124.

89. Bardaglio, "Shameful Matches," 114–115; "An Act Concerning Negro Slaves," in *Pro-ceedings and Acts of the General Assembly of Maryland, April, 1684–June, 1692*, ed. William Hand Browne (Baltimore: Maryland Historical Society, 1894), 546–549.

90. Because Massachusetts had no full-fledged code of laws to govern its enslaved in-habitants, its legal apparatus often dealt with bound people of African descent according to English laws governing servants. On Black testimony and judicial recourse, see Scott Han-cock, "'The Law Will Make You Smart': Legal Consciousness, Rights Rhetoric, and African American Identity Formation in Massachusetts, 1641–1855" (PhD diss., University of New Hampshire, 1999), 3, chap. 1; Hardesty, *Unfreedom*, 141; Edgar J. McManus, *Black Bondage in the North* (Syracuse: Syracuse University Press, 1973), 68; and Robert C. Twombly and Rob-ert H. Moore, "Black Puritan: The Negro in Seventeenth-Century Massachusetts," *WMQ* 24, no. 2 (April 1967): 224–242, esp. 228.

91. According to Sharon Block, the "few pre-Revolutionary sexual assault charges brought on behalf of black women" in colonial North America took place in Massachusetts. See Sharon Block, *Rape and Sexual Power in Early America* (Chapel Hill: University of North Carolina Press, 2006), 177.

92. *Sewall Diary*, 3, 128, April 24, 1717; William Henry Whitmore, *The Massachusetts Civil List for the Colonial and Provincial Periods, 1630–1774* (Albany: J. Munsell, 1870), 69.

93. For a sampling of the voluminous scholarship on the exploitation of enslaved women in the nineteenth-century South, see Thelma Jennings, "'Us Colored Women Had to Go Through a Plenty': Sexual Exploitation of African-American Slave Women," *Journal of Women's History* 1, no. 3 (Winter 1990): 45–74; Deborah Gray White, *Ar'n't I a Woman? Female Slaves in the Plantation South* (New York: Norton, 1999), 29–44; Saidiya Hartman, *Scenes of Subjection: Terror, Slavery, and Self-Making in Nineteenth-Century America* (New York: Oxford University Press, 1997), 79–112; Brenda Stevenson, *Life in Black and White: Family and Community in the Slave South* (New York: Oxford University Press, 1996), 236–243; and Stephanie M. H. Camp, *Closer to Freedom: Enslaved Women and Everyday Resistance in the Plantation South* (Chapel Hill: University of North Carolina Press, 2004), 41–43. For meditations on the psychological consequences of the abuse of enslaved women, see Nell Irvin Painter, "Soul Murder and Slavery: Toward a Fully Loaded Cost Accounting," in *U.S. History as Women's History: New Feminist Essays,* ed. Linda K. Kerber, Alice Kessler-Harris, and Kathryn Kish Sklar (Chapel Hill: University of North Carolina Press, 1995), 125–146. It is worth noting that the sexual coercion of bondswomen was carried out in New England not only by white men but also by Black men. For an enslaved woman raped by an African bondsman in her household (at the prompting of their enslaver), see Wendy Anne Warren, "The Cause of Her Grief: The Rape of a Slave in Early New England," *JAH* 93, no. 4 (March 2007): 1031–1049.

94. Joseph's brothers, James Otis and Samuel Allyne Otis, and his sister, Mercy Otis Warren, would all rise to prominence in the revolutionary era.

95. For a new and insightful analysis of this case, see Emily Jeannine Clark, "'Their Negro Nanny was with Child by a white man': Gossip, Sex, and Slavery in an Eighteenth-Century New England Town," *WMQ* 79, no. 4 (October 2022): 533–562.

96. Otis v. Hinkley, SF case 62026. *Oxford English Dictionary*, August 2021, s.v. "abroad," available at OED Online.

97. Thomas Jenkins's Deposition, SF case 169647.

98. For two reasons, it seems most likely that Isaac's mention of "some such Instances" to the miller was a reference to other households rather than to Isaac's own. First, a different deposition quoted Isaac as saying the very same thing with reference to other households. And, second, it is doubtful that Isaac would have wanted to draw attention to his own sexual abuse of Nanny at this time. However, it is possible, as Clark suggested, that Isaac was referring in this conversation to his own assaults on Nanny. For Isaac's statements, see Otis v. Hinkley, SF case 62026. See also Clark, "Their Negro Nanny was with Child by a white man," 551.

99. Otis v. Hinkley, SF case 62026.

100. Sharon Block argued that female servants and enslaved women were expected to "sexually serve" those who owned them throughout the mainland British colonies. See Block, *Rape and Sexual Power,* 65–74, quotation 66.

101. Otis v. Hinkley, SF case 62026. The proportion of Native laborers in Barnstable County was doubtless higher than it was in Suffolk County. See Gloria McCahon Whiting, "Race, Slavery, and the Problem of Numbers in Early New England: A View from Probate Court," *WMQ*

77, no. 3 (July 2020): 411–427, as well as Simeon L. Deyo, ed., *History of Barnstable County, Massachusetts, 1620–1890* (New York: H. W. Blake, 1890), 18, which states that Barnstable County had more than 500 Native inhabitants in the mid-eighteenth century. It is important to note that bound white women were also vulnerable to sexual abuse—both in Massachusetts and elsewhere in North America. See, for instance, Linda Marie Kealey, "Crime and Society in Massachusetts in the Second Half of the Eighteenth Century," 97–98, and Fischer, *Suspect Relations*, 101–110.

102. Examination of Phillis.

103. Examination of Mark; Examination of Phillis.

104. Examination of Mark.

105. In nearby Suffolk County, where slaveholdings were even larger than in Charlestown's Middlesex County, 942 households claimed 1,736 enslaved people during the middle of the eighteenth century (1725–1774). This means that the average enslaver bound 1.8 people. According to probate, there was little change from the second quarter of the eighteenth century to the third; enslavers claimed 1.8 bondspeople per household in both periods. During this same period of time, merely 12 of 942 estates (1.3 percent) claimed seven or more enslaved people.

106. For Tom, see John Hobby's inventory, 1712, SCPR, FS, vol. 17, 426. For Jemey, see Samuel Greenwood's inventory, 1722, SCPR, FS, vol. 22, 642, 644. For Sharper, see John Rogers's inventory, 1724, SCPR, FS, vol. 23, 360. For Will, see Charles Chauncy's inventory, 1711, SCPR, FS, vol. 17, 440–441.

107. Thadeus Maccarty's inventory, 1729, SCPR, FS, vol. 27, 228; David Ochterlony's inventory, 1766, SCPR, FS, vol. 65, 199; Thomas Smith's inventory, 1742, SCPR, FS, vol. 36, 124.

108. For Sharper and Nancy, see Arthur Savage's inventory, 1735, SCPR, FS, vol. 32, 206. For the "Back Garrett" and "Front Garrett," see Josiah Langdon's inventory, 1743, SCPR, FS, vol. 36, 314. For Phillis and Cato, see William Lambert's inventory, 1750, SCPR, FS, vol. 43, 387.

109. See Examination of Quacoe. Bedfellows were hardly unusual in eighteenth-century Massachusetts; other people, such as apprentices and children, slept together as well.

110. For Toney and Tom, see Elizur Holyoke's inventory, 1712, SCPR, FS, vol. 17, 408–411. For Pompey, see Samuel Greenwood's inventory, 1722, SCPR, FS, vol. 36, 69. For Boston, see Richard Hunnewell's inventory, 1748, SCPR, NS, vol. 27, 116.

111. In inventory after inventory, those beds not described as "Negro beds" are found in these lower rooms of the home. Of course, enslaved people sometimes slept together on the ground floor of their enslavers' houses as well; beds for Boston, Belinda, and Titus were found in the "North Back Chamber" of John Valentine's home, while the bedding of Joshua Wroe's bondspeople was in the kitchen. See John Valentine's inventory, 1724, SCPR, FS, vol. 23, 246; Joshua Wroe's inventory, 1730, SCPR, FS, vol. 28, 110.

112. *A Few Lines on Occasion of the Untimely End of Mark and Phillis, Who Were Executed at Cambridge, September 18th for Poysoning Their Master, Capt. John Codman of Charlestown* (Boston: Thomas Fleet [?], 1755).

113. John Winthrop, *Interleaved Almanac*, 1755, HUA.

114. *Boston Evening Post*, September 22, 1755, 4.

Chapter 6

Epigraph: Petition for freedom to Massachusetts Governor Thomas Gage, His Majesty's Council, and the House of Representatives, May 25, 1774, 1–2, Jeremy Belknap Papers, MHS.

1. For the remedies, see George E. Gifford Jr., "Botanic Remedies in Colonial Massachusetts, 1620–1820," in *Medicine in Colonial Massachusetts, 1620–1820* (Boston: Colonial Society of Massachusetts, 1980), 281, 273; Cotton Tufts, *Receipt Book of Cotton Tufts, 1773–1784*, sequence 66, B MS b11.1, Countway Library of Medicine, Boston, Massachusetts. For the custom of watching, see Erik R. Seeman, "'She Died Like Good Old Jacob': Deathbed Scenes and Inversions of Power in New England, 1675–1775," *Proceedings of the American Antiquarian Society* 104 (October 1994), 289–290. For the gunshots, see John Marrett, "Extracts from Rev. John Marrett's Interleaved Almanacs for 1775, and 1776, not elsewhere noticed," in *History of Middlesex County, Massachusetts, with Biographical Sketches of Many of Its Pioneers and Prominent Men, vol. 1*, ed. D. Hamilton Hurd (Philadelphia: J. W. Lewis, 1890), 676.

2. For the fever, see Samuel Sewall, *The History of Woburn, Middlesex County, Mass., from the Grant of Its Territory to Charlestown, in 1640, to the Year 1860* (Boston: Wiggin and Lunt, 1868), 573 n7. For Darby's birthdate, see Suffolk Deeds, vol. 387, 122 (September 9, 1835). For "tender," see Samuel Francis Batchelder, *Notes on Colonel Henry Vassall (1721–1769): His Wife Penelope Royall, His House at Cambridge and His Slaves Toby and Darby* (Cambridge, MA: publisher not identified, 1917), 74.

3. Marrett, "Extracts from Rev. John Marrett's Interleaved Almanacs," 675. Jacqueline Barbara Carr, *After the Siege: A Social History of Boston: 1775–1800* (Boston: Northeastern University Press, 2005), 13–42.

4. For Paul Revere's encounter with Mark's remains, see "A Letter from Col. Paul Revere to the Corresponding Secretary," in *Collections of the Massachusetts Historical Society, for the Year 1798* (Boston: Samuel Hall, 1798), 107–108.

5. Marrett, "Extracts from Rev. John Marrett's Interleaved Almanacs," 676.

6. Thomas C. Amory, "A Home of the Olden Time," *New England Historical and Genealogical Register* 25 (Boston: New England Historic Genealogical Society, 1871): 44–45.

7. Amory, "A Home of the Olden Time," 44–45. This exchange was first published in an article about the Longfellow House in 1871. The swinging boy was supposedly "Tonie Vassall," but the writer must have confused Anthony (the father) with Darby (the son). Anthony was most certainly not a "boy" when Washington lived in the Vassall mansion: He had already fathered several children, and, had he been a young man when Henry Vassall brought him from Jamaica to Massachusetts, he would have been around fifty-five years old in 1775. All clues indicate that the boy swinging on the gate in 1775 was, instead, Darby. First, Darby was actually a boy in 1775; he would have been six at the time. Second, the person who recalled this anecdote in print remarked that "Tonie lived to a great age," which was something that Darby did as well; he died at ninety-two, while both of his brothers died as young men. Third, Darby lived long into the nineteenth century, which means that a statement made by him about George's manners (or lack thereof) could have easily been remembered in 1871; Darby's death in 1861 preceded the print version of this story by only ten years. The anecdote rings true, in part because the divergence between the boy's understanding of his status and the general's ideas about bondage reflects the way in which slavery was transforming in the province at this very moment. It is not surprising that a local Black child who had left his enslaver's household better understood the dynamics of slavery and freedom in eastern Massachusetts than a southern man who had only just appeared on the scene.

8. For the groundbreaking study of how the American War for Independence emboldened people of African descent to claim independence themselves, see Benjamin Quarles, *The Negro in the American Revolution* (Chapel Hill: University of North Carolina Press, 1996).

9. A vibrant and growing body of scholarship sheds light on African American families and the process of emancipation. Most of it is situated temporally in the nineteenth century and tells stories of enslaved people in the South. This chapter seeks to complement it by examining freedom in a very different context. See, for example, Ira Berlin and Leslie S. Rowland, eds., *Families and Freedom: A Documentary History of African-American Kinship in the Civil War Era* (New York: New Press, 1998); Wilma Dunaway, *The African-American Family in Slavery and Emancipation* (New York: Cambridge University Press, 2003); Tera W. Hunter, *Bound in Wedlock: Slave and Free Black Marriage in the Nineteenth Century* (Cambridge: Harvard University Press, 2017); Annette Gordon-Reed, *The Hemingses of Monticello* (New York: Norton, 2008); Herbert Gutman, *The Black Family in Slavery and Freedom* (New York: Vintage Books, 1977); Dylan C. Penningroth, *The Claims of Kinfolk: African American Property and Community in the Nineteenth-Century South* (Chapel Hill: University of North Carolina Press, 2004); Elizabeth Regosin, *Freedom's Promise: Ex-Slave Families and Citizenship in the Age of Emancipation* (Charlottesville: University Press of Virginia, 2002); and Heather Andrea Williams, *Help Me to Find My People: The African American Search for Family Lost in Slavery* (Chapel Hill: University of North Carolina Press, 2016).

10. David Barry Gaspar, *Bondmen and Rebels: A Study of Master-Slave Relations in Antigua* (Durham: Duke University Press, 1993). Gaspar concluded that the plot was "not a figment of slaveowners' paranoia," 12. However, not all scholars are so confident. See, for example, Jason T. Sharples, "Hearing Whispers, Casting Shadows: Jailhouse Conversation and the Production of Knowledge During the Antigua Slave Conspiracy Investigation of 1736," in *Buried Lives: Incarcerated in Early America*, ed. Michele Lise Tarter and Richard Bell (Athens: University of Georgia Press, 2012), 35–59.

11. Alexandra A. Chan, *Slavery in the Age of Reason: Archaeology at a New England Farm* (Knoxville: University of Tennessee Press, 2015), 54; Gaspar, *Bondmen and Rebels*, 32–33, 35–36; Waldemar Westergaard, "Account of the Negro Rebellion on St. Croix, Danish West Indies, 1759," *Journal of Negro History* 11, no. 1 (January 1926): 55. I wish to thank Aabid Allibhai for the Westergaard reference.

12. Many years later, Anthony's son, Darby, would claim that his father hailed originally from Spain. See Batchelder, *Notes on Colonel Henry Vassall*, 62 n2. Darby maintained this until the end of his life; his death record specifies Spain as his father's birthplace. See *Deaths Registered in the City of Boston for the year eighteen hundred and sixty-one*, Massachusetts Vital Records, 1840–1911, number 3163, New England Historic Genealogical Society, Boston, Massachusetts.

13. No record of their marriage survives, but the couple made a commitment to one another in the middle of the eighteenth century that they—and others—long recognized as a legitimate union. In the 1780s, Anthony would call Cuba "his wife" in petitions he submitted to the Massachusetts assembly. Upon Anthony's death in 1811, the administrator of his estate would petition the local judge of probate on Cuba's behalf, stating that she was Anthony's "lawful married wife" and asking that she be "entitled to her apparel and such other of the personal estate of said deceased . . . according to her quality and degree." The judge would approve the request. The same year, Cuba would petition the state for permission to collect Anthony's pension, a request that was approved. And when Cuba herself died the following year, in 1812, Boston's *Columbian Centinel* would describe her as Anthony's "relict." See Petition of Anthony and Coby Vassall, MAC, vol. 186, 313–314, and Petition of Anthony Vassall, MAC, vol. 231, 115–117; letters to and from James Prescott, Judge of Probate, 1811, File Papers of Antony Vassall, #23335, Middlesex County Probate Records, MA Archives; Petition of Cuby Vassall,

Massachusetts Anti-Slavery and Anti-Segregation Petitions, Passed Resolves, Resolves 1811, c. 154, SCI/Series 228, MA Archives, https://nrs.lib.harvard.edu/urn-3:fhcl:12208688; and *Columbian Centinel*, September 19, 1812, 2.

14. No record of Flora's birth exists, but later records confirm that she was indeed the daughter of Cuba and Anthony. Her deed of emancipation confirmed her parentage explicitly. See Middlesex Deeds, vol. 73, 457 (December 9, 1772). And she is recorded as an heir of Anthony Vassall's estate alongside her siblings. See Anthony's real estate division, 1813, File Papers of Antony Vassall, #23335, Middlesex County Probate Records, MA Archives. As for Dorrenda, she died in 1784, possibly quite young. See Thomas W. Baldwin, *Vital Records of Cambridge, Massachusetts, to the Year 1850, vol. 2* (Boston: Wright & Potter Printing Co., 1915), 772. Although Dorrenda lived in the Vassall household and shared the Vassall surname, it is possible that she was unrelated; I have not been able to find conclusive proof linking her to the family.

It is extraordinarily difficult to reconstruct the family's early years, as the documentary record, so rich in evidence of the white Vassalls, is nearly silent on those they bound. Cambridge's Christ Church, which the Black Vassalls attended alongside their enslavers, did not record the children's baptisms. Cambridge's town clerk did not record the children's births. And neither Henry nor Penelope left much evidence of Anthony and Cuba's growing family. One of the only clues to the existence of the household's bondspeople at midcentury was produced by East Apthorp, Christ Church's pastor, who noted that Henry's "family" numbered ten persons in 1763. Henry and Penelope had only one child, so the tally suggests that the Vassall household had seven enslaved members. See William Stevens Perry, ed., *Papers Relating to the History of the Church in Massachusetts, A.D. 1676–1785* (Hartford [?]: privately printed, 1873), 502. Unfortunately, the minister did not list these seven enslaved people or provide any information about them. Were they all part of Anthony and Cuba's family, or were some unrelated?

15. See Batchelder, *Notes on Colonel Henry Vassall*, 38.

16. John Rowe, a prominent Boston merchant and friend of Henry Vassall, wrote about the gravity of Henry's financial situation in 1765. Diary entries spanning January 8 through March 23 mention a series of meetings he attended with Henry and others related to "the Settlement of Colo[nel] Henry Vassalls affairs." See John Rowe diaries, vol. 1, p. 92 (February 18, 1765), Ms. N-814, MHS. For the sale of the enslaved people on Antigua, see Rowe, vol. 1, p. 97 (February 28, 1765). For the sale of the Cambridge land, see Middlesex Deeds, vol. 65, 146–147 (October 28, 1765). For the mortgage of Henry's home, see Middlesex Deeds, vol. 67, 205 (September 30, 1767).

17. At some point, Flora was sold away from the family. Extant records do not indicate when this happened, but it seems likely that the sale was prompted by this financial crisis. Anthony purchased the girl's freedom from a Billerica couple in December, 1772. See Middlesex Deeds, vol. 73, 457 (December 9, 1772).

18. See Batchelder, *Notes on Colonel Henry Vassall*, 44, 74.

19. Some of the extended Vassall family overtly collaborated with British officials in the months leading up to the outbreak of the war. For instance, Thomas Oliver, brother-in-law of John Vassall, agreed to assume the post of lieutenant governor of Massachusetts, while John volunteered to serve on the so-called Mandamus Council of men appointed by the Crown to support the royal governor—a council that was wildly unpopular from its 1774 inception.

20. "Lieut[enant] Governor Oliver to Secretary Dartmouth," *Publications of the Colonial Society of Massachusetts, vol. 32* (Boston: Colonial Society of Massachusetts, 1937), 486. The farmers were angry that the Massachusetts Government Act limited the ability of colonists to elect local officials and representatives, and they were marching in response to the decision of the royal governor of Massachusetts to move stores of gunpowder out of the countryside into British-occupied Boston—that is, out of their reach.

21. J. L. Bell, *George Washington's Headquarters and Home, Cambridge, Massachusetts* (Washington, DC: National Park Service, U.S. Department of the Interior, 2012), 48, 50, and 86.

22. Petition of Anthony Vassall, MAC, vol. 231, 115–116.

23. Arthur Zilversmit contended that residents of Massachusetts understood the Quock Walker case as outlawing slavery. See Arthur Zilversmit, "Quock Walker, Mumbet, and the Abolition of Slavery in Massachusetts," *WMQ* 25, no. 4 (October 1968): 614–624. A. Leon Higginbotham Jr. summarized historical consensus in 1973 thus: "After the adoption of the Massachusetts Bill of Rights in 1780 and by subsequent judicial decisions declaring the freedom of Quock-Walker, slavery was abolished in Massachusetts in the 1780s." See A. Leon Higginbotham Jr., "Racism and the American Legal Process," *Annals of the American Academy of Political and Social Science* 407 (May 1973): 13. Because of this interpretation's long reign, offhand allusions to the Quock Walker case and the end of slavery in Massachusetts are common. For recent such mentions, see Kate Masur, *Until Justice Be Done: America's First Civil Rights Movement, from the Revolution to Reconstruction* (New York: Norton, 2021), 10, and Van Gosse, *The First Reconstruction: Black Politics in America from the Revolution to the Civil War* (Chapel Hill: University of North Carolina Press, 2021), 166.

24. For the documentation of Dick, see MAC, vol. 215, 378–379, 382–384, and 389a. For Dick as a "Free Negro," see 382.

25. This paragraph draws from my study of slaveholding in the probate records of Massachusetts's largest county, Suffolk. See Gloria McCahon Whiting, "Emancipation Without the Courts or Constitution: The Case of Revolutionary Massachusetts," *Slavery & Abolition* 41, no. 3 (September 2020): 458–478.

26. For a corroborating assessment that slavery on the eve of the American Revolution remained "firmly entrenched" in New England, see Joanne Pope Melish, *Disowning Slavery: Gradual Emancipation and "Race" in New England, 1780–1860* (Ithaca: Cornell University Press, 1998), 56.

27. John Vassall's inventory, 1778, File Papers of John Vassall, #23340, Middlesex County Probate Records, MA Archives; Penelope Vassall's inventory, 1778, File Papers of Penelope Vassall, #23342, Middlesex County Probate Records, MA Archives.

28. Whiting, "Emancipation Without the Courts or Constitution," 464–465.

29. *Independent Chronicle*, October 10, 1776, 2 ("HEARTY"); *Independent Chronicle*, January 9, 1777, 2, January 16, 1777, 4, and January 23, 1777, 4 ("Work"); *Independent Chronicle*, September 2, 1779, 4 ("labour"); *Independent Chronicle*, January 9, 1777, 2 ("Country").

30. *Continental Journal*, June 26, 1777, 3, and *Independent Chronicle*, June 26, 1777, 3 ("Free'd"); *Boston Gazette*, August 11, 1777, 3, August 18, 1777, 4, and August 25, 1777, 4 ("few"); *Evening Post and General Advertiser*, June 26, 1779, 4, and July 3, 1779, 4 ("seven").

31. *Independent Ledger*, September 13, 1779, 2, September 20, 1779, 4, September 27, 1779, 4, and October 4, 1779, 4 ("small"); *Independent Chronicle*, December 10, 1779, 3, December 16, 1779, 4, and December 30, 1779, 3 ("Boy").

32. *Continental Journal*, June 8, 1780, 3, and June 15, 1780, 1 ("age"); *Boston Gazette*, June 19, 1780, 3 ("time"); *Continental Journal*, August 24, 1780, 2, and August 31, 1780, 4, ("term"). These notices were posted in 1780, but before the state's constitution became effective.

33. *Boston News-Letter*, November 3, 1774, 3 ("indented"); *Independent Chronicle*, September 3, 1778, 4 ("bound").

34. *Boston Gazette*, August 11, 1777, 3, August 18, 1777, 4, and August 25, 1777, 4 ("large"); *Boston Gazette*, February 23, 1778, 3, and March 2, 1778, 4 ("good").

35. Boston was the center of print culture for all New England—and people posted for-sale advertisements from as far away as New York and freedom-seeker notices from as far away as South Carolina. This might help explain why such ads continued to be printed in Boston papers even after local practices of slaveholding appear to have come to an end. As for the advent of new ways of describing Black people and their bondage in this period, my observation is based on an analysis of 13,791 mentions of the term "negro" and about 800 mentions of the term "mulatto" (spelled eight different ways) in Massachusetts newspapers (most of which were printed in Boston) between 1704, when the first paper circulated, and 1790. Though every relevant newspaper archived in the *America's Historical Newspapers* database as of September 2020 was searched, this is an imperfect method by which to obtain all possible mentions of people of African descent in area newspapers for multiple reasons: not all newspaper issues survive, the database's search function is not fully reliable, and some advertisements might have used different terms or spelling. However, reading printed weeklies line by line determined that "negro" was the descriptor most often used by those looking to sell, buy, or find bound people of African descent in newspapers, which suggests—notwithstanding missing newspaper issues and missed hits—that such a search is a useful way to measure trends in discussing Black people in slavery or servitude.

36. For the recall of British General Thomas Gage, one-time military governor of Massachusetts, see John Richard Alden, *General Gage in America: Being Principally a History of His Role in the American Revolution* (Baton Rouge: Louisiana State University Press, 1948), 272–286.

37. Petition of Joseph Johnson, MAC, vol. 168, 445.

38. Petition of Cuba, MAC, vol. 168, 31–32.

39. RESOLVE FORBIDDING THE SALE OF NEGRO CAPTIVES, passed September 16, 1776, Chap. 324, in *Acts and Resolves, public and private, of the Province of the Massachusetts Bay* (Boston, 1918), 568; Massachusetts Historical Society, *Journals of the House of Representatives of Massachusetts, 1776, vol. 52, part 1* (Boston: Massachusetts Historical Society, 1985), 105–106, 109; and Resolve, MAC, vol. 215, 95–96.

40. Petition of Hugh Munro, MAC, vol. 166, 211.

41. It is worth noting that as a result of the 1772 Somerset case, once these two enslaved people arrived in Britain, they would enter a liminal state similar to what they might have experienced in eastern Massachusetts, and they would benefit from a legal guarantee that they could not forcibly be taken to slaveholding colonies.

42. Petition of Robert Pierpoint, MAC, vol. 167, 400.

43. Petition of David Mitchell, MAC, vol. 169, 77–79.

44. Petition of John Greenwood, MAC, vol. 223, 381–382. In various other instances, captured masters were prohibited from taking so-called "servants" off with them when they were released to go to England, but these bondspeople were not racially identified. See Petition of James Fulton, MAC, vol. 165, 291; Petition of James Kennedy, MAC, vol. 165, 292; Petition of Richard Pyne, MAC, vol. 165, 293–295a.

45. Petition of Richard Gridley, MAC, vol. 170, 414.

46. Petition of Betty Pote, MAC, vol. 221, 448–449.

47. Manumission of Cuff, Lincoln, Mass., MS A 6628, R. Stanton Avery Special Collections, New England Historic Genealogical Society, Boston. See also Manumission of Cato, Manumission of Corydon, and Manumission of Clouster, Papers of Jeremy Belknap, Folder 6, Box 1, 161.D, 013.4, Loose manuscripts, 1723–1799, MHS.

48. Petition of Benjamin Pemberton, MAC, vol. 185, 195 ("gone"); Petition of Allis, MAC, vol. 180, 218–219 ("went"); *Boston Gazette*, January 2, 1775, 4 ("strolling"); Inventory of Elisha Jones's estate, MAC, vol. 154, 55 ("left"); *Continental Journal*, November 14, 1776, 1 ("Visit"); Joseph Prout's Petition, MAC, vol. 183, 132 ("quietly"); Peggy's Habeas Corpus, SF case 102787 ("house"). For the increase in Massachusetts freedom seekers during the 1770s over previous decades, see Antonio T. Bly, "A Prince Among Pretending Free Men: Runaway Slaves in Colonial New England Revisited," *Massachusetts Historical Review* vol. 14 (2012): 92.

49. Peggy's Habeas Corpus, SF case 102787.

50. Cato v. Conant, SF case 92584. The court's ruling on this case has been lost.

51. John Fisher's inventory, 1784, SCPR, FS, vol. 83, 862.

52. Ellis Gray's will, 1781, SCPR, FS, vol. 80, 347. Others shared Ellis's confusion. See John Bradford's will, 1784, SCPR, FS, vol. 83, 579, and William Vernon's will, 1787, SCPR, FS, vol. 88, 500. For Ellis's role in the constitutional convention, see Massachusetts Constitutional Convention, *Journal of the Convention for Framing a Constitution of Government for the State of Massachusetts Bay* (Boston: Dutton and Wentworth, 1832), 8.

53. Elaine MacEacheren, "Emancipation of Slavery in Massachusetts: A Reexamination, 1770–1790," *Journal of Negro History* 55, no. 4 (October 1970): 304 n3.

54. Gary B. Nash, *The Urban Crucible: Social Change, Political Consciousness, and the Origins of the American Revolution* (Cambridge: Harvard University Press, 1979), chap. 9. Nash argued that the importation of bondspeople dropped suddenly at the end of the Seven Years' War (see p. 320). In contrast, Robert E. Desrochers Jr.'s study of the Boston slave trade as represented in the *Boston Gazette* suggests a boost in importation around 1760, but this importation—the "most intense" since the 1730s—was not long-lasting. See Robert E. Desrochers Jr., "Slave-for-Sale Advertisements and Slavery in Massachusetts, 1704–1781," *WMQ* 59, no. 3 (July 2002): 659–662, quotation 659.

55. Much scholarship on abolition in the Bay State has emphasized what T. H. Breen has termed a "heroic legal narrative," which saw lawyers and judges as the valiant champions of freedom. See T. H. Breen, "Making History: The Force of Public Opinion and the Last Years of Slavery in Massachusetts," in *Through a Glass Darkly: Reflections on Personal Identity in Early America*, ed. Ronald Hoffman, Mechal Sobel, and Fredrika J. Teute (Chapel Hill: University of North Carolina Press, 1997), 72–73.

56. This is Ellis Gray's formulation. See his will, 1781, SCPR, FS, vol. 80, 347.

57. Jeremy Belknap, "Queries Respecting the Slavery and Emancipation of Negroes in Massachusetts, Proposed by the Hon. Judge Tucker of Virginia, and Answered by the Rev. Dr. Belknap," *Collections of the Massachusetts Historical Society, vol. 4, 1st series* (Boston: Massachusetts Historical Society, 1795): 192. Jeremy sent "about forty copies" of a list of questions to "such gentlemen as it was supposed would assist in answering them." A comprehensive list of the recipients does not survive, but Jeremy mentioned as one of his "informants" Prince Hall, a leader of Boston's Black community. See Jeremy Belknap, "Queries Respecting the Slavery and Emancipation of Negroes," 199, 210. Some of the material Jeremy received in response to

St. George's questions survives, but Prince's responses have been lost, as have any others produced by people of African descent, if indeed they ever existed. For transcriptions of surviving responses, see Jeremy Belknap, "Letters and Documents Relating to Slavery in Massachusetts," *Collections of the Massachusetts Historical Society, vol. 3, 5th series* (Boston: Massachusetts Historical Society, 1877): 375–431.

58. Belknap, "Queries Respecting the Slavery and Emancipation of Negroes," 198, 200, 203.

59. Belknap, "Queries Respecting the Slavery and Emancipation of Negroes," 201.

60. Only one person signed the petition, a man, ostensibly bound, named Felix, but I use the plural here to discuss its authors because Felix introduced the entreaty as "the PETITION of many SLAVES, living in the Town of BOSTON, and other Towns in the Province" and used the plural throughout. See Lover of Constitutional Liberty, *The Appendix: or, some Observations on the Expediency of the PETITION of the AFRICANS, living in Boston, &c., lately presented to the GENERAL ASSEMBLY of this Province, TO WHICH IS ANNEXED, The PETITION referred to Likewise, THOUGHTS ON SLAVERY. With a useful EXTRACT from the Massachusetts Spy, of January 28, 1773, by way of an Address to the MEMBERS of the ASSEMBLY* (Boston: E. Russell, 1773), 11.

61. *Massachusetts Spy*, February 4, 1773, 205; February 11, 1773, 210; February 18, 1773, 214; February 25, 1773, 218; Isaiah Thomas, *The History of Printing in America, with a Biography of Printers, vol. 1* (New York: J. Munsell, 1874), 155.

62. *Massachusetts Spy*, January 28, 1773, 199.

63. John Allen, *An Oration on the Beauties of Liberty, or the Essential Rights of the Americans. Delivered at the Second Baptist-Church in BOSTON, Upon the last Annual Thanksgiving . . . And Remarks on the Rights and Liberties of the Africans, inserted by particular Desire* (Boston: D. Kneeland and N. Davis, 1773), 76.

64. *Boston Post-Boy*, May 3, 1773, 3; May 10, 1773, 4; May 17, 1773, 4; *Boston Evening-Post*, May 17, 1773, 3; *Boston Gazette*, May 17, 1773, 3; *Massachusetts Spy*, May 13, 1773, 3; May 20, 1773, 4.

65. Harry S. Stout called the orality of the *Oration* its "most important aspect" and characterized the author as standing in "striking contrast to virtually all other pamphleteers" of the era in his appeal to illiterate people. See Harry S. Stout, "Religion, Communications, and the Ideological Origins of the American Revolution," *WMQ* 34, no. 4 (October 1977): 537. For the ways in which the inclusion of the petition altered the tone of the *Oration* itself, from being wary of Black people's rights to embracing the freedom struggle of African-descended people, see David Brion Davis, *The Problem of Slavery in the Age of Revolution, 1770–1823* (New York: Oxford University Press, 1999), 276–277, and Chernoh M. Sesay Jr., "The Revolutionary Black Roots of Slavery's Abolition in Massachusetts," *New England Quarterly* 87, no. 1 (March 2014): 111.

66. Peter Bestes et al., "Boston, April 20th, 1773 . . . ," Broadside Portfolio 37, no. 16, Printed Ephemera Collection, Library of Congress. For insightful analysis of this broadside, see John Hannigan, "King's Men and Continentals: War and Slavery in Eighteenth-Century Massachusetts" (PhD diss.: Brandeis University, 2021), 179–181.

67. *Massachusetts Spy*, July 29, 1773, 1. The Boston paper made its way some twenty miles north to Salem, where the petition and its introductory heading were reprinted, word for word, in the *Essex Gazette*. See *Essex Gazette*, August 3, 1773, 4.

68. *Boston Gazette*, August 23, 1773, 4 ("Conscience"); *Massachusetts Spy*, February 10, 1774, 3 ("AFRICA"). For Caesar's appeal, see *Essex Journal*, August 17, 1774, 1.

69. For the January appeal, see *Massachusetts Spy*, September 1, 1774, 2. It is possible that the May 1774 petition was not published. More likely, based on the tenacity of the activists who wrote it—who placed all five other petitions they submitted to Massachusetts authorities between January 1773 and June 1774 in various forms of circulating print—the May 1774 petition was published, but the record of its publication has been lost. For a manuscript version of the May 1774 petition, see Petition for freedom to Massachusetts Governor Thomas Gage, May 25, 1774, 1–2.

70. Historians believed that this petition was never published, but it did in fact circulate in print within the community. See *Massachusetts Spy*, September 8, 1774, 1; also, Sesay, "The Revolutionary Black Roots of Slavery's Abolition," 123.

71. When Governor Thomas Gage dissolved the General Court on June 17, 1774, legislators had agreed upon a law preventing the slave trade, but they had not yet formally enacted the measure. See Massachusetts Historical Society, *Journals of the House of Representatives of Massachusetts, vol. 50* (Boston: Massachusetts Historical Society, 1981), 221, 271, 285, and 287–291. For analysis of the 1774 bill and its demise, see James J. Allegro, "'Increasing and Strengthening the Country': Law, Politics, and the Antislavery Movement in Early-Eighteenth-Century Massachusetts Bay," *New England Quarterly* 75, no. 1 (March 2002): 20–21.

72. It is difficult to measure the effect of this protracted public relations campaign on the thinking of the Black activists' white neighbors and legislators, but on occasion the actions of white people can be traced clearly to the influence of the petitions. For example, at a town meeting held on May 17, 1773, in Pembroke, a town south of Boston, inhabitants conveyed the following to their representatives to the Massachusetts General Court: "We think the Negro Petition Reasonable—agreeable to natural Justice and the Precepts of the Gospel, and therefore advise that . . . you endeavour to find a Way in which they may be freed from Slavery." See supplement to the *Boston Gazette*, June 14, 1773, 1. Likewise, a bill to abolish slavery drafted in 1777 by the Massachusetts General Court was stored among the papers of the court alongside a hot-off-the-press petition written by Boston's Black activists for the abolition of slavery. The activists' petition must have been read and considered by the lawmakers who composed the bill (which ultimately failed to pass because of concerns that abolitionist legislation would jeopardize the fragile union of the states). See Draft Antislavery Act, MAC, vol. 212, 130–132a.

73. Petition for freedom to Massachusetts Governor Thomas Gage, May 25, 1774, 1 ("naturel"); Allen, *An Oration on the Beauties of Liberty*, 78 ("noble"); *Massachusetts Spy*, July 29, 1773, 1; *Boston Gazette*, August 23, 1773, 4 ("Saviour").

74. For the descriptor "circular letter," see Allen, *An Oration on the Beauties of Liberty*, 76, 78. For an example of a rumor linked to abolition and the legislature that influenced the actions of freedom seekers during the early years of the Revolution, see Petition of Joseph Prout, MAC, vol. 183, 132. For the role of Black activists in circulating their petitions in pamphlet form, see Belknap, "Letters and Documents Relating to Slavery in Massachusetts," 387.

75. *Massachusetts Spy*, July 29, 1773, 1.

76. Petition for freedom to Massachusetts Governor Thomas Gage, May 25, 1774, 1.

77. *Massachusetts Spy*, September 8, 1774, 1.

78. Petition to the Council and House of Representatives, MAC, vol. 212, 132–132a.

79. *Massachusetts Spy*, July 29, 1773, 1.

80. Petition for freedom to Massachusetts Governor Thomas Gage, May 25, 1774, 1.

81. *Massachusetts Spy*, September 8, 1774, 1. For examples of petitioners in Connecticut and New Hampshire later borrowing the language and ideas of those in Massachusetts, see

Christopher Cameron, *To Plead Our Own Cause: African Americans in Massachusetts and the Making of the Antislavery Movement* (Kent: Kent State University Press, 2014), 65–66.

82. See, for instance, Nicole Eustace, *Passion Is the Gale: Emotion, Power, and the Coming of the American Revolution* (Chapel Hill: University of North Carolina Press, 2008).

83. *Boston Gazette*, August 23, 1773, 4 ("Children"); *Essex Journal*, August 17, 1774, 1 ("relatives").

84. *Essex Journal*, August 17, 1774, 1.

85. Allen, *An Oration on the Beauties of Liberty*, 77. These quotations are taken from a statement authored by someone with the pseudonym "CONSCIENCE," which introduces the petition.

86. Petition for freedom to Massachusetts Governor Thomas Gage, May 25, 1774, 1.

87. *Massachusetts Spy*, July 29, 1773, 1.

88. Petition to the Council and House of Representatives, MAC, vol. 212, 132–132a.

89. Indeed, some petitions that were likely signed in manuscript form were shorn of those signatures when printed, making personal identification impossible.

90. Lover of Constitutional Liberty, *The Appendix*, 10; *Massachusetts Spy*, July 29, 1773, 1.

91. See Emily Blanck, *Tyrannicide: Forging an American Law of Slavery in Revolutionary South Carolina and Massachusetts* (Athens: University of Georgia Press, 2014), 17.

92. *Massachusetts Spy*, December 23, 1773, 1.

93. The vital records database (see Note on Sources) counts 1,176 people of African descent who were married in an official capacity—that is, by a Boston minister or justice of the peace—at least once during the eighteenth century.

94. Belknap, "Queries Respecting the Slavery and Emancipation of Negroes," 203.

95. *Boston Evening Post*, July 19, 1773, 3, July 26, 1773, 4, August 2, 1773, 4 ("Company"); *Boston Evening Post*, June 6, 1774, 3 ("Wife"); *Boston Gazette*, February 6, 1775, 2 ("carried off").

96. Here I build on Kirsten Sword's contention that the attempts of Black men to establish patriarchal authority over their wives, as expressed in these revolutionary petitions, became a "route for inclusion" in revolutionary Massachusetts. See Sword, *Wives Not Slaves: Patriarchy and Modernity in the Age of Revolutions* (Chicago: University of Chicago Press, 2021), 236. My arguments about the importance of Black families to emancipation in Massachusetts, and about the rather sudden crumbling of slavery in the region, differ from the arguments of various other scholars who have trained their eyes on emancipation in the region, partly because I focus on the eastern part of Massachusetts, while my colleagues have taken on the state as a whole. For instance, Jared Ross Hardesty's argument that the Massachusetts constitution was a "'time bomb' aimed at destroying slavery" does not hold for Boston and its surrounds, where the constitution seems to have little altered patterns of slaveholding, but it seems to hold in the central and western parts of the state, where bondspeople had to sue for their freedom by appealing to the constitution. See Hardesty, *Black Lives, Native Lands, White Worlds: A History of Slavery in New England* (Boston: University of Massachusetts Press, 2019), 138. Likewise, Joanne Pope Melish's argument that the process of emancipation in Massachusetts was dependent on Quock Walker's judicial emancipation—but prolonged as white people worked to circumvent that decision—draws on evidence from across Massachusetts but not from the Boston area. See Melish, *Disowning Slavery*, 64–65, 76, and 95–96. As for Margot Minardi's nuanced account of emancipation in Massachusetts, it dates the Black exodus from slavery to the 1780s, after the 1780 constitution and the Quock Walker decision, which seems a plausible explanation for much of the state. See Minardi,

Making Slavery History: Abolitionism and the Politics of Memory in Massachusetts (New York: Oxford University Press, 2010), 14–20.

97. John Vassall's account, 1780, File Papers of John Vassall, #23340, Middlesex County Probate Records, MA Archives. The actual words were recorded by Thomas Farrington, but Anthony must have communicated this reality in order to persuade Farrington to compensate him for his care of his family.

98. Anthony's efficacy when it came to providing for his family in this revolutionary moment was prefigured by his ability to liberate his daughter, Flora, in the years before the war broke out. In 1772, the man persuaded Penelope to facilitate Flora's emancipation using money that he appears to have saved himself. John Nichols Jr. of Billerica, Massachusetts, recorded in a deed that he had "received" of Penelope twenty pounds "by the hands of Tony her Servant." See Middlesex Deeds, vol. 73, 457 (December 9, 1772).

99. Petition of Anthony and Coby Vassall, MAC, vol. 186, 313–314.

100. Petition of Anthony Vassall, MAC, vol. 231, 115–117.

101. Resolution on the Petition of Anthony Vassall, MAC, vol. 231, 114. Two years later, in October of 1783, Anthony was allocated a payment of twenty-four pounds from the estate of John Vassall. See Warrants on Absentees' Estates, MAC, vol. 154, 405.

102. A series of more famous petitions were sent to the legislature during this period by a woman named Belinda Sutton, who had been bound prior to the Revolution by Isaac Royall, Cuba's one-time enslaver. The success of the petitions—Belinda received multiple payments, though they seem to have come only sporadically rather than on the promised yearly schedule—indicates that the legislature did not automatically disqualify women household heads from support. (Belinda petitioned on behalf of herself and her ailing daughter, Prine.) See Petition of Anthony and Coby Vassall, MAC, vol. 186, 313; also, Roy E. Finkenbine, "Belinda's Petition: Reparations for Slavery in Revolutionary Massachusetts," *WMQ* 64, no. 1 (January 2007): 96, and Margot Minardi, "Why Was Belinda's Petition Approved?" Royall House & Slave Quarters website, https://royallhouse.org/why-was-belindas -petition-approved/. For Belinda's original appeal, see the Petition of Belinda, MAC, vol. 239, 12–14.

103. Anthony's state support appears to have been regular. When the man died twenty years later, Cuba apparently sought to obtain her annual stipend from the Massachusetts Treasurer only to be turned down because her name was not included on the original 1782 resolution. She therefore sent an appeal to the legislature. The Massachusetts General Court responded with a resolve stating that, though Anthony had died, "the reasons for granting the said annuity still remain in full force." Cuba was guaranteed a forty-dollar payment every February. See *Proceedings of the Massachusetts Historical Society, vol. 4* (1858–1860), 66; also Resolve on the Petition of Cuby Vassall, February 28, 1812, in Massachusetts General Court, *Resolves of the General Court of the Commonwealth of Massachusetts passed at the session begun and holden at Boston, on the eighth day of January in the year of our Lord, one thousand eight hundred and twelve* (Boston: Adams, Rhoades, & Co., 1812), 376.

104. For the house, see Middlesex Deeds, vol. 96, 84–85 (July 25, 1787). For the adjacent land, see Middlesex Deeds, vol. 105, 274–275 (August 3, 1791). For the acres across the street, see Middlesex Deeds, vol. 110, 199–200 (January 8, 1793).

105. Batchelder, *Notes on Colonel Henry Vassall*, 72. Several documents in Anthony's probate records refer to the man as a "yeoman." See File Papers of Antony Vassall, #23335, Middlesex County Probate Records, MA Archives.

106. For a discussion of the extent to which one might consider the 1790 census records as evidence of the end of slavery in Massachusetts, see Whiting, "Emancipation Without the Courts or Constitution," 461–462.

107. Gender and approximate age of white inhabitants were noted, but Black inhabitants were all enumerated together and recorded in one column.

108. To assess the shape and structure of Black families in Massachusetts in 1790, I read line by line through the census records of Boston and four neighboring towns: the Vassalls' Cambridge; Medford, where Cuba had lived on Isaac Royall's estate; the Bedunahs' Roxbury; and Charlestown, where Mark, Phoebe, and Phillis brought to fruition their desperate plot. In total, 907 Black people were enumerated in these towns, 551 of whom lived in Black-headed households and 356 of whom lived in white-headed households. Unfortunately, a significant minority of Black people in Boston lived in households that were described very poorly by census takers. Of Boston's 748 Black residents, 113 lived in households that were labeled "Negroes" or "Negroes & Mulattoes" rather than attributed to a specific household head. Often these households were quite large, composed of as many as 14 members. Apparently, the census taker came upon dwellings with many Black inhabitants and did not bother to try to sort out who belonged to which family. This sloppiness with recordkeeping makes it difficult to discern what the households of these 113 people were like.

109. Seven white people lived as subordinates in four households headed by Black men: those of Will[ia]m Clarke, James Morris, Will[ia]m Phillis, and Cato Clapham. All of these households were located in Boston.

110. Gloria McCahon Whiting, "Power, Patriarchy, and Provision: African Families Negotiate Gender and Slavery in New England," *JAH* 103 no. 3 (December 2016): 585–590.

111. For the material conditions of Darby's upbringing, see Anthony Vassall's will, 1811, File Papers of Antony Vassall, #23335, Middlesex County Probate Records, MA Archives. For the Black population of Boston, see Jared Ross Hardesty, "Disappearing from Abolitionism's Heartland: The Legacy of Slavery and Emancipation in Boston," *International Review of Social History* 65, no. S28 (April 2020): 145–168.

112. Church in Brattle Square, *The Manifesto Church: Records of the Church in Brattle Square Boston, 1699–1872* (Boston: Benevolent Fraternity of Churches, 1902), 269.

113. Lucy's father, Jupiter, was free at least as early as 1758, when he was baptized as a "free negro." See Mellen Chamberlain, *A Documentary History of Chelsea Including the Boston Precincts of Winnimsimmet[,] Rumney Marsh, and Pullen Point, 1624–1824, vol. 2* (Boston: Massachusetts Historical Society, 1908), 593. Based on Lucy's recorded age at death, she would have been born in or around 1776. (Lucy died in 1828 at the age of fifty-two.) See Baldwin, *Vital Records of Cambridge, Massachusetts*, 772.

114. Suffolk Deeds, vol. 387, 123 (September 9, 1835).

115. Sally Campbell Vassall was born on March 18, 1810, and baptized on May 6, 1810. For her birth record, see *Boston Births*, 355. For her baptismal record, see Church in Brattle Square, *Manifesto Church*, 231, which renders her name Sally Kimball Vassall. Flora had at least three children: Susanna Maranday, Margaret Maranday, and John Maranday. The latter two, described as "infants," were baptized on September 23, 1804. On the same day, their older sister, Susanna, an "adult," was baptized. See Records of Kings Chapel in *The Records of the Churches of Boston* (CD-ROM) (Boston: New England Historic Genealogical Society, 2002), 164. Cyrus's children, Eliza Flagg Vassall and Cyrus Anthony Gunther Vassall, were

baptized in Trinity Church in 1806 and 1809, respectively. See Andrew Oliver and James Bishop Peabody, eds., *The Records of Trinity Church, Boston, 1728–1830* (Boston: Colonial Society of Massachusetts, 1982), 680, 686. James appears to have had a child as well, as the census taker in 1810 recorded him as the head of a household of three—not two—persons of African descent. See United States Census, 1810, Boston Ward 6, Image 11 of 17. Catherine was the only living child of Anthony and Cuba who had not yet married in 1810. In the second decade of the eighteenth century, she would marry Adam Lewis of Cambridge. See Bell, *George Washington's Headquarters*, 34.

116. Darby's closest association was with the Brattle Street Church, which baptized and admitted him in 1796. He would marry Lucy in that church in 1802, and she would join the church in 1805. They would baptize most of their children there, and their one child to marry, Frances Holland, would choose to be wed by the church's minister. But Darby was active in other churches as well; he baptized two of his children in King's Chapel, and he maintained ties to Trinity Church, which was the church of Cyrus's family.

117. For the African Society, see *Liberator*, August 4, 1832, 124. For the school funding, see Petition of Primus Hall, Massachusetts Anti-Slavery and Anti-Segregation Petitions, Senate Unpassed Legislation 1812, Docket 4522, SCl/series 231, MA Archives, http://nrs.harvard.edu /urn-3:FHCL:11148848. For the independence celebration, see *Columbian Centinel*, August 31, 1825, 1–2.

118. Petition to the Massachusetts Senate and House of Representatives from the "Colored Citizens of Boston," Massachusetts Anti-Slavery and Anti-Segregation Petitions, Passed Acts, St. 1861, c.91, SCl/series 229, MA Archives, http://nrs.harvard.edu/urn-3:FHCL:1051 2596?n=200.

119. For the moniker "Daddy Vassal," see *Dollar Newspaper*, March 3, 1858, 2.

120. William, born in 1803, must have died sometime before April 1805, as Lucy bore another child at that time named William. This William appears to have died in August of 1805 at just under four months. For the second William's death, see Church in Brattle Square, *Manifesto Church*, 278. Darby's daughter, Sally Campbell, died in 1811, and his son, Richard Chardon, died in 1816. Both of these children were seventeen months old at their passing. See *Columbian Centinel*, October 19, 1811, 2, and *Columbian Centinel*, February 14, 1816, 2. Darby's children Charles Ward and Rhoda Goosby also likely died young, as Darby's household in 1820 numbered only three persons: Darby, his wife, Lucy, and their daughter Frances Holland. (The household had numbered nine in 1810.) For Darby's 1810 census record, see United States Census, 1810, Massachusetts, Suffolk County, Boston, Ward 7, Image 6 of 9. For Darby's 1820 census record, see United States Census, 1820, Massachusetts, Suffolk County, Boston, Ward 7, Image 2 of 13.

121. Darby Vassall in 1860 was listed in census records as a ninety-one-year-old "Waiter" living with his middle-aged daughter, Frances, and her husband, Jonas. Like Darby, Jonas worked: His recorded occupation was "Clothing." However, none of the three had any property, either real or personal, and their lack of property cannot be attributed to sloppy record-keeping, as others listed near them in the census had sizable assets.

122. Bell, *George Washington's Headquarters*, 41.

123. *Liberator*, November 22, 1861, 188.

124. For a contemporary counterexample, consider that the Black descendants of Thomas Jefferson are still prohibited, more than a century and a half after Darby's interment,

from being buried in the Monticello graveyard. See Leef Smith, "Monticello's Theories of Relativity: Jefferson Report Urges Against Taking Hemings Descendants into Group," *Washington Post*, May 4, 2002, B01.

125. Edward Doubleday Harris, *The Vassals of New England and Their Immediate Descendants: A Genealogical and Biographical Sketch Compiled from Church and Town Records* (Albany, NY: J. Munsell, 1862), 13.

Conclusion

1. Slavery was first legalized in the British Atlantic world five years earlier, in Barbados, which declared that people of African and Indigenous ancestry who arrived in bondage "should serve for Life, unless a Contract was made before to the contrary." The Bay Colony set out two other conditions under which slavery was legal: for prisoners of war and for "strangers" who "willingly selle themselves." See Jonathan A. Bush, "The British Constitution and the Creation of American Slavery," in *Slavery and the Law*, ed. Paul Finkelman (Lanham: Rowman & Littlefield, 2002), 382, and "A Coppie of the Liberties of the Massachusets Colonie in New England" (1641) in *Collections of the Massachusetts Historical Society, vol. 8, 3rd series* (Boston: Massachusetts Historical Society, 1843), 231. This is the ninety-first liberty.

2. The experiences of enslaved people in coastal New England more closely resembled the situation of enslaved people in Great Britain than it did that of enslaved people in the southern mainland colonies or in the Caribbean. See, for instance, Simon P. Newman, *Freedom Seekers: Escaping from Slavery in Restoration London* (London: University of London Press, 2022), and Gretchen Holbrook Gerzina, *Black London: Life Before Emancipation* (New Brunswick: Rutgers University Press, 1995).

3. For Boston's prerevolutionary economy, see Gary B. Nash, *The Urban Crucible: Social Change, Political Consciousness, and the Origins of the American Revolution* (Cambridge: Harvard University Press, 1979), chap. 9. For politics, see, for example, Richard D. Brown, *Revolutionary Politics in Massachusetts: The Boston Committee of Correspondence and the Towns, 1772–1774* (Cambridge: Harvard University Press, 1970), and T. H. Breen, *American Insurgents, American Patriots: The Revolution of the People* (New York: Hill and Wang, 2010), chap. 2. For the changes to the family ideal, see, for instance, Sarah M. S. Pearsall, *Atlantic Families: Lives and Letters in the Later Eighteenth Century* (New York: Oxford University Press, 2008), and Sarah Maza, "Only Connect: Family Values in the Age of Sentiment: Introduction," *Eighteenth-Century Studies* 30, no. 3 (Spring 1997): 207–212. For the language of sensibility, see Sarah Knott, *Sensibility and the American Revolution* (Chapel Hill: University of North Carolina Press, 2009), and Nicole Eustace, *Passion Is the Gale: Emotion, Power, and the Coming of the American Revolution* (Chapel Hill: University of North Carolina Press, 2008).

4. *Boston Evening-Post*, December 8, 1746, 2.

5. *Boston News-Letter*, April 18, 1751, 2; *Boston Evening-Post*, April 22, 1751, 2; *Boston Post-Boy*, April 22, 1751, 2. The wording is slightly different in the *Boston Gazette*, April 16, 1751, 2.

6. *Boston Evening-Post*, May 4, 1767, 3.

7. *Massachusetts Spy*, September 8, 1774, 1.

8. Lover of Constitutional Liberty, *The Appendix: or, some Observations on the Expediency of the PETITION of the AFRICANS, living in Boston, &c., lately presented to the GENERAL ASSEMBLY of this Province, TO WHICH IS ANNEXED, The PETITION referred to Likewise, THOUGHTS ON SLAVERY. With a useful EXTRACT from the Massachusetts Spy, of*

January 28, 1773, by way of an Address to the MEMBERS of the ASSEMBLY (Boston: E. Russell, 1773), 10.

9. *Massachusetts Spy*, September 8, 1774, 1.

10. Petition for freedom to Massachusetts Governor Thomas Gage, May 25, 1774, 1.

11. Frederick Douglass, *Narrative of the Life of Frederick Douglass, an American Slave. Written by Himself* (Boston: Anti-Slavery Office, 1845), 11, 119, 48.

12. Frederick Douglass, *My Bondage and My Freedom* (New York: Miller, Orton, & Mulligan, 1855), 60.

13. L. Maria Child, ed., *Incidents in the Life of a Slave Girl: Written by Herself* (Boston: Published for the Author, 1861), 59.

14. William W. Brown, *Narrative of William W. Brown, a Fugitive Slave* (Boston: Anti-Slavery Office, 1847), 27, 81, 49.

15. Harriet Beecher Stowe, *Uncle Tom's Cabin, or, Life Among the Lowly* (Boston: John P. Jewett & Co., 1852). Harriet Beecher Stowe, *A Key to Uncle Tom's Cabin: Presenting the Original Facts and Documents upon Which the Story Is Founded* (Boston: John P. Jewett & Co., 1853), 133.

16. For the argument that sentimental abolitionist literature bears the imprint of the so-called "slave narrative" genre, see Kerry Sinanan, "The Slave Narrative and the Literature of Abolition" in *The Cambridge Companion to the African American Slave Narrative*, ed. Audrey A. Fisch (New York: Cambridge University Press, 2007), 70–76.

Note on Sources

1. Suffolk County was much larger geographically in the seventeenth and eighteenth centuries than it is at present, encompassing the following towns for at least substantial periods of time: Bellingham, Boston, Braintree, Brookline, Chelsea, Cohasset, Dedham, Dorchester, Dover, Franklin, Hingham, Medfield, Medway, Mendon, Milton, Nantasket (which became Hull), Needham, Oxford, Roxbury, Sharon, Stoughton, Sutton, Uxbridge, Walpole, Weymouth, Woodstock, and Wrentham. See Nathaniel B. Shurtleff, ed., *Records of the Governor and Company of the Massachusetts Bay in New England . . .*, vols. 1 and 2 (Boston: William White, 1853), 2: 38; "An Act for Erecting, Granting and Making a County in the Inland Parts of This Province, to Be Called the County of Worcester, and for the Establishing Courts of Justice Within the Same," *The Acts and Resolves, Public and Private, of the Province of the Massachusetts Bay . . .* (Boston: Wright & Potter, 1874), 2: 584; "An Act for Erecting All the Lands Within the Town of Boston . . . ," *Acts and Resolves*, 969; D. Hamilton Hurd, *History of Norfolk County, Massachusetts . . .* (Philadelphia: J. W. Lewis & Co., 1884), 1–2.

2. The court did close for part of 1775 because of the British occupation of Boston, but it seems to have quickly made up for the lost time, processing a larger number of decedents' estates in 1776. See Gloria McCahon Whiting, "Emancipation Without the Courts or Constitution: The Case of Revolutionary Massachusetts," *Slavery & Abolition* 41, no. 3 (September 2020): 475 n34.

3. Probate records do not exist for all people who died in Suffolk County during this time. The property of both the poorer and the very wealthiest decedents was less likely to be inventoried than that of those in the middle, and only one-third to one-half of decedents whose estates were inventoried had written wills—though some whose estates were not inventoried left wills as well. Still, probate records provide insight into how enslaved people were spread throughout Anglo-American households, information that cannot be obtained elsewhere: No other type of record allows us to reconstruct the distribution of bondspeople in

Anglo-American households on a population scale in the region. See Gloria McCahon Whiting, "Race, Slavery, and the Problem of Numbers in Early New England: A View from Probate Court," *WMQ* 77, no. 3 (July 2020): 406–407.

4. See William Tinge's inventory, 1653, SCPR, FS, vol. 2, 144 ("Scotch"), 145; Widow Gross's inventory, 1654, SCPR, FS, vol. 2, 173 ("Irish"); Samuel Gray's inventory, 1708, SCPR, FS, vol. 17, 167 ("White"); William Phips's inventory, 1696, SCPR, FS, vol. 11, 202 ("negro"); Daniel Allen's will, 1715, SCPR, NS, vol. 19, 34 ("Indian"); Samuel Read's will, 1725, SCPR, FS, vol. 23, 539, 541 ("Spanish Indian"); Cromwell Lobdel's inventory, 1756, SCPR, FS, vol. 51, 256 ("molatto").

5. For racial labeling in seventeenth- and eighteenth-century Massachusetts and for the changing racial composition of the bound labor force as reflected in probate records, see Whiting, "Race, Slavery, and the Problem of Numbers," 411–427.

6. Gloria L. Main, "Probate Records as a Source for Early American History," *WMQ* 33, no. 2 (January 1975): 94.

INDEX

See "On Names and More" for the naming conventions followed in this book.

ACKNOWLEDGMENTS

Belonging has its genesis in the people who taught me over the years. Without Allison Sneider, I probably would not have studied history as an undergraduate at Rice University; I certainly would not have written an honors thesis and decided to pursue graduate work. I benefited as well from the mentorship of Edward Cox, Paula Sanders, and Richard Smith during my time at Rice. Evelyn Brooks Higginbotham, the very model of patience and generosity, guided me through my first year at Harvard University. Vincent Brown, Annette Gordon-Reed, Walter Johnson, and Jane Kamensky also played crucial roles in my intellectual development during graduate school, inspiring me with their thinking and devoting far more time than I deserved to sharpening my own. Jill Lepore pushed me to become a better historian and writer—her copious red ink was proof of how much she cared—and she empowered me to write the sort of book I wanted to write. As for Laurel Thatcher Ulrich, she believed in me when I most needed it; without her support, I might never have brought this project to completion. For these mentors and the others who taught me to love the historian's craft, I will always be grateful.

As I think back over the years of research that I undertook in order to write this book, I cannot help but reflect on how deeply indebted I am to those caretakers of the historical record who make the work of historians possible. Without the help of the librarians and archivists who facilitated my access to archival material, *Belonging* would never have come to be. I extend my gratitude to those who assisted me at the American Antiquarian Society, the Andover-Harvard Theological Library, the Andover Newton Theological School, the Boston Athenaeum, the Boston Public Library, the Congregational Library and Archives, the Connecticut Historical Society, the Harvard University Archives, the Maine Historical Society, the Massachusetts Historical Society, the Massachusetts Judicial Archives, the Massachusetts State Archives, and the Rhode Island Historical Society.

Of course, I could not have pursued a project requiring so much time in the archives without generous financial backing. For supporting my research and writing during graduate school, I would like to thank Harvard University, which provided resources through the Artemas Ward Fellowship, the Center for American Political Studies, the Charles Warren Center for Studies in American History, the Graduate School of Arts and Sciences, the History Department, and the Richard A. Berenson Graduate Fellowship. My graduate research was also funded by the American Antiquarian Society, the American Historical Association, and the New England Regional Consortium Fellowship. At the University of Wisconsin–Madison, I have been fortunate to obtain the time and resources necessary to continue my archival work and writing. Generous support for my research was provided by the University of Wisconsin–Madison Office of the Vice Chancellor for Research and Graduate Education with funding from the Wisconsin Alumni Research Foundation. I wish also to thank the Center for the Humanities, the E. Gordon Fox Endowment, the History Department, and the Institute for Research in the Humanities, all of which provided meaningful assistance.

During the years I was at work on *Belonging*, I found it helpful to publish parts of the book in article form. Doing so allowed me to refine my arguments, experiment with new bodies of evidence, and participate in scholarly conversations with others in my field. A portion of Chapter 2 was published as "Power, Patriarchy, and Provision: African Families Negotiate Gender and Slavery in New England," *Journal of American History* 103, no. 3 (December 2016): 583–605. Part of Chapter 4 and a segment of the Note on Sources were published as "Race, Slavery, and the Problem of Numbers in Early New England: A View from Probate Court," *William and Mary Quarterly* 77, no. 3 (July 2020): 405–440. And excerpts of Chapter 6 were published as "Emancipation Without the Courts or Constitution: The Case of Revolutionary Massachusetts," *Slavery & Abolition* 41, no. 3 (September 2020): 458–478. I extend my appreciation to all three journals for permission to include some of my already published material in this book, and I thank the editors and reviewers who helped me hone my arguments when I originally prepared those articles.

Audiences convened by a number of institutions have improved this book in important ways. For their probing questions and insightful ideas, I wish to thank the students, scholars, and members of the public assembled by the American Historical Association, Boston College, the Colonial Society of Massachusetts, the Massachusetts Historical Society, the Omohundro

Institute of Early American History and Culture, the Rhode Island Historical Society, the Schlesinger Library at Harvard University, the Society for Historians of the Early American Republic, the Society of Early Americanists, the University of Hull, the University of Massachusetts–Boston, the University of Michigan–Ann Arbor, the University of Minnesota–Twin Cities, and the University of Wisconsin–Madison. Many of those who presented alongside me offered invaluable suggestions, pushing my research in new directions. I especially wish to thank Cassandra Berman, Frederick Knight, Margaret Newall, Jerrad Pacatte, Jonathan Sassi, Felicia Thomas, Holly White, and Fay Yarbrough.

I deeply appreciate the generous historians who read portions of this work over the years and helped me make them better. Included in this group are Catherine Adams, Edward Andrews, Rhae Lynn Barnes, John Frederick Bell, Maria Bollettino, Jon Butler, Carla Cevasco, Stephanie Cole, Jason Eden, Crystal Feimster, Kirsten Fischer, David Gellman, Katharine Gerbner, Jared Hardesty, Bridget Heneghan, Susan Lee Johnson, Barbara Krauthamer, Ann Little, Joanne Pope Melish, Charmaine Nelson, Mary Beth Norton, Sarah Pearsall, Mark Peterson, John Wood Sweet, Alan Taylor, Joanne Jahnke-Wegner, Harvey Amani Whitfield, and Lisa Wilson. I extend my thanks to Aabid Allibhai, Edward Bell, Richard Boles, Sara Damiano, John Hannigan, Jared Hardesty, Alan Rogers, and Nicole Topich for answering my many questions and sharing sources. Serena Zabin provided an abundance of inspiration and practical guidance. Nicole Maskiell gave me the encouragement I needed to make it to the manuscript's end. Cornelia Dayton read the entire book with her characteristic close eye. Simon Newman pored over everything, sometimes more than once, offering invaluable feedback. And each page of this book bears the imprint of my exceptional editor, Bob Lockhart.

I have the good fortune of working in such a large and friendly department that I do not have the space to list all of the colleagues who have helped me over the years. Many have gone above and beyond, reading my work; providing timely advice; and sending flowers, cookies, and words of encouragement when I most needed them. I wish particularly to thank Simon Balto, Mou Banerjee, Ashley Brown, Cindy Cheng, Christy Clark-Pujara, Nan Enstad, Marcella Hayes, April Haynes, Patrick Iber, Steve Kantrowitz, Marc Kleijwegt, Jennifer Ratner-Rosenhagen, Jim Sweet, Matt Villeneuve, and Lee Wandel. Those who have chaired the History Department during my time on faculty deserve special recognition; Laird Boswell,

Anne Hansen, Leonora Neville, and Jim Sweet released resources in support of my scholarly development, emboldened me to say no to the nonessentials crowding out my writing time, and helped me navigate work while caring for my family through a pandemic. And Charles Cohen, my recently retired early Americanist colleague and dear friend, advocated for me and championed this project even before I set foot on campus. For such colleagues I am grateful indeed.

I have benefited from the support of others at the University of Wisconsin–Madison as well. Leslie Bellais performed first-rate work as a research assistant. Amelia Zurcher navigated a surprising amount of red tape to help me acquire images for this book. And my students have been a constant source of inspiration. They have listened well, and they have talked back, asking good questions, proposing alternate explanations, and coming to office hours to continue the conversations. Some have even offered to help. I am especially indebted to Max Herteen, Stella Lehane, and Ayuka Sinanoglu. As for Isaac Lee, he has been a crucial sounding board over the years; I am thankful for his assistance and humbled by his insight. It is my hope that this book will encourage graduate students like him, who make up the next generation of scholars of slavery. Therefore, all author's proceeds—whether from royalties, speaking engagements after publication, or any monetary awards—will go to the Darby Vassall Fund for the Study of Slavery at the University of Wisconsin–Madison. May the work carry on.

Friends near and far have sustained me during the time I have labored on *Belonging*. Jane Hendrickson has given wise counsel for a quarter century now, mainly from a distance. As for the local Madison community that has supported me through years of writing and revising, I am particularly grateful for Erika and Pete Anna, Mel and Mo Cheeks, Valentina Infante and José Varela, Jenna and Josh Lavik, Collette and Matt Lee, Erin and Brian Towns, and Jenny and Nick White—as well as all the kids. The meals, the texts, the walks, the prayers, and the offers to help (with my footnotes, no less!) have meant more than you know.

I am grateful, too, for my family. My thanks go to Joy and Daniel Geaslen and to Margaret and Andy Kalcic for their words of encouragement from this project's inception. Thank you to the extended Whiting and Taylor families—above all Don Taylor, Carey Whiting, and Jeffrey Whiting—for so deeply valuing my work. I am also appreciative of the aunts and uncles who have read my writing and urged me forward: Bart and Marilyn Drake, George Drake and Roberta Lombardi, Helen Drake and Randall Bausor, and Tom Drake and Leslie Waters. My parents deserve as much credit as anyone for enabling me to bring *Belonging* to completion. My dad, David McCahon, taught me to relish a good treasure hunt and came along to dig through the archives with me. My mom, Cynthia McCahon, helped me to find myself as a writer and inspired me with her example of what hard work can accomplish. The two of them, along with the incomparable Pam King, cared for my children and did so much more in order to allow me to write this book. My thanks are not sufficient.

Paul Whiting has been there through every archival find and frustration, cheering me as I poured a great deal of energy into an undertaking that, by any measure, made his life more complicated. I doubt I would have come to the end of this without his encouragement; God knew I needed a pathological optimist to walk alongside me through life. And for Elisa, David, and Audra: I appreciate your patience with me as I have had to write and write and write. Thank you for wanting to help me finish something that matters. I do wish it had not taken me so long, but I trust that one day you will understand why I needed to tell these stories. I love you, my family.